HISPANICS
IN THE AMERICAN WEST

Titles in ABC-CLIO's
CULTURES IN THE
AMERICAN WEST
Series

Scott C. Zeman, Series Editor

HISPANICS
IN THE AMERICAN WEST

Jorge Iber and Arnoldo De León

CULTURES IN THE AMERICAN WEST
Scott C. Zeman, Series Editor

A B C C L I O

Santa Barbara, California   Denver, Colorado   Oxford, England

Library of Congress Cataloging-in-Publication Data

Iber, Jorge, 1961–
   Hispanics in the American West / Jorge Iber and Arnoldo De León.
     p. cm. — (Cultures in the American West series)
   Includes bibliographical references and index.
   ISBN 1-85109-679-5 (hardcover : alk. paper) — ISBN 1-85109-684-1 (ebook) 1. Hispanic Americans—West (U.S.)—History. 2. West (U.S.)—History. 3. West (U.S.)—Ethnic relations. I. De León, Arnoldo, 1945– II. Title. III. Series.

  F596.3.S75I24 2006
  978'.00468—dc22
                          2005022932

09 08 07 06   10 9 8 7 6 5 4 3 2 1

This book is also available on the World Wide Web as an eBook.
Visit abc-clio.com for details.

ABC-CLIO, Inc.
130 Cremona Drive, P.O. Box 1911
Santa Barbara, California 93116-1911

This book is printed on acid-free paper.

Manufactured in the United States of America

*To Hispanics of all nations
who have shaped the U.S. West.
—ADL*

*This work is dedicated to my wife,
Raquel, our wonderful son, Matthew,
my father, Manuel, and in loving
memory of my mother, Bertha Iber.
—JI*

CONTENTS

CULTURES IN THE AMERICAN WEST

SERIES INTRODUCTION

Scott C. Zeman, Series Editor

In my classes on the history of the American West at the New Mexico Institute of Mining and Technology, we discuss the infamous Rock Springs Massacre of 1885 in which and angry mob killed twenty-eight Chinese workers and forced the rest out of the Wyoming mining town. My students are always a bit surprised when I mention that right here at home in Socorro, New Mexico, at about the same time, nativists denounced Chinese immigrants. The local newspaper declared the "Chinese Must Go!" and in the nearby mining hamlet of Kelly (now a ghost town), an anti-Chinese riot broke out (the mob apparently was enraged by the hiring of a Chinese cook—fortunately, the cook escaped harm and the mob leader was killed by his own men).

During its mining-town heyday in the late nineteenth century, Socorro boasted a diverse population of Hispanos, Anglos, African Americans, Slavs, as well as Chinese. Today, Socorro is home to New Mexico Tech University, the National Radio Astronomy Observatory, and other affiliated high-tech enterprises. New Mexico Tech's student body includes East Indians, Norwegians, Czechs, Vietnamese, Russians, Kenyans, Colombians, nuevo mexicanos, Native Americans, and Anglos. I use this perhaps self-indulgent example because it highlights the multicultural nature and history of the region. It is impossible to imagine Socorro's history—just as it is with the rest of the West—without this simple fact.

ABC-CLIO's Cultures in the American West Series, of which this volume is part, takes the same point of departure: to understand the West—to make sense of it—we must adopt a view that accounts for the incredible variety of its peoples.

The volumes in this series follow the lead of the New Western History, which brought to the forefront of western historiography issues of race, ethnicity, and gender. To use the words of one of the school's foremost historians, Richard White, "The American West is a product of conquest and of the mixing of diverse groups of people. The West began when Europeans sought to conquer various areas of the continent and when people of Indian, European, Asian, and African ancestry began to meet within the territories west of the Missouri that would later be part of the United States. The West did not suddenly emerge; rather, it was gradually created" ("*Its Your Misfortune and None of My Own": A New History of the American West,* p. 4).

The volumes in the series take on the challenging task of demythologizing the most heavily mythologized region in the United States. In *Gunfighter Nation: The Myth of the Frontier in Twentieth-Century America,* Richard Slotkin's monumental study of the myth of the frontier in modern America, Slotkin argues that "according to this [frontier] myth-historiography, the conquest of the wilderness and the subjugation or displacement of the Native Americans who originally inhabited it have been the means to our achievement of a national identity, a democratic polity, an ever-expanding economy, and a phenomenally dynamic and 'progressive' civilization" (p. 10). And, as Slotkin points out especially, "When history is translated into myth, the complexities of social and historical experiences are simplified and compressed into the action of representative individuals or 'heroes.'" The volumes in this series go far in helping deconstruct such a simplistic view of the history of the West.

Each volume in this series, written by experts in their respective fields, focuses on one of the many groups to call the West home. Volumes include discussions of origins, migrations, community development, and historical change, as well as short biographies. The volumes highlight key issues in the history of the groups, identify important historiographical concerns, and provide useful bibliographies.

Steven Danver of ABC-CLIO deserves the lion's share of the credit for this series. I would also like to thank him for being such a delight to work with. And thanks also to each of the authors of the volumes, without them this series would be still only an idea.

PREFACE

*H*ispanics in the American West is a book of history. It focuses on people coming from the Spanish-speaking countries of Latin America, save the nation of Brazil. Mainly, its subjects are Mexican-origin individuals, for of all the Spanish-speaking communities in the United States, Mexican Americans can lay claim to a lengthier presence in the wide expanse between the Mississippi River and the Pacific Ocean and they make up the largest percentage of that group. After World War II, immigrants from Puerto Rico, Cuba, and countries of Central America (particularly, El Salvador and Guatemala) began arriving in "the West," and so they also appear more prominently in the book's later chapters.

We confine our coverage to that region of the United States generally labeled "the West." We opt for the more recent definition of the term, which we interpret to encompass the American experience beyond the Golden State of California to include Hawaii. When we say "the West," we also have in mind a time frame that stretches well into the modern age of urbanization and industrialization. This perspective harmonizes with the thinking of modern-day scholars who break with the old view that "the West" and the frontier were synonymous and ended by the 1890s. Today's historians also conceptualize "the West" as culturally mosaic. We heed these current concepts to tell the story of a people who have shaped society as much as society in the West has shaped them.

Several features commend this book that is part of the Cultures in the American West Series published by ABC-CLIO. Importantly, it attempts to offer significant coverage of major movements that constitute the history of Hispanics in the U. S. West, highlights the role of leading Hispanics in the chronicle of the trans-Mississippi, and abides by the historical truism that ordinary people at times impact history as much as do those in power. Also, it relies on the most current scholarship in the field, as indicated in the bibliographic essays that follow each chapter and in the listing that constitutes the Select Bibliography. Enhancing *Hispanics in the American West* further is its reliance on some of the most recent historical approaches and interpretations being applied to the study of the West in general. It also profits from the scholarship produced by researchers in ethnic studies, among them the fields of literary criticism, folklore, race relations, gender, religion, anthropology, geography, and education. We have further tapped into sources of information unavailable to an earlier generation of historians, using Internet websites when available.

Our comprehensive coverage of the subject of Hispanics in the U.S. West yields several important lessons of relevance. It illustrates humankind's willingness to risk danger, injury, and even loss of life to travel toward a promised land, a scenario still played out along the U.S.-Mexico border. In their march *al norte* (to the north), those from Mexico, Central America, and even from South America brave thirst and hunger, bandits, the Border Patrol, and what some call "vigilantes" (actually border guard volunteers, primarily Anglo Americans, belonging to what is called the "Minuteman" Project) to achieve a start similar to one envisioned by their earlier predecessors. Others from Cuba and from other Caribbean islands chance perilous waters to reach the East Coast; many of them subsequently migrate to the U.S. West. From wherever they originate, these modern-day migrants attempt to reconstruct their lives once in the West; they transplant old ways and establish communities that duplicate ones left behind in the homeland. In so doing, Hispanics are today "browning America," a trend feared by many and one that ignites controversies (or "issues") about race, special treatment, and the merits of a multicultural society.

In writing a book that treats the topic of ethnicity and race, authors often face difficulty finding appropriate terminology. In our introductory chapter, we present a fairly lengthy explanation of what we mean by the terms "Hispanic" and "Latino." Trained in ethnic studies, we take for granted the connotations and meanings of words such as "white," "Anglo American," and "race," yet we recognize that to beginning readers such labels and words might be ambiguous and may even be offensive. The terms "white" and "Anglo American," as used in this work, refer to the majority population of the various states of the West, and are used interchangeably. We do not mean to imply that all "whites" were members of the economic and social elites in these locales. However, as will be made evident in the text, historians have recognized that, even for poor whites, the color of their skin (or, as some of our historical actors would have put it, their "race") tended to produce certain advantages (and thus better treatment)in a wide variety of social, legal, and economic interactions throughout the West.

Finally, a word about ourselves. We are both members of history departments, and as is the case with history professors, we teach a variety of courses in our field, though we specialize in what is generally referred to as "Chicano History." Our dissertations were on that subject, and over the years, our research and writing have continued to be on the history of Mexican Americans, though we have had to expand our knowledge to include other groups who fall under the general category of "Hispanics" or "Latinos." Being of Hispanic-descent, we feel close to the subjects we study. Readers might even find indications throughout the book that we write passionately about our topic. Should that be the case, we do not believe such sentiments to reveal defensiveness on our part, but rather a commitment to seeing that the role of Hispanics in the West be comprehensively and accurately told. Having read widely on the vast scholarship that exists on Hispanics in the United States, we hope that we have succeeded in doing that.

Jorge Iber
Texas Tech University
Lubbock, Texas

Arnoldo De León
Angelo State University
San Angelo, Texas

MAPS

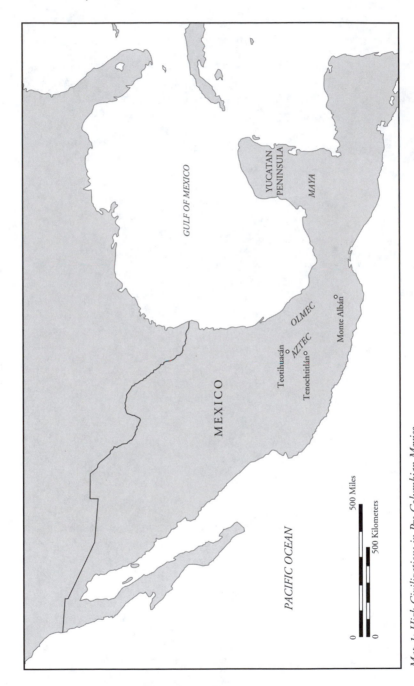

GULF OF MEXICO

YUCATAN
PENINSULA

MAYA

OLMEC

Monte Albán°

Teotihuacán°

AZTEC°

Tenochtitlán°

MEXICO

PACIFIC OCEAN

0   500 Miles

0   500 Kilometers

Map 1: High Civilizations in Pre-Columbian Mexico
Source: *Adapted from Lynn V. Foster, A Brief History of Mexico (New York: Facts on File, 1997), p. 8.*

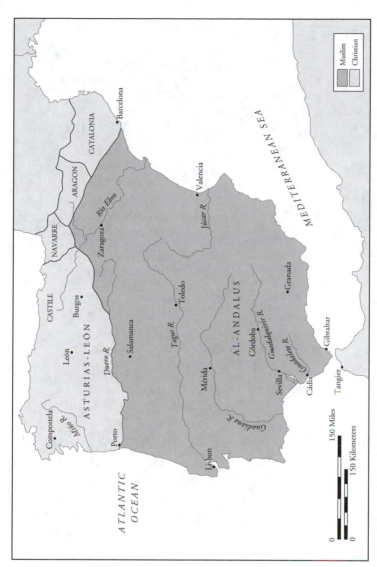

Map 2: Spain during the Reconquista
Source: *Adapted from Joseph F. O'Callaghan, A History of Medieval Spain (Ithaca, NY: Cornell University Press, 1975), p. 108.*

Map 3: The Route to New Mexico
Source: *Adapted from Marc Simmons,* The Last Conquistador: Juan de Oñate and the Settling of the Far Southwest *(Norman: University of Oklahoma Press, 1991), p. 94.*

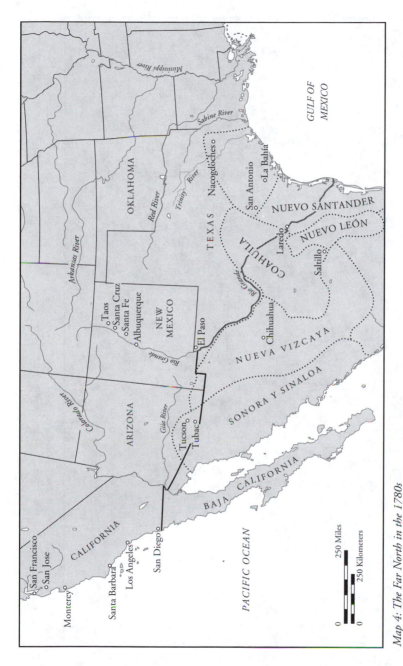

Map 4: The Far North in the 1780s
Source: *Adapted from John L. Kessell,* Spain in the Southwest: A Narrative History of Colonial New Mexico, Arizona, Texas, and California *(Norman: University of Oklahoma Press, 2002), p. 370.*

Map 5: The West under Mexico, 1821–1848
Source: *Adapted from David J. Weber, The Mexican Frontier, 1821–1846: The American Southwest under Mexico (Albuquerque: University of New Mexico Press, 1982), p. 2.*

CHAPTER One

HISPANICS: AN INTRODUCTION TO TERMS AND HISTORICAL BACKGROUNDS

This book is about the U.S. West and the role that Hispanics have played in that region. Immediately, this statement prompts two questions: What is the West and who are Hispanics? Certainly there is no solid agreement on what exactly the two terms mean. Over the years, historians, geographers, literary figures, government officials, and other interested observers have proffered different definitions of the West. Similarly, social scientists, educators, and local government leaders, as well as minorities themselves, have disagreed on the meaning of the word "Hispanic."

One way to make sense of these terms is to review the general understandings of them that have existed over the years and from that discussion attempt an explanation as to how this book employs the concepts. When most people hear about the West, they associate the term with that part of the United States beyond the Mississippi River. This definition is historically constructed, for it takes into account what has happened during the course of the expansion of the United States. At first the definition of the term shifted, being used for the area just beyond the limits of what was seen as civilization. It identified the expanse west of the thirteen states to the Mississippi River. After the war with Mexico (1846–1848), the California gold rush of 1849, and the ending of the Civil War, people streamed past the Mississippi River and implanted U.S. institutions there, turning the region into an appendage of American society. It was thus during the second half of the nineteenth century that the West came to be associated with the part of the United States beyond the Mississippi, and the characteristics of that place and time became part of the image of the West in the minds of most people. The West in this sense is the territory that then became the setting for Indian wars and gunfights, for adventurous mountain men, trappers, and miners, for cattle drives, and for wagon trains going to Oregon, California, or Montana. Even in the early twenty-first century, for most people these events and characters are what define the West.

There is also the West of the twentieth century, which contrasts dramatically with the West described above. People in the region between the Mississippi River and the Pacific Coast today live in immense cities such as Los Angeles and San Francisco. The region resembles much of the rest of the country in suburban living, congestion, pollution, skyscrapers, spaghetti freeways, and apartment housing. Crime is no less present there than it is in New York, Chicago, or Miami. An older cohort of Americans in cities such as Tulsa, or in the farm communities of Nebraska, question the morality of the young, just as do parents and grandparents in Baltimore and Philadelphia. Despite this lack of distinction from the rest of the country, we still refer to the area as the West, simply because it once was a zone where "civilization" met "savagery."

Closely associated with this image of the West is the West of fiction, myth, and imagination—the West as concocted by fiction writers and Hollywood moviemakers. This portrayal of the West is based on facts (garnered from the historical record), but they are exaggerated for the purpose of entertainment. Fiction is meant to sell, whether as books, short stories, or films, and so writers take the liberty of twisting historical facts for the benefit of a good yarn. In these works, the time period is often the latter half of the nineteenth century, and the stories feature white men as courageous protagonists fighting savage Indians on the Plains or battling cowardly Mexicans in Texas, Arizona, or California. Such a scenario has pioneering Anglo Americans conquering a wilderness land and civilizing it. The settlers bring with them character traits and moral values that contrast sharply with those of the people they meet in the West. White protagonists are honest, individualistic, democratic, enterprising, enlightened, and morally pure (especially the women), but the antagonists are corrupt, politically backward, lazy, ignorant, licentious,

Emigrants in oxen-drawn wagons head west across the American plains. (Library of Congress)

and so on. The fashion in these works of fiction that thus turn the West into myth includes cowboy hats and western boots, and if it be the twentieth century, the story line has the characters driving pickups or SUVs. In many minds, this depiction presents the "true West."

Human beings who lived in the region before the mid-nineteenth century held a perception of the West completely unrelated to those just described. First of all, they never used the term "the West." Then, population indigenous to these lands consisted of many peoples and each individual Native American tribe probably had its own notion of the nature of the world around them. To them, the area was their world, the natural world of which they saw themselves as a part, not conquerors. For most, the environment offered essential, and sometimes abundant food, usable commodities for the home, and items for trade. The same environment, on the other hand, was a setting for natural disasters (drought, tornadoes, dust storms, earthquakes, freezes, forest fires, and the like), famine, the threat of attacks, and other uncertainties. Once non-Indian population movements from east of the Mississippi River began during the early decades of the nineteenth century, the old homeland became a meeting point for invasion, conquest, forced removal, and dependency.

Anglo Americans, on the other hand, perceived the land west of the Mississippi as one inhabited by hostile (savage) Indians incapable of applying themselves to the productive use of the soil. During the 1840s, many sincerely believed (or at least they were informed by the architects of empire) that the West and its abundance ought to be part of the American kingdom. Throughout the rest of the century (the era of the "frontier"), westering Americans viewed the trans-Mississippi expanse as a bountiful space with unlimited natural resources waiting for man's exploitation. Prosperity was there for the taking. After all, was not the West generous with free lands, good soil for farming, feral livestock, green forests, untapped mines, virgin streams and rivers for trapping, and many other blessings? In the twentieth century, the West maintained its glamour as a land of new beginnings, as poor folks searched out work in agribusiness, the oil and logging industry, tourism, construction, and countless other enterprises. Whether native to the West or immigrants from the eastern United States, those with money, talent, and business insight conceived of the West as earlier immigrants had: as a place of unlimited possibilities for advancement. Still others looked at the region as less complicated than other parts of the country and as an area with more pleasant climate and more beautiful scenery. Many considered the West a healthy retreat for retirement.

European immigrants pictured the West in almost exactly the same way as Anglo Americans. For the masses, it was a place to find relief from one's misfortunes, even to transform one's destiny. In the case of the Amish, the Danes, and the Russians, to mention just a few examples, the West offered cheap land in amounts impossible to acquire in the Old World. For wealthier arrivals, it was a kind of underdeveloped outpost with the potential to enhance one's economic standing. For well-to-do Englishmen, for instance, the trans-Mississippi territory after the Civil War—where syndicate ranching saw an upswing—became a new outlet for financial speculation. Scottish aristocrats could not help thinking of the West as an ideal spot for sheep grazing and for multiplying their flocks. For those Europeans searching for a haven to practice unorthodox doctrines, the West offered the promise of toleration. Some coming from

Czechoslovakia wanted to find an arena wherein to practice freethinking, and the West seemed to be a better place for that than the more congested regions of the East Coast. In the twentieth century, the West for ethnocentric Europeans came to be a corner of the world to visit, stay in for a time, and make money, with the goal of returning to the old country for retirement.

Peoples of color have been attracted to the West as much as Anglo Americans and Europeans, and their vision of the West has been essentially similar. Most have come from lives of desperate poverty and have envisioned the region as ground space permitting them to achieve economic and social mobility through firm commitment to hard work, even if it be menial labor. The West for them offered a place of tolerance, one permitting them an autonomy wherein customs and traditions brought in from the country of origin could persist unmolested.

Whether as fugitive slaves, freedmen, or bona fide U.S. citizens after the Civil War, African Americans, to take one example, headed West in the belief that the region would not be a hotbed of prejudice, as had been the South, or the inner cities of the North. In the twentieth century, especially after World War II, African Americans defined the West as a land of opportunity, as new industries cropped up in California, Texas, Oregon, Washington, Colorado, and elsewhere, crying out for workers to come and end the labor shortages.

Asians, of course, were not literally going west but east in order to get to the Promised Land, particularly California, which during the nineteenth century the Chinese came to call Gold Mountain. Numerous other Asian groups have sailed east over the decades, not the least of which were the Japanese and Filipinos and, during the last decades of the twentieth century, the Vietnamese and Cambodians. To them, the West embodied a land of bounty, just as it did to European-descended peoples before them. As did others, some Asians dreamed of forging a new destiny, collecting their proceeds, and returning to the homeland with earned riches.

Hispanics, or Latinos (to use another common term), have seen the West both as a homeland and a place to seek refuge or Horatio Alger possibilities. To them, or course, the land did not go by "the West," but as the Far North, or more commonly, *el norte*. Whatever the term used, the

West is a homeland to Mexican Americans, since people of Mexican origin lived there long before the nineteenth century, when Anglo Americans arrived and gave the West its widely held name. But the fact of the matter is that much of the Hispanic population that exists in the West today has come subsequent to 1848, with an overwhelming proportion of that immigration occurring in the twentieth century, all newcomers looking for El Dorado. Other Latino groups have imagined the West as no less, and have also arrived in greater numbers during the last three decades or so of the twentieth century.

So what is the West? How is the West defined for the purposes of this book? We have noted that those who have lived in the region have seen it in various ways, though they have generally agreed on its main characteristic: that it is a land of promise. It is true that people who move into other parts of the country, say the South or the East, also have the understanding that those regions represent opportunity. Nevertheless, bountifulness is so strongly associated with the West that it makes sense to view it as a defining characteristic. And in the absence of consensus on precise geographical delineations, we will use, for purposes of this book, the standard definition of the West as the region of the United States west of the Mississippi River, the very definition that we mention is a historical construct and the area in which Hispanics have played an especially important role. Conscious of the expanding parameters that historians have given "the West" in recent scholarship, we also look at the Hispanic presence in Hawaii as part of our study.

Having explained our use of the term "West," let us go on to the second question at hand: "Who are the Hispanics?" In its simplest definition, the word "Hispanic" identifies people whose cultural antecedents lie first in Spain and then in the Spanish-speaking countries of Latin America, which include Mexico, Central America, all of South America except Brazil, and several Caribbean nations. Though the word has long been an entry in most dictionaries, it did not achieve widespread prominence as a label for public identification until after the 1960s. Before that era, society and government used nationality for reference. Instead of Hispanic, therefore, identifiable groups with roots in Latin America or Spain would have been called Mexicans, Cubans, Puerto Ricans, Nicaraguans, and so forth. Starting in the 1970s, however, departments of government, led by the Bureau of the Census, turned to the word Hispanic in order to distinguish those of Spanish/Latin American origin from white and black people in the United States. Such a usage made sense to government officials as they tried to identify underprivileged elements in need of government assistance, to determine funding for programs such as bilingual education, to redistrict local and state governments, and the like. The business sector quickly accepted the new nomenclature in targeting certain consumer groups, as it did not wish to alienate potential consumers with previously racially charged terms such as "Mexican." Many of Spanish/Latin American descent themselves endorsed the term, seeing it as a neutral reference appropriate for public discourse, or more specifically believing it would be useful as a way to give all Hispanic communities needed political empowerment.

It is more difficult to say how those called Hispanics can be recognized, though there are certain commonalities. Those in the United States who come from Spanish/Latin American stock may speak Spanish. They share cultures with those from the Iberian peninsula and with citizens of Latin America. Traditions and values that are extensions of those from the old homeland thrive in Hispanic communities. Spanish-language radio or television stations help spread the transplanted customs. The Catholic Church does the same, many times holding masses in Spanish and appointing Spanish-speaking priests to Hispanic parishes. Hispanics also tend to be "brown," that is, of a color that is distinguishable from that of Caucasians and African Americans. For the most part, Hispanics marry among themselves, thus biologically perpetuating their "race."

Once we get past this general description, accuracy dissolves. For one thing, Hispanics differ as a sociocultural group in an infinite number of ways. They may come from any one of the several countries in Latin America, for instance. They need not be Catholics, as the many Protestant religions have made inroads among the people of Latin America, as well as among Hispanic communities in the United States. Hispanics also differ by historical background, level of education, class and social standing, and date of arrival in the West.

Differences do not stop there. Although almost all in the United States whose roots are in Spain or Latin America outside Brazil do speak Spanish, there are varieties of Spanish spoken, so that someone from

Puerto Rico would communicate in a manner distinguishable from Mexico's Spanish speakers. Further, linguistic codes are used within Spanish-language communities. A person may employ one manner of speaking in formal situations, then use colloquialisms when interacting with peers. Moreover, there are Hispanics who speak only English. Others are bilingual.

Biologically, Hispanics also differ from one another. Most are a product of what in Latin America is termed *mestizaje,* or racial mixture usually between the aboriginal race of Native Americans and European Spaniards. People in Latin America thus come in different hues and physical looks. There are some who are of swarthy complexion, while others may be of a lighter skin tone. Some may have a European look, others recognizably Indian features. Africans also mixed with Europeans and with local Indian populations over the centuries, so that Hispanics may also be partly of African descent. This African heritage further diversifies the Latin American population from which Hispanics derive. Throwing things into further confusion is the fact that some Europeans, Indians, or Africans either never mixed with other races or did so minimally. Consequently, Hispanics may be purely European, Indian, or African, though their culture is Latin American.

Hispanics may also differ in the term they wish to use for themselves. One person or group may accept one identifier, but not another. Then a group may prefer a label it has ascribed to itself and reject one given to it by outsiders. Similarly, a community may employ one label while interacting in an informal situation, but use another while functioning in a formal setting. Politically, some terms may carry loaded meanings, while others may not. In some quarters, for instance, the word "Hispanic" is regarded as a euphemism used by those who deny or reject their indigenous roots or who feel somehow that the term elevates them socially. Critics of the word associate "Hispanic" with Spain and colonialism, linking it with the Spanish oppressors of the native Indian peoples. Persons of this political ilk may actually apply the term specifically to those Hispanics who appear to be too cozy with mainstream Anglo society. They consider those they call Hispanics as collaborators, as *vendidos* (sellouts), whose sympathies are not with those in the community who remain economically and politically marginalized, but with those who oppress them. These critics tend to be more politicized than most others in Hispanic communities and may opt to call themselves "Latinos," a term associated with the struggles waged by the poor and powerless. Among many university people, labor leaders, and political activists, "Latino" is a preferred term.

Some reasonable compromise on the term must be made for purposes of our discussion, and so in this book we use the word "Hispanic" as the census intends it. For the census, four major categories fall under the umbrella term of "Hispanic." They are "Mexican," "Cuban," "Puerto Rican," and "Other Hispanics." This book is primarily about U.S. citizens of Mexican descent and Mexican immigrants who inhabit the West, with chapter 8 touching upon the history of those who fall in the remaining three categories.

It may be useful to define these categories more precisely. Mexicans are descended at least partly from people who have migrated from Mexico. A few communities of Spanish-Mexican origin have existed in the West since the early seventeenth century, and the Spanish government established other settlements subsequently, so that certainly "Mexicans" lived there when Anglo Americans first began defining the West as the frontier beyond the Mississippi River. Immigrants from the country of Mexico looking for a new start in the United States either established newer communities in the nineteenth and twentieth centuries or replenished older ones. Given this growth in the population, together with natural reproduction, the population of Mexicans in the West far outdistances that of Cubans, Puerto Ricans, and "other Hispanics."

The long presence of Mexicans in the West serves to explain several things about the region's history. Spanish-Mexican *pobladores* (settlers) were the first Europeans to traverse what is the modern U.S. Southwest, and so many of the rivers and other landmarks there have Spanish names. Much adventure came out the pobladores' struggle with the wilderness before the coming of the Anglos, and as a consequence, there is a mystique about the region's "Spanish past." Mexicans and Mexican Americans have contributed in a multitude of other ways to the development of the West, many of them just being recorded by historians. Far more scholarly literature presently exists on Mexicans in the West than on any of the other three Hispanic groups. All of these reasons explain why the focus of this book is on Mexicans primarily.

The historical significance and numerical dominance of Mexicans and Mexican Americans in the West does not, however, mean that the other Spanish-speaking groups have left no imprint on the region. In order to provide a sense of proportionality, it makes sense, then, to briefly introduce the groups according to the extent and length of their presence in the area.

The scholarly literature on Puerto Ricans focuses, and rightly, on the group's highest areas of concentration: namely, the New York City, Philadelphia, Boston, and Chicago metropolitan areas. Nonetheless, historians and other scholars of the social sciences have examined a few pockets, some of long standing, of *boriquas* (as Puerto Ricans call themselves) in the U.S. West. The majority of the extant literature focuses on Hawaii and California, with scattered mentions of their presence in places such as Utah and Nevada. In many ways, the story of *Puertorriqueños* in these states mirrors that of Mexicans and Mexican Americans. Due to economic difficulties on the island at various points of the twentieth century, many boriquas traveled to the West as cheap agricultural labor (to work in the sugarcane fields in Hawaii and other agricultural pursuits in California) or mining labor (substantial numbers were recruited to Utah and Nevada during World War II) and through individual and communal diligence in overcoming adversity and discrimination, have constructed proud and positive communities, as well as achieving much social and economic improvement in places such as Los Angeles, San Francisco, Salt Lake City, and Las Vegas.

Although Cubans have lived in the United States since the early decades of the nineteenth century, their numbers have always been relatively small, especially in the West. The 1870 federal census estimated that a mere 7,000 Cuban-born individuals lived in the United States at that time. The overwhelming majority were concentrated in Key West, Florida, and New York City (mostly working in the cigar industry), with pockets in other port cities such as Tampa, Mobile, Baltimore, New Orleans, and Philadelphia. At the start of the enormous exodus after Castro's revolution (an exodus that started in the early 1960s), there were only about 124,000 people of Cuban descent in the United States. The lone substantial concentration of Cuban Americans located in the West was based in Los Angeles. The 1960s, however, witnessed the arrival of large numbers of Cubans seeking refuge from Castro's gulag (through the Peter Pan flights and the Freedom Flights of 1968–1973), and increasing numbers moved to (or were asked to relocate to) the West. Because of this migration, in addition to the expansion of the Los Angeles concentration, several new Cuban American clusters developed in the Las Vegas, Houston, San Diego, San Francisco, and Seattle metropolitan areas.

The Cuban American presence in the West is different in two significant ways from that of people of Mexican and Puerto Rican descent. First, by contrast with these other groups, it is more recent and smaller. Second, research by University of Miami geographer Thomas Boswell demonstrates that Cubanos living outside the "Cuban Mecca" of Miami-Dade County have higher socioeconomic standing than do Cubans living in southern Florida, a status nearly equal that of the general U.S. population. Cubanos, in the West and elsewhere, are, statistically, better educated and more affluent than other Spanish speakers. Still, although many Cubanos have experienced success, more recent immigrants (specifically, those who arrived during the Mariel boatlift of 1980 and subsequent waves during the 1990s) who have found their way West have not, by and large, experienced similar levels of social or economic progress.

The final cluster of Hispanics we examine contains some of the newest arrivals to the U.S. West and hence is the least well represented in the academic literature. This nebulous category of Spanish-speaking people includes individuals from all of the remaining Latin American nations (except, as always, Brazil). Among the largest groups found in parts of the West are El Salvadorians, Colombians, Hondurans, Guatemalans, and Nicaraguans. Many of these persons fled north during the 1970s in order to escape various vicious civil wars then raging in their homelands. Author Juan González, in his book *Harvest of Empire: A History of Latinos in America* (New York: Penguin Books, 2000), for example, notes that the Salvadorian community in Los Angeles ballooned from 30,000 in 1979 to roughly ten times that count by the late 1980s.

The numbers of "other Hispanics" have skyrocketed since the early 1980s, and now there are substantial concentrations in California, Texas, Nevada, and Utah. Like other people who came to the U.S. West before them, most of the Spanish-speaking "others" now residing in Los Angeles, Houston, Las Vegas, and Salt Lake City (and elsewhere) seek mainly to

improve economic and social opportunities for their children and themselves. The majority of such *recien llegados* (recent arrivals) have not come
to the United States seeking handouts, as some would have us believe, but
rather to seek fulfillment of the promises that our nation, and particularly
the region under consideration in this book, have offered to countless immigrants from other parts of the world. (See Table 1.1 for statistics on Hispanic population in the U.S. West, broken down by group and state.)

Table 1.1
Hispanic Population in the U.S. West, 2000

State	Mexican	Puerto Rican	Cuban	Other Hispanic
Alaska	13,334	2,649	553	9,316
Arizona	1,065,578	17,587	5,272	207,180
Arkansas	61,204	2,473	950	22,239
California	8,455,926	140,570	72,286	2,297,774
Colorado	450,760	12,993	3,701	268,147
Idaho	79,324	1,509	408	20,449
Iowa	61,154	2,690	750	17,879
Hawaii	19,820	30,005	771	37,163
Kansas	148,270	5,237	1,680	33,065
Louisiana	32,267	7,670	8,448	59,373
Minnesota	95,613	6,616	2,527	38,626
Missouri	77,887	6,677	3,022	31,006
Montana	11,735	931	285	5,130
Nebraska	71,030	1,993	859	20,543
Nevada	285,764	10,420	11,498	86,288
New Mexico	330,049	4,488	2,588	428,261
North Dakota	4,297	507	250	2,734
Oklahoma	132,813	8,153	1,759	36,579
Oregon	214,662	5,092	3,091	52,469
South Dakota	6,364	637	163	3,739
Texas	5,071,963	69,504	25,705	1,502,494
Utah	136,416	3,977	940	60,226
Wyoming	19,963	575	160	10,971

Source: Betsy Guzmán, *The Hispanic Population: Census 2000 Brief.*
C2KBR/01-3. "Table 2: Hispanic Population by Type for Regions, States, and
Puerto Rico: 1990–2000." (Washington, DC: U.S. Bureau of the Census, 2001),
p. 4.

INDIAN AND IBERIAN ORIGINS OF THE MEXICAN PEOPLE

Given that the category known as Mexican represents the central focus of this book, the rest of this introductory chapter is concerned chiefly with the racial and historical background of those who fall in that category. Almost all people of Latin American stock are products of the biological and cultural process termed *mestizaje,* discussed earlier. Sexual encounters between Spaniards and Native American women, whether in the West Indies, in Mexico, or in South America, occurred for a number of reasons, among them the violent propensities of the colonizers, the absence of Spanish women, and the human instinct to love and appreciate another person. As Spain imported Africans to perform plantation labor in Latin America, further mixing occurred, and so Africans added to the racial makeup of Mexicans, Cubans, Puerto Ricans, and "Other Hispanics." As the decades passed, the offspring of this racial fusion merged—either legally or illicitly—with other Spaniards, Africans, or men and women like themselves, further diversifying the Latin American racial constitution.

Mexicans, for the most part, descend from Indians and Spaniards. Here we do not reject an African racial and cultural contribution, for certainly African slaves lived in Mexico from the 1500s on, but anthropologists do not consider black-white miscegenation in Mexico to have occurred to the degree that it did in other Latin American countries. As to Indians, their contribution to the biological makeup of Mexico is probably greater than that of Spaniards, though culturally Mexico is more Spanish than Indian. Since both races feature prominently in the historical background of Mexican Americans in the United States, each deserves equal attention.

Indians came over the Bering Strait sometime between the years 40,000 and 15,000 BC. Although several different theories exist as to the provenance of early New World Homo sapiens, recent studies on DNA confirm that these people did in fact originate in Asia. Migration occurred in several stages and in different times, involving peoples with diverse biological backgrounds; they survived by relying on an array of small game, flora, and sea life in their new land. When, sometime between 8000 and 2000 BC, those who settled in Mesoamerica (that region extending from the northern deserts of what is today Mexico to upper Central America) mastered horticulture by learning to raise and harvest plants such as maize, beans, chiles, and squash, their nomadic existence ceased. Life in villages or small communities became the norm.

No specific characteristics may be given to all of the Indian peoples who lived in Mexico before the Spaniards' arrival. Indian cultures were too numerous and too diverse in development. Among the first to achieve more prominence were the Olmecs, who by the year 800 BC had risen to grandeur in the area of the modern states of Oaxaca, Tabasco, and Vera Cruz. Acknowledged as the civilization that influenced subsequent great societies in Mesoamerica, the Olmec nation—with rudimentary equipment—built imposing pyramids, sprawling urban centers, and huge stone figures (some of them 9 feet tall and weighing nearly 100,000 pounds) out of basalt rock transported over wide distances. They harvested maize and other farm crops and produced delicate pottery and ornaments, which they exchanged for other finished goods coming from Central America and other parts of Mexico. For unknown reasons, the Olmec civilization faltered sometime around 400 BC.

The Classic Era of pre-Columbian times (circa 200 BC–AD 800/1000) followed the age of the Olmecs. Unprecedented intellectual, scientific, artistic, and architectural strides marked this historical time period. Many were the civilizations whose achievements constituted the Classic Era, but those at Teotihuacán (in today's Mexico City), Monte Albán (in Oaxaca), and the Yucatán Peninsula (the Maya) surpassed all others in splendor and achievement. So awed were the Aztecs (discussed later) with the legacy of Teotihuacán (150 BC–AD 750) that they recognized it as the birthplace of the gods, the sun, and the moon. It is in Teotihuacán that one can find today the Pyramid of the Sun and the Pyramid of the Moon. At its prime, the city contained a population greater than 100,000 spread over 12 square miles. Its grandeur was only slightly greater than Monte Albán to the south (in the modern state of Oaxaca), however. Situated atop a mountain elevation, Monte Albán (AD 650–AD 900) contained pyramids, imposing religious temples, and sculpted art, as did Teotihuacán. Mystery surrounds the decline of both Teotihuacán and Monte Albán, at around the eighth and tenth century, respectively.

View of the Pyramid of the Sun from the top of the Pyramid of the Moon in Teotihuacán, Mexico. (Corel Corporation)

The most famous of civilizations in the Classic era was the Mayan. From about AD 200 to about AD 900, Mayan glory spread mightily throughout what later became the states of Yucatán, Chiapas, Tabasco, and Campeche. No single metropolis ever became the dominating center of Mayan power. Instead, numerous cities, many with populations of greater than 50,000 residents, gave evidence of the empire's intellectual progress. As accomplished as other contemporaries in town building, craft making, art, architecture, terracing, and the like, the Mayas surpassed them in intellectual discoveries. They excelled in keeping records, namely through the hieroglyphic writing they perfected. They pioneered the study of astronomy and paved the way in mathematics. Long before the Europeans became acquainted with the theory of the zero, the Mayas used the concept to plan their annual cropping (so as to feed their populations), pry into the mysteries of the solar system, and keep careful time, a practice permitted by the amazing accuracy of their calendar. Many arguments exist to explain the decline and fall of the Maya around AD 900. A recent school of thought puts the blame on unplanned urban expansion, for growth required cutting down forests, which in turn caused soil erosion, which then undermined the ability to feed increasing populations.

None of these early civilizations matched the power amassed by the mighty Aztec empire (AD 900–1521), which stood at the apex of its rule when the Spaniards reached the New World. Legend has them as late arrivals in the Valley of Mexico sometime in the fourteenth century, having started their migration from some northern land called Aztatlán, or Aztlán. According to the stories the Aztecs later told, their gods had instructed them to settle wherever they saw an eagle perched on a cactus, feeding on a serpent. They encountered this sight at Anáhuac (the Valley of Mexico). There the Aztecs found a receptive environment: agreeable climate, fertile soil, abundant forestlands, good water resources, and a central location in Mexico. They also encountered advanced civilizations such as Teotihuacán, which, though in decline, provided the means of growth to the ambitious Aztecs. They overcame what remained of the Teotihuacán civilization, then co-opted some of its religious beliefs, cultural practices, and knowledge, all the while building their own empire with its central city at Tenochtitlán (modern Mexico City). From Tenochtitlán the Aztecs launched military campaigns against neighboring peoples, subduing most and bringing them under the Aztec banner. By the early 1510s, the Aztec Empire sprawled throughout most of Central Mexico and also extended into parts of Central America.

Aztec civilization puzzles the modern observer. As a people, the Aztecs tended to have a warrior mentality and were inclined to barbarism and cruelty. At times, their wars had as their purpose only the goal of capturing enough victims to satisfy their gods through the ritual of human sacrifice. Class and gender equality had no place in the precepts of Aztec life. Instead, social stratification and oppression of women were guiding principles. Yet at the same time, countless enlightened traditions and practices offset these more baneful aspects of their civilization. They instituted compulsory education, discouraged immoral behavior, and took pride in the fairness of their judicial system.

Moreover, they left a mark of accomplishment that commends the Aztec name even today. They had developed a reliable enough system for treating the problems of the sick (by using local herbs) that it is still used in contemporary Mexico. Archaeologists have found evidence that they performed successful brain surgery. Their skill as farmers helped prevent possible food shortages for the people. Their merchants engaged in a flourishing trade that extended to far-off points in the empire. Sophisticated sculpture, elegant craftwork, and soothing music spoke to their aesthetic sensibilities. Their capital city of Tenochtitlán housed some 60,000 to 80,000 people, and its magnificence was appreciated by the Spaniards who conquered them, as it still is by those who visit the historic site today. Pyramids, well-kept residential areas, clean streets, and beautifully maintained gardens constitute only a partial list of the features that enhanced the city's grace.

It would be pleasant to think that those of Mexican origin today were descended exclusively from such magnificence as the Olmecs, Mayas, and Aztecs represent. But the fact of the matter is that, biologically speaking, Mexican Americans who inhabit the U.S. West inherit (in addition to Aztec blood) the blood of lesser-known peoples who lived in lands outside the Valley of Mexico and the Yucatán Peninsula. Still, it is with the cultures of these high civilizations that most people of Mexico, and thus Mexicans in the United States, identify. Some of these cultural legacies will be discussed in subsequent chapters of this book.

Naturally, Mexican Americans also identify with Spaniards, but the Spanish heritage itself needs elaboration. The earliest inhabitants of the area of the modern country of Spain (often referred to as the Iberians) derived from Mediterranean stock. Sometime during the sixth century BC, Indo-Europeans known as the Celts migrated into the peninsula and over the ensuing generations mixed with the Iberians to produce what have come to be known as Celt-Iberians. Other Mediterranean civilizations planted colonies in Spain subsequent to this time, among them the Greeks, who remained in Spain (and influenced life and culture) from about the seventh century BC to about the second century AD.

The most influential of the peoples who were part of early Spanish history were the Romans, whose empire throve across Europe from about 200 BC to AD 400. To the Romans, Spain owed much, not least its name—in Latin *Hispania,* which evolved over the years into *España.* As elsewhere, it was the Romans who brought Christianity. No one knows exactly when the new religion first appeared in the country. Stories circulated—none of them documented—that the Apostle Paul, sometime between 63 and 67, traveled through Spain and there preached the Christian word. The most famous of these legendary accounts holds that St. James the Apostle proselytized in Spain, and though this story is similarly problematic, there is little question that Christianity was very much a part of Spanish life by the second century.

The Romans also imposed their language on the peninsula, and their codes of law almost completely supplanted all preexisting legal systems, customs, and traditions. Literature flowered during the Roman period, and Spain made its own contribution to the splendor of Roman civilization by producing renowned poets, writers, philosophers, and historians. The cities of Spain bustled with activity and compared favorably in business and urban dynamic with metropolises of similar size in other parts of the Roman Empire. It is no exaggeration to state that the Romans left an indelible impression on Spain. Historians note that by the time their stay ended, few traces of pre-Roman civilizations remained.

Germanic invasions beset Europe starting around the fifth century, and they did not spare Spain. Into the peninsula swept several of these barbarian groups, the fiercest being the Visigoths. Proponents of a warrior cult, they suppressed all resistance they encountered and had soon overcome the entire peninsula. But they left implanted little of their way of life. On the contrary, they were completely won over to the Roman way of life entrenched there, absorbing Christianity, Latin, and Roman laws and decrees.

Not so with the Muslims, followers of the Islamic faith, who crossed the Mediterranean and overpowered Spain, starting in 711. The Moors, as the Spaniards called them, referred to their conquered land as al-Andalus. They swiftly spread their brand of Arabic civilization in those regions under their control, and as some of them intermixed with the indigenous peoples there, altered the racial stock of the "Spaniards." During the tenth century, Muslim Spain reached a peak of greatness. Cities in different quarters of al-Andalus became frenzied scenes of business activity. Manufacturing plants produced woolen or silk textiles, leather, assorted weaponry, paper, and glass for trade in African and Mediterranean markets. Such prosperity in turn transformed many cities throughout al-

Andalus—among them Toledo, Córdoba, and Zaragoza—into some of the most highly civilized and fastest growing urban centers in Europe. Farms yielded crop surpluses, and agricultural goods also became very much a part of the era's international trade.

The Muslims' imprint on Spain was to be indelible. They developed methods for working the range and managing livestock, while at the same time introducing innovations applicable to farm work and large-scale gardening. They discovered new treatments and cures for sickness and diseases and spread their knowledge of medicine to other parts of the Mediterranean. Their preferred architectural styles are readily identifiable worldwide even today. The patio, complemented with attractive water fountains and decorated with multicolored Spanish tile, is a Muslim contribution, as is the "Moorish roof" one finds on homes throughout Latin America and the U.S. Southwest. Many attitudes the Spaniards (and later Mexicans and Mexican Americans) subsequently held about women derived from Muslim influences. Señoritas were to be proper, pure, and innocent, and must be protected by men from shame, insult, and their own waywardness. The Spanish tradition of taking a midday siesta is of Muslim origin.

But Christian Spain never completely accepted the Muslim way of life, especially Islam, and a counteroffensive to retake the homeland began soon after the Arab occupation. Called the *Reconquista* (reconquest), this campaign originated in the northern regions of the peninsula, which the Muslims had failed to bring under their power. Around the ninth century, the Reconquista took on an obsessive character, as Spaniards committed themselves to regaining the kind of life they knew before their ignominious defeat. Spanish culture, language, traditions, and laws were to be rescued at all costs. Civilizations now clashed, as Spaniards and Muslims fought with equal fanaticism in defense of their respective heritages.

The Reconquista also took on religious overtones, as the Christians vowed to return Spain to its former status as a glorious Catholic kingdom. Spaniards, led by those from Castile, fused the passion of Christianity and pride in their homeland into one holy cause as they struck against the despised occupiers. They were inspired in their struggle by the supposed discovery around 900 of the tomb of St. James (called in Spain

Saint James the Great, apostle and martyr, at the battle of Santiago de Compostela, Spain. By Martin Schongauer (c.1430–1491). (The Art Archive/Bibliothèque des Arts Décoratifs Paris/Dagli Orti)

Santiago) in the kingdom of Galicia, an event that soon transformed Santiago into Spain's patron saint. Soldiers in battle now reported St. James fighting alongside them against the insufferable infidels or at least seeing him in the skies mounted on his white horse urging them on.

The Reconquista shaped Spanish life in still other ways. The seven centuries of conflict made a central virtue of machismo, or masculine prowess, for instance. Common soldiers, for example, could well win social promotion by their display of valor in the face of grave risk. The Castilian determination to oust the Muslims further made honor, chivalry, self-discipline, sacrifice, and military service supreme virtues. Spaniards, whether rich or poor, accepted these qualities so wholeheartedly that they became traits of the Spanish character. Despite what appears to have been a fanatical Spanish resolve to rid the peninsula of the Muslim foes, it was not until the last decade of the fifteenth century that the Reconquista was completed. It took coordination between the newly united kingdoms of Aragon and Castile to achieve this goal. Led by King Ferdinand and Queen Isabella, a more unified Spain launched a last formidable campaign against Granada, the remaining Muslim stronghold, and in 1492 the Moors capitulated.

THE CONQUEST OF MEXICO

By a coincidence of history, Spain that same year made contact with the landmass that in Europe came to be called the New World. The *conquistadores* (Spanish conquerors) who followed in the wake of Christopher Columbus thus sailed across the Atlantic with the same sense of adventure and search for glory as had obsessed the soldiers of the Reconquista. Aside from that, they came to claim new kingdoms and convert new infidels for the mother country, then at the apogee of international influence and might in Europe. A conquistador named Hernando Cortés led the charge for the domination of Mexico and the conquest of the Aztec Empire. Upon reaching the mainland, he encountered some friendly peoples who, as a token of their good will, presented Cortés and his army of about 550 men with several young maidens, among them one who was christened as Doña Marina, but in Mexican history has been known derisively as *La Malinche* ("the traitor," derived from Malintzín, Doña Marina's Aztec name) for the assistance she rendered the Spaniards. Cortés then founded, on April 21, 1519, what came to be known as the city of Vera Cruz, and by August commenced a march toward the interior and Tenochtitlán. Defeating resistance along the way, he arrived in the Valley of Mexico in November 1519.

Awaiting the Spaniards with some trepidation in Tenochtitlán was the Aztec emperor, Montezuma. He had expected visitors to come from the eastern shores one day, for one of their ancient gods—named Quetzalcoatl (the Feathered Serpent)—had once promised to return from banishment and redeem the Aztec Empire from corruption, profligacy, and the baneful practice of engaging in human sacrifice. Legend held him to be a man with white skin and a beard, and reports to Montezuma described the strangers as such. When Cortés and his contingent arrived in Tenochtitlán on November 8, 1519, Montezuma welcomed them, not risking offending strangers whom he considered to be gods.

Hernando Cortés and Aztec ruler Montezuma meet in November 1519 on Cortés'
expedition to conquer Mexico. (Library of Congress)

Montezuma treated the Spaniards with special hospitality, behavior that did not ease the conquistadors' anxiety, for after all, were they not in a precarious situation, surrounded by thousands of people who could not be trusted? For self-protection, Cortés took Montezuma hostage, an act that angered the emperor's subjects and ended the Spaniards' welcome. The Aztecs, bound on recapturing their besieged city, launched an attack on the heart of Tenochtitlán in June 1520. In the frenzy of battle, Montezuma was killed (legend says accidentally), but the Aztecs chased the Europeans from Tenochtitlán on July 1, 1520, in what Mexico's history refers to as *la noche triste* (the sad night).

By no means did the Spaniards despair, however. Cortés, with significant reinforcements from the West Indies, arrived on the periphery of Tenochtitlán in December 1520. Cuauhtémoc, Montezuma's successor, coordinated the city's defenses, but Spanish forces and weapons, reinforced by Indian allies, proved too powerful. Tenochtitlán's defenses collapsed on August 21, 1521.

The conquest of Mexico had immediate repercussions for New Spain, as the new colony came to be called by the Spanish government. Millions of Native Americans throughout the land died in the aftermath of the defeat at the hands of the conquistadors. Scholars attribute the catastrophe to a number of causes, chief among them disease. The most devastating of these plagues were smallpox, measles, and typhus, against which the Indians had little natural protection, as these were Old World diseases. Entire villages succumbed to the diseases, leaving families shattered, communities leaderless, and the fields with not enough workers left to harvest the crops. Hunger thus took its toll of lives as well, a calamity exacerbated as the Spaniards moved native villagers from productive farmlands. Human cruelty accounted for still more deaths, as the Spaniards engaged in homicide, launched military actions, and pressed the Indians into hard labor in the mines and on rural estates. The Catholic Church added to the tragedy by either killing or endorsing the deaths of those whom it considered agents of the devil. A last cause that students of New Spain's colonial era find responsible for the decimation of the indigenous population is loss of will. So many people surrendered to the tragedy that befell them so completely that they simply sickened and passed away. According to one scholar's calculation, the population in the Valley of Mexico stood at approximately 1.5 million on the eve of the conquest, but within a century had declined to slightly less than 200,000.

For the survivors of the tragedy, fate brought harsh work and labor exploitation. In the decades immediately following the conquest, the victorious conquistadors received *encomiendas,* or rights over Indian villages to be used for making a profit. In return, the *encomendero* had the responsibility of Christianizing and Europeanizing his charges, a task he seldom fulfilled. Instead, the Indians endured sexual abuse, overwork, and conditions that approximated enslavement. The encomienda system lasted only until the last years of the sixteenth century, by which time the original conquistadors had died. By then, the system had left its mark on colonial New Spain, and the ruling classes found it easy enough to duplicate it in other forms.

As a replacement, the *repartimiento* (giving the Spaniards the authority to use Indian labor) emerged. The crown gave its blessing to the repartimiento system, given the shortage of labor in New Spain. Mine owners, farmers, and ranchers, as well as government officials in charge of overseeing urban projects, were only too eager to seek the Indians as an exploitable work force and not long after repartimiento was instituted, the system began to cause horrible human misery. Emerging along side the repartimiento was the *hacienda,* or rural estate. As Spaniards received lands from the crown for ranching and farming, they recruited laborers from among the poverty-stricken Indian villagers, who could do little other than accept in the face of increasing hunger. Many swiftly found themselves in debt to the *hacendado,* who was only too happy to keep them in a perpetual state of dependence.

The conquest also produced a mestizo race. Cohabitation between Spanish men and Indian women began almost immediately. Whether consensual or forced, racial mixing between the two races occurred to such a degree that the progeny of the two peoples soon became a visible element in colonial Mexican society. Within a generation or two after the conquest, at least three distinguishable races were present in New Spain, and literally thousands of other groups that were the offspring of the admixture of these three. There were the Europeans (Spaniards), who arrived at a steady pace from Spain to assume positions in government and the church, to start in Mexico anew as miners, farmers, or ranchers, to reinforce the king's armies, or simply to pursue adventure. There were the masses of Indians, the ones falling victims to disease and doing the harshest labor for the Spaniards. And there were hundreds of Africans. Making up the fastest growing segment of the population were the mestizos, generally the progeny of Spanish men and Indian women who in turn mixed with fellow mestizos, other Indians, Africans, or Europeans to beget a group given the label of *castas* (all possible racial mixtures). Demographers today suppose that close to 80 percent of Mexico's population is a product of racial mixing, with Indian genes predominating.

The fate of the mestizos, whose numbers soon multiplied to the point that they constituted the dominant ethnic element in New Spain, was social subordination. Spanish colonial society recognized differences based on racial makeup. At the top stood the Spaniards, whether they were *peninsulares* or *criollos*. No difference in genetic constitution distinguished these two groups, nothing but place of birth. The former were born in Spain, the latter in the New World, but criollos were considered inferior to their parents, for the homegrown Spaniards believed the climate of the New World somehow weakened their own children. Notwithstanding this baseless supposition, the colonial mentality regarded the criollos as white, and so along with the peninsulares they lorded it over the mestizo population, which both deemed contemptible.

Mestizos to the Spaniards represented the fruits of man's base impulses, iniquity, and immorality. Spain since the Reconquista had subscribed to the idea of racial purity (*limpieza de sangre;* literally, "cleanness of blood"), and the Catholic Church had accentuated the sacredness of marriage. Mestizos consequently bore the stigma of both mongrelization and illegitimacy, and for all intents and purposes they were lumped with the lowly Indian peoples. Most worked alongside the Indians and mulattoes (the offspring of an African and an Indian) in the mines or haciendas, went without schooling, and had little hope of improving their condition. Colonial society was not so closed as to keep all mestizos from social improvement, but the lot for the majority of Mexicans was one that created discontent and perpetual resentment of the ruling class.

A Mestizo Heritage

So what was the significance of the above conditions to the plain people of Mexico and subsequently to those pobladores (settlers) who migrated toward the Far North (as the area we know as the U.S. West is called by borderlands historians), either during the colonial era or in modern times? Two things might be noted here. First, people of the lower stratum, the majority of them mestizos or Indians (who continued intermixing with each other), came to be branded as peons, and as such less deserving of opportunities for social betterment. Spaniards identified them as a people of color and associated them with crude and uncultivated manners. Second, subjugation produced a modified version of European culture, for indeed, the Spaniards sought to wipe out as much of the native way of life as possible. The lower classes came to practice Catholicism, accept Spanish customs and traditions, participate in Spanish entertainment forms, help erect buildings in the European manner, and dress as the

Spaniards dictated. Cotton breeches for men and the loosely fitting Indian blouse (called a *huipil*) for women surfaced as the acceptable fashion for the masses.

It was, nevertheless, a syncretic culture that people of Spanish/Mexican descent exported into frontier areas such as Mexico's Far North during the colonial era and that migrants continue transplanting to the United States even in the twenty-first century. This culture, a product of the conquest and the generations' process of mestizaje, took much from the Spanish past but also preserved much of the Native American way. Examples of each civilization's input stand out readily in *lo mexicano* (the Mexican way of life).

Spanish is the most obvious contribution made by the conquerors. The Latin spoken by the Romans during their occupation of Spain between 200 BC and AD 400 was the basis of the language Spain brought to the New World, since not even the seven centuries of the Muslim occupation had changed that feature of Spanish civilization. But the Muslims did influence the Spanish language, so that many words Hispanics use today (and take for granted as being Spanish) actually derive from Arabic words. Under Spanish and Mexican rule, the states located in the modern U.S. West were governed by *alcaldes* (city mayors) and policed by the *alguacil*. Throughout the U.S. West, the Spaniards built *acequias* (irrigation canals), used *norias* (waterwheels) to bring the water to their crops, made homes of *adobe* (sun-dried brick), and resided in barrios (urban neighborhoods). As late as the nineteenth century, many Mexicans from Texas to California made their living as *arrieros* (wagon drivers). Throughout Latin America (and the U.S. West), people can hardly do without *azucar* (sugar), *arroz* (rice), *zanahorias* (carrots), or *naranjas* (oranges). The word *tarea*, referring to some kind of task, is frequently employed by youths having to do their homework, including their *álgebra* (an Arabic word also adopted in English), so that they can then spend time around the *alberca* (the swimming pool). The list of Arabic-derived Spanish words appears endless.

Another aspect of Spanish civilization that entrenched itself in Mexico was Catholicism. Both through force and teaching, the Spaniards attempted to supplant the indigenous pagan religions with Christian doctrine. They succeeded in making Catholicism New Spain's primary religion, at least among those who lived in towns and accepted European ways to any extent, for many Indian tribes either escaped the missionaries' proselytizing or rejected the European religious view altogether. As in the case of language, vestiges of Arabic influences (minimal though they were) remained in Catholic thought, especially in expressions. Commonly among people of Mexican descent one hears, *"Si dios quiere"* (if God wishes it), to which the listener responds, *"Ojalá"* (usually translated "I hope so!"). Here the second person is, usually without knowing it, invoking the power of Allah, the Muslim counterpart to the Christian God. The appeal to God in the phrase *"Que dios los guarde"* (may God take care of you) also comes from Arabic declarations of good wishes.

Also imposed on life in the New World by the Spaniards were legal traditions traceable to the Roman stay in the old homeland. To take one example, the law made it reasonably easy for orphans to be readily adopted into a family. Allegiance to the concept of community property meant that husband and wife could lawfully claim (with equal right) any moneys or property they amassed while married. If a woman earned money on her own, it could not be claimed solely by the husband, as was the case in the British colonies of North America, for instance. Should a divorce occur, any earnings accumulated by man and wife would be split equally. Those under financial duress could expect protection from the legal system if unable to meet their financial commitments, as Roman tradition prohibited creditors from taking debtors' homes or their means of making a living. The legacy of this Spanish tradition remains in the U.S. West today.

To the Spaniards the people of Mexico owe numerous forms for expressing civility, gratitude, and good wishes. Custom and courtesy dictate that older persons, or those of some prominence, be addressed formally as *usted,* and not with the less formal *tu.* Colonial society came to use the terms *don* and *doña* as formal titles given to people of social rank or to elderly folks deserving of esteem. Much of Mexican etiquette is of Muslim origin. Not infrequently does one hear someone say *esta es su casa,* "this is your home," or perhaps *está en su casa,* "you are in your home." Before beginning a meal, a family member at the table may say *buen provecho,* a wish that the sustenance may yield good health.

What, on the other hand, have people of Mexican origin inherited from their Native American parents? Their name, "Mexicans," is one of the first things that comes to mind. The word *Mexicano/a* is deeply rooted in Aztec lexicon, for after all, the Aztecs referred to themselves as the *Mexica* (or *Meshica*), and Mexicans named their country *México* after the ancient *Meshica*.

Indian religious traditions have also blended into Mexico's Catholicism. No other event in the history of Mexico's indigenous people has had a deeper influence on the country's beliefs than the appearance of the Virgin Mary to Juan Diego. As the story has been told through the centuries, the Indian Juan Diego witnessed the apparition of the Virgin in 1531, near the outskirts of Mexico City. The Virgin asked the distressed Indian to build a chapel in her honor there on the spot where she had appeared, but no one believed the lowly Juan Diego. Thereupon, the Virgin (a woman of dark skin) reappeared and gave Juan Diego visible proof of her mysterious revelation, which Juan took to the Bishop. The Virgen de Guadalupe thus became the patron saint of Mexico, and the Catholic Church observes December 12 as the *día de la Virgen de Guadalupe* (day of Our Lady of Guadalupe). In Mexico and in the U.S. West, Mexicans sometimes refer to her as *la morenita* (the brown-skinned lady).

Numerous indigenous foods are part of the diet of Mexicans and Hispanics, including tortillas, tamales, and *atole* (gruel), all of which are made of maize, a staple of Aztec sustenance, which people crushed on the metate, an Aztec word for a grinding stone. Also very familiar to Mexican meals are frijoles, chili, tacos, and enchiladas. Foreign in Europe at the time of the conquest but well known to pre-Columbian people in the Valley of Mexico were such edibles as *cacahuates* (peanuts) and *camotes* (sweet potatoes) and the intoxicants mescal and tequila, made from native plants.

In addition, several common words in Spanish are of Aztec derivation, not of Iberian origin: *nopal* (cactus), *mecate* (rope), *papalote* (a kite), *guajolote* (turkey), and *zoquete* (mud). Also, it is not uncommon to find clubs, business establishments, ranches, newspapers, and a wide array of other concerns adopting names that invoke the Aztec past. To be found in Mexico and among Mexican American communities in the U.S. West are Club Chapultepec, Tortillería Cuauhtémoc, and a periodical by the name of *Azteca del Norte.*

Aztec mythology also has been part of the Mexican (and the Hispanic) experience since the colonial era. Many people in Mexico, as well as Mexican-origin residents of the United States, still retain a belief in the legend of La Malinche. This story, which resembles other such folkloric tales, tells how Doña Marina despaired when Hernando Cortés deserted her, leaving the Indian mistress with their sons. Forlorn, she killed the boys, but then spent the rest of her days in grief and looking for them in the streets of the once splendid Aztec capital. Superstitions that remain both in Mexico and among Mexican-descent persons are also traceable to Aztec beliefs. *Brujería* (witchcraft) exists today within some Mexican American communities in the U.S. West, as believers in the occult seek the help of *brujas* (witches), who are supposed to be able to inflict evil on those responsible for harm. Many also still rely on *curanderos* and *curanderas* (faith healers). Curanderos appeal to spirits and rely on native herbs, many of which the Aztecs themselves used for medical treatment.

LA MALINCHE/DOÑA MARINA

Among the most remarkable figures from pre-Columbian history to have relevance to the Mexican American experience is a woman known both as *La Malinche* and *Doña Marina.* Her story is applicable to Hispanics in the U.S. West, first because Mexican Americans are of Indian heritage and she was in fact an Aztec woman. Then, Mexican American history has part of its roots in the history of Mexico, and few textbooks about Mexico ignore her presence (indeed, survey texts on Mexican Americans also include her story, as this text does).

How exactly is Malinche portrayed historically? Sympathetic interpretations see her as a loyal ally of the Spaniards who brought enlightenment and Christianity to the Aztec pagans. More commonly, however, she is seen as a traitor who collaborated with the foreigners to trample her own people (the Native Americans) by colluding with Hernando Cortés and indeed giving birth to an infant fathered by the conquistador. The term *malinche,* in fact, connotes betrayal or disloyalty, and the term designates those who abet the enemy or defect to the opposition.

Recently, however, women scholars in Mexican American history have questioned the latter portrayal. They call for a reconsideration of Malinche in light of changing understandings about women that have unfolded during the course of the last few generations. To these scholars, she should be seen as a historical personage, and not a symbol of one political ideology or another. Further, she should be accepted as many women are today: as independent-minded individuals who resist male standards that suppress their potential. The historian Cordelia Candelaria goes so far as to see her as a "prototypical Chicana feminist." (Cordelia Candelaria, "La Malinche, Feminist Prototype," *Frontiers: A Journal of Women Studies* 5 No. 2 (1980), p. 6) Only a teenager when she encountered the Spaniards, Malinche was by then quite confident, intelligent, resourceful, persuasive, dynamic, and a survivor by instinct. Furthermore, revisionist writers point out, her contemporaries (that is, other Native Americans who knew her or knew of her deeds) hardly considered her a traitor. To the contrary, they referred to her as *Malintzín*, a name suggesting distinction. Indian recollections and later artwork also characterized her in a positive manner.

Who exactly was this woman that is the center of such controversy? She was born around 1505 (and died sometime between 1527 or 1528) to an Aztec family of noble standing and received the name of *Malinal*. As a young girl, she attended school, as permitted by Aztec tradition for those of privilege. Her widowed mother, however, sold Malinal, who now found herself amidst the Mayas in the province of Tabasco, where her status deteriorated to that of a slave. In 1519, Malinal became the servant of Hernando Cortés, having been given to him by the people of Tabasco, whom Cortés had just defeated. The Spaniards christened her as Doña Marina.

How specifically, did she aid the Spaniards? Doña Marina traveled every mile of the road with Cortés and the conquistadors from the coast to the Aztec capital of Tenochtitlán, and she retreated with them on la noche triste. She became Cortés's translator immediately, for she spoke her native Nahuatl (Aztec language) and several dialects used in Yucatán by the peoples of Tabasco, as well as Spanish, which she learned quickly. She functioned as the eyes and ears of the

Spaniards, detecting on more than one occasion talk of conspiracy among the Indian nations that the expedition encountered. Doña Marina acted as an intermediary between Cortés and Montezuma, the Aztec emperor, when the two met face-to-face in Tenochtitlán. She persuaded some of her people that resistance against the Europeans was useless, given that the gods had preordained the Indians' defeat. Cortés even came to view her as a confidant, and she counseled him on the ways of the Indians and even advised him on military strategy. She cared for the Spaniards' physical well-being following bloody battles.

Was Doña Marina aware that she was committing an act of betrayal, as future generations of Mexicans would believe? According to Professor Candelaria, the historical moment determined her actions and not any disloyalty to the indigenous people of Mexico. She was first of all a product of her upbringing, for her culture taught women to be obedient, as indeed Malinche came to be when she was presented to Cortés as a servant. Second, Malinche (like many others) despised the Aztec nation for its oppressive policies. The Aztecs callously inflicted injustices upon those they dominated, raiding the many settlements beyond Tenochtitlán and demanding taxes, confiscating prized possessions, and carrying off victims for human sacrifice. Doña Marina thus saw the Spaniards as a liberating power. Moreover, religion dictated her actions. Like many others in Mexico, she believed in the legend of Quetzalcoatl and fully considered Cortés to be the long-expected god coming to redeem his kingdom from Aztec wickedness. What else could she do but join in fulfilling what she believed to be a predetermined destiny?

Mexican American scholars, then, have sought to rehabilitate Doña Marina, feeling her depiction as a traitor to be unwarranted. What should be noted, they argue, are her intelligence and her intuitive knack for adjusting to the circumstances confronting her from moment to moment. Her instincts explain her actions, and not a selfish desire to betray her own countrymen and put them at the mercy of Spanish colonialism. Further, she is deserving of a more prominent role in history. Her personal attributes proved of immeasurable value to the conquest, yet history books give her little credit. Instead, the focus remains on the conquistadors, who happen to have been men.

The Aztec heritage is also celebrated as a proud component of Mexican history. Several of the national murals painted by Diego Rivera, David Alfaro Siquieros, and José Clemente Orozco, Mexico's brilliant artists of the 1920s and 1930s, extol pre-Columbian life and are among the most awe-inspiring of Mexico's treasures. They daily attract countless tourists, and many of these murals serve as the models for Mexican American art found in the large urban areas of the U.S. West. The emblem of the eagle and the serpent found on the Mexican national flag acknowledges the Aztec search for a homeland, mentioned above. Since the 1970s at least, elements within Mexican American communities (mainly literary figures) have found kinship with the Aztecs, as seen in their identification with Aztlán, the land that the Aztecs left as they searched for a new home in the Valley of Mexico. These members of the intelligentsia apply the word *Aztlán* to the spiritual commonality they perceive as existing among those whose heritage is Mexican.

A FINAL WORD

Who, then, are Hispanics in the U.S. West? The overwhelming majority of them are of Mexican extraction, but no particular characterization applies to all. Physically speaking, Mexican Americans may range anywhere from displaying heavy Indian features to being *güeros,* that is, Anglo-looking. There exists disagreement as to what label is the best group reference. While some accept the term "Hispanic," others stridently reject it, maintaining that it connotes Spanish colonialism of the Indian and mestizo populations of Latin America with whom they identify.

Nonetheless, it is clear that the heritage of all Hispanics who are considered Mexican Americans is a combination of their pre-Columbian Indian and Spanish roots. Although the process of mestizaje did not always involve the highest civilizations of Mesoamerica (after all, most of these had perished soon after the conquest), Mexican Americans nonetheless identify—knowingly or unknowingly—with aspects of their Aztec past. Many may not know, for instance, that the term *Mexicanos,* the word they use to identify themselves in Spanish, is Aztec in derivation. Numerous folk traditions of pre-Columbian origins made their way into the religion introduced by the Catholic priests into Mexico. Catholicism today thus accepts such miracles as the apparition of our Lady of Guadalupe (among the most successful religious associations to be found in local parishes throughout the U.S. West are Guadalupana societies). The foods typically associated with Mexico are ones traditional to the Aztec diet, and today the Mexican restaurant business is a thriving enterprise throughout the United States. Aztec words sprinkle the vocabulary that Spanish speakers employ in everyday conversation with other Hispanics.

The Spanish heritage is even more pronounced among Mexican Americans than is the Mexican Indian contribution. The Spanish colonizers brought to the New World a European civilization influenced by the Greek, Roman, and Muslim presence in the peninsula and then imposed it on the Indians and mestizos, either through persuasion or force. Language ranked as the Spaniards' foremost cultural offering to Latin America, and though varieties and unique linguistic codes abound within Mexican American communities, Spanish is an identifiable feature of *Hispanidad.* Catholicism follows language as the most prominent contribution that Spain made to its New World colonies, and even though pre-Columbian beliefs have been integrated into Church teachings, the religion that the Spaniards imposed on Mexico retains the essential doctrine and ritual as known in Europe. Social rules of public courtesy, social decorum, and proper etiquette also derive from Spain's interaction with different cultures that occupied the country for centuries at a time.

Hispanics, thus, come from a background molded by the influence of two civilizations, the Spanish and the Mexican Indian. In the U.S. West, their culture has been further shaped by American ideals, politics, education, mass culture, and the like. Despite acculturation, the heritage of Spain and Mexico persists, giving the West its own blend of multiculturalism. Such a feature of the region is not of recent development. It began in the 1520s when Spaniards explored northward from Anáhuac, and that pattern of exploration and settlement is studied in the chapter that follows.

BIBLIOGRAPHIC ESSAY

As noted in the text, much disagreement exists on an exact definition of the West, but there is a rich body of works that elaborate on the spectrum of images we hold of the region. A good beginning point might be the many surveys available on the history of the trans-Mississippi, among them classics by Ray Allen Billington such as *America's Frontier Heritage* (Albuquerque: University of New

Mexico Press, 1974), and Ray Allen Billington and Martin Ridge, *Westward Expansion: A History of the American Frontier* (sixth edition; Albuquerque: University of New Mexico Press, 2001). Other equally capable studies written more recently include *The New Encyclopedia of the American West,* edited by Howard R. Lamar (New Haven, CT: Yale University Press, 1998); Gerald D. Nash, *The American West in the Twentieth Century: A Short History of an Urban Oasis* (Englewood Cliffs, NJ: Princeton-Hall, 1973); and *Ethnicity on the Great Plains,* edited by Frederick C. Luebke (Lincoln: Published by the University of Nebraska Press for the Center for Great Plains Studies, 1980). One of the most recent syntheses is Richard White, *"It's Your Misfortune and None of My Own": A History of the American West* (Norman: University of Oklahoma Press, 1991), a sweeping account that covers themes such as environment, urbanization, racial minorities, gender, and many others.

The equally problematic definition of the term "Hispanic" has attracted much attention since the 1970s. One good starting point for elucidation might be José Cuello, *Latinos and Hispanics: A Primer on Terminology* (Detroit, MI: Wayne State University Press, 1996). Each of the many different Hispanic communities has attracted its own body of literature, and here we can only list a select number of surveys that may be useful as guides to the reader. Works attempting to cover all groups include Juan González, *Harvest of Empire: A History of Latinos in America* (New York: Penguin, 2000); Sylvia A. Marotta and Jorge G. García, "Latinos in the United States in 2000," *Hispanic Journal of Behavioral Sciences* 25, no. 1 (February 2003); L. H. Gann and Peter J. Duignan, *The Hispanics in the United States: A History* (Boulder, CO: Westview, 1986); Roberto Suro, *Strangers among Us: How Latino Immigration is Transforming America* (New York: Albert A. Knopf, 1998). Two of the better surveys on Mexican Americans include Rodolfo Acuña, *Occupied America: A History of Chicanos* (fifth edition; New York: Pearson Longman, 2004), and Manuel G. Gonzales, *Mexicanos: A History of Mexicans in the United States* (Bloomington: Indiana University Press, 1999). Readings on non-Mexican origin peoples include Luis Antonio Cardona, *A History of Puerto Ricans in the United States of America* (Bethesda, MD: Carreta Press, 1995); James S. Olson and Judith E. Olson, *Cuban Americans: From Trauma to Triumph* (New York: Twayne, 1995); Max J. Castro, *The New Cuban Immigration in Context* (Coral Gables, FL: Dante B. Fascell North-South Center, University of Miami, 2002); Jacqueline Maria Hagan, *Deciding to be Legal: A Mayan Community in Houston* (Philadelphia, PA: Temple University Press, 1994); and Ramona Hernández, *The Mobility of Workers under Advanced Capitalism: Dominican Migration to the United States* (New York: Columbia University Press, 2002).

The literature on pre-Columbian history would cover volumes. Thorough coverage of the Indian heritage of the Mexican American may be gleaned from such solid and reliable surveys as Michael C. Meyer, et al., *The Course of Mexi-*

can History (seventh edition; New York: Oxford University Press, 2003); Lynn V. Foster, *A Brief History of Mexico* (New York: FactsOnFile, 1997); Ramón Eduardo Ruiz, *Triumphs and Tragedies: A History of the Mexican People* (New York: W. W. Norton, 1992); Robert M. Carmack, *The Legacy of Mesoamerica: History and Culture of a Native American Civilization* (Upper Saddle River, NJ: Prentice Hall, 1996). General histories of Latin America can also prove useful, for many also treat Mexico from Colombian times through the colonial period. Among these is Benjamin Keen and Keith Haynes, *A History of Latin America* (sixth edition; Boston: Houghton Mifflin Company, 2000). Old classics with good factual content include John Francis Bannon et al., *Latin America* (fourth edition; Encino, CA: Glencoe Press, 1977), and John Edwin Fagg, *Latin America: A General History* (third edition; New York: Macmillan, 1977). On *La Malinche,* much of the literature on this historical personage is reviewed and analyzed in Sandra Messinger Cypess, *La Malinche in Mexican Literature: From History to Myth* (Austin: University of Texas Press, 1991). The new revisionist perspective is advanced in Cordelia Candelaria, "La Malinche, Feminist Prototype," *Frontiers* 5, no. 2 (1980).

The history of Spain is similarly voluminous, but the connection between Iberian experience (before the conquest of Mexico) and Mexican Americans may be deduced from sources such as Américo Castro, *The Spaniards: An Introduction to Their History* (Los Angeles: University of California Press, 1971); Joseph F. O'Callaghan, *A History of Medieval Spain* (Ithaca, NY: Cornell University Press, 1975); Samuel H. Mayo, *A History of Mexico: From Pre-Columbia to Present* (Englewood Cliffs, NJ: Prentice-Hall, 1978), as well as from the classic surveys of Latin America noted above.

The makings of a mestizo people at the time of colonial New Spain is covered comprehensively in any book that surveys the history of that country, among them the ones by Ruiz, Foster, and Meyer and Sherman listed above. Useful also to the discussion of cultural mestizaje are Luis Leal, "In Search of Aztlán," in *Aztlán: Essays on the Chicano Homeland,* edited by Rudolfo A. Anaya and Francisco Lomelí (Albuquerque, NM: Academia/El Norte Publications, 1989), and Guillermo Lux and Maurilio E. Vigil, "Return to Aztlán: The Chicano Rediscovers His Indian Past," in the same work.

FROM TENOCHTITLÁN TO THE FAR NORTH: EXPEDITIONS, 1520s–1780s

Once Tenochtitlán fell, the Spaniards fanned out in different directions, ultimately making their way into the Far North (the modern U.S. West). What dynamics motivated the thrust outward from the Valley of Mexico? There existed the thrill of more adventure. The possibility of greater fortune called. The mystery of what lay beyond the conquered region beckoned. The gains of conquest needed to be consolidated and then protected from competitors. "Savagery" demanded to be defeated and replaced with Spanish civilization. Heathenism invited missionary work. All these impulses produced permanent settlements in modern New Mexico by the 1590s and in Texas, Arizona, and California during the eighteenth century. By the time that the United States acquired these areas in the mid-nineteenth century, Spain and Mexico had left a permanent imprint on them.

THE FIRST *ENTRADAS*

Myths of wealthy kingdoms, Edenic places, and exotic lands rank high among reasons spurring the early conquistadors into explorations of the Far North. In the age of conquest, Europeans were inclined to hold true tales and stories that modern civilization would dismiss as fictitious narratives, fairy tales, figments of the imagination. Accounts of such fantasies as the Fountain of Youth, El Dorado, and a Land of Quivira were thus credible to people living in the sixteenth century, as indeed was the fable of the Isle of the Seven Cities, or Antilia. As the story of Antilia goes, a

Portuguese archbishop, six fellow bishops, and several settlers had escaped the Muslim occupation of the Iberian peninsula and had sailed across the Atlantic Ocean and established the Seven Cities of Antilia. It was this mysterious dominion that many believed Columbus had discovered in 1492. The region now known as the West Indies was thus first known as the Antilles.

Equally fascinating for Europeans of the sixteenth century was a tale apparently traceable to the ancient Greeks, according to which a civilization ruled by women named the Amazons lay somewhere to the east, possibly around modern Turkey. In 1510, or thereabouts, there appeared a book in Spain that lent credence to the old Greek legend. The new version speculated that an island existed in the proximity of the Indies, that a woman named Calafia ruled over it, and that abundant wealth blessed this kingdom, known as California. Seduced by this story, the Spaniards in their explorations north searched specifically for such a paradise, and in an 1535 expedition that took them to what is now Baja California, named that peninsula "California." The Spaniards in 1542 extended the same name to the area of the modern U.S. state of California.

The New World harbored its own rumors of fabled spots, and the Spaniards listened to them inquisitively. One tale emanated from the Aztecs themselves, who related to the Spaniards their saga of a place named Aztlán, wherein the Aztecs had originated. This homeland, supposedly situated somewhere to the northwest of Tenochtitlán, was a setting of material splendor. People lived harmoniously among trees, fresh water springs, and Seven Caves while enjoying bountiful crops, as well as many fowl and fish. Appropriately, the site had been given the name "place of Herons." In search of this mythical land of the Seven Caves, two Franciscan friars by the name of Juan de la Asunción and Pedro Nadal journeyed north, and in 1538 they may have reached the part of the Colorado River that separates California from Arizona. The expedition returned to the heartland empty-handed, though the friars carried back other tales of settled communities in the area around the regions they had traversed.

The Indians whom the Spaniards encountered as part of the early exploration of the Far North also circulated stories about settlements such as Cíbola and Quivira. First to hear of such mysterious lands was Álvar

Marooned on Galveston Island since 1528, Álvar Nuñez Cabeza de Vaca and his companions trekked westward toward Mexico in 1534 and reached the Pacific Coast in 1536. They were the first Europeans to cross the North American continent on foot. Cabeza de Vaca's account of his stay in Texas and that of his travels contains the first descriptions of Texas geography, flora, fauna, and native culture. The explorer also brought back rumors of fabulous riches that encouraged further Spanish expeditions into what is now the United States. (North Wind Picture Archive)

Núñez Cabeza de Vaca, the first European to have walked across what is now the U.S. West. Marooned in Texas in 1528 with four others following the Florida shipwreck of his crew, Cabeza de Vaca wandered into Culiacán (a Spanish outpost in what is now the Mexican state of Sinaloa) in 1536, reporting to Spanish officials rumors of prosperous Indian communities situated in the northern hinterlands. Such accounts were enough to spark entradas (expeditions) in search not only of these mysterious settlements but of the legendary Seven Cities of Antilia.

To ascertain the veracity of these stories, Fray Marcos de Niza headed north in 1538. Upon his return the next year, he reported to officials that he had in fact seen a magnificent city known to the Indians as Cíbola and that it constituted part of a constellation of seven cities. To follow up, the government in 1540 authorized a nobleman named Francisco Vásquez de Coronado to claim these Seven Cities of Cíbola. Coronado never did find them, even after two years of exploration in the middle of the North American continent. The Indians in the lands he covered raised his curiosity further, one of them informing Coronado of the existence of Quivira, another idyllic place, which also eluded the conquistador.

Aside from legends of New World paradises, other forces pushed the Spaniards northward from Tenochtitlán. Booty in the form of human slaves for work in public projects or the haciendas of central Mexico led Spaniards hundreds of miles from the kingdom of the Aztecs. Indeed, the first Spaniards that Cabeza de Vaca encountered in Culiacán in 1536 were men engaged in a slave roundup, an operation that Cabeza de Vaca found abhorrent. A more important material lure drawing the Spaniards northward was silver. According to well-documented accounts of the episode, in 1546 Indians in the Zacatecas region whom the Spaniards had befriended showed the foreigners what proved to be iron deposits. Overnight, the Zacatecas region became a magnet for miners, assorted entrepreneurs, shysters, and settlers. The mining boom soon expanded into Guanajuato and Chihuahua, where more settlements seemed to appear overnight. In Chihuahua, the Spaniards founded the town of Santa Bárbara in 1567, from which several expeditions into what is today the United States were later launched.

The desire to save souls also served as an impetus pushing the Spaniards toward northern frontiers. Particularly passionate about winning converts to Christianity were the Franciscans, an order of missionaries that had been active among the Muslims during the Reconquista and whose zeal now stirred them into wanting to Christianize lands beyond Chihuahua. At Santa Bárbara in Chihuahua, stories had filtered down for years about established Indian nations residing along the upper Rio Grande. Peaceful farmers living in self-sustaining villages reportedly made up the population of such settlements. This land of the Pueblo, the Navajo, and the Zuñi Indians, among others, was destined to earn the name of New Mexico, as it reminded so many of the sedentary communities that marked the interior of New Spain.

It was, then, the determination to "save souls" that produced in 1581 an expedition into the upper Rio Grande Valley of what is now New

Mexico, led jointly by the Franciscan Agustín Rodríguez and by a military officer named Francisco Sánchez Chamuscado. The explorers entered the territory of the Pueblos along the Rio Grande, and returned to Santa Bárbara reporting little of material value. But two of the friars stayed behind to work among the Indians, a calling as far as the Franciscans were concerned, but a grave miscalculation in the minds of both church and government officials. To insure the safety of the missionaries, another expedition led by Antonio de Espejo returned to Pueblo country in 1582, only to find that the Franciscans had met martyrdom at the hands of the Indians. The Espejo undertaking proved significant to the crown, nonetheless, as it brought back more precise reports about the region of New Mexico and present-day Arizona, as well as tales of illusory wealth in the form of silver.

The desire to convert souls, pursue new fortunes, and achieve imperial goals all played a hand in the crown's decision, by 1583, to enter the land of the Pueblos and take possession of it. But the plan did not materialize until 1595, when a frontiersman named Juan de Oñate received authorization from Spanish officials in Mexico City to head into enchanting New Mexico. Oñate brought admirable credentials to the assignments. Son of Cristóbal Oñate, a notable silver baron from Zacatecas, the younger Juan (about fifty years old) had his own wealth, had distinguished himself in service to the king by fighting Indians, and now displayed an irrepressible zest for the task before him.

By negotiating a contract with Oñate for the exploration, conquest, and settlement of New Mexico, the crown expected to finally establish a claim to the northern lands and simultaneously launch a program of proselytizing among the Indian nations therein. The Catholic Church, a copartner in any frontier movement in Latin America, was to be the agent of Christianization. The crown risked little financially under this agreement, paying only the expenses of the missionaries who would be accompanying the expedition, for Oñate bore the greater cost of the enterprise. Even though he had to pay for every possible expense necessary for the journey north—including but not limited to recruitment of soldiers and settlers, wagons, carts, livestock, food, supplies, tools, and defense—Oñate stood to profit handsomely. The king granted Oñate numerous honors and titles, among them that of *adelantado* (a title given to persons investing their own resources in order to conquer an area; wealth found therein would belong to the adelantado and his followers), and that of governor of New Mexico. With so many concessions given him, Oñate visualized establishing a family empire in New Mexico and amassing greater wealth than he already possessed. As to the common people who were to inhabit Oñate's colony in New Mexico, the chance to start anew influenced their decision to uproot themselves, borrow money for their undertaking, and join the march north. In New Mexico, they might find valuable minerals, receive an encomienda (or the privilege to rely on Indian settlements for making economic profit) of Indians and grow prosperous, get government appointments, and (for men) earn titles such as *hidalgo* (a level of nobility earned after five years of living in New Mexico).

In Zacatecas, Oñate and his associates prepared for months before undertaking the 1,200-mile journey to the upper Rio Grande Valley. Among other things, planning involved soliciting and receiving recruits, purchasing and storing provisions, rounding up livestock, amassing a military force, and waiting for the friars. It also meant tolerating complaints from the restive settlers ready to move out, dealing with insubordination, and having to agonize over a meticulous inspection (designed to ensure that Oñate had abided by his contract) to be conducted by a royal representative. In the summer of 1596, the caravan finally lumbered down the Camino Real (the Royal Road) toward Santa Bárbara, a distance of 400 miles from Zacatecas. Moving along the trail hardly brought the settlers a break in the old waiting routine, however, as politics intruded to keep Oñate from making headway. Nor did traveling coalesce the disparate elements constituting the expedition. Some of the settlers despaired of ever reaching New Mexico and deserted the column, while others absconded with essential supplies. Wagons broke down and had to be repaired, or livestock wandered off and had to be rounded up. But still, the pioneers pressed on toward Santa Bárbara.

On January 26, 1598, the entrada departed from Santa Bárbara, destination New Mexico. The procession stretched for several miles, and included *carretas* (carts), covered wagons, beasts of burden and livestock numbering close to 7,000, and of course, a motley assemblage of hardy frontier folks (an estimate of 400 men, with about 130 of these bringing their families along), 129 soldiers, 8 missionaries, and many Indian servants and allies. As a group, the pobladores (settlers) experienced one obstacle after another. North of Santa Bárbara they braved the currents of the Conchos River, but people, livestock, and wagons made it safely across. Next, the formidable Chihuahuan desert stood between them and El Paso. The wasteland made them lose their way temporarily, but more dreadfully, inflicted thirst and hunger on all concerned. As they approached the Rio Grande, they encountered sand dunes difficult for carts with heavy loads to traverse, yet they surmounted this barrier as well.

In early May, Oñate and his colonists crossed what is now the boundary that separates Texas and New Mexico. The march up the trail brought further problems and tribulations, among them hardship to both man and beast, as the physical environment, including a stretch of land called the Jornada del Muerto (Dead Man's Journey) took its toll. Food and water supplies dwindled, and many suffered hunger and thirst. Tragedy struck families with the loss of a loved one. Accidents and breakdowns caused slowdowns and despair. Insubordination persisted. Finally, on August 18, 1598, Oñate's pobladores arrived at a site they named San Juan, which later acted as the capital of the colony that Oñate the conquistador hoped to develop into a huge empire.

Actually, San Juan was a Pueblo village, but the Spaniards made themselves literally at home by moving in with the Indians. Situated close to the confluence of the Rio Chama and the Rio Grande, and some twenty miles from what is today Santa Fe, it appeared a logical place for Oñate. It stood at a central location from which Oñate could conduct exploration for new lands and even for an outlet to the sea. The mountains nearby held out the promise of silver deposits. Surrounding lands seemed fertile enough to provide essential crops for the colony's survival. The Indians, moreover, were friendly enough to be counted upon in desperate times. The village itself, however, seemed likely to be too small for Oñate's purposes, so the Spaniards in the spring of 1599 wrested from the Indians a pueblo (with some 400 dwellings) located across the river. They christened the new community San Gabriel and modified it to their liking. They redid some of the homes, built a church and accommodations for the Franciscans, and altered the town's layout to conform to that of other frontier settlements in New Spain.

Life in San Gabriel hardly approximated the one the pobladores had visualized for themselves. Though they lived among friendly hosts, not all Native Americans were accepting of their presence, and in fact threats from hostile Indians posed a constant danger. The pioneers faced the most trying conditions in the hinterlands. In the summer, they lived amidst heat and the annoyance of insect parasites, as well as fleas, flies, and mosquitoes. During winter, they endured the terrible New Mexico cold while facing shortages of corn, squash, and other foods, lacking proper attire, and having insufficient firewood to keep warm. The struggle for survival entailed having to improvise on just about everything from cooking and equipping their small households to finding medical care for their sick children. To exacerbate matters, the local lands failed to yield enough edible crops (grain, corn, and beans) to support the entire community. Cattle ranching seemed impossible in the region where Oñate had settled them. Far removed from the source of new supplies, moreover, they had no place to turn, and supply carts arrived from the interior only irregularly. They had dreams of growing wealthy, yet nothing of value had yet been discovered. They had not even acquired the encomiendas they had been promised, for the neighboring Pueblos had nothing to give the Spaniards as tribute.

Thus simmering discontent pervaded much of San Gabriel from the beginning. The Franciscans had not been as successful in converting the natives as expected, and their own suffering caused them to consider abandoning the work among the Pueblos. Even soldiers in Oñate's force wondered about continuing to defend a land that had little value to the crown. So many pobladores reconsidered their reason for coming (and staying) to New Mexico that soon a conspiracy to defect spread throughout the colony. Indeed, in October 1601, a contingent of pobladores left San Gabriel without Oñate's approval and hurried back to Santa Bárbara and more comfortable circumstances.

The deserters told such damaging accounts of colonial corruption, mismanagement, and neglect under Oñate that the conquistador's aim of gaining fame and fortune in New Mexico seemed less and less attainable. His faithful colonists of no more than 200 still kept San Gabriel viable, and their presence acted to assert Spain's visible claim to the borderlands.

But sometime around 1607 or 1608, they also despaired of living there and began a gradual relocation to a spot on the Santa Fe River, a tributary of the Rio Grande that ran some twenty miles south of San Gabriel. As to Oñate, Spanish officials in 1609, after years of hearing complaints regarding his abuse of his command, finally issued orders to recall him. Don Pedro de Peralta replaced Oñate.

Peralta arrived in New Mexico late in 1609. On the north side of the Santa Fe River, across from where the San Gabrieleños had staked their claim, the new administrator in 1610 formally founded Santa Fe, the second oldest living town in the continental United States, after St. Augustine, Florida (1565). Peralta followed carefully crafted colonization laws and abided by specific royal decrees. The viceroy in Mexico City had given him specific directions:

> When he [Peralta] shall have arrived at said province he shall inform himself of the conditions of said settlement endeavoring before anything else [to lay] the foundation and settlement of the Villa . . . so people may begin to live there with some cleanliness and stability, in which he shall allow the citizens to elect four councilmen, and two ordinary [regular] alcaldes each year who shall try civil and criminal cases which may occur in said Villa and within five leagues around it. . . . The said ordinary alcaldes and councilmen of said Villa may mark out for each resident two lots for house and garden and two *suertes* for vegetable gardens and two more for vineyards and for an olive grove and for a *cavaleria* [*sic*] of land
> . . . They shall mark out as belonging to said Villa six *vecindades* and one square of the streets for the purpose of erecting Royal Buildings and other public buildings. (Gilbert R. Cruz, *Let There Be Towns: Spanish Municipal Origins in the American Southwest, 1610–1810* (College Station: Texas A&M University Press, 1988), p. 24)

Several features commended Santa Fe's location. The site could be reached easily enough from all directions, especially by supply trains coming from the interior of New Spain. It met certain stipulations dictated by Spanish policy as essential for success. Open range spread to the south, and fertile farmlands lay nearby. The local woods provided foraging for livestock and wood supply for residents. Further, the Rio Grande meandered close to the settlement.

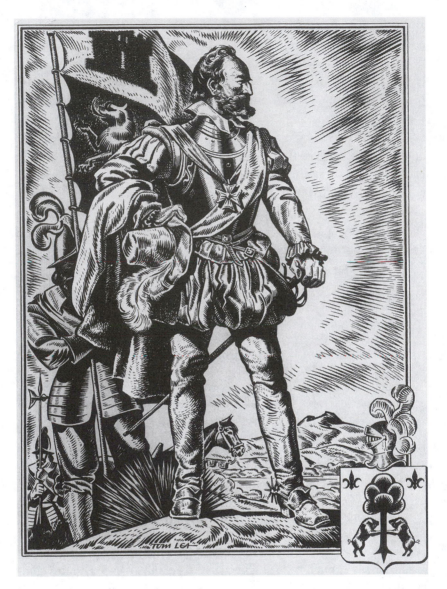

Portrait of the Spanish conqueror Juan de Oñate (1550–1630), who established the colony of New Mexico for Spain. (Bettmann/Corbis)

NEW MEXICO IN THE SEVENTEENTH CENTURY

Peralta departed New Mexico four years after his arrival, having stabilized things in the province. Governed subsequently by different royal appointees coming from the heartland, the people of New Mexico went about the task of nation building. Most of the pobladores (just a few hundred, including some of the missionaries) lived in Santa Fe, the only recognized *villa* (a chartered community, though not having the status of a *ciudad,* or city, which had a larger population) in the province. With crown permission (settlers could not pick up and relocate voluntarily), some of the Oñate colonists built homes in farmsteads and ranch settlements that extended along the Rio Grande from as far north as Taos to what is now Albuquerque in the south. Proximity to water or to a supply of Indian labor generally determined the beginnings of these scattered sites. According to recent scholarly estimates, the entire population in New Mexico totaled about 1,000 at mid–seventeenth century, and then increased to about 2,500 at its highpoint in the 1660s.

From what historians can determine, those who constituted New Mexico's population during the colonial era descended from immigrants from Spain, as well as from mestizos and other mixed-bloods from Mexico. Additionally, some (about 10 percent) were of African descent. Few from the outside made their way into New Mexico throughout the seventeenth century, excepting friars and government officials who spent terms of service on the frontier. Thus, much of the growth resulted from natural reproduction and racial mixing between civilian men, soldiers, and even the friars with local Pueblo women (always taken as paramours in the case of the clergy, in some other instances as Indian wives), as well as from the custom of adopting orphaned Indian children. The products of miscegenation generally joined their mothers' society, though European fathers might recognize their offspring and accept them into their households. One historian posits that as of 1680, as high as 90 percent of the Hispanic population had actually been born in New Mexico (France V. Scholes, "Civil Government and Society in New Mexico in the Seventeenth Century," *New Mexico Historical Review* 10 (April 1935), p. 97).

Class distinctions also existed within the small colony. At the top of the social hierarchy were the missionaries (only a handful in the realm at any one particular time), government appointees such as the governor, lower bureaucrats, or military officers, and an identifiable coterie of founding families. This latter element derived its power from a number of sources, among them their standing as charter colonists and their unwavering loyalty to seeing crown intentions materialize. The latter goal they pursued by fulfilling their duty under the governor's supervision as soldier-citizens, acting as military protectors of the colony, guardians of the missionaries, and company commanders tracking down Indian raiders. Some thirty-five of them were encomenderos—having received that position from the governors that followed Oñate—and as such derived tribute, in the form of food and raw cloth, from the many Pueblo families under their "guardianship." Others of the upper class owned *estancias* (landholdings) in the region to the southwest of Santa Fe. Some of these land grants embraced thousands of acres of good grassland and featured rangeland of a kind familiar to those who had come from Spain.

DOÑA TERESA DE AGUILERA Y ROCHE

In seventeenth-century New Mexico, the majority of colonists sought to eke out a hardscrabble existence from small-scale farming and ranching. There did exist a small class of landowners, who together with the few government officials composed an aspiring gentry, but generally speaking, most people in New Mexico possessed little wealth or recognized social standing. Outsiders were few in New Mexico, for little immigration took place. Detached from life in the interior, the pobladores lacked education and cultural refinement. Males dominated the social order. Although Spanish law did extend to women many rights guaranteeing property, patriarchy governed relations between the sexes, and men expected deference from women.

In the midst of these surroundings lived a woman by the name of Doña Teresa de Aguilera y Roche, wife of Don Bernardo López de Mendízabal, the governor of New Mexico (1659–1661). She appeared out of place in such a primitive environment. For one thing, she was better off than others. Her husband, as did many governors on the frontier, engaged in corruption–such as exploiting local Pueblo labor—that netted the couple a fair revenue. Doña Teresa fashioned herself as New Mexico's "first lady" and dressed in a manner becoming such a position. Additionally, she had her own servants, who helped mitigate the crude life on the frontier. She was, furthermore, not a native of New Mexico, but rather European born. As one of privilege in the Old World, she had received a proper education and been raised in cultivated circles. She and the governor had brought to New Mexico an extensive library, and they took great pride in maintaining it. Doña Teresa understood male-dominated society in New Mexico, but was fully capable of independence.

Doña Teresa's stay in New Mexico was marred (along with her husband's) with accusations directed at her by the Franciscan missionaries. Off to Mexico City the couple went, and there officials jailed the two in April 1663. Then, on October 26, 1663, the Inquisition (a religious body that investigated cases of heresy among the population) leveled formal accusations against Doña Teresa. She spent the next fourteen months in a Mexico City jail, defending herself against charges she considered without merit.

The Inquisition compiled a total of forty-one articles accusing Doña Teresa of a number of transgressions. The most serious charges alleged that she and her husband engaged in the practice of Judaism. The intelligence on which the charges were based had been gathered by the Franciscan missionaries from testimony given them by the Pueblos, many of them servants of the governor and Doña Teresa. Seemingly, the two had the habit of bathing every Friday, and they did so secretively as if to be concealing some proscribed deed. On that same day of the week, the governor Don Bernardo would have a complete change of clothing, while Doña Teresa herself made it a point to replace the tablecloth as well as the linen in the household. On Saturday, a day to be observed according to religious custom, Doña Teresa instead committed the further sacrilege of meticulously grooming and dressing herself.

Further complaints leveled at Doña Teresa included her use of the paranormal. For instance, she resorted to concoctions (presumably acquired from the Pueblos) in order to entice her husband into romance. She also used onion peels on her feet for mysterious reasons. The articles alleged further that Doña Teresa and her husband were not good practicing Christians. They failed to attend Church as expected, to say grace at the dinner table, or to engage in daily prayer. They

displayed a lack of concern for Catholicism by further
shunning its rituals and disrespecting religious objects such as
statues. Doña Teresa delighted in reading foreign language
books from the couple's library, the articles elaborated,
perhaps because of their irreligious content.

Dona Teresa, the self-assured aristocrat from New Mexico,
did not accept her indictment passively. Rather, she
counterattacked forcefully in a series of responses given during
a thirty-day period from late October through late November.
Regarding the family's propensity for bathing, getting into
clean clothing, and replacing the household linen on Friday,
nothing sinister should be attached to the routine, she
rebutted. In fact, Don Bernardo changed his clothing,
especially his shirt, several times during the week. Neither
should her compulsion for spending time making herself
attractive imply disrespect for Saturday. Simply put, Sundays
did not afford her enough time to prepare appropriately for
mass. Doña Teresa denied absolutely any interest or
involvement in the occult. The onion layers she used on her
feet, for example, had no purpose other than to relieve
discomfort caused by calluses. She then derided the
accusations that she was remiss in her Christian faith. Of
course she was a believer, she avowed, worshiping at Santa Fe
on Sundays alongside the rest of the community. Any breach
of obligation to weekly mass could be explained by illness or
by some other unexpected occurrence. Her reading of books
in a foreign language held no particular meaning. Some of the
works she read were in Italian, her mother tongue, and she
simply wished to remain knowledgeable in the language.

But Doña Teresa did not stop at explaining the reasoning
behind her "controversial" actions. On January 1664, she
added details explaining possible motives for the accusations
made against herself and Don Bernardo. Political enemies in
Santa Fe had conspired to defile the family name and
reputation, she asserted. The Franciscans in particular wished
to exploit Indian labor and had resented her husband's
intervention on the Pueblos' behalf. New Mexican society,
moreover, hosted wanton characters and lowlifes who
engaged in moral turpitude, adulterous liaisons, infraction of
laws, and criminal activity. They despised people such as
herself and her husband, who symbolized integrity and who
through their authority enforced royal decrees. Her rejoinders

apparently swayed the Inquisitors, so that in December 1664 they suspended the case against her.

What does the case of Doña Teresa de Aguilera y Roche illustrate? At the individual level, it shows that Doña Teresa was a woman of unflagging confidence fully capable of defending herself against the most serious allegations that could be mustered by one of Spain's most powerful institutions. She presented a convincing argument (through defense attorneys, of course) before that body and won. Further, Doña Teresa's example draws attention to the existence of many women in colonial New Mexico who could be bold, brash, daring, and assertive. At a more general level, the case reveals the tolerance that Spanish society granted women, especially those of the elite class, who could make use of the legal system and be confident of being heard fairly.

On this land, owners tended to small herds of livestock that included cattle and horses, as well as a few burros and mules, which not only served the New Mexicans as a work force and food source, but also as commodities useful in trading with some of the far-off settlements in northern New Spain. But the mainstay of the ranch was sheep, especially the *churro,* with its coarse wool, which the pioneers had introduced into Pueblo country and then found to thrive on the New Mexico range. Sheep yielded hide, which the New Mexicans could use for making jackets, for local bartering, or for exchange. From wool, the New Mexicans manufactured clothes, blankets, and other useful products. For assistance in working their flocks, the *estancieros* (estate owners) turned to native Pueblo labor, as well as faithful, trained sheepdogs brought from either Europe or New Spain.

The overwhelming majority of New Mexicans were not landowners but ordinary people who spent their time struggling to stay alive. The division of labor assigned Hispanic women to the household, where they cared for the children, prepared meals (from scratch), improvised at making clothes or footwear, and even protected the home from hostile attacks. Menfolk, meantime, worked at any job they could find, including that of day laborer. During time off, men had to build their homes (generally adobe structures of one or two rooms) or make improvements upon them. Homes in New Mexico generally consisted of adobe or stone material, clay floors, basic windows and door openings, and fireplaces. The inhabitants outfitted them with makeshift beds, tables, benches, and other kinds of simple furniture. Men also had to contribute their labor to the establishment of public edifices, including churches and missions.

A typical day in frontier New Mexico, however, saw most male heads of households (whether landowners or common settlers) and their sons (at an early age) tending to sheep and cattle or tilling the earth from dawn till dusk. To be sure, cultivation posed many problems for the pioneers. For one thing, fertile farmlands did not abound in New Mexico, so that taking up farming meant dispossessing the Pueblos, who already lived on the most productive soil. It also required irrigation, and Spaniards turned to the old reliable system of using acequias, or ditches, to water their crops. Winter weather also afflicted New Mexico, especially during spring, and the New Mexicans learned to replant should early frosts destroy the seedlings.

The primary fare for the Pueblos had been corn, beans, and squash, which the Spaniards quickly adopted, but the newcomers supplemented these staples with foods they imported, such as peach, plum, and apricot trees. Favorite vegetables brought from Europe by the first pobladores would be commonplace on any table today: lettuce, cabbage, carrots, radishes, peas, turnips, and onions, to take a few examples. Similarly, the New Mexicans introduced to the borderlands many foods indigenous to New Spain, among them chiles, beans, and corn. The latter two commodities differed from the ones known in New Mexico, but considering the desperate food shortages that plagued people, little distinction over time came to be made at the dinner table. While no real incentive to farm for profit existed in New Mexico due to isolation, the demand for sustenance required that genuine attention be given to insuring a good harvest.

Ranch and farm products served a function other than providing sustenance to the pobladores, as they also acted as commodities for exchange. In New Mexico a money economy never took root in the seventeenth century, so that sales and purchases invariably involved the bartering of farm and ranch products. The latter came from range animals (such as bovine stock, sheep, and swine) which either the small "aristocracy" or their immediate forbears had introduced into New Mexico. A cow might obtain a family some corn (either from fellow pioneers or the Indians), draft animals could get someone a captured Indian slave, or a horse might be traded for a finished product that made its way up the trail from New Spain. Many other kinds of raw materials—produced in the province either by the New Mexicans or neighboring Indian peoples—could be readily acquired with ranch or agricultural goods. Among these were wool and cotton (including the *manta,* Indian cloth made from cotton and wool) salt, tallow, buffalo hides, bows and arrows, and so forth.

Isolation also offered practically no opportunity for intellectual enrichment. Only a few of those who had accompanied Oñate could have claimed any education, and as time passed, their children received practically none, for indeed, there were no schools in the province at that time. Even some of the soldier settlers could not sign their names. Without an ability to read and deprived of contact with news and information from the heartland, people who lived out their days in New Mexico were essentially backwater folks, informed only by the lessons of life. The missionaries were highly educated men, but their instruction targeted the Indians, not the settlers. The governor and support personnel also came from educated backgrounds, but they did not see themselves as responsible for enlightenment of the masses.

The remoteness of New Mexico also helped preserve Spanish culture, at least in a modified form. Spanish remained the language of discourse among the settlers, Catholicism the acknowledged religion, imperial institutions the norm, and an array of customs and traditions the core of a person's heritage. But the great distance from the motherland compelled acceptance of the tried and tested ways of the aboriginal population, so that the Spaniards borrowed culturally from the Indians, just as the Indians did from the Spaniards. Each community, for instance, relied on the other for such necessities as medicinal cures, garments, footwear, kitchen utensils, building materials, house-building techniques (such as the manner of making adobe dwellings), wild game, livestock, vocabulary terms, and more. The Spaniards came to prefer the practical bow and arrow that the

Indian used to hunt buffalo. They accepted Indian recipes but altered them to suit their own tastes, especially those requiring the corn ingredient. They adopted *punche,* a weed that the Indians smoked in lieu of tobacco, as well as *tesgüino,* an alcoholic beverage that derived from fermented corn. The Spaniards further grew fond of *amole,* obtained by pulverizing the roots of the yucca plant and then swishing the powder in water to produce shampoo. Despite this interdependence, New Mexico in the seventeenth century remained a society divided along racial lines, with the Indian population living as a dependent or colonized people.

For contact with New Spain's heartland during the seventeenth century, the pobladores relied on a supply system used by the Franciscans to equip and restock their Catholic missions in New Mexico. These wagon caravans traveled from Mexico City to New Mexico (stopping at spots in between) irregularly, sometimes every three to five years, and took almost eighteen months to complete the return cycle. The wagons brought essential materials for the missions, and also needed goods for the settlers on the frontier (among them livestock), and returned with commodities for sale by New Mexicans, among them raw leather goods, hides, piñon nuts, salt, candles, wheat, native blankets, and Indian slaves. New colonists, bureaucrats, soldiers, and missionaries either went north in these caravans or accompanied them on their return voyage.

An Indian uprising, known historically as the Pueblo Revolt, interrupted the routine of life in New Mexico in 1680. Historians have advanced a number of causes for this unexpected backlash against the Spanish occupation. Some have attributed the upheaval to anxiety and discontent emanating from natural calamities, such as drought and attendant crop losses, to diseases, and to attacks from other Indian nations (among them the Apaches) competing for scarce resources. Other scholars see Franciscan attempts to replace the Pueblo's own religious system with Catholicism as a major catalyst for the uprising. As the Pueblos resisted Franciscan attempts to eradicate Pueblo religious beliefs, the missionaries escalated their efforts to wipe out paganism, only to alienate Indian true believers. During the revolt, the Indian did in fact kill several priests—and not before blaspheming them and vandalizing the Catholic churches—in a display of hatred toward Christianity. Still other writers point to the role of Popé, the organizer of the Pueblo Revolt, as being the instigator of the drive to oust the Spaniards. Had it not been for the leadership skills of Popé, these writers argue, the revolt might not have attained the success it did.

Popé began the Pueblo Revolt on August 10, 1680, coordinating the insurrection from Taos. He and other instigators had as their purpose ridding New Mexico of the foreigners and regaining it for Native Americans. To that end they wiped out entire families (as well as friars) wherever they encountered them throughout the farmsteads and ranch hamlets that had sprouted along stretches of the Rio Grande. Beleaguered New Mexicans who could escape the wrath of the insurgents made their way to two pueblos, one of them Santa Fe, the other Isleta, a Pueblo settlement located downriver from Santa Fe. Those who went to Isleta, some 1,500 of them who could more easily beat a retreat, soon hastened on to El Paso del Norte on September 14, 1680. Those in Santa Fe (about 1,000 of them) put up a brave defense throughout the rest of the month of August against some 2,000 Pueblos, but seeing their homes, government buildings, and churches burned and destroyed, ultimately decided upon withdrawal as well. Given the option by the besiegers of facing death or returning to the old homeland, the New Mexicans filed out of Santa Fe on September 21 and also headed for El Paso. By the time the Pueblos had succeeded in driving out the Spaniards, they had killed some 380 of them as well as 21 of the 32 priests assigned to the province.

In the area downriver from El Paso (today's Ciudad Juarez), some 2,000 of the New Mexican expatriates established themselves amidst the small civilian population already living there. Dispossessed of almost all their worldly goods, the refugees made temporary housing from whatever materials (sticks and rocks, for instance) could be found in the vicinity. They faced shortages of provisions and essential foods, poor crop harvests, and constant Indian attacks. They knew not what fate held for them now and could only hope for a return to the only homeland most had ever known. But it was not to be for most. The only move left for them was another fallback into the interior of New Spain, or to El Paso proper, to which many were relocated in 1684. By 1690, only half of those who had arrived in the El Paso region ten years before remained.

THE SPANISH BORDERLANDS, CIRCA 1690S TO 1780S

Too much lay at stake for New Mexico to be forsaken, however. To start with, Spain felt it imperative to protect its empire's northern periphery from competing international powers. The Pueblos needed to be chastised and those among them still receptive to conversion must be Christianized. Despite Spanish failures to find wealth in the Far North, moreover, lingering reports of possible silver mines in New Mexico induced officials to pursue attempts to discover them. Then, there was personal aggrandizement, for whoever might reconquer New Mexico would gain titles, power, and elusive wealth.

These many reasons explain why a Spaniard named Diego de Vargas headed north in the fall of 1692. His initial inspection of the province proved favorable, and in the fall of 1693, he led a resettlement expedition numbering some 800 people that included about 100 military personnel, 18 missionaries, and 70 founding families, as well as immense numbers of livestock: mules, cattle, and horses. Some of the civilian settlers that constituted the caravan were returning from El Paso to their old homes, though Vargas had recruited most of the families from Mexico City and its environs.

The journey north for the new pioneers was no less harsh than it had been for the first pobladores who had accompanied Oñate back in 1598. The settlers faced the usual breakdown of vehicles, illness among the young, shortages of supplies and food reserves, the emotional stress that long voyages cause, and harsh winter weather. Upon arriving in Santa Fe in December 1693, Vargas ousted the Pueblo occupiers of the villa by a combination of persuasion and force and saw to it that his settlers moved into the vacated Indian homes. From Santa Fe, Vargas proceeded toward other pueblos; these were defended obstinately by Native American dwellers, but in hard fought battles, he brought New Mexico back into the imperial fold by 1696.

During lulls in the fighting, Vargas went about founding other settlements along the Rio Grande, among them Santa Cruz in 1695. For this villa, situated some twenty miles north from Santa Fe, Vargas turned to about forty-four families (identified by recruiters as *españoles mexicanos*) of artisans and skilled craftsmen who had arrived from the interior in June 1694. Albuquerque's birth also stemmed from the reconquest, though that occurred after Vargas had been replaced as governor of New Mexico in 1697 and had died in 1704. In Albuquerque at the government's direction in 1706, some thirty-five families settled and called their new home Alburquerque (Anglos later altered the name to its modern spelling, without the first *r*). Like Santa Fe and Santa Cruz, the new community received the designation of *villa*. From these three larger settlements, New Mexicans dispersed in all directions, though they stayed close to the Rio Grande during that early period. Taos grew from migration originating from Santa Cruz, as did other small hamlets established to the east of Santa Cruz. People choosing to leave Albuquerque or Santa Fe for ranches and farmsteads went south, east, and west, seldom venturing too far from the Rio Grande.

Almost at the same time that it acted to populate New Mexico, Spain hurried to lay claim to Texas. At least two reasons lay behind the impulse to settle this newer land. They included the threat from the French empire and the desire to bring Christianity to the "kingdom of Teja," that is, to the Caddo Indian peoples who lived in today's eastern Texas and western Louisiana.

The French peril derived from the explorations of the area of Texas by one René-Robert Cavelier de La Salle (known historically as La Salle). As this well-known story goes, La Salle wished to assist France in expanding that country's New World empire by founding an outpost somewhere along the Gulf coast of North America, preferably at the mouth of the Mississippi River. Establishing such a base would allow France to launch an assault on New Spain from the north. Whether by error or intent, in February 1685 La Salle with some 180 settlers landed on the Texas Gulf coast in what is today Matagorda Bay. He then erected what the French called Fort St. Louis, in the area that is today Vanderbilt, Texas.

For Spain, such an encroachment was not to be countenanced. A French occupation of Texas posed the danger of an attack on New Spain's northern silver mines and jeopardized Spanish commerce on the Gulf of Mexico. To oust the French from Texas, therefore, Spain sent Alonso de León on several expeditions, but it was not until 1689 that de León found Fort St. Louis. By then, all that remained of the outpost were traces of once grand designs by La Salle to settle Texas and from there to launch destabilizing campaigns on New Spain.

French imperial aims, then, explain Spanish interests in staking claims to eastern Texas. But a second factor—religion—also prodded the Spaniards to settle the area, for in undertaking the expeditions to find La Salle, de León and his men had heard that the people of the Caddo confederacy, situated along the Texas-Louisiana line, had expressed eagerness for Christianization. At least two missions thus went up by 1690 among the prospective converts, but the institutions did not last long, for the Spaniards had miscalculated Caddo interest in conversion. Within three years, eastern Texas had been abandoned once again.

But the Spaniards did not lose sight of Texas for too long, as the French threatened once more in 1714. Father Francisco Hidalgo, who had conducted missionary work among the Caddo during the 1690s, longed to return to eastern Texas and had written a letter to the French in Mobile, Alabama, asking for their help in Christianizing the Indians. Pretending to be following up on this inquiry, a Frenchman by the name of Louis Juchereau de St. Denis surprised the Spaniards in July 1714 by arriving at San Juan Bautista, Spain's northernmost settlement, situated close to what is now Eagle Pass, Texas, announcing a French desire for trade. Stunned twice within three decades, the crown could no longer leave eastern Texas exposed. Government officials now feared French illegal goods (coming from down the Mississippi) enticing people in the northern frontiers and breaking up Spain's control on those hinterlands. A possible French assault on New Spain's mines also alarmed officials.

Thus the need to shield Spain's northern periphery from the French led to the founding of the earliest permanent settlements in Texas. Appointed in charge of the expedition to eastern Texas was Domingo Ramón, son of the officer in command of San Juan Bautista. Accompanied by a total of 75 people, including missionaries, military personnel, and civilians, he departed the Rio Grande in April 1716. Within two months Ramón and his pobladores had arrived at their destination and with diligence built a presidio and six missions to act as buffers against further French advances. Ramón located one of the missions amidst the community of the Nacogdoche tribe (of the Caddo confederacy), thus the origins of the name given to the town, Nacogdoches. There in eastern Texas, the Caddos lived in permanent villages and might still be converted to Christianity, certainly more readily than could the wandering tribes in the Far North. If alliances could be negotiated with them, moreover, the Caddos and others in the confederacy could help bring to nothing the unwavering French determination to push west beyond Louisiana. The pobladores, meanwhile, would act as a support unit in the region, harvesting crops and raising livestock for themselves, the soldiers, and the Franciscans.

Spanish officials realized the vast distance that separated Nacogdoches from San Juan Bautista and that a station midway between the two would serve their operation better. To establish such an outpost, royal officials selected Martín de Alarcón, the governor of the state of Coahuila, who departed the Rio Grande on April 9, 1718, for central Texas. He headed a force of some 72 persons and several herds of horses, mules, cattle, and sundry other livestock. In what is now San Antonio, Alarcón erected a complex of missions, a presidio, and a civilian settlement.

So few people manned Nacogdoches and San Antonio, however, that the crown deemed it imperative to strengthen the two settlements with added personnel from the interior. Furthermore, the Gulf coast, where La Salle had planted his little colony years earlier, remained vulnerable to invasion. In March 1721, therefore, the crown ordered a wealthy nobleman named Marqués de San Miguel de Aguayo to carry out the task of reinforcing the two colonies and protecting the coast. To Texas Marqués de Aguayo brought numerous families and such plentiful numbers of livestock that some historians call it the first real cattle drive in the state's history. Historians have also credited Alarcón for stabilizing things in Texas, for by the time he left, the Marqués had added more people to the region, increased the number of missions and presidios, and founded La Bahía near Matagorda Bay to guard against attacks from foreign rivals.

The last coordinated effort on the part of crown officials to solidify their control of Texas during the early eighteenth century occurred in 1731, when they implemented plans to settle pobladores from the Canary Islands at San Antonio. The *Isleños* (Islanders)—some 55 of them—hoped for a fresh start in life. Spain, on the other hand, intended to augment the Texas population with their numbers. To insure that things went well for both parties, therefore, the government equipped the caravan adequately at Saltillo. There the Islanders received mounts, draft animals, farm equipment, and other supplies needed for the journey into the hinterlands. Their grueling trip ended in March 1731, and following that year's harvest, they proceeded to found the villa of San Fernando de Béxar alongside the older settlement (of some 200 people) that had been established earlier in 1718. In accordance with previous agreements, the Canary Islanders got some of the better lands available in the vicinity for farming, titles of nobility, and other special rewards.

The crown undertook no further initiatives to colonize Texas once the Canary Islanders had located in San Antonio in 1731. As of that date, therefore, only the small total of about 500 people represented crown authority in the province. Certainly, military personnel (accompanied by their families) rotating into frontier service arrived regularly from northern Mexican states such as Coahuila and Nuevo León. Franciscans, some of them coming directly from Spain, also entered the province to staff the various missions. Civilians also drifted into Texas occasionally, but they did so without crown authorization and not as part of any colonization effort. Some were merchants seeking new markets, others individuals looking for life improvement for themselves and their families, and still others may have been men evading the law. Reproduction, complemented by irregular but steady migration from the New Spain proper and even European countries, thus accounted for increases in population throughout the several decades after the 1730s. A census taken in 1784 placed the total number of people living in the civilian settlements of San Antonio, Nacogdoches, and La Bahía (and their environs) at approximately 2,800.

The census enumerators identified about 1,600 of these 2,800 as Spaniards, about 180 as mestizos, some 400 as being of *color quebrado* (of African, Indian, and Spanish mixture), and the remainder as being Indian converts or slaves. In actuality, practically none of the *españoles* had been born in Spain, and those who did have Spanish parents were Mexico-born. "Spanish" at that time designated a social category, and was applied to people of good standing in the community. Though such people might have Indian ancestry, their family connections and their position in society, politics, or the military nonetheless earned them the designation of *español.* On the frontier, persons of mixed blood could upgrade themselves to the status of "Spaniards" by achieving distinction on the battle-field, by the accumulation of wealth, or by marrying into prominent families. The conclusion that only 180 mestizos lived in Texas after several generations, therefore, is misleading. In fact, a good majority of the 2,800 pobladores were probably of mestizo extraction. Even the Canary Islanders by the 1780s had mixed through intermarriage with the local population, so they also were not truly Spaniards (Oakah L. Jones Jr., *Los Paisanos: Spanish Settlers on the Northern Frontier of New Spain* (Norman: University of Oklahoma Press, 1979), p. 51).

Although these 2,800 pobladores living in Texas during the 1780s formed the core of Spanish colonial society in the area, mention must be made of a fledgling community and some ranch hamlets existing in an area of a jurisdiction (the state of Nuevo Santander, or modern-day Tamaulipas) along the Rio Grande that later became part of Texas. These settlements derived from a colonizing project undertaken by José de Escandón, an experienced frontier administrator, who in the 1740s received approval from the crown to colonize both sides of the Rio Grande, starting from about present-day Nuevo Laredo to the downriver village of Mier. Escandón hoped to found communities in this area that would act to discourage further foreign designs on the Far North and to help deal with some of the Indian nations that from their bases along the Texas coast constantly harassed the northern settlements of Nuevo Santander. Families from the states of Coahuila and Nuevo León responded to Escandón's call for volunteers, lured by the possibility of acquiring free land, receiving compensation in the form of a small monetary allowance, and escaping visits by tax collectors.

The result of this activity was six settlements, two of them on the north bank of the Rio Grande, one of which became Laredo, Texas. Established in 1755 by a man named Tomás Sánchez, one of Escandón's lieutenants, this villa by the 1770s contained a population of nearly 700. The nucleus of ranch communities extending from the Rio Grande Valley to the Nueces River came into being during the next decades when the crown granted pastureland to leading citizens of Nuevo Santander who wanted to expand into large scale ranching on the north bank of the Rio Grande. By the 1780s, several ranches dotted the region that is today called South Texas.

Whether living in Nacogdoches in eastern Texas or along the north bank of the Rio Grande, *Tejanos* faced as much difficulty as their counterparts in New Mexico in wresting a livelihood in the remote Far North. The land obviously offered the most practical avenue to survival, but farming without the manpower, proper implements, and needed seed did not entice many. Ranching had its own drawbacks, being vulnerable to Indian attacks and a lack of local markets, but it nonetheless served as the bedrock of the Texas economy. Until the mid–eighteenth century, ranching consisted mostly of rounding up wild cattle (*mesteños*), either for food or barter, but the enterprise then began bearing returns around the San Antonio River valley, the very location with which early Texas ranching by Spaniards is associated. After that period, ranchsteads appeared, as grantees built small dwellings around which relatives and workers established their own shacks for mutual protection.

Ranchers could find markets for their horses, mules, sheep, and cattle at the local presidio, as well as among townsfolk and sundry other local buyers. But more of a profit could be made by exporting their animals. Thus did the people in Nacogdoches engage in contraband trade with Louisiana, but those in the Béxar region preferred traveling south. By the 1770s they had developed commercial ties with the neighboring state of Coahuila, exporting hides, tallow, jerky, and other commodities produced on the frontier. Yearly, Tejanos took such goods to the Saltillo Fair (in Coahuila) and, on their return, brought home a variety of finished items and essential supplies, among them ranch gear, blankets, salt, and kitchen utensils.

Ranch owners who had received grants of land for cattle raising were the closest thing to an elite class in colonial Texas, along perhaps with a small group of merchants and traders found in the urban economies of Béxar, Nacogdoches, La Bahía, and Laredo. Aside from these two elements, however, most Tejanos were just plain folks accepting any sort of employment to provide for their family's well-being. Many worked on the range or even rented land. Young men could also join the local military. A military career not only provided a living but entailed doing what many civilians did anyway: defending against Indian attacks and guarding against foreign threats. Other men worked with oxen and mules, transporting goods across hostile terrain. Experienced carpenters, blacksmiths, masons, and other artisans always found demand for their services. As for women, they were not always relegated to domestic tasks. There lived in colonial Texas a number of women who owned ranches, having gotten them either through grants (if they were heads of households), inheritance, or widowhood. Many examples exist of ranch women who capably administered their lands, managed work crews, and tended to ranch business. Traditionally, however, women's duties involved doing housework and raising families, though women also earned livelihoods as seamstresses, laundresses, servants, and the like.

In New Mexico, meanwhile, Hispanic society and community during the eighteenth century continued to be shaped by the frontier environment. Compared to Texas in the eighteenth century, the population in New Mexico soared, standing at 16,000 according to the census of 1790 (considered by historians to be one of the most reliable censuses taken during the eighteenth century). During this time period, the population remained more or less concentrated in the same region colonized in the 1690s and 1710s (that is, from Taos in the north to the several communities just south of Albuquerque). The foci of Hispano civilization in New Mexico in 1790 still encompassed the old villas of Santa Cruz, Santa Fe, and Albuquerque, but these towns had grown considerably in size during the century (respectively, their populations in the early 1790s stood at 3,116, 3,660, and 6,153). Newer rural settlements, moreover, had been founded by families to the east and west of the Rio Grande.

Census takers during the eighteenth century persistently labeled the majority of those in New Mexico as being españoles, but as in the case of Texas, such a label was a misnomer. The name was simply given to those who through the generations acquired lands, won appointment to government position, earned distinction as Indian fighters or military men, or simply insisted on being distinguished from the Indian peoples in the kingdom. In point of fact, few people lived in New Mexico who could claim racial purity by having arrived there directly from Spain. Of all those listed in the 1790 census, for instance, only two declared themselves to have been born in Spain. Actually, population increases were due to racial mixing with the Pueblos and other indigenous peoples, for there occurred little immigration from the interior, and certainly not from Spain.

Scholars estimate that during the eighteenth century perhaps 80 percent or more of New Mexico's inhabitants were of mixed heritage.

Among the españoles, class distinctions existed, with a category of noblemen constituting the top tier. This nobility owned the better parcels of land, raised flocks of sheep, and often had Indian slaves working for them. Members of this "aristocracy" referred to each other by titles of respect (for instance, hidalgo; or *don* for males, *doña* for women), intermarried, and held exclusive social functions when possible. Despite such displays, a lack of identifiable wealth blurred their difference from the bulk of common folk, who themselves pretended to be españoles (so as to be set apart from the Indian populations), even though they might have nothing more than small plots of land. At the bottom of New Mexico's colonial society was a class composed of *genízaros,* that is, Indian peoples absorbed into Hispanic life who worked as servants, slaves, or peons.

Whether the pobladores considered themselves españoles or not, survival required that all engage in physical labor of some kind, so that even landowners, government officials, presidio soldiers, and the missionaries had to perform work in order to feed themselves and those dependent upon them. Naturally, the land provided the most practical means of livelihood, but ranching in New Mexico never became a gainful vocation as it was in Texas, and sheep instead of cattle generally served as the mainstay of most *ranchos.* Farming was not a profitmaking enterprise either, but more farmers than ranchers lived in New Mexico, planting maize and vegetables for their own sustenance or trade. Day laborers who did not own land took jobs such as herders or servants and supplemented their incomes with produce from small gardens situated close to their homes.

Although urban dwellers such as merchants, crown officials, and skilled craftsmen were not directly tied to the land, their living nonetheless serviced (or derived from) an agrarian-based economy. Artisans included carpenters, blacksmiths, and masons. Weavers in the city created beautiful woolen products (made from the wool of sheep raised in surrounding ranches), among them attractive blankets that could be used for sale, barter, or exchange in the markets of the interior. Despite their various occupations, city dwellers themselves had to work the land in some way or another to supplement small earnings.

New Mexico did produce enough goods to enable traders in the latter decades of the eighteenth century to participate in the annual fair held in Chihuahua every January. During the summer, the New Mexicans came together in Taos for trade with the Pueblos and other Indian nations from the Plains. In exchange for their woolen blankets and clothing, corn, knives, and some livestock, the New Mexicans received hides, buffalo robes, weapons, and slaves. The New Mexicans then joined the yearly caravan for Chihuahua, carrying the wares acquired in Taos as well as their own homemade goods. As did the Tejanos on their return from the Saltillo Fair, the New Mexicans brought home a variety of kitchen items, manufactured clothing, hardware, calendars, and other merchandise coveted on the frontier.

Though not too different in its social and economic structure from Texas, culture in New Mexico displayed its own distinctive forms. The Spanish vocabulary in New Mexico contained archaic terms and words that persisted even into modern times, as for example the use of the verb *facer* for *hacer* (to do, or to make). People from particular parts of Spain also seem to have been a greater component of the New Mexico colony than of Texas. Although not uncommon in other parts of the United States West, surnames such as Archuleta, Vigil, Apodaca, Luján, Baca, Barela, and Romero appear to be more frequently found in New Mexico. A kind of popular art—the making of *santos*—also flourished in New Mexico to a degree not perceptible elsewhere. Starting in the eighteenth century, New Mexico has been identified with the making of *retablos,* that is, depictions of santos (saints) on flat wooden surfaces (and later painted on tin materials). New Mexico also produced what were called *bultos,* or statues of saints whittled out of cottonwood or pine.

Why did such cultural forms take root in New Mexico and not in other parts of the borderlands? A significant discussion on the matter has arisen among scholars in recent years that has taken the name of the Hispano Homeland Debate. On the one hand, there is a school that argues that settlers came to New Mexico more than 100 years before they did to Texas (and almost two centuries before they arrived in modern-day California and Arizona) and that those who arrived with Oñate (and even Vargas) came directly from Spain. Being more isolated from New Spain than any other subsequent group would be, these earliest pobladores preserved aspects of their Iberian heritage more successfully than would have been possible for those born in the New World. But a counter school of thought sees New Mexico's "distinctiveness" as only a regional variation of what exists among other Hispanic communities in the U.S. West. Proponents of this point of view note that similar relics of an Iberian past are to be found in parts of northern Mexico, and perhaps even among older Mexican communities established within the continental United States during the late eighteenth or early nineteenth centuries. Two powerful pieces of evidence on the side of this argument exist: most of those who settled New Mexico were not in fact españoles, and New Mexico was never so isolated as to insulate a transplanted culture.

Whatever may be the actual case, it is fact that by the 1780s the New Mexicans had been able to provide for themselves without much help from communities in the heartland. They had dealt with the varied problems of isolation, food shortages, the weather, the terrain, and antagonistic Indians. Their numbers had multiplied over the decades, guaranteeing Spain's claim to the upper Rio Grande region of the borderlands. They had further implanted an enduring Hispanic culture rich in vocabulary, customs, foods, folklore, and entertainment forms. *Nuevomexicanos* had realized, to the extent possible on the frontier, the human ambition to create a society where economic mobility was possible and where people felt comfortable with the political culture around them.

While New Mexico and Texas had reached a fair level of stability by the latter decades of the eighteenth century, such was not the case in Arizona and California, which were then in the incipient stages of colonization. The crown had several reasons for wanting to assert the Spanish presence in these two regions. As always, there lived heathens (Indians) in those frontier areas who needed to receive the Christian word. Then, there lurked (as to the east of Texas) a foreign menace. California seemed especially vulnerable to possible penetration by Russia, England, or even Holland. Missions, presidios, civilian settlements, and ranchos could carry out missionary and defensive goals, as they in fact had done in New Mexico and Texas.

First of these two northwestern lands to see early settlement was Arizona. The name *Arizona* seemingly comes from *Arizonac,* a name given to a mining district (the *Real de Arizonac*) that existed during the 1730s in

Pimería Alta (today's southern Arizona), which got its own name from the presence of the Pima Indians living around the Tucson region. Among the earliest Europeans to take seriously what then existed as a jurisdiction of the state of Sonora was Father Eusebio Francisco Kino, who during the 1680s and early 1710s conducted missionary work among the Pimas and other Sonoran Indian nations. But the crown was more interested in smashing the Pimas, for they constantly harassed the Sonoran frontier towns. As a deterrent to Indian attacks, therefore, government officials established the presidio San Ignacio de Tubac in 1752 on the Santa Cruz River, and around it sprouted a civilian post. As of 1757, a total of 411 soldiers and civilians lived at Tubac, though a general decline followed after 1776 when the military relocated the garrison. San Agustín del Tucson then took Tubac's place, as royal officials wanted a fortification that would be strategically placed to deal with Indian raids, protect the friars working in Pimería Alta, and be a link in the colonization efforts undertaken from Sonora to California. The presidio/pueblo complex there established proved to be the beginnings of present-day Tucson, Arizona. As of 1778, seventy-five soldiers manned the garrison, and they lived in an adjoining village along with their families.

Toward the end of the eighteenth century, Arizona remained a sparsely settled outpost in the Far North, and its standing as a colony hardly compared with that of New Mexico or Texas. But it proved to have both short-term and long-lasting significance. From Tubac and Tucson departed some of the ambitious expeditions that resulted in the permanent settlement of California by civilians. Then, of course, culture had gained a toehold in another borderland region that today contains a strong Hispanic ambience.

The first initiatives designed to assert a claim to California occurred in 1769, when the crown ordered a mission and military station erected in the area around what is now San Diego. By 1773, this attempt at affirming a right to California had led to the establishment of a total of five missions throughout the province, as well as one presidio in Monterey in 1770. Still, although these two institutions served the crown in securing California and attending to the need of converting Indians, they lacked support from civilian settlers, the ones who might plant the necessary crops and raise the needed livestock for everyone's survival.

Juan Bautista de Anza was a Spanish explorer and the official founder of San Francisco in the late eighteenth century. (Corbis)

Moreover, there was a need for civilians who—through constant immigration and reproduction—could help populate the frontier in a manner that missionaries and detachments of presidial soldiers could not.

The task of leading pobladores into California fell to Captain Juan Bautista de Anza, then a presidio commander in Tubac, Arizona. Finding most of his recruits in Sinaloa, Anza departed from Tubac in October 1775 and headed north toward Tucson. About 240 people made up his expedition, as did hundreds of heads of cattle, horses, and mules, and a plentiful stock of supplies. They headed overland along the Gila River until it intersected with the Colorado River, then continued west, ultimately to Monterey, where the caravan arrived in March 1776. The colonists immediately began setting up households in the presidio, marking the first time that civilian pioneers had made their way to California with the intent of staying permanently.

In actuality, these first pobladores were too few in numbers, and in any case, the crown desired formal civilian settlements. Towns not only would be tangible signs of a Hispanic presence in the borderlands, but would also help foster farms and ranches that could produce the food and livestock needed by California's Franciscans and soldiers. From this necessity resulted the founding of the cities of San José and Los Angeles. San José came to be peopled in 1777 by some of the families brought initially to Monterey by Juan Bautista de Anza as well as by families belonging to some of the presidial soldiers. As of 1778, sixty-eight persons were reported living there. Los Angeles, on the other hand, was settled by pioneers brought in from Sinaloa and Sonora in 1781. Its founders (eleven families, or a total of forty-four persons) carefully laid out the town according to royal blueprints, as was the case with the founding of other borderlands towns such as Santa Fe and San Antonio. Thus, as of the 1780s, the future Golden State consisted of two fledgling settlements, several ranchos, nine missions, and four presidios, among them San Francisco, also built in 1776.

LEGACY

Though the settlement of Arizona and California came late in the eighteenth century, Spain still left a lasting imprint there. A syncretic culture melded from European and indigenous roots flourished from Texas to California by the late eighteenth century. Almost every river and stream, and many a mountain and valley from California to Texas bore a name given to it by a Spanish explorer or early pioneer. Ranching had already made an impact on cattle herding, though Mexicans later left a greater stamp on the vocation. Civic-minded citizens throughout the U.S.

Presidio of San Francisco, America, from Picturesque Travels around the World *(1822), by Otto von Kotzebue, Russian naval officer who circumnavigated the earth three times. (The Art Archive/Navy Historical Service, Vincennes, France/Dagli Orti)*

Southwest today display their admiration and fondness for their antecedents by renovating and preserving presidios, missions, government buildings, and other historically significant structures. Spain's destiny in what is now the U.S. West suffered a political setback in the early 1800s, but its culture has continued steadfastly.

BIBLIOGRAPHIC ESSAY

There are numerous specialized studies that treat the period of what the great historian Herbert E. Bolton called the "Spanish Borderlands," the area settled by Spanish and Mexican settlers during the era from the time of the first Spanish entradas to about 1821. Among these are John Francis Bannon, *The Spanish Borderlands Frontier, 1513–1821* (New York: Holt, Rinehart, and Winston, 1970), and more recent works by John L. Kessell, *Spain in the Southwest: A Narrative History of Colonial New Mexico, Arizona, Texas and California* (Norman: University of Oklahoma Press, 2002); David J. Weber, *The Spanish Frontier in North America* (New Haven, CT: Yale University Press, 1992); Oakah L. Jones, *Los Paisanos: Spanish Settlers in the North Frontier of New Spain* (Norman: University of Oklahoma Press, 1979); and Gilbert R. Cruz, *Let There Be Towns: Spanish*

Municipal Origins in the American Southwest, 1610–1810 (College Station: Texas A&M University Press, 1988).

There also exists a corpus of literature focusing more precisely on specific states of the U.S. West. By far, more has been written on New Mexico, in part because New Mexico was settled by the Spaniards more than a hundred years earlier than was Texas, and much earlier than Arizona and California. Among the many excellent publications on the earliest years of colonial New Mexico are the works of Marc Simmons, such as *The Last Conquistador: Juan de Oñate and the Settling of the Far Southwest* (Albuquerque: University of New Mexico Press, 1991), and *Coronado's Land: Essays in the Daily Life in Colonial New Mexico* (Albuquerque: University of New Mexico Press, 1991). The acknowledged expert on colonial New Mexico remains France V. Scholes, whose most important works include "Civil Government and Society in New Mexico in the Seventeenth Century," *New Mexico Historical Review* 10 (April 1935), and "Troublous Times in New Mexico, 1659–1670," *New Mexico Historical Review* 15 (October 1940). Scholes translated many of the original documents of the era from Spanish to English and relied extensively on those translations for his writings. Much of what is known today of Doña Teresa de Aguilar y Roche comes directly from Scholes' research, for instance. Other good studies for the period of the seventeenth and eighteenth centuries are Carroll L. Riley, *The Kachina and the Cross: Indians and Spaniards in the Early Southwest* (Salt Lake City: University of Utah Press, 1999); and Ramón A. Gutiérrez, *When Jesus Came, the Corn Mothers Went Away: Marriage, Sexuality, and Power in New Mexico, 1500–1846* (Stanford, CA: Stanford University Press, 1991). Works that look at New Mexico during the eighteenth century (following the Pueblo Revolt) and that are informative as to social life in that province are Adrián Bustamante, "'The Matter Was Never Resolved': The Casta System in Colonial New Mexico, 1693–1823," *New Mexico Historical Review* 66 (April 1991); John Chávez, "Aztlán, Cibola, and Frontier New Spain," in *The Lost Land: The Chicano Image of the Southwest* (Albuquerque: University of New Mexico Press, 1984); and Antonio José Ríos-Bustamante, "New Mexico in the Eighteenth Century: Life, Labor and Trade in la Villa de San Felipe de Albuquerque, 1706–1790," *Aztlán: International Journal of Chicano Studies Research* 7 (Fall 1976).

The famous Pueblo Revolt of 1680 is a topic all its own in New Mexico's history, and an extensive bibliography on the subject exists. Among the recent careful studies of the episode is Andrew L. Knaut, *The Pueblo Revolt of 1680: Conquest and Resistance in Seventeenth-Century New Mexico* (Norman: University of Oklahoma Press, 1995). Those interested in the historical debate on the revolt's causes and meanings should consult David J. Weber, *What Caused the Pueblo Revolt?* (Boston: Bedford/St. Martin's 1999).

An issue of contention in the history of colonial New Mexico is the theory that colonial New Mexico was a unique "Hispano Homeland," preserving the culture of Spain more purely than any other area in the New World. The foremost advocate of such a position is Richard Nostrand, *The Hispano Homeland* (Norman: University of Oklahoma Press, 1992); the thesis is also supported by Marc Simmons, Fray Angélico Chávez, and others in "Rejoinders," *Annals of the Association of American Geographers* 74, no. 1 (1984). Those who question this unique position of New Mexico articulate their case in J. M. Blaut and Antonio Ríos-Bustamante, "Commentary on Nostrand's 'Hispanos' and their 'Homeland,'" *Annals of the Association of American Geographers* 74 (1984). A recent discussion of this debate is found in Phillip B. Gonzales's review of Charles Montgomery's book *The Spanish Redemption: Heritage, Power, and Loss on New Mexico's Upper Rio Grande* (Berkeley: University of California Press, 2002), in *New Mexico Historical Review* 78 (Summer 2003).

Texas has its own scholars, who have produced splendid studies on the Lone Star State during the Borderlands period. Among the best of such recent works are Donald E. Chipman, *Spanish Texas, 1519–1821* (Austin: University of Texas at Austin, 1992), and Jack Jackson, *Los Mesteños: Spanish Ranching in Texas, 1721–1821* (College Station: Texas A&M University Press, 1986). The New Social History, which considers the lives of ordinary folks to be as worthy of study of that of elites, is represented by Jesús F. de la Teja, *San Antonio de Béxar: A Community on New Spain's Northern Frontier* (Albuquerque: University of New Mexico Press, 1995), and Armando Alonzo, *Tejano Legacy: Rancheros and Settlers in South Texas, 1734–1900* (Albuquerque: University of New Mexico Press, 1999), which studies South Texas following its settlement during the 1730s and 1750s. Works on Arizona and California for the eighteenth century are not as plentiful, simply because they were only settled in the later decades of the eighteenth century. Those origins, however, are expertly covered in some of the books mentioned above, among them the ones by Jones, Weber, and Kessell.

CHAPTER THREE

THE WEST
UNDER MEXICO,
1780s–1848

Beginning about the 1760s, bold moves took place at the imperial level that influenced the course of events in the Far North. These changes emanated from the so-called Bourbon reforms. In the short run, these new policies assisted in stimulating economic growth in the old colonies of New Mexico and Texas, as well as in the younger settlements of Pimería Alta and California. In the end, the Bourbon initiatives injured relations between Spain, the mother country, and all the Latin American colonies, including New Spain. When Mexico won its independence in 1821, the Far North fell under its sovereignty and remained so until the United States acquired the land west of the Mississippi in 1848.

The Bourbon reforms get their name from the Bourbon kings who implemented them. Led by Carlos III (1759–1788), government officials (many of them disciples of the Enlightenment) enacted a series of measures that had as their purpose making the administration of Latin America more efficient and Spain itself more powerful. These plans followed an inspection tour of Mexico made by José de Gálvez, visitor general from Spain, between 1765 and 1771. From Gálvez's recommendations followed a number of new strategies, among them the establishment of an intendancy system to be headed by appointees from Spain, a better corps of tax collectors not vulnerable to corruption, and free trade to be permitted among all constituting the Spanish empire. To ascertain the problems that afflicted the northern frontier, the crown dispatched the Marqués de Rubí (1766–1767) with the task of inspecting all missions, presidios, civilian settlements, and ranches therein. His findings produced what came to be called the New Regulations of Presidios in 1772, which proposed the reorganization of the northern frontier of New Spain. These recommendations in turn led to the creation of the *Provincias Internas* (Interior Provinces) in 1776, an administrative unit under a commandant general that embraced most of the northern Mexican states and the colonies in the Far North. The Regulations also called for a war against the *indios bárbaros* (barbaric Indians) who wreaked terror on those entrusted with defending the crown's lands. In any event, however, campaigns against the Indians alternated between actually waging war and trying to mollify them with gifts and various forms of diplomacy.

Government representatives (responsible for carrying out bureaucratic orders) and pobladores (who made up the military forces in frontier wars) during the last two decades of the eighteenth century turned to gift giving to placate (and even control) the indios bárbaros, reasoning that such approaches cost less in money and lives than waging war. Moreover, the Indians themselves seemed to have preferred this formula, as it was a way for them to acquire weapons, alcohol, textiles, trinkets, and the like. Frontier people also dealt with the hostile Indian nations by forging alliances with the more willing ones against intransigent tribes unwilling to accept the friendly policy of trade and gift offerings. They negotiated such pacts by either defeating the Indians on the battlefield or winning them over by allowing them to participate in the new commerce, in trade fairs, and in the festivity of gift sharing. The pobladores in Texas, for one, made peace with the Comanches in order to smash the troublesome Apaches. In New Mexico, similar treaties were formed with the Comanches and the Utes in order to deal with the Navajos and with the Pueblos to contend with various other tribes that rejected Spanish policies. By the 1790s, relations between the pobladores and the indigenous peoples appear to have entered a friendlier era, as peace became more common, due to the policy recommendations that had emanated initially from the Bourbon reforms.

Peace with the Indians, precarious though it was, allowed for more profitable ranching, farming, and business transactions, so that the Far North experienced a healthy upswing in its economy. Commerce among

the several territories within the Provincias Internas expanded simultaneously. The pobladores of the Far North sent some of their own goods
south—among them cattle products, sheep, wool, wheat, and Indian
blankets—and brought back from Chihuahua, Sonora, and Coahuila assorted manufactured goods. Even trade with the Indians increased, to the
point that some of the pobladores in northern New Mexico traveled into
what is now Utah to barter.

A more direct impact on the Far North was created by the discontent
that the Bourbon reforms caused in New Spain, for it was that discontent
that (in part) led to a war for independence and eventually the Far North
coming under the rule of Mexico. The people of New Spain had not been
too happy about governance managed from afar. Further, the criollos
(those born in the New World of Spanish parents) resented the crown appointees who arrived in Mexico to execute the reform measures. The
gachupines (as those of the New World derisively called those from the
peninsula) looked down on the locals, an absurd attitude so far as the
criollos were concerned, since they considered themselves as good as those
from the mother country, and indeed their equals.

MIGUEL HIDALGO AND THE DIEZ Y SEIS DE SEPTIEMBRE

Actually, the Bourbon reforms only aggravated strained relations between
mother country and colony. They did not cause the war for independence. Rebellion occurred, instead, due to a series of events that took
place in Europe and Spain in the late eighteenth century and in the early
years of the nineteenth century. Charles IV, successor to Charles III,
proved unable to handle domestic affairs and soon saw his monarchy
mired in corruption. The French Revolution of 1789, with its violence
and execution of Louis XVI, brought a response from conservative Spain
in the form of a declaration of war in 1793. Defeated by its neighbor,
Spain now faced a new war with the British, a problem that demanded
new revenue and sacrifices from the colonies. Then the entire country fell
to French occupation under Napoleon in 1808. The Spaniards revolted
on May 2, 1808 (known in Spanish history as the *Dos de Mayo*), and subsequently called for Spanish subjects everywhere to form juntas to govern

until the return of Ferdinand VII, successor to Charles IV who had abdicated. In Mexico, those elements that had been dissatisfied with the administrative policies of the Bourbon reforms and alarmed over the events unfolding abroad began seriously to contemplate independence.

Long-standing resentment among the various social classes would impress itself onto the turbulence that uniquely distinguished New Spain's war for independence from parallel movements in Latin America. There prevailed, for instance, smoldering hatred between the lower classes (composed of the mestizos, and castas, Indians, common workers, and the unemployed populace) and the peninsulares and criollos who made up society's upper crust. To complicate matters, there was the deep contempt between peninsulares and criollos. The crises of the 1790s and early 1800s had exacerbated differences between these two sectors. When Napoleon overthrew Ferdinand in 1808, the criollos intensified talk of independence, on the grounds that the king's absence permitted self-rule. Independence for them would end the domination of the despised gachupines. The criollos would then govern Mexico unimpeded.

With this goal, criollo conspirators met regularly in Querétaro (state of Querétaro). Among those involved in planning the expulsion of the gachupines was Father Miguel Hidalgo y Costilla, the parish priest in Dolores, Guanajuato. Though a criollo himself, Hidalgo felt genuine compassion for the lower classes, for he daily viewed the poverty and misery of their lives. When royal authorities discovered the conspiracy and acted to arrest the plotters, including Hidalgo, the priest decided upon prompt action lest all be lost. On the morning of September 16, 1810 (the *Diez y Seis de Septiembre*), Hidalgo addressed his parishioners and informed them that the time was at hand to end the injustices that afflicted them under peninsular rule.

Off to war against the ruling classes (both peninsulares and criollos) went the masses. Almost immediately the war for independence planned by the criollos became a social rebellion, as Hidalgo's army targeted all that smacked of oppression, including haciendas, the homes of the wealthy, businesses, government offices, and the like. Hidalgo found himself unable to control his unruly followers, who now sought out Spaniards to amend centuries of wrongs. For months, the motley army of mestizos, castas, and Indians ran amok through central Mexico, until a royal army defeated them in March 1811. Officials arrested Hidalgo, tried him for conspiracy and treason, and executed him.

Other leaders took up Hidalgo's struggle, however, among them another priest named José María Morelos. But by 1815, royalist forces had also apprehended Morelos and executed him. Guerrilla leaders, among them Vicente Guerrero and Guadalupe Victoria, remained defiant throughout the rest of the decade, and carried on the dream of equality and nationhood. Then, almost abruptly, the end of fighting came when a coalition of factions and social classes—unwilling to live under a liberal constitution forced upon Spain in 1820—united on behalf of independence. The war's closing in 1821 hardly brought about the implementation of the ideals that Hidalgo had championed. On the contrary, Mexico's war for independence proved only a conservative change at the top, with criollos replacing gachupines.

In the territories of the Far North, the war for independence went unnoticed, except in Texas. In San Antonio, those who sided with Miguel Hidalgo included first, Juan Bautista de Las Casas, and then, Bernardo Gutiérrez de Lara. In January 1811, Las Casas effectively rallied part of the Béxar population that was discontented with provincial Spanish rule. This element resented the governor's interference with contraband, his efforts to dilute the powers of the town council, and his general capriciousness. But not everyone in Béxar was prepared to take the extreme step of joining a revolutionary movement against the crown, and the result was a backlash that landed las Casas in the hands of the authorities and his decapitated head at the end of a pole for the public to view as a warning to would-be traitors in Texas. Two years later, Bernardo Gutiérrez de Lara led the "Republican Army of the North" from Louisiana into Texas, captured Nacogdoches, La Bahía, and Béxar, only to experience defeat in August 1813 at the hands of the royalist commander José Joaquín Arredondo. Why the two movements failed to gather greater support for independence may be explained partly by the fact that the Tejanos placed greater importance on local matters than they did on what unfolded hundreds of miles—if not across the ocean—from their daily lives. As a provincial people, furthermore, they disapproved of outsiders. They were inclined to back politics that could potentially improve their conditions but abandoned those politics if they became detrimental to their well-being, as was the case with the las Casas revolt and counterrevolt.

COMMUNITY BUILDING IN THE FAR NORTH

The person most responsible for gaining New Spain's independence had been a royalist officer named Agustín de Iturbide. A faithful combatant against the insurgent independence forces led by Hidalgo, then by Morelos, and then the *guerrilleros,* he had been converted to the wisdom (as were many in New Spain's upper classes) of making a final break with the mother country by the desire to prevent Mexicans from being subject to life under Spain's liberal constitution of 1812. Issuing a proclamation labeled the Plan de Iguala in February 1821, he won over disparate elements favoring independence and in July 1821 proclaimed Mexico free.

Supporters of the Plan de Iguala had agreed upon a constitutional monarchy for Mexico, with an elected congress to govern until a qualified prince from Europe was found to serve as first emperor. Iturbide, meanwhile, took the helm of government as its executive, until the evening of May 8, 1822, when a crowd gathered outside his palace, calling for his elevation to emperor of Mexico. He accepted the emperorship of Mexico when the congress, bending to popular insistence, offered him the post the next day.

The provinces of the Far North, all under governors appointed by the crown during the 1810s, acceded to the new political order. But government under Iturbide did not last long, as many in Mexico resented his arbitrary rule, among them members of the congress who entertained republican ideas and rejected monarchy. When Iturbide dissolved the legislative body, he found himself face to face with supporters of the Plan de Casa Mata, a political manifesto advanced by a military commander by the name of Antonio López de Santa Anna, who promised the establishment of a republic. Opposition forces proved too strong for Iturbide to overcome, and he left Mexico in March 1823.

The unity that produced Iturbide's ouster lasted only briefly, for soon two philosophically different political factions vied for the right to govern. On the conservative side stood what in Mexico's politics of the 1820s through the 1850s were known as the Centralists. This group favored the centralization of government at the national level and sought the restoration of a social order resembling the one existing in the colonial era, wherein land owners, the clergy, and the military presided over the masses. Opposing them were the Federalists. They advanced a liberal position that gave greater power to the states while weakening the administration in Mexico City. Their hope was to establish a republic based upon the ideas embodied in the Spanish Constitution of 1812 and the U.S. Constitution of 1787. It was this element that won the power struggle, creating Mexico's constitution of 1824 and seeing it ratified.

Under this constitution, the settlers of the Far North had to accept a dependent political status. New Mexico and California, for instance, became territories within the Mexican republic, while Texas settled for being a part of Coahuila. Tejanos did not fare badly under Federalist rule. They worked jointly with Federalist leaders in Coahuila to ensure their prosperity through Anglo American immigration, hoping that settlers from the United States would help advance agriculture and ranching, fend off Indian raiding, and develop commercial ties with markets beyond Texas. At least until 1834, they felt optimistic about the course of their plans.

An end to their expectations came in 1834 when Antonio López de Santa Anna, the same person who had overthrown Iturbide behind the Plan de Casa Mata, removed the Federalists from national offices and within two years imposed a Centralist regime on Mexico. The Centralists made all states into departments to ensure greater control from the center of power in Mexico City, and their conservative politics reigned almost uncontested in Mexico for the next dozen years or so. Most communities in the Far North resented Centralist policies.

To be sure, these communities remained relatively small in numbers. The region with the most inhabitants was New Mexico, containing about 42,000 as of 1821. California then followed with 3,320 pobladores, and Texas ranked right behind it with 2,500. Arizona lagged with a population of slightly higher than 750. Though historians still cannot accurately ascertain the correct size of the Hispanic population at mid-century, in what was by then the U.S. Southwest, they have ventured estimates. One study shows the population to have been as follows for the year 1850:

New Mexico—62,000 to 77,000; Texas—13,900 to 23,200; California—9,100 to 14,000, and Arizona—1,000 to 1,600. [Oscar J. Martínez, "On the Size of the Chicano Population: New Estimates, 1850–1900," *Aztlán* 6 (Spring 1975): 50–56.]

For the most part, the pobladores during the Mexican era remained concentrated more or less in the areas in which they had settled during the initial colonization. A rural society persisted, with only a handful of towns (such as Albuquerque, Santa Fe, and perhaps San Antonio) with Mexican populations greater than 1,500. But even these "cities" lacked those amenities generally associated with urban life today, among them mercantile establishments, banks, department stores, food markets, and the like.

In New Mexico, the core of life was still in the north. The main communities remained the old villas of Santa Cruz, Santa Fe, and Albuquerque, the latter two about the only cities in the province to experience discernible demographic expansion during the Mexican era. As noted previously, settlement over the years had dispersed from these centers, and numerous rural villages had sprouted to the east and west of the Rio Grande and to the north beyond Taos. The southern half of New Mexico below today's Belén remained relatively uninhabited, however.

The other regions of the Far North mirrored New Mexico's pattern of population concentration in the original pockets of settlement. The Californios still hugged the coast, as they had since the earliest entradas of the 1770s. Most people lived in the old towns of Los Angeles, San José, and Branciforte (1797), and in settlements close to the presidios at San Francisco, Santa Barbara, San Diego, and Monterey. Only Los Angeles and San José experienced population increases during the 1820s through the 1840s, though not much, from 650 to 1,250 and 415 to 700, respectively. In Texas, the majority of Tejanos remained around Nacogdoches, La Bahía, and the main community of San Antonio, though several farmsteads were to be found along the San Antonio River. On the border, people stayed closed to the village of Laredo, as well as along the Rio Grande, where numerous ranching units had been established. In Arizona, Mexican people had not succeeded in expanding into the northern reaches of the province due to Indian attacks, and so the main centers during the period of the 1820s through the 1840s remained Tucson and Tubac.

Street scene in Santa Fe, New Mexico, in the 1860s. (North Wind Picture Archive)

Historians puzzle as to why greater migration from the interior did not occur during the Mexican era (or previous to it, for that matter) to secure the Far North from the Indian tribes that harassed the pobladores regularly or from Anglos who began trickling in at that time. One possible answer is that land was plentiful closer to their homes in the interior. Why risk life by uprooting themselves? Unlike today, moreover, little pressure existed demographically to thrust people into frontiers. Furthermore, most people in Mexico found it an expensive proposition to pick up in one area and locate to another. Then, so much political turmoil existed in Mexico during this epoch that government officials found it almost impossible to coordinate colonization projects. Finally, of course, the hinterland offered an uncertain fate. There lingered the possibility of Indian attacks, a scarcity of food supplies, and few employment opportunities. Given these circumstances, frontier people did not overrun the North.

But this did not imply neglect by politicians, for Federalists and the Centralists each attempted the peopling of the northern Mexican periphery, and even the governors of the Far North attempted to achieve expansion that would offer some semblance of security for their citizens. In Arizona, for instance, Mexican administrators during the 1820s distributed land grants to rancheros in areas neighboring Tucson and Tubac, as well as in the valley to the east of these two urban sites, though such settlements did not thrive, due to the aforementioned Indian dangers.

The interior government also felt an obligation to California, as Russia in 1812 had established a foothold close to San Francisco Bay and since then announced it had no intentions of pulling out. The Russians did indeed withdraw in 1841, but Mexican officials did not wait that long to initiate a colonization program to thwart Russians plans. In 1834, they assigned leadership of the project to José María Híjar and José María Padrés, and prepared to subsidize expenses for the scores of settlers who participated in the enterprise.

On April 15, 1834, about 300 settlers departed from Mexico City, filing out in a long caravan that resembled the ones that Juan de Oñate, Diego de Vargas, or Juan Bautista de Anza had led to the Far North during the days when Spain ruled the borderlands. Some distance on the way to the Pacific coast, the colonists found their wagons unable to navigate the terrain, so they made the rest of the journey on foot. At the port of San Blas, the group boarded two separate ships, the *Natalia* and the *Morelos,* and sailed for California, on August 1, 1834.

After an exhausting and unpleasant trip (Híjar himself had become seriously ill with seasickness), the 129 people accompanying Híjar sailed into San Diego on the *Natalia* on September 1, 1834. The would-be defenders of northern California found shelter among the local population, biding their time until Híjar recovered from his seasickness and they overcame the effects of the voyage. Finally recuperated, Híjar led his settlers toward Monterey, ordering them north in small groups, each band of pioneers leaving a few days after the previous one. The colonists had to walk or go atop oxcarts, with a few fortunate ones getting to ride horses. The *Morelos,* meantime, sailed into Monterey on September 24, 1834, carrying Padrés and 120 passengers. They went ashore in no better condition than had the earlier arrivals into San Diego, and like their counterparts, received a good reception from the local villagers, who also put them up for their brief stay. They departed by land for San Francisco in November, also traveling by oxcarts and on foot, as was the mode in those frontier days, and arriving at their destination in a month's time. The San Diego colonists, in the meanwhile, lagged on their way to San Francisco, many getting no further than Monterey.

Despite the best intentions of all involved, the attempt to neutralize the Russian presence in the proximity of San Francisco faced an uncertain fate by December 1834. Little could be expected financially from the new administration in Mexico City, which had toppled the old one responsible for the colonization plan. The native Californios, meantime, distrusted the project as threatening their own economic well-being. They feared that Híjar and Padrés had come with the authority to distribute the best lands in the province to their own colonists and that the two colonizers intended to control California commerce. The California governor, to exacerbate matters, suspected the two of political intrigue, and he had them arrested and deported to Mexico. In March 1835, national officials sounded the death knell to the dream of planting a civilian outpost in northern California, proclaiming that the Híjar-Padrés settlers could settle anywhere in the province, should they wish to do so. Most did in fact remain permanently in California, with some establishing homesteads in the San Francisco area.

In Texas, the Federalists also promoted colonization programs during the 1820s and 1830s. The most famous of these enterprises, to be discussed later, brought Anglo Americans to Texas starting in 1821, but the most successful one undertaken from the interior involved Martín de León. In 1824 he received a contract from the provincial deputation (a legislature at the provincial level) in Texas to bring in forty-one families from Tamaulipas. De León was the only one to receive such a contract, as the life of the Texas deputation ended when Texas became part of Coahuila later in that year. De León, acting as impresario, was to establish a colony on the Guadalupe River by recruiting the stipulated number of people, selecting land for them (each family received a league and a *labor* of land, or some 4,600 acres) within the boundaries of his colony, and ensuring their good conduct and their observation of the law.

From Tamaulipas, de León led his family and the rest of the migrants toward Victoria, the name that Mexican officials had given the little colony on the Guadalupe. The trip toward Texas was made by mule train, and like other such caravans heading to the Far North, it included as much as would be necessary for the trip and for the early months that it took to found a settlement—food supplies, seeds for farming, agricultural equipment, and livestock. Upon arriving on the Guadalupe in the spring of 1825, de León went about the task of laying out the town according to specifications called for by old Spanish law and custom. He established a town square and set aside home plots for his grown children and the other pobladores. Then he distributed ranch properties along the Guadalupe River. More families arrived at the de León colony during the next few years, some of them from Europe (especially Ireland), so that by 1828 Martin de León's plans to gain a new beginning in Texas had been achieved.

Aside from projects that originated in Mexico City to people the northern frontier, there were efforts undertaken by some of the governors to do the same. Among the most ambitious efforts at internal colonization were ones undertaken in New Mexico, mainly during the administration of Governor Manuel Armijo (1837–1846). Historians have taken different positions regarding Armijo's motives for using land grants to settle New Mexico and defend it from Indians and westward-moving U.S. citizens. Some have argued with conviction that Armijo was a corrupt and self-seeking administrator who used the abundant lands of New Mexico for personal profit. Other scholars, however, see a well-intentioned and carefully crafted design behind his land grant and settlement program. For instance, most of the land grants he distributed went to Nuevomexicanos and naturalized Mexicans (that is, Anglo Americans and Europeans who had accepted citizenship in Mexico). It is true that he gave what might seem a disproportionate amount of land to Anglos and Europeans, but those who received land from him had been faithful residents of New Mexico for many years, having married into local families or worked dutifully for the public good of the Mexican nation. Moreover, he distributed lands for the specific purpose of settling those parts of New Mexico that were sparsely populated. Doing so would help stake claims to the hinterlands and make them buffer areas against the indios bárbaros. Among the best known of such grants was the one given to Guadalupe Miranda and Charles Beaubien (a Canadian) in 1841. Armijo knew Beaubien as a respected member of New Mexican society, took the precaution of including Miranda as a partner, and designated lands for them woefully in need of possession. The Miranda-Beaubien grant lay in northeastern New Mexico and extended into what is today Colorado.

The governors of California, under authority given them by legislation issued by Mexico's congress during the 1820s, similarly undertook land grant programs during this time period. As was the case elsewhere, they did so for the purpose of protecting the frontier and providing security to the settlers. Much of the land given out to prospective rancheros occurred after 1833, when Mexico's government, through a policy called secularization, ended the Catholic Church's control of the missions, thus freeing church property for distribution to private citizens. Californios saw profit to be made from owning ranchos and then selling cattle hides and tallow to foreigners, who by then were visiting California with the purpose of developing trade opportunities. The prospect of an easy income led many to request new lands, so that in the years 1843 to 1844, for instance, the California government distributed rancho grants to more than a hundred Californios.

The location of these fledgling ranchos served the intended purpose of solidly claiming the whole of California. Before 1833, people preferred receiving land around Los Angeles and Monterey, as both towns were situated close to missions and both had convenient access to the sea. After secularization, however, not only did people ask to receive the old mission lands (the missions had been scattered throughout California), but property all along the California coastline and even acreage in the interior of the province so long as it was not too distant from the ocean. By the 1840s, therefore, California rancheros had moved into the inland valleys of Napa and Sacramento. A few foreigners also participated in the expansion of that decade, though as in New Mexico, many were Mexicanized gringos.

ENTREPRENEURSHIP

The ending of the Spanish era produced an increased amount of economic activity in the Far North. Spain had imposed too many barriers on the northern settlers, closely overseeing commercial activities therein and otherwise stifling an entrepreneurial spirit. The dawn of the Mexican era brought less supervision and greater encouragement to those wishing to share in the lucrative prospects that surfaced during the 1820s and after.

Some of these newer opportunities derived from the start of the Santa Fe trade. In 1821, an American trader named William Becknell arrived unannounced in Santa Fe, New Mexico, peddling a number of U.S.-made articles which the Nuevomexicanos found enticing. Other American merchants followed Becknell, their goods welcomed in New Mexico. Items popular among the people were U.S. clothing fashions, tools, books, weapons, and farm implements. In exchange for such products, the New Mexicans offered mules, sheep, furs, and their own homegrown textiles.

By the latter part of the 1830s, some of these successful New Mexican entrepreneurs were referring to themselves as *capitalistas* (capitalists). They had made the best of their connection with U.S. merchants and developed close ties with their counterparts in some of the eastern cities, if not beyond the United States, to include markets as far away as Europe. Not only that, but they had taught Americans the Mexican system of freighting and packing and made them appreciate the value of mules as the preferred draft animal for the business.

Commercial ties also extended south to Mexico. From the 1820s through the 1840s, long caravans reminiscent of those of the colonial period departed New Mexico in late summer and fall for Chihuahua and parts beyond along the Old Spanish Royal Road. Convoys consisted of merchants, muleteers, Indian servants, private citizens, and sundry hangers-on. They carried with them woven textiles, socks, blankets, hides, skins, hats, and blankets. Sheep became the most significant export by the 1840s, as the Nuevomexicanos herded south somewhere in the vicinity of 30,000 to 40,000 of the sheep annually. The forty-day journey proved no less formidable than the excursions of earlier centuries, with the same danger of Indian attacks, the same need to camp out (since practically no accommodations existed along the route), and the same necessity of surviving on provisions prepared along the way (ordinarily, beans, tortillas, and a little meat), as eating establishments such as those found today were hardly present on the frontier.

In California, meanwhile, profit seekers during the period of the 1820s through the 1840s saw opportunity in the arrival of foreigners, many of them Americans, who sailed into the California coast to hunt otters and seals and to dispose of manufactured goods. In exchange for fin-

Mexican freighters. Engraving of Mexican teamsters with teams of oxen and mules, by Armand Welcker. (University of Texas, Institute of Texan Cultures at San Antonio, 074-0485)

ished products imported from the United States and even Europe, the Californios eagerly bartered (since money was practically nonexistent on the California frontier) their abundant supply of cattle hides, a commodity in demand in the United States for making leather products such as boots and saddles. The Californios also turned a profit by selling bags of tallow, that is, the beef fat that frontier people of the that era found useful for making soap and candles. After mission secularization, the Californios also had an increased number of horses for sale, and they found ready demand for their stock in Mexico and among Anglo Americans slowly drifting into the province.

Despite what seems a profit motive behind the kind of commerce practiced in New Mexico and California (as well as other regions of the Far North), historians still debate the character of the frontier economy. Was it preindustrial, developing capitalist, or capitalist? One school of thought lays the whole emphasis on the capitalism at work long before the mid–nineteenth century, and as noted earlier in this chapter, some of the Nuevomexicanos were referring to themselves as capitalistas during the 1830s. Another group of scholars believe that the economy was shaped chiefly by lingering elements of feudalism, among them debt peonage, a dependent work force compensated not in wages but in material assistance, and profits used not for capitalist investment but for providing immediate comforts to the landed gentry and their families. Such a debate is not likely to end in the near future, but it is certainly true that entrepreneurship was playing a larger role than it had before.

Culture on the Northern Frontier

Social distinctions remained in the Far North as they had since the time of the first settlements, but as earlier, the frontier acted to equalize matters. By the 1830s a discernible class of *ricos* (rich folk) was appearing in California and New Mexico, due to increased trade with Mexico and the United States, mission secularization, and an increased amount of smuggling undertaken in league with the *Americanos* and foreigner intruders. In Texas, the situation was somewhat different because Anglo Americans had displaced Tejanos (by then Tejanos were a minority, though a large one) from positions of commercial influence after the war for independence of 1836, but nonetheless there lived ranch owners who clung to earlier property and thus still constituted an element a cut above the rest of Tejano society.

The majority of Mexicans in the Far North derived their livelihood from occupations essential to frontier survival. Many were *carreteros* (cartmen), day laborers, artisans, miners, ranch hands, servants, water carriers, *pastores* (shepherds), and migrant sheepshearers. In New Mexico, sheepherding was one way of sustaining the family unit, but many of the pastores found a life of debt as part of the *partido* system. Under this arrangement, sheepherders assumed responsibility for large sheep flocks, with the understanding that profits would be shared at the end of year, at which time the herd would naturally have multiplied. Generally, however, so many sheep would have been lost that sheepherders found themselves perpetually in debt. Arrieros (mule drivers) and packers in New Mexico fared only slightly better. They made up an integral part of the Missouri and Chihuahua trade, and they gained renown for their skills at managing the mules used in commercial freighting. They had no match at packing mules that would carry heavy loads over long distances, and in fact dominated the freighting networks in the U.S. West until the railroads arrived there after the Civil War. Indeed, Americans involved in long-range hauling adopted the Mexican method for mule freighting, and even borrowed terms from the Mexican teamsters. Despite such skills, Mexican muleteers hardly made enough money to escape the poverty they faced as members of the lower class.

The overwhelming majority of people on the frontier had always been mestizos, and so the pobladores could hardly make racial distinctions among themselves. Unlike the U.S. South during that period, people of different "races" lived and worked together. No particular racial doctrine existed in the Far North delineating a master or peon class. But that race consciousness prevailed there is not a matter of debate. As the censuses taken by both the Spanish and Mexican governments indicated, many preferred to consider themselves españoles, a people different than the *indios* and the few biracial (mulatto) settlers who lived among them. Race sensitivity, however, seldom acted to deter persons of color from bettering themselves on the frontier.

The culture that continued in the Far North after independence was mainly that perpetuated by civilian pobladores, for although soldiers and missionaries had been very much a part of the movement northward, noncivilians generally remained there only temporarily. Many soldiers did retire in the borderlands, but they customarily married into local families and readily melted into the general civilian population. A religious or military culture thus never greatly influenced *paisano* (common folk) culture.

What was life like for common people under Mexico's government? Materially, it remained more or less an extension of things that existed before independence. For clothes, the pobladores improvised as best they could. Most wore homemade garments, ordinarily made of cotton, or perhaps silk. Shoes tended to be of leather, with the poor inclined to use sandals, for they were easy and inexpensive to make from cowhide.

For homes, the settlers necessarily relied on what nature offered them in the form of timber and other natural commodities. In some places in the North, people used adobe brick and straw to fashion their modest *jacales* (huts), while in other regions they turned to stones, mesquite trees, reeds, and other natural materials capable of offering protection from the

A father, mother, and their daughters stand in front of their thatched roofed house, called a jacal, *near the Rio Grande border of Mexico and United States, ca. 1915. (Corbis)*

weather. Most houses tended to be no more than two rooms (on the frontier, cooking took place outside), lacked windows, and featured dirt floors. Common objects that one takes for granted in building homes today were scarce on the frontier. These included nails, cut lumber, hinges, glass, plumbing materials, among many other essentials, though such items did make their way west with the Santa Fe trade. Increased economic ties with the United States after the 1830s also brought to the Far North such manufactured home improvement materials as finished doors and glass windows.

The interior of homes reflected their makeshift nature, as indeed furnishings were roughly crafted. Men generally hand made the household's beds, chairs, stools, and tables. Bunks *(bancas)* many times served for eating purposes, as family members of necessity ate sitting on the floor. Wall decorations might be crosses, altars, or other religious objects such as bultos (discussed later). As they did with the building materials that made their way west by the 1830s, homeowners (at least among the wealthy) began purchasing factory-made furniture, clocks, tableware, dishes, and other such commodities from the United States.

Austere frontier living meant lack of schooling for the general population, as indeed, very few educational institutions could be found on the frontier. As had been the state of affairs during the colonial period, only government officials, the friars, and some soldiers could claim literacy. Any instruction that occurred during the Mexican period, therefore, fell to the literate elements in society, most of them bureaucrats. Also employed was the Lancastrian system of education, wherein those who had acquired a semblance of learning (presumably from the bureaucrats) taught the illiterate. But such learning only occurred at the elementary school level, and in any case, lack of finances everywhere acted to curtail grand plans for an educational program. Still, some of the wealthier families in the Far North did find the means to send their sons to school, either in Mexico or the United States

The lack of formal education on the frontier by no means stifled creativity. Literature generally existed in oral forms: *poesía* (poetry), *pastorelas* (shepherd plays), *canciones* (songs), and *cuentos* (short stories). Those able to read, generally members of the expanding rancho class, imported books and accumulated libraries. Written literature was not abundant in the borderlands, but it was not completely absent. Fray Gerónimo Boscana in 1831 wrote *Chinigchinich,* an ethnographic account of the California Indians at Mission San Juan Capistrano, for whom Boscana cared for many years. During the 1830s, another Californian named Joaquín Buelna wrote poetry to pay homage to the California ranchero class.

Literate people did wish to stay abreast of events by reading newspapers, and though Spanish-language newspapers did not proliferate until the latter decades of the nineteenth century, they did exist in New Mexico and California by the 1830s. In actuality, the first Spanish-language newspaper appeared in Texas in 1813 under the title of *Gazeta de Texas,* established in Nacogdoches (albeit briefly, as only one issue was ever published) by revolutionaries wanting to spread republican ideas throughout Mexico during New Spain's war for independence. A more ambitious journalistic endeavor appeared in Santa Fe, New Mexico, in 1834, where Ramón Abreú began publishing *El Crepúsculo de la Libertad* (The Dawn of Liberty) before turning over the venture in 1835 to Father Antonio José Martínez of Taos. In Taos, Father Martínez continued *El Crepúsculo,* but expanded his enterprise to the printing of materials important to his work as a priest and educator, among them instructional manuals and prayer books. Indeed, Martínez has been credited with having published the first book in New Mexico, one titled *Cuaderno de Ortografía* (actually a speller, translated as Book of Orthography, 1835). Three years later, Martinez issued his memoirs under the title of *Relación de Meritos del Presbítero Antonio José Martínez*. (An Account of the Merits of the Priest Antonio José Martínez). At the same time that Abreú started *El Crepús-culo,* a Californian by the name of Agustín V. Zamorano imported a printing press to California and commenced publishing a number of materials, among them administrative regulations and a book by Governor José Figueroa titled *Manifesto to the Mexican Republic* (1834). Figueroa's manifesto declared California's right to determine its own political matters without the intervention of the central government.

For sustenance, people continued relying on time-tested staples, many of them corn products. As is the case today, people enjoyed eating corn tortillas, corn bread, and corn on the cob, as well as a variety of dishes made from corn such as tacos, enchiladas, and tostadas. The corn tortilla, while popular on the frontier during this time period, came to be rivaled by the wheat tortilla, for the latter took less time, preparation, and labor than did the former. Wheat tortillas could be whipped into dough, rolled out, and cooked on a griddle in a brief period of time, perhaps minutes.

Other delicacies popular during the Mexican era (and which continue to be commonplace in modern times) would include *menudo* and *barbacoa.* The former, made from beef entrails (cleaned out thoroughly, of course) and embellished with traditional spices and hominy (made from corn), is still eaten today, generally in the morning (though it may be eaten at any time). Barbacoa (the counterpart to this dish in the United States would be the American pit barbecue, and in fact the word "barbecue" is derived from *barbacoa*), on the other hand, might be made from beef, mutton, pork, or wild game such as deer. The meat to be cooked would be wrapped in a flame-resistant covering (perhaps corn leaves, and later burlap sacks, and today aluminum foil) and left in an earthen pit to roast for several hours. Secret recipes would of course set one person's barbacoa apart from that of a neighbor's.

Women and men carried on familiar roles during the Mexican era, and each acted out parts that the young were expected to learn. Girls

Mexican women making tortillas, New Mexico, 1800s. Printed color lithograph. (North Wind Picture Archive)

learned about religious beliefs and traditions, housekeeping tasks, gardening, matters of health and healing, and basic education from their mothers, and they in turned passed on such knowledge to their offspring. By associating with older women at religious occasions or family get-togethers, girls integrated themselves into a support network of mothers, aunts, and grandmothers who could sustain them in time of travail. Women understood the limitations placed upon them by a male-dominated patriarchal society, among them discouragement from professional careers and exclusion from office and the franchise. Catholic teachings, moreover, emphasized the husband's preeminence within the family unit. Nonetheless, women also knew about their right to inherit, transfer, and own property (and many of them indeed held property) and to use the courts. Women turned to the judicial system to gain relief from intolerable nuptial obligations, or to complain of adultery and the irresponsibility of husbands. Women similarly understood that their confinement to a woman's sphere was in many cases simply a formality, and so they became Indian fighters, ranch owners, range hands, and entrepreneurs, among the latter being the legendary Doña Gertrudis Barceló (La Tules), who in the New Mexico of the 1840s made thousands of dollars as a saloon keeper, gambler, and astute financier. Thus, while young girls learned that certain duties belonged primarily to them, they also recognized that the openness of the frontier allowed them opportunities outside what traditional Spanish and Mexican culture dictated.

Young men, meanwhile, followed the example of their fathers and brothers. Being a man in the nineteenth century meant knowing much about survival in the wilderness, for few people could persevere without requisite outdoor skills. A man had to be a jack-of-all trades and master of them all, including fishing and hunting small game (like deer and elk), or larger animals such as the buffalo. Similarly, they had to be adept at farming, working livestock, building homes, and fighting Indians. Men also kept their word (*la palabra de hombre;* "the word of a man"), an ethic that young men learned early in life. Few men could have maintained a respectable standing in their community had they given their *palabra,* then gone back on it.

There were other customs by which people lived, many of then traceable to the pobladores' Spanish ancestors. Proper etiquette, for instance, required that people courteously inquire as they partook of food or drink, "Gusta usted?" "Would you like to share?" Adults instructed young people to remove their hats when speaking to elders. The midday siesta, when taken, also revealed something of the Moslem imprint. On the borderlands, the pobladores had no objection to taking a break from hard toil at midday, dining, and then taking a siesta.

For relaxation, the pobladores engaged in various festivities and pastimes. Several were the types of festivals held in the Far North, most of them extensions of similar activities practiced during the colonial era. People celebrated birthdays, baptisms, holy days, and Christmas in grand style when possible. On occasions when entire communities participated, the town plaza became the center of activity. Therein, revelers treated themselves to a wide choice of foods, bought from a variety of wares offered (whether fireworks or horse saddles), engaged in enticing games of chance, and gave their attention to motivating orators. The Diez y Seis Septiembre, Mexico's independence day, was already being celebrated in

Texas by the 1820s, and on that day, Tejanos many times took the day off from hard work. In San Antonio, people gathered for a lengthy procession down the center of town and then enjoyed music and festivity, while community leaders regaled them with stories of the glorious homeland.

Entertainment throughout the Far North also included games of horsemanship. Veteran horsemen and young cowboys tried to show off their skills by competing in the *corrida del gallo* (cock-pulls, a game requiring a rider mounted on horseback and galloping at full pace to pull out of the ground a rooster buried up to its neck), the *corrida de la sandía* (the watermelon race), or some kind of rodeo sport. Bullfights and cock-fights entertained many, as did traveling circuses that brought to the frontier agile tumblers called *maromeros.*

Frontier folks also reveled in dancing. To be sure, people danced for reasons other than delight. Scholars believe that dancing met a social need out on the frontier, as on the outback people lacked ready recourse to organized entertainment activities like those that existed in the heartland. Dancing also filled a gender need, for life on the borderlands was male-dominated, with few leisure outlets for women except those connected to the home. Dancing had no particular gender bias, furthermore—indeed it could function only with the participation of women—and so it had broad appeal and popularity. Overall, dancing was a social gathering, but it could also have class connotations. *Bailes* (dances) in California, for instance, were often the domain of people with higher social standing. Rancheros held them in their large homes or on outdoor platforms, and restricted the list of invitees to those of property. By contrast, *fandangos* were held throughout the Far North, which all could attend. Blaring music, spirits, gambling, and carousing all marked this raucous form of revelry, and during the Mexican era, it came to be the favorite kind of dance pastime. Social correctness was suspended momentarily as disparate elements joined in the merriment, including women, children, Indian fighters, sheepherders, peons, and even priests.

More solemn were religious dances such as *Los Matachines,* a dramatization traceable to the Old World, when Spain fought the Muslims during the Reconquista. This Spanish drama, which used swords to symbolize battle, reenacted on an open-air stage the conflict between good and evil, but it had been readjusted in the New World to reflect the Christian conquest of the Indians. In New Mexico, with which it is still identified today, the Matachines dance included Indian actors. The exhibition portrayed the history of Hispanos and indigenous peoples as they had historically interacted with each other on the northern frontier.

Drama also was a form of popular entertainment during this time. On occasion, traveling groups passed through the Far North to offer stage dramas in the form of one-act plays or comedies. Native (and unique) to New Mexico, however, were the dramas—performed by local actors—that commemorated two famous historical events in the region's past. In *Los Comanches,* the people of New Mexico celebrated an epic defeat they had inflicted on the Comanche people back in the 1770s. In the second drama, *Los Tejanos,* the pobladores recalled the capture by local military forces of Texans who invaded New Mexico in 1841, intending to incorporate the province into the Republic of Texas during the presidency of Mirabeau B. Lamar.

By the 1830s, the last of the Franciscan friars had left the borderlands, leaving the pobladores with few ways to fulfill their desire to satisfy their religious obligations. Secular clergy still worked there, but never enough to care for the entire frontier. The exception was New Mexico, where a native clergy replaced the Franciscans by the 1830s. Young men who had been born and raised in New Mexico journeyed to the seminary in Durango during the 1830s and 1840s for religious instruction and preparation for the priesthood, so that by 1846, New Mexico could claim some nineteen clerics in the region, a greater number than could be found elsewhere in the Far North.

Apparently, the presence of these *curas* in New Mexico was not enough to meet spiritual needs, for a more popular religiosity came to be visible there. People displayed their faith in their religion by building *altarcitos* in honor of special saints, for instance. Generally, candles would burn at the altarcito as part of this demonstration of faith.

The most popular expression of popular religiosity surfaced among the Brothers of Our Father Jesus, a fraternal organization that seems to have first appeared in New Mexico between 1790 and 1810, then spread into southern Colorado. Given the scarcity of priests to say mass, administer the sacraments, and bury loved ones, the Penitentes, as people called the Brothers, founded their own chapels and developed their own rituals, liturgy, and practices in an effort to fulfill the needs of those who wanted spiritual reinforcement. Apparently their teachings derived from the lessons of the Franciscans who had ministered to New Mexico for almost two centuries. Rites included prayers and penance and public demonstration of their piety. Inclined to secrecy, the Penitentes engaged in such customs as self-flagellation, a practice much condemned by ecclesiastical authorities in the interior of Mexico.

PADRE ANTONIO JOSÉ MARTÍNEZ

During the 1830s and 1840s, he came to be known throughout New Mexico as a gifted and courageous priest who stood up both to ecclesiastical and government officials when their policies clashed with his work. As a parish priest, he spoke proudly of his role as representative and defender of the faithful in the Taos. He reportedly assisted the Penitentes as they attempted to provide religious services to those New Mexicans neglected by the institutional church. Politically, he called for a greater separation between church and state. As a member of New Mexico's territorial assembly, he championed the cause of the common people. At the same time, he spoke openly in opposition to the Anglo American and European foreigners arriving in New Mexico during this time period, for they asserted too much influence by developing economic alliances with the ricos and acquiring land grants from the governor. His name was Padre Antonio José Martínez, known in history as the *cura* (priest) of Taos. He was a priest of high intelligence, a man immensely sure of his convictions, and a person confident of the righteousness of his ways. His parishioners admired him for his compassion and education, but his opponents in government and the church considered him a maverick and a troublemaker.

Padre Martínez was a product of northern New Mexico, born there in 1793 and raised in the region until he left to study for the ministry. He yearned for learning, and of necessity he taught himself to read and write, availing himself of whatever literature existed on the frontier. At age nineteen, he married, but within two years he found himself widowed. In 1817, he opted for the priesthood, and left for Durango to pursue his studies. At the Tridentine Monastery of Durango, he impressed both his classmates and teachers with his intellect and erudition, earning his ordination in 1822. In 1823, he returned to his native land, ultimately winning an assignment as the cura of Taos in 1826.

During the 1830s, Padre Martínez began to make his mark on New Mexico's history, playing a leading role as a member of the territorial assembly, as a community activist, and ultimately as a spokesperson against foreign encroachment on New Mexico. In the legislature, Padre Martínez worked to lighten taxes being levied on common citizens, to establish schools one way or another, and to find ways to deal with marauding Indians, whose attacks he blamed on the diminishing size of their hunting grounds, brought on by land squatters and swindlers. Empathizing with parishioners, especially those in the countryside who had little contact with the priesthood, Padre Martínez remonstrated at the means used by some of his fellow priests to collect money, such as threatening worshippers with the denial of the Eucharist, church marriages, and burial in the *campo santo* (holy cemetery). He tolerated and even supported the Penitentes, despite the fact that higher church officials condemned the group as extralegal and engaged in practices proscribed by the Catholic hierarchy. In his parish in Taos, he opened up in the 1830s a small school for children. In 1833, he established Our Lady of Guadalupe Seminary, with the purpose of preparing young boys for studying for the priesthood in Durango. Two years later, he acquired a printing press and set out not only to make available educational and religious materials but also to launch a newspaper. Taking the name of *El Crepúsculo de la Libertad* (The Dawn of Liberty), the newspaper turned out to be short-lived, but it still deserves recognition as the first such effort undertaken in New Mexico.

For his efforts, Padre Martínez gained much praise from his superiors, to the extent that he was authorized to oversee the confirmation of parish children, a power generally reserved for bishops. Then, in 1842, Padre Martínez received from his superiors in Durango the post of pastor for life in Taos. Secure in his appointment, he accelerated his involvement in politics, becoming an outspoken opponent of the government for its willingness to give so much land to foreigners, and worse yet, foreigners who nonetheless incited the nomadic Indian peoples against the New Mexicans. He rebuked government officials for their inability to protect the region from increased Indian attacks on farms, homesteads, and villages. To remedy things, he advocated a peace policy toward the indigenous nations, emphasizing the need to teach them skills in horticulture and ranching. Hearsay and legend also link Father Martínez to the Taos Rebellion of January 1847, a resistance movement against the U.S. occupation after the American takeover of New Mexico in 1846.

Martínez's life of involvement and controversy did not abate following the U.S. acquisition of what was now to Americans "the West" in 1848. Rather it escalated in direct proportion to appointments made by U.S. and European church officials, especially that of the Frenchman Jean Baptiste Lamy as vicar apostolic of New Mexico in 1851. With Lamy, who looked condescendingly on the New Mexicans and some of their church practices, Martínez waged a running battle. He opposed the Bishop's tithing practices, his denunciation of the Penitentes, and his appointment of parish priests who did not understand Nuevomexicano culture. In the late 1850s, Bishop Lamy excommunicated Martínez, but the cura of Taos simply set up his own chapel in the town and continued to minister to those faithful to him and not to the Bishop's appointees. Martínez passed away in 1867.

Also in New Mexico, and for the same reasons, folk art that had first appeared during the late eighteenth century flowered during the Mexican period. This revival was due to the work of *santeros*, or New Mexican craftsmen who sought to meet the needs of pobladores calling for sacred icons, or of people neglected by the Catholic Church or unable to pay for images that came through official channels. Santeros produced replications of Christ and the santos (saints) in the form of bultos and retablos for use in church buildings and private homes. Bultos were carved statues made from trees, especially cottonwood, and became extremely valuable among ordinary folks who sought ways to express their religious sincerity and who desired tangible images of the saints to which they could appeal for intercession in periods of tribulation. Retablos were paintings on wood, generally pine. Neither pretended to be fine art, but that was of little importance, for people coveted them for their spiritual value, as they reinforced one's religious faith. Bultos and retablos generally represented a village's patron saint, or one who might be instrumental in bringing relief to a stricken person or population. Farmers facing droughts, for instance, might want a bulto of a saint who could bring relief; another common need was for one who could protect them from disease or Indian attacks.

Santero art in the classic form it assumed during the first half of the nineteenth century declined after 1848 when priests arriving in the borderlands from either the U.S. or Europe condemned this Mexican American craft as medieval and pagan. But it continues until today, though it is now more apt to be appreciated for its aesthetic value than for its religious meaning.

Folklore, which embraced folktales, fictional anecdotes, legends, and the like, constituted a significant aspect of popular beliefs held by the pobladores. Among the most established legends was that of *La Llorona*, which told of a weeping woman searching for her lost children. People in the Far North (as did those in Mexico itself) reported hearing her *llantos* (wails) as she moved through the darkness lamenting having killed her youngsters in a fit of rage. Settlers feared for their own children, lest the frightful woman also kill their little ones. It was considered a bad omen to have La Llorona pass by one's home, for her visit meant the possible death of a close family member.

On the frontier, people confronted an array of difficulties that potentially caused health problems and even epidemics. No systematic plan for trash collection existed, nor for animal control and proper waste disposal, for instance. The pobladores could not count on the central government for help, and adequate medical attention could hardly be provided at the local level. Settlers consequently resorted to popular means of caring for the sick and wounded. The most common treatment was provided by what were called curanderos (who are believed to cure by virtue of having received a special power from God), or by *sobadores* (who cure by massaging or rubbing the body). These folk healers, women (curanderas) as well as men, were generally members of the local community who had learned their work as apprentices to established healers and then won the trust of their fellow pobladores. At the very least, curanderos, curanderas, and sobadores, not to mention *parteras* (midwives), provided emotional comfort to the infirm, and some purportedly effected miraculous cures. Using herbal medicines (taken from local plants, including roots), as well as items such as cobwebs or animal

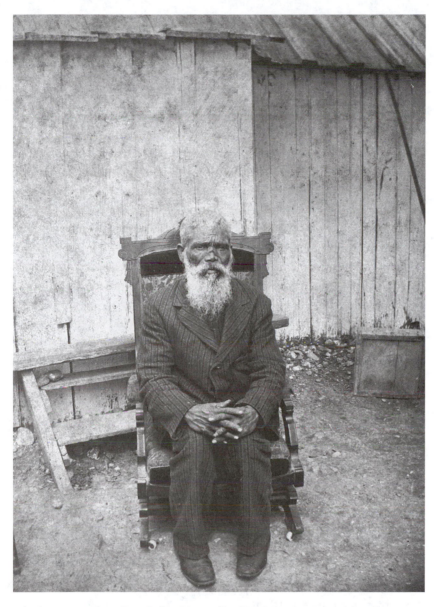

The famous curandero *"Don Pedrito" Jaramillo of South Texas, seated outside a frame building. San Antonio, Texas, 1894. (University of Texas, Institute of Texan Cultures at San Antonio, 087-0239)*

by-products (oils, for example), the curanderos and curanderas tended to every kind of ailment or emotional problem, among them indigestion, broken bones, and *susto* (fright).

THE POBLADORES AND OTHER PEOPLES

Though far removed from the heartland, pobladores had regular contact with other people, including politicians from the central government in Mexico City who could well determine the politics of the region. Certainly, the connection between communities in the "departments" of the north and government in the interior remained somewhat strained after 1834, the year in which Santa Anna assumed power in Mexico City for the Centralists. Texas, California, and New Mexico had all subscribed to the principles of federalism, for this doctrine promised them a measure of regional autonomy and self-rule. Rebellion, discontent, and uneasiness between the northern regions and the motherland thus marked the period of the 1830s and 1840s.

In Texas, Mexican oligarchs during the 1820s and early 1830s had worked alongside Anglo American newcomers to foster progress in the province. But questionable behavior on the part of Anglos had led Mexico to reconsider the colonization policy that the government of Coahuila y Tejas had implemented in 1825 to encourage U.S. immigration. By the late 1820s, Mexico could no longer countenance some of the activities underway in Texas. Anglos defended slavery even while Mexico sought to abolish it, governed themselves in their communities according to U.S. political traditions, took the lands provided to them by the government and speculated with them, engaged in forbidden smuggling, and in other ways made themselves unwanted. By the same token, the immigrants maintained that economic growth was impossible without slavery, that guarantees made under the federalist Constitution of 1824 had been violated, and that Mexico was too politically backward for them. Such attitudes, along with other factors, begot an independence movement in Texas by the summer of 1835.

The rebellion placed Tejanos in an awkward position. Should they join the rebels, remain loyal to their native land, or align themselves with neither side? Some supported the banner of independence, among them Juan Seguín, who led companies of Tejanos at the Siege of Béxar in the fall of 1835 and at the Battle of San Jacinto on April 21, 1836. Others who sided with the independence efforts included José Francisco Ruiz and José Angel Navarro, who signed the Texas Declaration of Independence on March 2, 1836, as did Lorenzo de Zavala, an exile from Yucatán who had come to Texas to care for his landed property. Also opting to fight with the Anglos were about nine Tejanos who lost their lives on March 6, 1836, at the Battle of the Alamo. A smaller group of Tejanos, on the other hand, sided with the Centralist forces, for a number of reasons. They shared a common heritage and ethnicity with Mexico, distrusted the intentions of Anglos with whom they had experienced bad relations, or had relatives fighting with the Centralists. The majority of Tejanos remained neutral, however, adopting a wait-and-see attitude toward the conflict.

At the Battle of San Jacinto, the Texans (as the Anglo inhabitants of the area called themselves) won independence for Texas by defeating the army of Santa Anna. The stand that Tejanos took on the Texan war for independence mattered little. After 1836, most became part of a subaltern class, as vengeful Texans defrauded Tejanos of their land, destroyed the Mexicans' private property, expelled them from their homes, and committed violent acts against them. Even Juan Seguín took refuge in Mexico in 1842 to escape the wrath of accusers who believed him to be a conspirator with Mexico against the Republic of Texas.

The native Californios who now replaced old colonial officials appointed by the crown also resisted Centralist rule, but federalist opposition there did not reach the level of seriousness it did in Texas. For the most part, the Californios wanted a greater hand in determining their own destiny, and in the summer of 1836, under the leadership of Juan Bautista Alvarado, they overthrew the Centralist governor there. Later that same year, the Californios repeated their act of expulsion by ousting a second Centralist appointee.

Not all Californios played a hand in these acts of defiance and resistance. As in Texas, some opposed such exploits, while most remained neutral. Especially suspicious of such escapades were those who lived in southern California, for they saw anti-Centralism as the work of those in the north (the area from about Santa Barbara to the San Francisco region). Californios in the south feared being outvoted by the *norteños* in an independent confederation led by Alvarado (or any other Federalist, for that matter), so they resisted involvement in the schemes of their northern compatriots. Finally, in June 1837 the Centralists in Mexico negotiated a truce with Alvarado, allowing him to stay as governor in return for his loyalty to Mexico City. Alvarado so remained until 1842, when the new Centralists replaced him, but the new Centralist governor was himself sent packing in February 1845. Such was the relation between California and the motherland when the Mexican era ended.

Dissatisfaction in New Mexico with the Centralist administration of the mother country never amounted to the discontent experienced in Texas or California. A rebellion against the Centralist governor of New Mexico did break out in August 1837, but it did not spread outside the ranks of the lower stratum, where poor people complained about unaffordable taxes, impressments to fight Indians, and general oppression. After having gotten rid of the Centralist governor, the rebels sought recognition from officials in the interior, but with no success. To their dismay, by September 1837 they had to contend with a counterresistance from within New Mexico, as loyalist members of the New Mexican rico class sought to quell the disturbance. By January 1838 the opposition, aided by a few Centralist soldiers recently arrived from Mexico, brought the disorder to an end by executing the masterminds behind the upheaval.

A combative struggle for livelihood had always shaped relations between the pobladores and the indigenous Indian nations in the borderlands, and in the nineteenth century, frontier folks in the north still found it difficult to reconcile with the indios bárbaros. On the one hand, the pobladores continued their reliance on some of the Indian nations, among them the Navajos, the Pueblos, and even the Apaches, to acquire slaves or servants (generally women and children) to be used as slaves or servants. Many colonists believed, furthermore, that the Indians should be relocated elsewhere and perhaps even exterminated, as they impeded demographic expansion and economic growth. Alternatively, the Indian population continued to see the settlers as intruders on their traditional hunting grounds, as well as potential sources of foods and supplies not generally available to those making their living as nomads. Thus Indians incessantly launched attacks on farms and ranches, attacks that yielded them such items as crops, horses, mules, sheep or cattle, and farm equipment.

In California, relations with Indians remained both contentious and reasonably friendly. On the one hand, people lived in fear of insurrection, attack, and possible massacre at the hands of former mission Indians (such as the Shoshone tribes) and other native peoples who had never accepted conversion. On the other hand, California was the scene of Indian integration. Intermixing had occurred between Indian women and the mestizo population to such an extent that the offspring of such unions who successfully joined mainstream society became eligible for land and citizenship upon the secularization of the missions. Indeed, many of them received such property in the 1830s, though many lost it to greedy and unscrupulous members of the *gente de razón* (people of reason, or the Mexican population) soon after. Further, the Californios came to accept Indians into their defense forces. Deprived of troops from the interior, California enlisted acculturated Indians known for their riding adroitness and marksmanship. Moreover, the Californios had long integrated Native Americans into their society as menial laborers. Acculturated Indians worked in the homes of the gente de razón, as well as on ranches and farms, not to mention public works projects. To be sure, a good many of those doing such work had been forcibly pressed into service, generally after having been plied with liquor, then disciplined for their indiscretion by being forced to work out their punishment. Still, the situation was relatively harmonious.

Relations between the pobladores and native tribes differed markedly in the other provinces of the Far North. In Arizona, New Mexico, and Texas, indios bárbaros refused capitulation and continued raining terror upon the settlements, stealing and destroying whatever the settlers possessed, including their livestock and field crops, and attacking and murdering pioneers at will. In Texas, the Comanches, Kiowas, and Apaches preyed upon the people of San Antonio and Goliad until after the war for independence in 1836 and wandered as far south as the Rio Grande settlements into mid-century. The scene was similar in Arizona, where the Hopis, the Pimas, and especially the Apaches terrorized the colonists until well after the end of Mexican rule in 1848. In New Mexico, the settlers contended with nomadic tribes such as the Navajos, the Utes, and the Comanches, who, equipped with firearms acquired from U.S. citizens, attacked the exposed ranchos. Pobladores coexisted in an uneasy truce with the Pueblos, each people claiming their own territoriality, though the pobladores expanded into portions of Pueblo lands during the first half of the nineteenth century.

With the Mexican government now providing little protection (compared to the Spanish government, which had financed presidios during the colonial period), the pobladores relied on volunteer militias to battle the hostile tribes. Those who joined such volunteer companies perforce had to possess their own fighting gear, including weapons, horses, and camp equipment. But it proved not to be a difficult choice for men to join these militia companies that paid no salary, for often it meant the difference between saving one's property or seeing it lost or demolished.

Interactions with westering Anglos entering the borderlands from about the 1820s through the 1840s have been described as being both belligerent and accommodating. On the one hand, there was a cohort of these immigrants that did not look very favorably upon the pobladores. This group included trappers, hunters, travelers, and even frontier farmers going west with intention of occupying land as squatters. They painted the indigenous Mexicans in rather unsavory terms, making racial slurs based on the color of their skin and so forth, and imputing to them numerous faults, such as backwardness, ignorance, laziness, immorality, cowardice, superstition, depravity, and cruelty. Many of these Anglos condemned Mexicans as inclined to religious fanaticism and too addicted to the song and the chase, as well as vice.

But there came to live in the borderlands another element from the United States that coexisted amiably with the pobladores. Lawyers, men of commerce, and merchants quickly integrated themselves into Mexican society by forming ties with elites throughout the Far North. Business alliances with local leaders and property owners, whether in Texas, California, or New Mexico, offered infinite possibilities for profits. Anglos could gain business advancement, land from the government of Mexico, and even citizenship. For the elites, such partnerships meant possible connections to the U.S. economy and even international markets.

Alliances between Mexicans and Anglos also involved intercultural marriages. Throughout the borderlands, existing class differences within Mexican communities discouraged marriage between the daughters of elites and those belonging to the lower class, so that many rancheros welcomed unions between their daughters and Anglo traders, bankers, or lawyers. Anglos willing to accept Mexican culture in turn perceived advantages for themselves in marrying into the local population. They could acquire land grants, integrate themselves into local political networks, and gain support in establishing a local business.

Of course, economic advantage was only one reason the two groups found intermarriage desirable. Myth held that Mexican women preferred Anglos because of their physical features: white skin, blue eyes, greater height, and the like. Love obviously played some part, for not every marriage that occurred (or every relationship that developed) involved women of the upper class. But whether marriage involved economic motives, physical attraction, or true love, the preparation for nuptials required conformity to Mexican customs and protocol. Courtship was always the initial step toward matrimony; after a successful courtship, the prospective groom would ask for his bride's hand in marriage, for the consent of the parents to wed was essential among the propertied classes. Even among the propertied classes, however, not every case of courtship conformed to such rituals, as there were numerous instances wherein Anglos and Mexican women simply entered into informal unions. Many such arrangements involved women of the lower class living with trappers, struggling merchants, or itinerants who had decided to stay a spell on the Mexican frontier.

THE WAR FOR THE FAR NORTH

Even outside Texas life under Centralist rule came to an end in the Far North with the U.S. defeat of Mexico in 1848. War erupted between the two countries in 1848 due to a complex set of reasons. The United States had cast eyes on what it thought of as the West for a number of years, having annexed Texas (which had been a Republic since 1836) in 1845 despite protests from Mexico, which had never recognized Texas independence. About the same time, the United States had made it known to Mexico that it was prepared to buy California, if not take it by force. Such aggressive behavior derived from the U.S. sense of Manifest Destiny, the notion that it was the country's obvious destiny to expand from the Atlantic Ocean to the Pacific Ocean. Mexico, on the other hand, found itself having to defend its integrity and honor, lest it be exposed as a pathetically feeble country unable to defend its own lands. Anglos continued arriving in California, with the intentions, Mexico feared, as the ones that had produced the loss of Texas. More ominously, the U.S. Navy had captured Monterey in 1842, and although the occupation (carried out on the mistaken belief that Mexico and the United States were at war) was short-lived, it illustrated to Mexico the shameless ways by which the Americans were capable of taking foreign territory.

War between the two countries began in April 1846, following a skirmish between U.S. and Mexican troops in South Texas. From the Rio Grande Valley, the United States carried the war toward Mexico's interior, though troops simultaneously headed for New Mexico, Arizona, and California. Leading U.S. forces into New Mexico in August 1846 was Stephen W. Kearney, who faced little resistance from the territory's governor, Manuel Armijo, though he had as many as 4,000 New Mexicans prepared to fight the *Americanos*. Historians still debate Armijo's motives for refusing to fight. Some assert that he recognized the futility of standing up to a superior force, while others argue as strongly that he feared disrupting his own business operations, which were tied to the Santa Fe trade. Later in the year, however, resistance to the U.S. occupation broke out, and before U.S. troops could put down the insurrection by January 1847, the rebels had killed the newly appointed U.S. governor.

In California, meantime, a "Bear Flag Rebellion" erupted in June 1846, led by Anglo settlers living in the territory. They immediately declared California independent from Mexico, and they were soon assisted by the U.S. Navy, which blockaded all California ports. In the fall of 1846, however, a native resistance involving California *guerrilleros* repelled troops from much of southern California. But reinforcements arrived in short order from the United States, and so by early 1847, all of California had fallen to Anglo American firepower.

Hostilities between the two countries ended in the fall of 1847, when the U.S. military entered Mexico City triumphantly. In the Treaty of Guadalupe Hidalgo (February 2, 1848), Mexico conceded the Far North to the United States. The treaty provided that those of Mexican descent living in the conquered region, and who within one year decided to remain therein, would have all the rights of U.S. citizens.

BIBLIOGRAPHIC ESSAY

Among the most fascinating topics in Mexico's history is the great upheaval that occurred in 1810 against Spain, the mother country, and which subsequently led to Mexico's rule from 1821–1848 over the "West." A most recent and quite exhaustive work is Eric Van Young, *The Other Rebellion: Popular Violence, Ideology, and the Mexican Struggle for Independence, 1810–1821* (Stanford, CA: Stanford University Press, 2001). Other equally informative studies include Colin M. MacLachlan and Jaime E. Rodríguez O., *The Forging of the Cosmic Race: A Reinterpretation of Colonial Mexico* (Berkeley: University of California Press, 1980); Lester D. Langley, *The Americas in the Age of Revolution, 1750–1850* (New Haven, CT: Yale University Press, 1996); Ramón Eduardo Ruiz, *Triumphs and Tragedy: A History of the Mexican People* (New York: W. W. Norton, 1992); and the older history of Charles C. Cumberland, *Mexico: The Struggle for Modernity* (New York: Oxford University Press, 1968).

Relations existing between colony and mother country obviously affected events in the Far North during the period from the 1780s through 1820s, and there is a credible list of works presently available chronicling conditions and affairs therein. One of the best known of these works is David J. Weber, *The Spanish Frontier in North America* (New Haven, CT: Yale University Press, 1992), respected for its exhaustive bibliography and the supportive detail included in the endnotes. Another is Ramón Gutiérrez, *When Jesus Came, the Corn Mothers Went Away: Marriage, Sexuality, and Power in New Mexico, 1500–1846* (Palo Alto, CA: Stanford University Press, 1991), which, though it focuses more specifically on New Mexico, nonetheless insightfully covers the era extending from the Bourbon Reforms to the start of the U.S. war with Mexico. Also quite useful is Thomas D. Hall, *Social Change in the Southwest, 1350–1880* (Lawrence: University Press of Kansas, 1989).

More specifically focused on the time period covered in this chapter is David J. Weber's classic, *The Mexican Frontier, 1821–1846: The American Southwest under Mexico* (Albuquerque: University of New Mexico Press, 1982). Several works supplement Weber's well-respected and often cited monograph. Among those focusing on specific U.S. states are Richard L. Nostrand, *The Hispano Homeland* (Norman: University of Oklahoma Press, 1992); James E. Officer, *Hispanic Arizona, 1536–1856* (Tucson: University of Arizona Press, 1987); Ana Carolina Castillo Crimm, *De León: A Tejano Family History* (Austin: University of Texas Press, 2003); Armando Alonzo, *Tejano Legacy: Ranchers and Settlers in South Texas, 1734–1900* (Albuquerque: University of New Mexico Press, 1998); and Lisbeth Haas, *Conquest and Historical Identities in California, 1769–1936* (Berkeley: University of California Press, 1995).

New Mexican entrepreneurial involvement in the Santa Fe Trade has recently been the subject of some interesting work, with Susan Calafate Boyle, *Los Capitalistas: Hispano Merchants and the Santa Fe Trade* (Albuquerque: University of New Mexico Press, 1997), being perhaps the most useful. Articles that complement Boyle's monograph include David A. Sandoval, "Gnats, Goods, and Greasers: Mexican Merchants and the Santa Fe Trail," *Journal of the West* 28 (April 1989), and Sterling Evans, "Eastward Ho!: The Mexican Freighting Commerce Experience and the Santa Fe Trail," *Kansas History* 19 (Winter 1996–1997). An overview of economic activity among the pobladores is provided by Juan Gómez-Quiñones, *Mexican American Labor, 1790–1990* (Albuquerque: University of New Mexico Press, 1994).

The scholarship that addresses culture during the first half of the nineteenth century is not extensive, but it is growing yearly. A good starting point is Arthur L. Campa, *Hispanic Culture in the Southwest* (Norman: University of Oklahoma Press, 1979), although it places disproportionate emphasis on New Mexico. Works offering overviews of literary developments include Charles M. Tatum, *Chicano Literature* (Boston: Twayne, 1982); Joseph Sommers and Tomas Ybarra-Frausto, *Modern Chicano Writers* (Englewood Cliffs, NJ: Prentice Hall, 1979); *Pasó Por Aquí: Critical Essays on the New Mexican Literary Tradition, 1542–1988,* edited by Erlinda Gonzales-Berry (Albuquerque: University of New Mexico Press, 1989); and A. Gabriel Meléndez, *So All Is Not Lost: The Poetics of Print in Nuevomexicano Communities, 1834–1958* (Albuquerque: University of New Mexico Press, 1997).

Interest in gender studies has generated exciting investigations into the role and status of Mexican women in Mexico's Far North, with the most informative at the moment being Deena J. González, *Refusing the Favor: The Spanish-Mexican Women of Santa Fe, 1820–1880* (New York: Oxford University Press, 1999). Equally enlightening is Albert L. Hurtado, *Intimate Frontiers: Sex, Gender, and Culture in California* (Albuquerque: University of New Mexico Press, 1999). An example of works at the dissertation level is Miroslava Chávez, "Mexican Women and the American Conquest in Los Angeles: From the Mexican Era to American Ascendancy" (Ph.D. dissertation, University of California at Los Angeles, 1998), and there also exist solid articles like Janet Lecompte, "The Independent Women of Hispanic New Mexico, 1821–1846," *New Mexico Historical Review* 12 (January 1981) and Richard Griswold del Castillo, "Neither Activists Nor Victims: Mexican Women's Historical Discourse: The Case of San Diego, 1820–1850," *California History* 74 (fall 1995). Useful on the Mexican American family is Richard Griswold del Castillo, *La Familia: Chicano Families in the Urban Southwest, 1848 to the Present* (Notre Dame, IN: University of Notre Dame Press, 1984), which despite its main focus on the post-1848 era, offers valuable information about the Hispanic family during the Spanish and Mexican periods.

The numerous leisure activities of the pobladores, following long days of work, have gotten attention. In "Béxar: Profile of a Tejano Community, 1820–1832," *Southwestern Historical Quarterly* 89 (July 1985), Jesús F. de la Teja and John Wheat touch on civic celebrations in San Antonio, Texas, while Anthony Shay in "Fandangos and Bailes: Dancing and Dance Events in Early California," *Southern California Quarterly* 64 (Summer 1982) explains the role of dance in California communities. Religious observations often included dance performances, among them the Matachines dance. This is discussed extensively in Sylvia Rodríguez, *The Matachines Dance: Ritual Symbolism and Interethnic Relations in the Upper Rio Grande Valley* (Albuquerque: University of New Mexico Press, 1996).

Much of the work on the pobladores' Catholicism has been limited to New Mexico, and it includes Robert E. Wright, O.M.I., "How Many Are 'A Few'?: Catholic Clergy in Central and Northern New Mexico, 1780–1851," in *Seeds of Struggle/Harvest of Faith: The Papers of the Archdiocese of Santa Fe Catholic Cuatro Centennial Conference,* edited by Thomas J. Steele, S. J., Paul Rhetts, and Barbe Awalt (Albuquerque, NM: LPD Press, 1998); Marta Weigle, *The Penitentes of the Southwest* (Albuquerque: University of New Mexico Press, 1976); J. Manuel Espinoza, "The Origins of the Penitentes of New Mexico: Separating Fact From Fiction," *Catholic Historical Review* 79 (July 1993); Ross Frank, "The Life of Christ and the New Mexican Santo Tradition," *Catholic Southwest: A Journal of History and Culture* 7 (1996); and William Wroth, "The Flowering and Decline of the New Mexican *Santero,* 1780–1900," in *New Spain's Far Northern Frontier: Essays on Spain in the American West, 1540–1821,* edited by David J. Weber (Albuquerque: University of New Mexico Press, 1979).

The contact made between the pobladores and other peoples living (or arriving) in the region is discussed extensively in Weber's *Mexican Frontier.* Other works addressing such interaction include Raymund A. Paredes, "The Mexican Image in American Travel Literature, 1831–1869," *New Mexico Historical Review* 52 (January 1977); Douglas Monroy, *Thrown Among Strangers: The Making of Mexican Cultures in Frontier California* (Berkeley: University of California Press, 1990); Leonard Pitt, *The Decline of the Californios: A Social History of the Spanish-speaking Californians, 1846–1890* (Berkeley: University of California Press, 1970); Deborah Moreno, "'Here the Society is United': 'Respectable' Anglos and Intercultural Marriage in Pre-Gold Rush California," *California Historical Quarterly* 80 (spring 2001); David Montejano, *Anglos and Mexicans in the Making of Texas, 1836–1986* (Austin: University of Texas Press, 1987); Rebecca McDowell Craver, *The Impact of Intimacy: Mexican-Anglo Intermarriage in New Mexico, 1821–1846* (El Paso: Texas Western Press, 1982); and the book by Deena J. González mentioned above, *Refusing the Favor.*

As to the war with Mexico (1846–1848), a discussion of causes, campaigns, and negotiations is given in Donald S. Frazier, *The United States and Mexico at*

War: Nineteenth-Century Expansionism and Conflict (New York: Simon and Schuster Macmillan, 1998). The accord that ended the war is explained in Richard Griswold del Castillo, *The Treaty of Guadalupe Hidalgo: A Legacy of Conflict* (Norman: University of Oklahoma Press, 1990).

Padre Antonio José Martínez, the subject of the biography on page 97 of this chapter, remains a controversial personality in New Mexico's history. Early writers on Martínez tended to be critical of his independent manner in Taos, but revisionism has rehabilitated his image. Much can be learned about the cura of Taos from works such as Paul Horgan, *Lamy of Santa Fe: His Life and Times* (New York: Farrar, Straus and Giroux, 1975); David J. Weber, *The Edge of Empire: The Taos Hacienda of los Martínez* (Santa Fe: Museum of New Mexico Press, 1996); Fray Angélico Chávez, *But Time and Chance: The Story of Padre Martínez of Taos, 1793–1867* (Santa Fe, NM: Sunstone Press, 1981), and the revisionist essays in E. A. Mares (ed.) *Padre Martínez: New Perspectives from Taos* (Taos, NM: Millicent Rogers Museum, 1988).

Chapter Four

NEW CONQUERORS, 1848–1880

People used to living with Spanish-Mexican legal and political traditions, to valued customs, folkways, and modes of conduct handed down for generations, and to familiar ways of conducting business transactions now, in the wake of the Treaty of Guadalupe Hidalgo's ratification, had to examine, assess, and accept or resist the new Anglo American authority. Introduced into the borderlands by westering Anglos in the wake of the conquest was a belief in democracy as the highest form of governance and a society rooted in the premise of equality, albeit not for all racial groups. A different culture, language, and religion, as well as bigoted notions on race, accompanied these tenets.

This era, extending from about mid-century until the latter decades of the nineteenth century, preceded the great age of national and international expansion associated with the Industrial Revolution and the Progressive Era. Put differently, the old Spanish-Mexican borderlands remained essentially a frontier region up until 1880. Most people who trekked west from east of the Mississippi traveled not by train or any other comfortable means of transportation, but by wagon, often pulled by oxen. Small-scale farming and ranching constituted the main means of livelihood. Mining, initially sparked by the California gold rush, acted as an ancillary element of the rural economy. The Civil War, and then the Reconstruction that followed it, dominated the politics of the West, as it did the rest of the country, retarding economic growth and prolonging the frontier condition. Indian wars, which escalated during the late 1860s and did not end for nearly two decades, similarly gave the West the image of a hinterland, a meeting place between "civilization" and "savagery."

By the 1880s, the frontier was changing, or had changed. The age of the Cattle Kingdom, fueled by the demand for beef in the East following the Civil War, now saw rapid decline. Investors turned to farming instead, and a veritable farm revolution occurred, encouraged by irrigation and reclamation projects that turned previously unproductive lands into farming empires. Massive influxes of "foreigners" came from every corner of the earth, including Asia, despite deep concerns among westerners of a possible "yellow peril." Urbanization accompanied immigration, as older municipalities attracted newcomers or new ones sprung from nowhere to rival eastern cities. Railroad building, which came west with seriousness after the Civil War, expanded after the 1880s, connecting not only the regions but also the Atlantic to the Pacific coast. Western mining also made monumental strides in the waning decades of the nineteenth century, as corporations sought new profits from the extraction of copper and silver. By the 1890s, the West could boast of its connection to the world economy, including the Far East and Latin America, something that had not occurred during the frontier epoch.

MIGRATION AND DEMOGRAPHIC PATTERNS

No one knows precisely the number of people of Mexican descent who lived in the West as of 1850, the first time federal officials took a census of the region. Even the size of the population in 1880 is difficult to ascertain, given the numerous obstacles involved in census taking. To begin with, it was a costly undertaking for the federal government. Census takers were often not the most determined and lacked the initiative needed to execute their work. Many could not communicate in Spanish. Some of them faced difficulties reaching isolated villages and settlements or at times completely missed family members (of whom some were migrant workers out on the trail, others were simply ducking the *Americanos* prying into domestic matters) who constituted a household. To make matters even more difficult, the Bureau of the Census did not categorize Mexicans separately, instead aggregating them with others of the white race. For historians, geographers, or demographers, this practice means that a hand count might yield a more precise figure, but as noted, census taking was so flawed that even if researchers painstakingly tallied the actual lists of names and counted the Hispanic ones, the raw census still would not yield proper results.

The last effort undertaken to approximate the Mexican American population in the West for the late nineteenth century is now thirty years old, but it still remains the most dependable estimation. Those calculations, made by the historian Oscar J. Martínez, put the entire Mexican-descent population in 1850 at somewhere between 86,000 and 116,000 and then at around 226,000 and 327,000 by 1880 (Martínez, "On the Size of the Chicano Population," p. 56). The number of Spanish-speaking inhabitants who lived in each state was given earlier, in chapter 3. Martínez does not give figures for each state for 1880, and so it is difficult to determine growth. One source does put the Mexican-origin population in Texas in 1880 at 70,653 and another study places the number in New Mexico at about 109,000 for that year.

The increase in numbers obviously is explained not only by natural procreation but also by migration from the homeland, Mexico. To be sure, there occurred a "back to Mexico" movement for a brief period after 1848. In California during the 1850s, conditions for the Californios deteriorated due to general economic and political displacement, land loss, and growing violence. There, repatriation groups formed and negotiated with the Mexican state of Sonora for the opportunity to found new colonies, but only a few of these attempts at returning to Mexico reached fruition. At the same time, concerns in Mexico City that the pobladores ought not to be abandoned and left to the mercy of the new conquerors also prompted repatriation plans. Government officials thus drafted proposals to have people relocate to colonies in Mexico. One of the best known (and researched) of these deeds involved the Hispanos of New Mexico, who responded quite positively to inquiries by a commissioner sent there in 1849 to gauge interest in a colonization project in Chihuahua. The arrangement called for granting lands to the new settlers, and soon the town of Guadalupe was founded on the south bank of the Rio Grande near today's El Paso. In 1849, the settlers, some 1,500 of them in Guadalupe, plus others in neighboring settlements in the El Paso region, found themselves right back under U.S. jurisdiction when the Rio Grande changed course and placed these communities on the north bank of the river. Meanwhile, other Nuevomexicanos on their own, though soon after assisted by the Mexican government, resettled in what is called the Mesilla Valley, then northern Chihuahua, but today in southern New Mexico. The people of the Mesilla Valley, an estimated 1,900 as of 1852, similarly became U.S. citizens again when the United States bought that strip of land from Mexico in 1853.

The fact of the matter, however, is that the migration in the decades between 1850 to 1880 was overwhelmingly north to the United States and not south to Mexico. Why was this so? Historians have advanced numerous causes for the phenomenon. In 2003, Gilbert G. González and Raúl A. Fernández published a provocative study reviewing the numerous explanations advanced in the scholarly literature to account for migration, dismissing most of them and advancing their own premises. They firmly criticized what is called the push-pull thesis, which posits that certain forces (among them poverty, peonage, and political oppression) exist in the mother country "pushing" people into the Southwest while simultaneously "pulling" forces (such as economic and political opportunity) in the United States draw people northward. They play down such an explanation (and its offshoots) for a variety of reasons, among them that migration to the United States did not begin in large numbers until the twentieth century and that Mexicans come to the United States even during times when prosperity is general in Mexico. Other advocates of this position attribute cross-border movement to agency among migrants and in so doing, also reject push-pull influences. They hold that people on their own, regardless of push and pull variables, make the monumental decision to migrate in an effort to improve on their material circumstances. As historical actors, they find their way into a certain locality in the United States, then sink roots there and start anew.

González and Fernández argue that the reason for the direction of migration is not to be found in push-pull factors or basic human instinct but in U.S. capitalist domination of Mexico. Over the years, the United States made Mexico an economic colony, and among the things the United States has exploited for generations is Mexico as a cheap source of labor. Beginning in the years after the U.S. Civil War (1861–1865), González and Fernández observe, American investors started considering Mexico, the country the United States had just defeated in 1848, as a possible source of wealth. Porfirio Díaz, who became the president of Mexico in 1876 and served until 1911, wished to modernize his nation and thus permitted the United States opportunities to build railroad lines in Mexican northern states. For the United States, these railroad lines meant that companies engaged in investments in Mexico's economy could readily ship farm goods and raw minerals from Mexico's interior to markets north. González and Fernández see the 1870s as the time when the connection was forged between the U.S. and Mexico that explains the large-scale migration that commenced in the twentieth century and continues unabated today.

The González and Fernández thesis as explicated above might account for twentieth-century movements north, but what lies behind migration between 1848 and 1880 before U.S. intervention in Mexico occurred? Certainly there would have been forces compelling people to uproot themselves in Mexico and strike for the United States. Indeed, the period from the late 1840s through the 1870s was one of political crisis and military conflict in Mexico. First, the country had to live with the humiliation of defeat by the United States. Then, when reformers imposed a new liberal constitution on Mexico in 1857, a backlash occurred from conservative elements in the country, and civil strife in the form of the War of the Reform (1858–1861) ensued. Almost as soon as President Benito Juárez imposed stability on the land, France invaded Mexico. Repulsed initially by a Texas-born army officer named Ignazio Zaragoza at the Battle of Puebla on May 5, 1862 (celebrated still as the Cinco de Mayo), the French nonetheless returned the next year to rule Mexico under Maximilian. Juárez and his followers ultimately defeated the French in 1867, but calm hardly followed. He and his successors now had to deal with the reconstruction of the country, not a minor undertaking for a poverty-stricken nation. In part, uncertainty and danger explain why some people in Mexico considered a better start in the U.S. West.

But other reasons besides politics and war account for the decision to trek toward the U.S. West. Mexico still remained a society divided along class lines, with the wealthier elements dominating almost every aspect of the nation's political and economic infrastructure. Not much future existed for common folks living in urban areas or who worked in the countryside on haciendas (rural estates) or in the mines. In fact, a good many of those who labored on haciendas had the status of peons and were tied to the estates (and the landlords) by debt peonage. The same applied to mine workers, many of whom possessed skills that earned them no more than a living wage and a debt at the company store. Still another factor motivating people in Mexico to consider journeying north were the persistent Indian wars that made daily living perilous. Other miscellaneous reasons behind migration north would be a search for seasonal work, the need to take a wait-and-see attitude given domestic unrest in Mexico, or just simply the desire to be close to relatives who had already moved to the U.S. West.

Also lying behind the northward movement was the appeal of promising opportunities not available in Mexico. There was the chance of literally striking it rich as early as 1849, the year of the California gold rush. Miners from states in Mexico closest to California, among them Sonora and Zacatecas, quickly made the decision to make the long trip toward the gold mines. Some 20,000 such miners reportedly flooded the diggings. Unfortunately, along with the gold they found much xenophobia and jealousy, creating such a hostile environment that many simply returned to the homeland.

But the gold rush of '49 was not the only enticement in the West. For one thing, mining as a magnet persisted, as other gold finds followed, among them ones in Arizona, Colorado, and Nevada, all of them seducing those who wanted something better than the perpetual turmoil in Mexico. Also inviting workers from Mexico were possibilities offered by the expanding railroad lines from the Mississippi River to the Pacific Coast. Railroad companies had relied initially on Chinese labor, but a nativist campaign against Asians surfaced by the late 1860s. A promising alternative source of labor was Mexico, and recruits from Mexico did indeed respond to the call.

Other opportunities within the frontier economy further "pulled" people into the U.S. West during the era between 1848 and about the 1880s. This was the era of the Cattle Kingdom, especially in Texas, and a great need surfaced for cattle hands. The number of vaqueros already available did not meet landowners' needs, so again migrants from Mexico answered the call. New farmsteads cropped up in Texas, Arizona, and California (as well as Colorado and New Mexico), all of them requiring

Group of vaqueros outside Santa Ynez Mission in California, 1800s. (North Wind Picture Archive)

expansion of the workforce. Again new arrivals from Mexico filled the demand. The U.S. government built military posts throughout every region of the West, and in many cases, especially in border areas, it was Mexicans who provided the auxiliary labor pool. The new economy also stimulated urban growth, and jobs in the cities enticed people from Mexico with the promise of improved wages and of finished goods produced by U.S. factories. In the city, Mexican men did the backbreaking tasks of building the numerous retail stores, hotel, banks, and other establishments that became part of the cityscape. Port cities also required an unskilled staff, and Mexicans could be found working the San Diego or San Francisco waterfronts in California or the docks in Brownsville and Corpus Christi in Texas.

Not all Mexicans came as workers. The migration north also included people of means wanting to establish new operations (say in freighting, trade, or journalism) in cities such as Tucson, San Antonio, and Los Angeles. Some from this entrepreneurial class saw possibilities for a cross-border connection between enterprises in the United States and Mexico.

Much of what has been said so far about motivation can be summed up as hope for a land of abundance—the hope held by so many immigrants to the West. No particular obstacle, either geographical or political, existed to stop migrants from crossing the international border. In Texas, people could ford the Rio Grande, and from New Mexico to California the boundary was more or less imaginary. As for political factors, Mexico had no specific policy to deter out-migration, while the United States subscribed to an open-door policy to help facilitate the movement of laborers required for developing the region. No agency like the Immigration and Naturalization Service (INS) existed then.

People from Mexico, the majority of them poor, could thus freely follow the human instinct for material betterment. In this sense, they differed little from American settlers, from African Americans wishing to escape the suffocating oppression of the U.S. South, or from European and Asian immigrants who similarly looked at the West as a land of grand possibilities. Mexicans were lured north by the idea that they would be able to give loved ones material security. At the very least, the West provided more diversity of jobs, among them freighting, mining, and ranching (with which the newcomers were already familiar) or new occupations in commerce or in other jobs in the city. Social mobility might even be a possibility in the U.S. West, the migrants believed. The hope for schooling, the belief that it might be possible to acquire a skilled trade, and the possibility of owning land, all played a role in the many defining decisions to strike north.

Opting to leave the homeland held somber consequences, as it does for today's migrants who decide to relocate to the United States. Uprooting oneself and family entailed leaving friends and community behind and forsaking the environment one had grown up in. It meant arriving in a land of unfamiliar institutions. It called for a swift recovery (both psychological and physical) upon arriving on the western frontier, though for

Mexicans the presence of already established Spanish-speaking communities in the U.S. West and the knowledge that they could readily return to their native soil eased such problems.

Once having decided to move, the immigrants faced a tortuous course on the road to the U.S. West. In contrast to the colonial period, when caravans of settlers marched toward the borderlands under the guidance of an experienced colonizer, the journey now tended to be ill-planned and disorganized. Men might make the journey by themselves, or they might bring their immediate family of wife and young children. Or several families might agree to make the trip together. Whatever the arrangement, the pioneers counted on the hospitality of villagers living along the path north. Most of the émigrés walked, carrying few belongings with them, while the more fortunate might have the luxury of riding a burro or a mule. Danger haunted them as they traveled. Some got lost. Indians and road agents lay in wait. Of necessity, survival had to be improvised. Some of the travelers got sick, especially the very young. Death was not unknown. The migrants hoped to find work and set up housing quickly, until they recovered enough from the journey to look for something better

The immigrants did not all flock to any one location in the West. Instead, they headed for that area of the frontier closest to their region of origin. Thus, folks from the states of Durango, Chihuahua, Sonora, and other northwestern Mexican states set off for California; those from Tamaulipas, Nuevo León, and Coahuila departed for Texas. Whatever U.S. state was their selection, newcomers tended to congregate in preexisting Hispanic settlements. Consequently, almost two-thirds of the Spanish-speaking population came to live in the southern areas of California during the last decades of the nineteenth century. It was there that much of the Mexican population had been clustered since the colonial period. From California, on the other hand, Mexicans, whether native or foreign born, could decide to migrate further, as indeed many did during the 1860s and 1870s, to work in the mines of Nevada, Arizona, and Colorado where more possibility of success beckoned.

In Texas, the counties between the Nueces River and the Rio Grande attracted the most immigration. In that area, extending west into the Laredo district, the population increased from about 9,000 in 1850 to

51,826 in 1880. Almost 85 percent of the population there was of Mexican descent, working in fledgling towns or on the many ranches then being established by recently arriving Anglos or on ranchos belonging to old-line Mexican families. But Mexicans found other areas of the state equally capable of extending them a livelihood. Central Texas, which included the old city of San Antonio, kept growing after the Civil War, and it enticed the migrants, though never in such numbers as did the trans-Nueces. West Texas, stretching from San Antonio to El Paso, by the 1870s was issuing calls for workers to man sheep and cattle ranches and burgeoning farms. In West Texas, the population was equally divided between Anglo and European whites and Mexican residents.

According to research, the number of immigrants arriving each year in the Arizona Territory jumped from 4,348 in 1870 to 9,330 in 1880. (Richard Griswold del Castillo, *La Familia: Chicano Families in the Urban Southwest* (Notre Dame: University of Notre Dame Press, 1984), p. 58). They were responding to opportunities available in the new silver, gold, and copper mines. For the most part, the immigrants and their American-born counterparts remained clustered around Tubac along the border with the Mexican state of Sonora. Resembling settlement patterns elsewhere, southern Arizona remained an overwhelmingly Hispanic locale.

The immigration and demographic dispersal patterns discernible in California, Texas, and Arizona do not apply to New Mexico or to southern Colorado. Growth therein was internal, with very little immigration from Mexico, since these two territories did not experience mining, ranching, and railroad booms between 1848 and 1880 as did California and Texas. Those who did enter New Mexico gravitated toward the north, that is, the environs of Taos and Albuquerque, where the closest ties to the U.S. economy existed. Population growth, as well as encroachment into old land grants by arriving Anglo settlers, did, however, compel the Hispanos to diffuse toward all corners of the territory, if not beyond. From the settled villages of northern New Mexico, the search for richer grazing grounds and abundant water resources for sheep took the pobladores to the Colorado border. Some, indeed, spilled into the Colorado Territory to establish farms and new communities. Small towns in southern Colorado such as Trinidad trace their beginnings to this northward thrust from New Mexico during the 1850s and 1860s.

Dispersal also occurred in all the other directions. Pressure to find fertile sheep ranges pushed some New Mexicans toward the northeastern sections of the Territory and into the Texas Panhandle, for instance. This same need, alongside population growth and continued immigration from the United States that infringed on old settlements, produced movement toward the northwest as far as northeastern Arizona. The expansion south led to the founding of communities such as present-day Ruidoso in southeastern New Mexico, as well as many other rural plazas along the Rio Grande in the direction of El Paso, Texas.

CULTURES MEET

Wherever Mexican-origin people already lived or decided to settle, or whatever their citizenship status, interaction on the borderlands now involved contact with groups other than unfriendly Native American people and a small number of pioneering Anglos and Europeans. African Americans and Chinese also came to constitute the racial makeup of the West following the signing of the Treaty of Guadalupe Hidalgo, albeit only as a small minority. To be sure, the pobladores still contended with attacks from the Native American nations, for, as mentioned earlier, the so-called Indian Wars did not end in the West until many years after the Civil War. Thus Mexicans in southern Arizona, northern New Mexico, and western Texas still lived in fear of strikes from the Comanches and Apaches. In California, by contrast, where the old indigenous people did not create a threat such as that posed by the Plains tribes, Mexicans many times worked alongside Indians who eked out a living as itinerant ranch- and farmhands in the new economy. Deprivation, poverty, and neglect became the fate of the California Indians, and they ultimately disappeared (at least from the public eye) either through natural death, murder, or gradual absorption into other minority communities.

Contact with African Americans was infrequent for several reasons. For one thing, communities in the West now tended to be segregated along racial lines, with all races keeping (either by law or by choice) to their own people. While African Americans migrated West starting with the gold rush of 1849, their numbers were never so high that they came in close contact with Mexican American villages and barrios. Furthermore, African Americans were not inclined to settle in those regions of the West where Mexicans already lived. In Texas, for example, the pattern was to join existing black communities in East Texas, so that few went west of San Antonio. Given these circumstances, social interaction between African Americans and Mexicans is difficult to ascertain, though historians point to one case in the West Texas county of Presidio during the 1870s where black soldiers mixed easily with the local Mexican inhabitants. Racial intermarriage and informal relations with Mexican women became the norm there, as all those involved (including white soldiers) came to grips with the isolation and the need to count on each other for the sake of self-preservation.

Mexican American association with Chinese communities was similarly sporadic, probably for reasons akin to those that explain the low degree of interaction with African Americans. Mexican workers did come face to face with the Chinese on the labor front, though, as both competed fiercely for openings in the very exacting and at times dangerous tasks in the mines and railroad lines then being built across the West. The instinct to survive, therefore, could well incite clashes, as it did in Calabasas, Arizona, in 1882, when Mexicans attacked a camp of Chinese railroad hands in a drive to expel them from the area. Along with a contingent of white laborers, the Mexicans destroyed the site and successfully eliminated the Chinese as potential competitors for what amounted to no more than low-paying occupations.

The most common contact Mexicans had in the West was with white people, of course, who now made up the majority of the population in the old Mexican Far North. Many were the enticements that brought whites (among them Europeans) to the West, including the ones explaining the Mexicans' trek to the north. The gold rush had lured the first wave of Anglo Americans, but new and infinite possibilities for growth in the region account for the sweeping migration that unfolded in the last half of the nineteenth century. Whatever the reasons for the influx, it was impressive enough that the fate of Mexicans (as well of African Americans and Asians) was now determined by the newcomers who laid out ambitious strategies for developing the trans-Mississippi frontier.

Anglo Americans imported racial views and understandings that did not bode well for Mexicans. How did such notions take shape? Historians advance a number of explanations. For one thing, almost three centuries of English-Spanish rivalry over world colonization had had its effect; the English had come to hold very disparaging attitudes toward Spaniards, considering them cruel, bigoted, and degenerate. Spaniards were not a pure race in English eyes; their blood was mixed with that of the Arabs. Anglo Americans held them guilty of the additional transgression of mixing with the native New World inhabitants. Those Anglos who had recently arrived in the West considered Mexicans the degraded offspring of a Spanish and Indian mixture, by nature incapable of improving the region. In Anglo Americans' considered judgment, Mexicans had failed miserably to improve it over the course of two centuries. Some even associated them with savagery, linking Mexicans with Mexico's indigenous civilizations that had engaged in cannibalism and other barbarous acts. The Americans' impulse was thus to treat Mexicans as racial inferiors, and indeed, Anglos tended to lump the old aristocracy that had presided over Spanish-Mexican society with commoner Mexicans or with the new arrivals from Mexico or other parts of Latin America. For many Anglos, dark-hued Mexicans ranked just one level above African Americans.

More immediate events fueled such already ingrained feelings. The Texas War for Independence in 1836 had left Americans with unforgiving sentiments toward Mexicans, for the Mexican army had committed what many Americans considered unwarranted atrocities at the Alamo and at Goliad. Manifest Destiny, that feeling in the United States during the 1840s that the United States was fated to extend from coast to coast (which had culminated in the Treaty of Guadalupe Hidalgo), gave Americans a sense of victory and a conviction that Mexicans in the West were no more than a conquered people. They saw themselves as arriving in the West driven by the call to redeem the hinterlands from the defeated Mexicans, whose indolence had only retarded progress. If there was to be a place for Mexicans in the new West, it was as manual laborers and not much else.

Protestantism acted to further demean and subordinate Mexicans. Protestant Americans saw Mexicans as suffering from the many disadvantages of Catholicism, which they tended to consider a backward religion. To Protestants, Mexicans appeared a childlike people under the influence of the priesthood. Protestants further found Mexicans morally decadent and their values short of those expected of civilized humanity.

Missionaries acted as though the West was a foreign land and the Mexicans inhabiting it must be rescued from primitivism and superstition.

Mexicans in the West were subjected to numerous wrongs as a result of Anglo American prejudices. For one thing, Anglos put Mexican landowners on the defensive by forcing Mexicans to prove legal title to lands they had owned or worked for generations. In South Texas, many of the old grantees successfully beat back such efforts—launched by Euro-American ranchers, merchants, and lawyers—when land commissions, court decisions, and the legislature sided with Tejano proprietors. Not until the 1880s, according to certain historians, did some of the old South Texas rancheros lose their lands, a misfortune due to a combination of forces, among them Anglo intrigue, natural calamities, and the Hispanic tradition of dividing up land among heirs.

The situation was much worse in New Mexico and California. Many Anglos believed that the conquest gave them the right to supplant native landholders, and many brazenly moved onto private property as speculators, ranchers, or squatters to lay first claim to what they considered open lands. In California, lawyers made it a profitable practice to either defend the interlopers against the Californios (then in the process of adjusting themselves to the U.S. legal system) or to take on the Californios as their clients.

The Land Act of 1851 established a three-man commission to investigate the legitimacy of the old land grants, and it proved a challenging process for the Californios. Most lacked the necessary paperwork to prove legal title to their lands. A common understanding and a family's working of a rancho had earlier been good enough to establish a claim to one's domain, but that was no longer enough in the new California. The only option for the Californio grantees now was to hire Anglo lawyers, who charged the unsuspecting defendants exorbitant fees, often forcing them to relinquish part of their estates to pay their legal expenses. Worse yet, some Mexican landowners signed papers (which at times they did not understand), not realizing that they were thereby surrendering title to their lands. The new "proprietors" then made a profit by renting out their new acquisitions to Anglo ranchers needing to graze their livestock.

The contemptuous feelings Anglos brought west, augmented by contacts that at times turned out to be unpleasant, resulted in numerous other kinds of indignities for Mexicans. White society crafted a kind of justice that favored Americans and Europeans at the expense of Mexicans and, for that matter, other minority groups. The courts and law enforcement mechanisms in many cases became the exclusive province of whites. Consequently, Mexicans found themselves more frequently victimized by the law, shown in their being convicted more often than whites. They were also often targeted by extralegal groups who took the law into their own hands.

According to one recent study, some 350 Mexicans across the West met their death via lynching in the period between 1850 and 1880, among them a California woman named Juanita (also known as Josefa) who fell victim to a white mob in 1851. As history records the episode, Juanita (in fear of a physical attack) killed a white intruder who wanted to get into her cabin at a Downieville, California, mining camp. Within hours, an ad hoc hearing got underway and convicted her of murder, the jury sentencing her to death by hanging, a penalty that "executioners" carried out immediately. An equally egregious (though legal) miscarriage of justice involved a Texas Mexican woman named Chipita (or Chepita) Rodríguez near Nueces County in 1863. The facts in this case involved the murder of a white man, allegedly killed by Chipita at her home according to the prosecution, for money he was carrying. Despite the scanty evidence against her, the court condemned Chipita to hanging, and law authorities carried out the sentence in November 1863.

RESISTANCE ON MANY FRONTS

Reaction by Mexicans to the repercussions of the conquest manifested itself in several forms in the period from 1848 to 1880. These expressions included resistance, retaliation against injustices perpetrated upon Mexican American communities, and accommodation to the new order of things. Throughout the West, response to U.S. rule included both rejection and approval.

Resistance came in the form of what Anglos called Mexican outlawry, but which Mexican Americans considered justifiable retaliation. There are several examples of such cases, but the person who has intrigued historians most in recent years has been Joaquín Murrieta. Exhaustive research by some historians depicts the Sonora-born Murrieta coming in 1850 as a miner to the gold diggings with his wife and half-brother, only

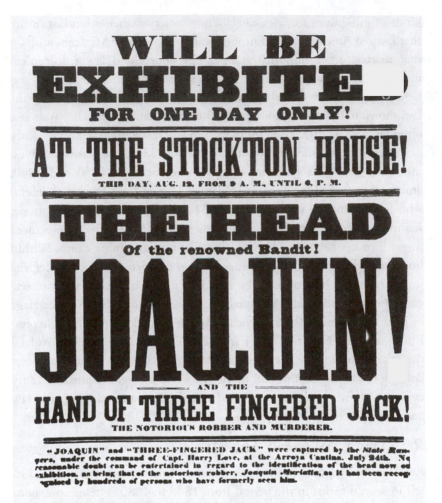

WILL BE EXHIBITED

FOR ONE DAY ONLY!

AT THE STOCKTON HOUSE!

THIS DAY, AUG. 12, FROM 9 A. M., UNTIL 6, P. M.

THE HEAD

Of the renowned Bandit!

JOAQUIN!

AND THE

HAND OF THREE FINGERED JACK!

THE NOTORIOUS ROBBER AND MURDERER.

"JOAQUIN" and "THREE-FINGERED JACK" were captured by the *State Rangers*, under the command of Capt. Harry Love, at the Arroyo Cantina, July 24th. No reasonable doubt can be entertained in regard to the identification of the head now on exhibition, as being that of the notorious robber, *Joaquin Murietta*, as it has been recognised by hundreds of persons who have formerly seen him.

Reward poster announcing the display of the head of bandit Joaquín Murrietta and the hand of Three Fingered Jack, one of his gang members, 1853. (American Stock/Getty Images)

to be victimized by the chaos that was part of the gold rush. Allegedly, white men raped his woman, lynched his sibling, and whipped Murrieta almost to death. To avenge these crimes, Murrieta took up his gun and terrorized California *Norteamericanos* by raiding ranches, murdering people, and attacking mining camps. His death came at the hands of a posse in 1853, but legend holds that Joaquín did not meet his end in this manner, but that he returned to Sonora, where he lived on for many more years.

Other scholars argue just as adamantly that no such person existed, that the fabled Joaquín was a creation of folklore, or that he was a composite of several individuals named Joaquín. If a Joaquín Murrieta did indeed live, then he was no heroic figure, but a scoundrel who led a gang of thugs in stealing horses and attacking and killings Anglos, Chinese, and even fellow Mexicans. His goal was to acquire money in the most convenient manner, including holding up those who possessed it. By no means, according to this interpretation, was Murrieta a Robin Hood, a social bandit type retaliating against those of special privilege to make up for atrocities committed on fellow Mexicans.

Mexicans also revealed their displeasure with the post-1848 West by challenging exploitation on the job. Among such episodes is the work stoppage that occurred in 1865–1866 in the New Almadén mercury mine in Santa Clara County in California. The labor force there consisted mostly of Californios and skilled miners recently arrived from Sonora who performed dangerous work underground, risking falls from ladders, health hazards, and explosions. For these dangers, the miners received meager wages, hardly enough to provide for the welfare of their families. Things deteriorated further in 1863, when a U.S. company bought the New Almadén mine and implemented "reforms" that made life worse in both the workplace and the village. To demonstrate their discontent, therefore, the miners initiated strike activity in 1865. Some of the Sonoran miners used strong nationalist language during the course of the strike, equating the company's exploitation of workers with the imperialism of the French then occupying Mexico. Management counterattacked by calling upon local law authorities, dismissing the principal spokespersons, and eventually replacing the workforce with European miners. The resistance fizzled out by 1866, but the strike pointed to a Mexican willingness to challenge unsatisfactory circumstances in the new U.S. West.

Common folks also resisted the Americanos in cases where Anglos became too invasive and disrupted old ways of living. One such case was the El Paso Salt War of 1877, during which poor people in West Texas rebelled against a clique of Anglo entrepreneurs who wished to control local salt

lakes that had provided villagers with a source of livelihood for generations. A more prominent case of resistance involved country folks in
northern New Mexico skirmishing against the Maxwell Land Grant and
Railway Company during the 1870s and after. For decades, poor villagers
had lived on land belonging to Lucien B. Maxwell, a French Canadian
(but a naturalized citizen of Mexico) who had married into the prominent
Beaubien family of New Mexico in 1844. Under Maxwell, villagers held
the status of common laborers (actually peons working for Maxwell) but
had possessed the right to use the vast lands and pastures on Maxwell's estate. Workers also enjoyed a degree of security, knowing that they could
live in their semiautonomous villages without fear of arbitrary expulsion.

In 1869, however, Maxwell and his wife María de la Luz sold their
grant to the Maxwell Land Grant and Railway Company. In contradis-
tinction to Lucien Maxwell, the firm's stockholders displayed little interest in respecting village ways. They desired profits and looked upon the
resident population as a ready proletariat capable of producing dividends
for the venture. Company officials, moreover, saw the old communal
properties as a source of revenue and acted to deny villagers their use. Beginning in the 1870s, therefore, life changed abruptly for the villagers,
who now had to work for Maxwell Land Grant and Railway Company
owners at low wages, buy from the company's stores, forsake a traditional
form of living, and even vacate the very lands that for generations had
sustained them. Villagers resisted the new reality by engaging in pro-
tracted guerrilla war against the intruders.

In a struggle that continued into the 1890s, they shot at Company
officials, killed livestock, destroyed fences and barns, and otherwise sabo-
taged business operations. The company fought back by reinforcing its
security forces and bringing lawsuits against the malcontents. Years of
fighting produced few gains for villagers, many of whom found themselves having to compromise by leasing their old lands from the Maxwell
Land Grant and Railway Company.

ACCOMMODATION IN THE MULTICULTURAL WEST

The majority of Mexicans sincerely hoped to become part of the new
West. Both plebeians and those of the upper crust worked on becoming
familiar with U.S. laws and government bureaucracies. Those with a spe-

cial attraction for politics sought places for themselves, either as leaders or as grass-roots activists. They understood the odds against their ambitions, as Anglos controlled most of the political machinery in the West. But such crusaders saw virtue in the constitutional government based on the principles espoused in the United States by figures like George Washington, Alexander Hamilton, and Thomas Jefferson. If their experience before 1848 in New Mexico, California, Colorado, Arizona, and Texas had been one of general neglect by the central government or one of disorder in the homeland if they were newly arrived from Mexico, then these Mexicans viewed the new democracy with optimism. They could call attention to those problems that plagued them by holding mass gatherings, rallying the discontented, lobbying their legislators, taking their grievances to the courts, and persuading town dwellers, villagers, or ranch and farm folks to vote for a particular platform.

Thus Mexican communities approached the politics of the post-1848 period in much the same way as did other groups in the West. Some found politics fascinating and pursued a place in government, others participated in it because they felt it their duty, and still others considered politics irrelevant. But whatever the case, Mexicans were politically present to some degree or another in every area in which they lived. In areas or communities where they constituted a majority, whether it be in South Texas, southern Arizona, or in southern California towns, Mexican Americans took an interest in politics by campaigning and running for positions, either as part of independent factions, political rings, or the local Democratic or Republican parties. They further served in a variety of posts, some of them elective and others appointive. In localities where they constituted a substantial part of the population, they occupied positions in commissioners' courts, town councils, and school boards or served as election judges, justices of the peace, policemen, surveyors, or representatives in legislatures.

To be sure, those most likely to pursue a place for themselves in the political structure of the post–Mexican War era were members of families active in government affairs before the conquest, as with José Antonio Navarro and Santos Benavides in Texas. But that was not always the case, especially some twenty years after the conquest, when the older generation passed into old age and a new one raised under U.S. laws set its sights on the new politics. Further, recent arrivals from Mexico could try their hand at U.S. politics, as in the case of Estevan Ochoa of Tucson, Arizona, an immigrant from Chihuahua. Ochoa learned the English language early on and became a U.S. citizen, then went on to serve in the Arizona territorial legislature during the 1860s and 1870s and in 1875 won the office of mayor of Tucson, at a time when the city was in the process of becoming a predominantly Anglo town.

Among others certainly desirous of negotiating with the new U.S. order were men and women who had been economically successful in Mexico's Far North before the war, or in Mexico itself, and now wished to continue doing business under U.S. rule. There is the example of Mexican Americans in Tucson, Arizona, among them the aforementioned Estevan Ochoa, whose business fortunes actually increased while possibilities for success constricted for Mexicans elsewhere. Ochoa came to make much of his money in the mercantile, ranching, mining, and freighting business. It was he (and others like him) who in the post–Civil War era helped the U.S. government supply its military garrisons in the West and facilitated the transport of goods to and from isolated ranches and remote mining camps.

The most successful of Hispanic entrepreneurs up until the 1880s were those in New Mexico who had participated in the Santa Fe Trade before 1846. Historians who have studied this cohort point to several wealthy families, among them the Chávez, Armijo, Otero, Perea, Yrizarri, Baca, and Barela. These families succeeded in the face of Anglo competition for several reasons. They learned to form alliances with Anglo Americans who had political connections in the Territory. These elites maintained their ties with merchants in Chihuahua, Zacatecas, and other Mexican states, just as they had in the 1820s through the 1840s, and thus continued profiting from an expanding international trade that involved taking wool and other Mexican products east and returning west and to Mexico with merchandise such as hats, clothes, ammunition, weapons, shoes, dishes, and wines. They never severed ties with the U.S. (and even European) commercial houses that had handled their transactions during the height of the Santa Fe Trade, and as a result, commerce persisted without much interruption. Lastly, these merchants diversified their ventures, going into sheep raising and banking. Starting in the 1860s, however, these same families faced the reality of more difficult times, though by no means did they see financial ruin. The Civil War, for one thing, stifled business growth. After the war's end, they encountered greater competition from Anglo capitalists. The railroad making its way West undercut them. Then, many of the old entrepreneurs died and divided their business concerns among family members whose priorities lay outside the commercial sector.

Equally inclined to integrate themselves into the new economy were common folks, equipped with not much more than old skills or a willingness to learn the new occupations that accompanied urban growth in the West. These included vaqueros, miners, sheepshearers (who might migrate into Washington and Wyoming), farm hands, day laborers, grubbers (those who clear land), dishwashers, construction workers, wagon drivers, and in the case of women, laundresses, servants, waitresses, and seamstresses. Others created their own kind of work, maybe as peddlers of Mexican foods or as water haulers, to mention only some of the more creative types of undertakings. As a group, Mexicans counted on the ethic of hard work to get ahead in a world of enterprising go-getters.

Unfortunately, the fate for the majority of the population of Mexican descent in the West came to be one of unattained prosperity. Most Mexicans came to constitute an immense working class with limited opportunity for upward advancement. Some remained peons on ranches like those in South Texas and in New Mexico, beholden to new owners who combined the old labor relations with newer approaches geared to produce revenue. Such was the arrangement Lucien Maxwell forged in northern New Mexico, where for some twenty-five years after the mid-1840s Maxwell ran his ranch as a hacienda, holding his workers to the land through debt peonage. Those laborers able to find openings in nonagricultural pursuits such as in mining and railroad building faced no better a fate than the peons. They worked as hard but earned lower wages than did their Anglo coworkers. Historians refer to this relegation of Mexicans to the lowest stratum of the occupational ladder as "proletarianization."

RETENTION OF THE MOTHER CULTURE

Mexicans sought accommodation in the new West, but they retained their ethnic identity, unwilling to jettison a generations-old heritage.

Being a Mexican meant adhering to those beliefs, customs, and traditions passed on to them by their Spanish and mestizo forebears. It involved having pride in the accomplishments of the homeland, its history and institutions, and its contributions to the arts and literature. Communities insisted that members of the group still be faithful to the Catholic religion, appreciate ethnic music, perpetuate in-group folklore, rely on the delicious foods historically cooked by their parents and grandparents, and celebrate religious and secular festivals as always.

Indeed, much of what has been discussed in previous chapters about Spanish/Mexican culture continued with only minor modifications when the West became part of the United States. Most communities remained primarily Spanish-speaking, though some people therein learned the English language, or at least enough of it to become active players in politics and society as well as dependable wage earners. Accepted conventions about courtesy and respect toward others did not fall by the wayside just because of the new governance. Protestant sects attracted only a few Catholics. Reverence for our Lady of Guadalupe hardly diminished. Words inherited from the Muslims or the Aztecs remained as commonplace as they had since the first Spanish/Mexicans pobladores arrived in the Far North. Foods that had their origins in the Iberian Peninsula or in parts of the Spanish empire and later the Mexican nation still made up the dishes set at the dinner table. Aztec mythology and orally transmitted folklore scarcely faced obliteration. In fact, Anglo American society saw merit in some of things that were Mexican and accepted them. Architectural styles, entertainment forms such as the card game monte, games of riding skills, ways of handling cattle or sheep on the range, and techniques used in mining operations—all became part of the cultural landscape of the U.S. West after mid-century.

By their presence, therefore, either as natives to the land or new immigrants entering it after 1848, Mexicans made an imprint on the West despite campaigns to disfranchise them politically or disarm them economically. Culturally speaking, Mexicans were much more visible in post-1848 society than they were in the political and economic spheres. Anglos did not always appreciate the ways of those whom they had just conquered, but the fact of the matter is that Mexican cultural traditions survived intact through the transitional decades following the Mexican

War, nourished as they were by immigration and a desire by Mexican-descent inhabitants to maintain the old way of life. To be sure, Mexican culture in the West took several shapes. Some Mexicans were purely ethnic, as they spoke only Spanish and adhered completely to entertainment styles grounded in the Mexican past and to customs traceable to their Spanish/Arab/Native American heritage. Others were bicultural, having accepted elements of the U.S. milieu into their identity. But in whatever form, the resilience of lo mexicano made a major contribution to making the West a multicultural world.

Belief in the ideal of the family structure and the values that nourished it remained a bulwark of Mexican American living in the West. As was the case with other people entering the region during this era of change, family arrangements among Mexicans varied. According to data drawn from the federal censuses, the nuclear family remained the ideal, and indeed, most family units consisted of the husband, the wife, and their immediate offspring. There were also extended families, featuring grandparents, as well as grown siblings with their own families living under one roof. Some households had women as heads, whether because husbands were away engaged in seasonal work, because of widowhood, or because women preferred living alone and raising their own children. There is some indication that the number of women-headed households increased after 1848, a fact that would have empowered women somewhat, as they now assumed a role traditionally occupied by men. No doubt this assumption of a new role occurred in some cases, but for the most part, Mexicans (as was the case with other groups in the West) continued believing in the subservience of women.

Long-standing precepts regarding the place of women and wives in society changed little, therefore. Nonetheless, there are many examples of independent women and of wives and mothers who transgressed established standards. Those from the elite class seemed to have more easily overcome limitations placed upon women, or at least they had greater opportunity to exercise their innate abilities. Such was the case with María de la Luz Beaubien Maxwell, wife of Lucien B. Maxwell (the Mexican government had initially granted what came to be known as the Maxwell Land Grant to Carlos Beaubien, Luz's father). As copartner of the grant she had inherited, she continued to be involved in several of the estate's transactions, including new purchases of land after she married Lucien in 1844, and indeed she signed the contract that transferred much of the hacienda to the Maxwell Land and Railway Company in 1869. After her husband passed away in 1875, Luz continued her business interests, amassing large herds of livestock, and in fact gaining a reputation as a kind of "cattle queen."

Even though Mexican patriarchy dictated limitations for women, allowances were made for those in extenuating circumstances. Widows could remarry without disgrace being cast upon them, and under frontier conditions where life offered uncertainty, many did in fact marry two or three times, having another family with each new spouse. Society, on the other hand, discouraged women (as had been the custom before 1848) from having premarital relations, though in practice people condoned such informal unions in cases where the practical thing in a frontier environment was to live together without the marital commitment.

Intermarriage, usually involving Mexican women and white men, also came to be acceptable. Few studies, however, exist on this topic. What little has been written (mainly on New Mexico) lists several reasons for interracial liaisons. Anglo men and Mexican women lived together because of the human instinct to love and acquire the support of loved ones. They also became involved due to sexual imbalances: not enough white women lived in the West, so that Anglo men chose Mexican women. Economic motives might also account for such unions, as a marriage to an Anglo man might mean material improvement and better financial security for Mexican women. Catholicism apparently also entered into consideration, as the number of Irish Catholic men married to Mexican women appears disproportionate. Scholarly investigations also show that intercultural contact, generally between Anglo men and Mexican women, occurred in the context of a hostile environment between the races, that associations between whites and Hispanic women were not exclusive to the upper class, and that only a small percentage of Mexican women in New Mexico actually entered into these unions, though a majority of Anglo men did so. In Santa Fe, for instance, the great majority of Mexican women married men from Spanish-speaking communities, and even when women married Anglos, Mexican American culture persisted among their offspring unless the married couple relocated to another part of the West. If the family stayed in New Mexico, or those parts of the West featuring a Mexican majority (southern California, southern Arizona, or South Texas, for instance), then children almost certainly would inherit the mother's culture. Under those circumstances, it was the Anglo husband who invariably acculturated himself in his adopted society.

The great majority of Mexicans in the West remained true to the faith of their forebears and thus remained Catholic. Church officials from the United States now managed the affairs of the Catholic Church in the U.S. West, a change that did not augur well for Spanish-speaking parishes. Often, the church gave priority to the needs of other regions in the country or failed to grasp the importance of ministering to Mexican Catholics in the West. European priests often were the ones assigned to Catholic communities, and though some did their work effectively, others proved to be bigoted and intolerant of the cultural ways of their flock, criticizing Mexican folk beliefs, as well as people's values and morals, if not their lifestyle.

Catholics did the best they could under such circumstances. Most times they abided by the wishes of their pastor. Those preferring to express reverence in their own way might seek out alternative means to worship, as in the case of some New Mexicans who still continued supporting the Penitentes. Many others improvised to maintain traditional methods of worshipping, as in the case of those in remote areas of the West where priests seldom made appearances. Mexican rancheros in South Texas during this period, for instance, built their own chapels, where the local population might meet to meditate and pray or implore the Lord for spiritual support. Poor folks constructed their own home altars, which they adorned with images of their favorite saints, votive candles, and crucifixes. People often had to bury their loved ones without a priest's presence, but they expressed their faith and devotion to the church by embellishing the family plot with handcrafted statues of saints, fresh flowers, and simple headstones. Itinerant priests passed through these isolated villages and settlements periodically to administer the sacraments, including that of marriage and baptism.

Protestant sects did little to proselytize among Mexicans, and so Catholicism remained deeply rooted for that reason as well. The Presbyterian, the Methodist, and the Methodist Episcopalian Churches made some attempts to convert Spanish-speaking Catholics, but no massive conversions followed. Several reasons would explain the failure. Protestant mission boards did not always give priority to Mexicans as prospects for conversion, instead focusing on Irish or German Catholics in the West. Many of the Protestant missionaries had a low regard for the Mexicans' intellectual capacities and their overall lifestyle. At the same time, Mexican Catholics rejected Protestantism outright as a heretical belief system. They often ostracized the few within the Mexican American community who converted to Protestantism, among them close friends and even relatives. Overall, Mexican-origin pobladores were not prepared to forsake their ancestors' faith.

The pobladores expressed creative thoughts, nationalist outlooks, individual and community feelings, historical recollections, and views of history through various methods. Those of the lower class, given their illiteracy, tended to vocalize their sentiments (instead of setting them down on paper) by a reliance on folk songs, accompanied by either a violin or guitar. In Texas, the *corrido* (ballad) became a very popular form of musical display, as through it Tejanos could conveniently verbalize their personal understanding of things around them. Among the corridos best known to scholars are ones that tell the adventures of particular historical figures, such as Juan N. Cortina, a Tejano who in 1859–1860 led a mini-revolt against Anglos then arriving in the Lower Grande Valley and displacing Mexicans economically and politically. Others recounted events such as the cattle drives to Kansas, for Mexicans had made up some of the work crews going north to the Plains states during the 1860s and 1870s. Folk songs might also include what are called *coplas* (a couplet, or stanzas of four or more lines). These narrated other types of historical adventures, among them Mexico's resistance against the French occupiers during the 1860s.

IGNACIO ZARAGOZA

Who should be celebrated as the greatest Tejano military hero in history? Mexican Americans from Texas have always lived up to their reputation for bravery, a quality they have displayed in all wars, especially World War II, when five individuals of Mexican descent from the Lone Star State won

Ignacio Zaragoza, nineteenth-century Mexican general, overcame the French on May 5, 1862. (The Art Archive/National History Museum, Mexico City/Dagli Orti)

the Medal of Honor. Almost forgotten is Ignacio Zaragoza, hero of the Battle of Puebla (Mexico), who was known throughout the U.S. West by the last decades of the nineteenth century, and who continues to be toasted today as the commander who defeated French forces invading Mexico on the Cinco de Mayo (Fifth of May) in 1862.

Ignacio Zaragoza was born to a military family in Goliad, Texas, on March 24, 1829. At that time, Texas belong to Mexico, though not for long, as in 1836 Anglo Texans won their independence from that country and established an independent republic. With the turn of events, the Zaragoza family retreated to Mexico, where Miguel G. Zaragoza, Ignacio's father, resumed his career in the armed services. In Mexico, Ignacio himself pursued different career interests, finally settling in 1853 for service in the Mexican army, thus following in his father's footsteps. During the civil war of the 1850s, Zaragoza sided with the forces of Benito Juárez, which at the time were advocating an administration based on liberal democratic principles.

Juárez succeeded in implementing such a constitutional government by 1861. But his troubles (and those of the Mexican people) had hardly ended, as France in 1862 laid out ambitious plans to expand its empire to Mexico. When French forces landed in Vera Cruz in January of that year, President Juárez dispatched Zaragoza east with orders to protect the region. Skirmishes occurred as the French pushed inland, continuing until Zaragoza retreated to Puebla, a city of some 80,000 inhabitants situated between the Gulf of Mexico and Mexico City. There, Zaragoza with some 6,000 troops began preparations to ward off an all-out offensive expected from the 6,000-man French force. Heavily armed forts stood on the way uphill to Puebla, but the French infantry fought valiantly until Zaragoza's cavalry dispersed the attackers. When the French withdrew, Zaragoza proclaimed the day as having belonged to Mexico. Sadly, Ignacio Zaragoza died of typhoid fever on September 8, 1862. Moreover, the French took the city the next year and made Mexico part of the French empire until 1867.

But so significant was the victory considered when it took place that President Juárez on September 11, 1862, decreed the Cinco de Mayo a national holiday. Its hero was a man from Goliad, Texas, a fact not overlooked by Hispanic communities in the U.S. West, though formal commemoration of his bravery did not come to Zaragoza from Texans until late in the twentieth century. In 1980, the people of Texas erected a ten-foot bronze statue in Goliad State Historical Park to honor Zaragoza.

Less officially, Mexicans in Texas, California, and Arizona began commemorating Zaragoza's grand deed on a yearly basis starting no later than the 1880s. Immigrants from Mexico recalled their history and roots and made certain that the past persisted in their adopted land. Generally, a local association or club (perhaps the Sociedad Mutualista Ignacio Zaragoza) took the lead in organizing the festivities. Or it might be community leaders who took command of preparations, for in every *colonia* (as Spanish-speaking communities were collectively called) lived persons recognized by neighbors and friends as capable figures able to get things done, among them attending to barrio issues by negotiating with those in power. In towns and villages, the local plaza or perhaps someone's property would act as the setting for the fiestas. Out in the countryside, a house yard or barn might do for the event.

Wherever held, however, the Cinco de Mayo became an occasion for dressing up in a national fashion, reminiscing about times in the old land, and spending time socializing with close acquaintances. Folks gathered to hear patriotic speeches, listen to music, and mill around food booths where sumptuous homemade dishes could be bought. Those born in the U.S. West and having little knowledge about the old country joined in the fun, simply acknowledging the day to be part of their ethnic heritage. But through the years, Americanized Mexicans came to insist that the observation have some relevance to their experience in the United States. Thus, playing American music, holding contests to determine the best performer in the latest dance craze, or permitting declamations in English came to be slowly accepted as part of the celebration as the decades passed.

In modern times, Ignacio Zaragoza lives on in the annual Cinco de Mayo commemorations held wherever Mexican American ethnic enclaves have sprouted, including regions of the Midwest. With immigration constantly invigorating old communities, people hardly lose touch with a heritage that is very much a part of being Mexican American. Indeed, organizers, many of them U.S. born, make sure to invite dignitaries from Mexico, or perhaps film or music celebrities from that country. Also accompanying these modern events are folkloric dances, Spanish-language music, Mexican foods, and of course, the national colors of Mexico.

Recently, many Cinco de Mayo festivities in the larger cities have expanded beyond their early intent. They have evolved into occasions serving purposes beside that of remembering Ignacio Zaragoza and the victory that stirred Mexico into waging a four-year war against the French. For one thing, the Cinco de Mayo fiesta acts as a kind of refresher course for increasingly acculturated youngsters. In the public schools, teachers observe the date as part of a multicultural curriculum that also includes Martin Luther King Day, César Chávez Day, and President's Day. Then, the Cinco de Mayo commemoration also has become an auspicious time to make money. Large corporations get into the act, hoping to advertise their product by sponsoring a favorite event. Civic groups attempt to raise funds for scholarships, while church clubs sell tamales or other enticing dishes to finance a variety of parish programs.

Once upon a time, then, common folks, many of them recently arrived from Mexico, held Cinco de Mayo feasts in a genuine effort to laud the exploits of Ignacio Zaragoza. Despite the commercialism that has infiltrated them over the years, these annual commemorations today nonetheless remind both young and old that a great Tejano figure, fighting for Mexico in 1862, is the person being feted.

Those of the upper crust with command of the written word, on the other hand, penned their feelings on issues of the day or called on their artistic powers to create literature reflecting life in the U.S. West. All wrote in Spanish, though the works of some, as in the case of the following three figures, were immediately translated into English. During the 1850s, José Antonio Navarro, a leading oligarch from San Antonio who had assisted the Texans in the war for independence of 1836, published in serial form what many years later (1869) appeared as *Apuntes históricos interesantes de San Antonio de Béxar* (Commentaries of Historical Interest on San Antonio de Béxar). Distressed over what he perceived as the misrepresentation of Mexicans in the history of Texas by Anglo American authors, Navarro sought to record for posterity a corrected version of events as Tejanos remembered them or as he had personally witnessed them. For Navarro, Anglos writers were not giving Tejanos due credit for their contribution to the Texas story. Then in 1858, Juan Nepomuceno Seguín, issued his *Personal Memoirs of John N. Seguín* in order to clear his name of accusations that he had turned traitor to the Republic of Texas, the country he helped create by his gallantry at the Battle of San Jacinto (1836). The aforementioned Juan Cortina in 1859 issued two proclamations in South Texas denouncing injustices being committed against Texas Mexicans by newly arrived Anglo Americans. In truth, another person wrote these public statements, but it is generally agreed that the pronouncements contain Cortina's own ideas and that he read them out to a scribe, possibly one of his relatives.

In California, Antonio María Osio, a government official during the 1830s and 1840s, finished in 1851 a 110-page manuscript, which he never published (scholars recently rediscovered the document at Santa Clara University). Titled *La Historia de Alta California,* the work covered the period of Mexican California from about the mid-1820s until just after the Mexican War. Researchers find Osio's history valuable, not only because it points to the literary record left by the Californios, but also because it reveals much about social and community life in old California. It is a firsthand account of historical events, furthermore, revealing at least some of the Californios' feelings about the arrivals of the conquerors in 1846. Osio did not temper his thoughts about the occupation, freely expressing anger and resentment at the way the Americanos treated the Californios as a conquered people.

Different from all the above is the novel published in 1872 by María Amparo Ruiz de Burton, a native of Baja California (born in 1832), who in 1849 had married an Army man named Henry S. Burton in Monterey. Titled *Who Would Have Thought It?* and written in English, the novel does not have the Hispanic West as its setting, nor Mexican Americans as its main characters. Rather, it is set in New England in the decades before and during the Civil War and revolves around prim aristocratic society there. The novel's satiric portrayal of New Englanders is meant as a critique of the United States as a whole, as Ruiz de Burton denounces American hypocrisy, crassness, ethnocentrism, and imperialism. The novel seems out of place in Mexican American literature, for it does not conform to the type of literary expressions mentioned above (corridos, memoirs, and histories written in Spanish). As such, it calls for a broader definition of Mexican American literature.

Other venues that perpetuated Mexican culture included newspapers, folklore, festivals, entertainment activities, and the like. Mexican American journalism directed at a Spanish-speaking public made its own appearance during the early 1850s, accelerated somewhat during the 1870s, and then really came into its own by the latter decades of the nineteenth century. San Antonio, Texas, and Los Angeles and San Francisco, California, by midcentury had very active newspaper editors who addressed a number of issues of concern to Mexican American communities, among them politics, Anglos' mistreatment of Mexicans, and lack of appropriate educational opportunities for Mexican Americans. Most vociferous of the journalists during this period was Francisco P. Ramírez of *El Clamor Público* (Los Angeles) who from about 1855 to 1859 unceasingly berated the new political order in California, denouncing Anglos for land theft, violence inflicted on the Californios, miscarriage of justice, distortion of history, neglect of education for Spanish speakers, and so many other misdeeds. By the 1870s, New Mexico had taken its place alongside Texas and California in journalism, with the most prominent newspapers being located in Taos and Santa Fe. Like their counterparts in other parts of the West, Nuevomexicano newspapers also highlighted the problems of inadequate education, poverty, disfranchisement, and ethnic subordination. But they also promoted ethnic awareness by circulating news of great achievements taking place in Mexico, by enthusiastically publicizing ethnic functions and the national holidays of Mexico, by defending Mexican American life, which seemed constantly under disparagement by Anglo society, and by accentuating the magnificent components of the Spanish/Mexican heritage, such as the Spanish language.

The old way of life also persisted in the observations of old entertainment forms. Certainly, people acknowledged religious holy days (for example Easter, and the *día de la Virgen de Guadalupe,* December 12) as they had before the conquest, celebrating with solemn prayer, community gatherings, and tributes to the local village's favorite saint. The Christmas season called for special feasts, such as presenting pastorelas (dramas) and holding *posadas* (rests) that reenacted Joseph and Mary's quest for shelter.

Mogollón, New Mexico, celebrates Cinco de Mayo with a parade on their main dirt road through town, circa 1914. (Corbis)

But occasions other than religious ones also meant fun times, as in the case of traditional family gatherings. A person's birthday or a couple's wedding anniversary might become a reason for festivities. For such events, families and relatives pooled their meager resources to rejoice on a grand scale, offering much food and delectable dishes such as tamales and fine pastries. Many times folks would just come together, perhaps on weekends, for some kind of public dancing, whether in urban areas or farm settlements. Or it might be the end of the crop year, or a special Mexican holiday, such as the Cinco de Mayo (May 5) or the Diez y Seis de Septiembre (September 16). At such ethnocultural events, people might come from miles around to hear nationalistic speeches and patriotic declamations while socializing, catching up on gossip, and enjoying fireworks, abundant food, and entertaining music.

There were of course less formal ways to pass the time. In California for a while after the conquest, Mexicans continued to enjoy bear fights, although such sports were discontinued by law after some time. Men, primarily, attended cockfights, another sport perceived as inhumane by Anglos. But Mexicans held them clandestinely.

TWO WESTS

Between the year of the conquest and the penultimate decade of the nineteenth century, Hispanics held at least two images of the U.S. West. Many were inclined to see the region with trepidation, for the conquerors brought xenophobia and hostility with them. Many Mexicans saw the West under the U.S. government as a closed society, characterized by intolerance, violence, land theft, and a denial of opportunity. In the face of such a perception, the most disgruntled among Mexicans chose a path of forceful resistance. As indicated in this chapter, there were those who chose banditry as a manifestation of their discontent. Others sought to carry out vigilante justice against those they believed were depriving them of their lands or denying them usage of grounds they had long farmed. Laboring men talked labor strike when conditions in the workplace deteriorated to an intolerable level.

On the other hand, many others saw the West under the U.S. government as a fitting place to continue striving for a decent livelihood; if they were immigrants, they saw it as a hopeful setting wherein they could stake out a niche and begin life afresh. Such inhabitants accepted the West as settler-friendly and made the effort to become part of it. Accommodation for this group seemed a better option than resistance, and so learning the language of the conquerors, adjusting to the new economic system, and adapting to society's laws and governance appeared in order.

Whether rebels or accommodationists, Mexicans in the West steadfastly refused to dissolve ties with their cultural past. Belief in Mexican family values, faith in the Catholic religion, reliance on songs and music to express community feelings, and an appreciation for their native language thus persisted alongside the process of Americanization. Biculturalism did not exist before 1848, but it has become a fact of life for the Hispanic community since then.

BIBLIOGRAPHIC ESSAY

There exist countless studies explaining the transition that occurred in the U.S. West for the period circa 1848 to the latter decades of the nineteenth century, among them the classic studies mentioned in the bibliographic essay for Chapter 1. Still, we found Howard Roberts Lamar, *The Far Southwest, 1846–1912: A Territorial History* (New Haven, CT: Yale University Press, 1966), particularly relevant to this chapter. Dr. Lamar has long been an important interpreter of western history, and his many other works are worth consulting, among them a volume he edited, *The New Encyclopedia of the American West* (New Haven, CT: Yale University Press, 1998).

The migration that occurred during this period from Mexico into the U.S. West has not attracted a great deal of attention, but the few studies that are currently available offer cogent explanations of the causes behind the movement north. They include Arthur F. Corwin, *Immigrants and Immigrants: Perspectives on Mexican Labor Migration to the United States* (Westport, CT: Greenwood Press, 1978); Lawrence A. Cardoso, *Mexican Emigration to the United States, 1897–1931: Socio-Economic Patterns* (Tucson: University of Arizona Press, 1980); and of course, Gilbert G. González and Raúl A. Fernández, *A Century of Chicano History: Empire, Nations, and Migration* (New York: Routledge, 2003), discussed in the text. Only a few studies presently exist on emigration from the West to Mexico in the aftermath of the war of 1848; they include Martín González de la Vara, "The Return to Mexico: The Relocation of New Mexican Families to Chihuahua and the Confirmation of a Frontier Region, 1848–1854," in *The Contested Homeland: A Chicano History of New Mexico,* edited by Erlinda Gonzales-Berry and David R. Maciel (Albuquerque: University of New Mexico Press, 2000). Richard Griswold del Castillo, *Los Angeles Barrio, 1850–1890: A Social History* (Berkeley: University of California Press, 1979), contains a brief discussion of repatriation efforts undertaken by the Californios in the wake of the conquest.

The relationships of Mexicans with other ethnic groups from all over the United States in the period after 1848 has received some scholarly attention. The new contact of Mexicans with African and Chinese Americans is the subject of Arnoldo De León's *Racial Frontiers: Africans, Chinese, and Mexicans in Western America, 1848–1890* (Albuquerque: University of New Mexico Press, 2002). The reasons for the hostility toward Mexicans on the part of the Anglo American majority are explained in Raymund Paredes, "The Origins of Anti-Mexican Sentiment in the United States," in *New Directions in Chicano Scholarship,* edited by Ricardo Romo and Raymund Paredes (La Jolla: University of California at San Diego, 1978).

What happened in light of these negative responses to Mexicans is a matter that has been studied at some length; a recent account of some of the events is given in Stephen J. Pitti, *The Devil in Silicon Valley: Northern California, Race, and Mexican Americans* (Princeton, NJ: Princeton University Press, 2003). The great amount of brutality inflicted on Mexicans during that period is summarized vividly in William D. Carrigan and Clive Webb, "*Muertos por Unos Desconocidos* (Killed by Persons Unknown): Mob Violence against Blacks and Mexicans," in *Beyond Black and White: Race, Ethnicity, and Gender in the U.S. South and Southwest,* edited by Stephanie Cole and Alison M. Parker (College Station: Texas A&M University Press, 2004). The unique setting in West Texas that allowed for cooperation among Anglos, Mexicans, and Africans is described in Paul Wright, "Population Patterns in Presidio County in 1880: Evidence from the Census," *Journal of Big Bend Studies* 7 (January 1995).

Scholarly attention on the way some Mexicans responded to the conquest and to the prejudice and cruelty that accompanied it through banditry has often focused on the person most closely associated with the use of force against the occupation, the legendary Californio Joaquín Murrieta. A brief discussion of what the literature says about Murrieta may be found in Richard Griswold del Castillo, "Joaquin Murrieta: The Many Lives of a Legend," in *With Badges and Bullets: Lawmen and Outlaws in the Old West,* edited by Richard W. Etulain and Glenda Riley (Golden, CO: Fulcrum Publishing, 1999). The arguments in the continuing debate over Murrieta's motives for turning to banditry may be found in John Boessenecker, "California Bandidos: Social Bandits or Sociopaths?" *Southern California Quarterly* 80 (1998).

The most prominent of the strikes that constituted another form of resistance to Anglo domination (the New Almadén mine strike of 1865) is given much deserved notice in Pitti's book mentioned above, *The Devil in Silicon Valley.* The resistance put up against American companies by poor settlers in New Mexico facing encroachment on village lands is covered in María E. Montoya, *Translating Property: The Maxwell Land Grant and the Conflict over Land in the American West, 1840–1900* (Berkeley: University of California Press, 2002), and in Robert J. Rosenbaum, *Mexicano Resistance in the Southwest: "The Sacred Right of Self-Preservation"* (Austin: University of Texas Press, 1981).

That people of Mexican origin who had the resources adjusted to the new circumstances of the age is now common knowledge, given the great amount of scholarly work done on what are termed the elites of Mexican society. Among such studies are Thomas E. Sheridan, *Los Tucsonenses: The Mexican Community in Tucson, 1854–1941* (Tucson: University of Arizona Press, 1986); Manuel E. Gonzales, *The Hispanic Elite of the Southwest* (El Paso: University of Texas at El Paso, 1989); and the more recent monograph by Susan Calafate Boyle, *Los Capitalistas: Hispano Merchants and the Santa Fe Trade* (Albuquerque: University of New Mexico Press, 1997).

Those of the poorer class adjusted in their own way, namely by adopting cultural strategies that permitted them to find a place in the U.S. West while they remained faithful to their Mexican heritage. Their continued allegiance to Catholicism has been documented in monographs such as Arnoldo De León, *The Tejano Community, 1836–1900* (Albuquerque: University of New Mexico Press, 1982) and Armando Alonzo, *Tejano Legacy: Rancheros and Settlers in South Texas, 1734–1900* (Albuquerque: University of New Mexico Press, 1998). Reasons for Protestant failure at proselytizing among Mexicans are discussed in Juan Francisco Martínez, "Origins and Development of Protestantism Among Latinos in the Southwestern United States, 1836–1900" (Ph.D. dissertation, Fuller Theological Seminary, School of World Mission, Pasadena, CA, 1996).

Adherence to family traditions (as well as the changes that occurred within families after 1848) is the subject of Richard Griswold del Castillo, *La Familia: Chicano Families in the Urban Southwest, 1848 to the Present* (Notre Dame, IN: University of Notre Dame Press, 1984). Other important works that look at the Mexican American family for this time period are Alonzo, *Tejano Legacy,* mentioned in the previous paragraph, and Arnoldo De León and Kenneth L. Stewart, *Tejanos and the Numbers Game: A Socio-Cultural Interpretation from the Federal Censuses, 1850–1900* (Albuquerque: University of New Mexico Press, 1989).

Women and their role within the Mexican American family during the latter half of the nineteenth century have not received due attention, but there is increased interest in doing them justice. The independent role of women, especially the case of María de la Luz Beaubien Maxwell, is discussed in Montoya, *Translating Property,* mentioned in the sixth paragraph of this bibliographic essay. Marriages between Mexican women and Anglo men are studied in Darlis Miller, "Cross-Cultural Marriages in the Southwest," *New Mexico Historical Review* 57 (October 1982), and Deena J. González, *Refusing the Favor: The Spanish-Mexican Women of Santa Fe, 1820–1880* (New York: Oxford University Press, 1999).

The continuation of folkloric patterns and the Mexican American allegiance to them, especially in music, is discussed brilliantly by the famous folklorist Américo Paredes, in *A Texas-Mexican Cancionero: Folksongs of the Lower Border* (Austin: University of Texas Press, 1976). The writings of those who recorded their memoirs or their thoughts during this particular time period that are discussed in the text have gained the interest of different scholars, and published works include *Defending Mexican Valor in Texas: José Antonio Navarro's Historical Writings, 1853–1857,* edited by David R. McDonald and Timothy M. Matovina (Austin, TX: State House Press, 1995); *A Revolution Remembered: The Memoirs and Selected Correspondence of Juan N. Seguín,* edited by Jesús F. de la Teja (Austin: Texas State Historical Association, 2002); Jerry D. Thompson, *Juan Cortina and the Texas-Mexico Frontier, 1859–1877* (El Paso: Texas Western Press, 1994); and Rose Marie Beebe and Robert M. Senkewicz, "The Recovery of the First History of Alta California: Antonio María Osio's *La historia de Alta*

California," in *Recovering the U.S. Hispanic Literary Heritage,* vol. 2, edited by Erlinda Gonzales-Berry and Chuck Tatum (Houston, TX: Arte Público Press, 1996). The book itself was published as Antonio María Osio, *The History of Alta California: a Memoir of Mexican California* (Madison: University of Wisconsin Press, 1996). The novel by María Amparo Ruiz de Burton discussed in the text is discussed in Anne E. Goldman, "'Who ever heard of a blue-eyed Mexican': Satire and Sentimentality in María Amparo Ruiz de Burton's *Who Would Have Thought It?*' in *Recovering the U.S. Hispanic Literary Heritage,* vol. 2, edited by Erlinda Gonzales-Berry and Chuck Tatum (Houston, TX: Arte Público Press, 1996). The novel was first published in, and has recently been reissued, edited by Rosaura Sanchez and Beatrice Pita, by Arte Público Press, in 1995. Spanish-language journalism in New Mexico is the focus of A. Gabriel Meléndez, *So All Is Not Lost: The Poetics of Print in Nuevomexicano Communities, 1834–1958* (Albuquerque: University of New Mexico Press, 1997). Francisco P. Ramírez and his newspaper, *El Clamor Público,* receive close consideration in Griswold del Castillo, *The Los Angeles Barrio,* and in Leonard Pitt, *The Decline of the Californios: A Social History of the Spanish-Speaking Californians, 1846–1900* (Berkeley: University of California Press, 1966).

Ignacio Zaragoza, the hero of the Battle of Puebla, has been the subject of many works in Spanish, but very few in English. Nonetheless, something can be learned about him from reading surveys such as Jasper Ridley, *Maximilian and Juárez* (New York: Ticknor and Fields, 1992), and Ramón Eduardo Ruiz, *Triumphs and Tragedy: A History of the Mexican People* (New York: W. W. Norton, 1992). On the Cinco de Mayo celebrations across the generations, see José M. Alamillo, "More Than a Fiesta: Ethnic Identity, Cultural Politics, and the Cinco de Mayo Festivals in Corona, California, 1930–1950," *Aztlán: A Journal of Chicano Studies* 28 (Fall 2003), and Arnoldo De León, *Ethnicity in the Sunbelt* (2d edition; College Station: Texas A&M University Press, 2001).

CHAPTER FIVE

PROLETARIANIZATION, RESISTANCE, AND AMERICANIZATION: 1880–1930

The half century spanning the years from 1880 to the beginning of the Great Depression in 1930 generated much change in the reality of the lives of Spanish-speaking people in the U.S. West. As Americans completed the process of consolidating their commercial, social, and political hold over the lands captured from Mexico, the status of most men and women of Mexican descent in the West continued to decline, often leading them into the margins of American life. During this era, the Spanish-surnamed people who inhabited the region were subjected to a new way of life. Part of the metamorphosis featured the imposition of a different economic, industrial, and agricultural milieu, which channeled the majority of Spanish speakers into low-skilled, low-paying, and menial occupations. It was true that many former elites met this fate. However, the start of the 1900s attracted large numbers of people from Mexico as well to work in such jobs. Still, as we will note, they resisted such changes (individually and through unions and cultural, community, and religious organizations) with tenacity. In addition to such changes, the years from 1910 to 1930 also witnessed the "Great Migration" (precipitated by the Mexican Revolution and opportunities for unskilled labor brought about by the economic transformation of the West), which channeled Mexicans into nearly every corner of the region. The infusion of new blood from *Mexico Viejo* (Old Mexico) altered social relations both within and outside western barrios.

This chapter, then, not only focuses on how life changed for Hispanics already living in the West but also recounts the process of Mexicano migration into territories and states with an already substantial Spanish-speaking presence (such as Texas, California, and New Mexico), in addition to prompting dispersal into newer locations of settlement, such as Utah, Nevada, Oregon, Wyoming, Hawaii, and elsewhere. In retracing the footsteps of such people, we will address issues such as what pulled thousands of *solos* and *familias* into the various territories and states. Also, we will focus on how newly arrived Mexicanos interacted with U.S.-born Spanish speakers, Anglos, and other neighbors after arriving at the various destinations and discuss whether interactions were friendly or hostile.

The scholarly literature, moreover, offers analysis of class, religious, and political differences within communities, as well as noting the processes of community and coalition building in various locations. Also, we will examine both the cultural and daily lives of Spanish-surnamed men and women of Mexican heritage in the U.S. West during this era and address these questions: (1) What adjustments did they (and their children) make to their new surroundings? (2) How much of their culture did they retain? (3) What cultural traits and traditions did they jettison in the process (sometimes under duress imposed by Anglo authorities) of adapting to a new life in el norte (the north).

Before proceeding with this part of our story, however, it is necessary to note that the amount of information describing the entry of Puerto Ricans into the West during the late nineteenth and early twentieth centuries is scant. Most of the information available deals with Hawaii and California. In regard to Cuban Americans, anthropologist Vincent Edward Gil has argued that there were almost no Cubanos living west of the Mississippi River prior to the commencement of the totalitarian Castro regime in 1959. Census figures estimate the number of Cuban-born individuals living in the United States prior to 1960 at around 30,000; the overwhelming majority lived in Florida, with identifiable pockets of concentration in Miami, Jacksonville, Tampa, Key West, and Pensacola. Additionally, there were Cuban American communities in New York City, New Jersey, Boston, Mobile, and New Orleans. Although some scholars (such as James S. and Judith E. Olson) mention Los Angeles among such pockets of concentration, Gil (whose dissertation focuses on Cuban immigration to Los Angeles after 1960) counters that "there is no record of there being any significant number of Cubans in . . . Los Angeles . . . Small numbers . . . no doubt were dispersed throughout the . . . basin before then, but not nearly in sufficient numbers to be considered a Cuban *community*" (Gil, "The Personal Adjustment and Acculturation of Cuban Immigrants in Los Angeles," pp. 53–54). Therefore, as delineated in the opening of this text, our focal point for this particular time frame will be the experiences of Mexican Americans and the Mexicanos who arrived during the years before 1930; information on Puerto Ricans will be included as relevant and available.

THE NEW ECONOMIC MILIEU

Numerous and substantial inquiries have been done on the commercial transformation of the West and its influence upon the lives of Mexican Americans in Texas, California, Arizona, New Mexico, and elsewhere during the era covered in this chapter. Such studies provide an effective prologue to our scrutiny of these economic trends for two significant reasons: first, they provide an overview of the arrival and early development of vital industries (such as railroads, extractive industries, and commercial agriculture) in various parts of the West, and second, they catalog the drastic and pervasive decline of the social, economic, and political fortunes of the population of the West that shared a Mexican heritage.

Before focusing on examples from specific states and communities, however, a brief synopsis of the entire region's economic changes between 1880 and 1930 is necessary, and Richard White's *"It's Your Misfortune and None of My Own": A New History of the American West* provides an effective beginning for our discussion. The history of the West's economy during these years highlights one of the primary themes discussed in this work: although many Americans often painted the region as a virtual El Dorado for all who were hardy enough to venture there, the reality of economic life, especially for Hispanics, was much harsher. As White notes, this transformation "produced losers as well as winners," with people of Mexican descent suffering mightily in the new "economy plagued by excessive competition and a shortage of capital" (White, *"It's Your Misfortune,"* p. 236).

In order to carry out such a grandiose undertaking, it was often necessary to clear out the "old order," which frequently meant that Hispanic farmers, who often produced only enough for their own needs were ridiculed and purged by Anglo newcomers who saw their way of life and economic arrangements as mere "relics of backwardness and barbarism" (White, *"It's Your Misfortune,"* p. 236). As noted in the previous chapter, and as we will examine further in the following pages, this process of removal and redistribution of land to more "appropriate" purposes and ownership took several decades and was accomplished not only by the market process, but also by the legal chicanery and violence used against those of Mexican descent throughout many parts of the West.

As the land was slowly "cleared" of remaining undesirables, the new economic order eventually blossomed. Again, Richard White's words provide an adroit synopsis of the end result of this painful process. Richard White's description of the transportation infrastructure that was needed to complete this transformation incidentally makes clear what the transformation created: "Without the railroads, commercial agriculture, most mining, cattle raising . . . for a national market remained unprofitable. The modern western extractive economy began with the railroads" (White, *"It's Your Misfortune,"* p. 246).

The impact of this transformation upon Hispanics and their lands was, to say the least, cataclysmic. People of Mexican descent lost enormous tracts of land throughout Texas, California, Arizona, and New Mexico. This development, although with its own individual and important idiosyncrasies in each locale, effectively and eventually rendered impotent most of the economic, social, and political capacity of Californios, Tejanos, Nuevomexicanos, and other Spanish-speaking people. We now turn to a series of brief examinations of this process in several locales.

In 1987 David Montejano published *Anglos and Mexicans in the Making of Texas, 1836–1986,* his excellent analysis of the process through which many of the nineteenth-century Tejano elite of southern Texas lost their lands to recently arrived Anglos. Although Montejano recognizes that sometimes there was outright fraud in the taking of such lands, he argues that fraud was not entirely to blame. Rather, there were both official and commercial factors that helped destroy the power and prestige of most rancheros between 1865 and 1900. First, the Tejanos faced a new legal process and system (especially the sheriff's sale to settle tax arrears) that often meant that thousands of acres of land were sold to pay off debts of less than twenty dollars. The next two factors, lack of capital availability and wild price fluctuations in the cattle market, worked in tandem to transfer enormous tracts to Anglo control as well. One example Montejano provides is that of Victoriano Chapa, who in 1901, at the age of eighty-nine, was forced to sell his animals and lease his land in order to raise funds. The old Tejano bemoaned his fate, stating that "'My roots go deeper than those of any mesquite growing up and down this arroyo. When a man belongs to a place and lives there, all the money in all the world cannot buy him anything else so good'" (Montejano, *Anglos and Mexicans*, pp. 60–61). Two days before having to turn over his ranch, the elderly Chapa committed suicide. Montejano summed up the process of land loss by rancheros in southern Texas thus: "Because the Mexican landowners were unable to secure the capital for continuous improvements necessary in a developing and unpredictable cattle industry, their precarious market position became particularly clear during periods of a depressed cattle economy or a natural disaster" (Montejano, *Anglos and Mexicans*, p. 52).

Another historian who has noted this pattern is Armando C. Alonzo in his work *Tejano Legacy: Rancheros and Settlers in South Texas, 1734–1900.* Here Alonzo catalogs, to take one example, the lending pattern of a large broker, H. P. Drought & Co. of San Antonio, and argues that, "during the period from about 1885 to 1908, out of hundreds of loans only thirty-nine loans were made to rancheros south of the Nueces River" (Alonzo, *Tejano Legacy*, pp. 237–238). Although, Alonzo explains, many of these ranch owners tried to diversify into farming, sharecropping, and commercial farming, by around 1900 "the erosion of the land base of the ranchero class, particularly the elites, represented the most crucial factor in the ultimate decline of the Tejanos. By 1900 only a few Tejano landowners could in fact compete for loans or wait out the depressed economy until stock prices improved to reenter ranching on a moderate scale" (Alonzo, *Tejano Legacy*, p. 257). Having lost control of most of their lands in southern Texas, those of Mexican descent in the region had little to offer but their labor to the new owners of rancho lands. Their labor sufficed for a couple of decades, until about the early 1900s, when a new era, one of commercial agriculture, began in South Texas and required even larger numbers of Mexican Americans and Mexicanos as laborers.

Analogous conditions existed in California, as historians Leonard Pitt, Lizbeth Haas, and Albert Camarillo (among others) have noted. The arrival of Anglos in California and the U.S. triumph in the Mexican War did not instantaneously bring about the decimation of Californio elites. However, as in the Lone Star State, the economic and social eradication of competitors to white domination (often through the imposition of land taxes as well as costs associated with perfecting land titles) proceeded between the 1850s and 1870s, as discussed in chapter 4. One significant factor in helping bring down the old order was that "California state law enabled squatters to preempt uncultivated land until titles to grants had been confirmed. When patented, the grantee was obliged to pay squatters for the cost of improvements they had made on the land" (Haas, *Conquest and Historical Identities,* pp. 64–65). Thus, even if Spanish-surnamed owners of Mexican descent managed to hold on to property, they would often have to reimburse those who had trespassed on their land for improvements they had not ordered.

Though clearly external circumstances put intense pressure on the Californios' finances, elites also contributed to their own downfall by spending lavishly on furnishings and other luxury items during times of high beef prices (such as during the years of the gold rush). Unfortunately, for these Spanish speakers and their progeny, by the early part of the 1860s the "final blow to already-strained assets was dealt when the majority of their cattle died between 1861 and 1864, years of drought and flood. Many were ruined by the unregulated and high interest rates that fed off an economy that was cash poor" (Haas, *Conquest and Historical Identities,* p. 66). The end result, as noted by Albert Camarillo, is that "by 1870 many once wealthy rancheros had been reduced to subsistence farming on rented land" (Camarillo, *Chicanos in a Changing Society,* p. 37). As more and more Anglos arrived in places like Santa Barbara, "the traditional Mexican pastoral economy was being replaced by Anglo American capitalism" (Camarillo, *Chicanos in a Changing Society,* p. 47). The net effect of this trend was a decline in political power, as well as the relegation to menial occupations of most Spanish speakers in Santa Barbara and elsewhere in California.

Occasionally, they worked as vaqueros . . . and in other related jobs throughout the county. They managed to eke out a living by subsistence gardening and other odd jobs. Significantly, the expansion of agricultural production . . . began creating a demand for a seasonal farm labor force. Likewise, the expanding tourist trade in the city developed a new need for service-worker labor force and construction workers. (Camarillo, *Chicanos in a Changing Society,* p. 51)

In Arizona, according to historian Thomas E. Sheridan, the need to create an effective fighting force against Apache raids mitigated ethnic tensions between Anglos and Spanish speakers through the early 1860s. This need even provided a social setting in which some women of Mexican heritage married Anglos. However, as the menace subsided, land ownership and a struggle for economic control of the Tucson and surrounding areas became divisive issues, creating a cleavage between the former allies. In January 1881, for example, the U.S. Indian Service ordered Mexican ranchers and farmers (who lived on lands that were part of a Papago Indian reservation) off lands that many families had occupied for decades. The economic changes brought about by the entry of a market-driven economy into southern Arizona worked its evil magic here as well as in Texas and California and, in the end "the amount of capital necessary to make a living as a rancher and farmer steadily rose until only the larger, more efficient operations could survive. Most small holdings, Mexican or Anglo, simply could not compete with the land and cattle companies and agricultural development spreading across the region" (Sheridan, *Los Tusconenses,* pp. 70–73).

Ultimately, in Arizona and elsewhere, many of the Spanish-speaking people who lost control of their lands wound up migrating to the developing urban areas of the West. Here, they became "miners, railroad workers, laundresses, or small businessmen. Most, in fact, mastered a number of trades" (Sheridan, *Los Tusconenses,* p. 76).

Finally, there was New Mexico. As Armando C. Alonzo notes, the process of taking away Nuevomexicano lands "consumed more time" (Alonzo, *Tejano Legacy,* pp. 259–260), though it still produced results similar to those noted above. Alonzo mentions four specific causes for the divergence in the New Mexican experience from that of Spanish speakers in other locales: the length of occupation, land grants made to groups, not individuals, the same lands being granted on more than one occasion to settlers, and finally, the property rights of preexisting Pueblo communities. Nuevomexicano landowners had held their land longer; land grants there were made to groups, not individuals, and groups had more power to resist; settlers were granted the same lands more than once, giving them a greater chance of having legal proof of the grant; and communities of Pueblo Indians sometimes had preexisting rights to the land.

These factors combined to slow down the process of land loss, but at the same time they contributed to turning U.S. adjudication of *mercedes* (land grants) into a legal conundrum filled with endless possibilities for lawyerly chicanery and thievery. In addition, the inexactness of grants during both the Spanish and Mexican eras further contributed to a chaotic situation. All told, scholars have estimated that the Nuevomexicanos lost control of approximately 80 percent of their lands. The expenses and time involved in lengthy and Byzantine legal proceedings drained much of the landowners' economic reserves and weakened their ability to compete in the new commercial order. The stage was then set, with the removal of the old elite, for the advent of a new economic arrangement and, as historian Sarah Deutsch notes in her work, *No Separate Refuge: Culture, Class and Gender on an Anglo Hispanic Frontier, 1880–1940*, this change had a dramatically negative impact on the lives of Hispanic men and women (by forcing them into wage labor) and on the village life that many Nuevomexicanos had held so dear.

While the process of land dispossession helped limit the influence of the Hispanic population in the West, the development taking place in the region eventually served as a magnet that attracted millions of unskilled Mexicanos to areas now populated not only by fellow Spanish speakers, but by an increasing numbers of Anglos and other groups. In order to fill the labor requirements of the industries developing in the U.S. West, owners of capital eventually instituted a dual wage system. "The top tier consisted of managerial positions and skilled work and was the domain of white workers. The bottom tier consisted of arduous but unskilled, low paying jobs. . . . This bottom tier was disproportionately the domain of nonwhite workers" (White, *"It's Your Misfortune,"* p. 282). It was in this bottom that many Americans saw Chinese, Japanese, and Filipino workers as fitting, and ultimately, native born Spanish speakers and Mexicanos.

The cumulative effect of these trends was to severely curtail the possibility of Hispanics in the West being able to bring to reality the fantasy that the region supposedly would reward with economic prosperity all who would work hard. The net result was that the majority of Spanish-speaking men and women wound up ensnared in low-paying jobs that provided little in the way of upward mobility.

With this brief overview of the major economic changes and their impact upon Hispanics in the West by the late nineteenth century, we can now turn our attention to the arrival of large numbers of Mexicanos (and Puerto Ricans as well) in the region during the last years of the 1800s and the early decades of the twentieth century.

MIGRATION INTO THE WEST

In his research on the economic transformation of Texas (especially the southern part of the state), David Montejano argues that, by the end of the nineteenth century, many Anglos who helped destroy much of the commercial and political power of the Tejano elite were themselves confronting the substantial weight of market forces. The ranchos that many of these people now owned had to struggle through the dramatic cycles of a capitalist economy, just as Spanish speakers had in years previous. Still, the new landowners had investment options usually not available to Hispanics and it was "against the backdrop of fluctuating and discouraging cattle and cotton prices [that there] were hopeful signs of new possibilities" (Montejano, *Anglos and Mexicans in the Making of Texas*, p. 106). Among the potentialities was the development of commercial agriculture.

Montejano cites the story of a turn-of-the-century farmer in Dimmit County who planted Bermuda onions and realized a profit of about one thousand dollars per acre, whereas many of his neighbors working with cotton earned profits of less than fifteen dollars per acre. Financial recompense such as this, as well as the effective promotion of the St. Louis, Brownsville and Mexico Railway, eventually attracted thousands of farmers (many from the Midwest) to South Texas. While the rewards for Anglos able to invest in such new developments were often quite high, for the people of Mexican descent this trend signaled the end of a difficult era of land loss and accommodation to a new order, and the commencement of an even harsher one, during which the overwhelming majority of

Spanish speakers in the southern section of the Lone Star State endured relegation to agricultural labor and to being "treated as an inferior race, segregated into their own town quarters and refused admittance at restaurants, picture shows, bathing beaches, and so on" (Montejano, *Anglos and Mexicans in the Making of Texas,* p. 114).

Commercial agriculture in the West obviously was not limited to the southern section of Texas. With the passage of the Newlands Reclamation Act of 1902, millions of acres in the region in time came under cultivation, eventually turning many formally arid areas into rich, productive farmlands. As we will detail briefly below, large portions of western states and territories began producing an enormous variety of foodstuffs during the later part of the nineteenth and the early decades of the twentieth century. As the level of production developed, it generated enormous demand for menial laborers.

At first, farmers attempted to use native white labor to fill this need, and later they turned to Asians such as Chinese, Japanese, and Filipinos to work these crops. With the passage of the 1882 Chinese Exclusion Act and the Gentlemen's Agreement of 1908, which further restricted the procurement of Chinese labor, however, along with the "unfortunate" propensity of Filipinos to join unions and of the Japanese to buy land and strike out on their own, it became necessary for farmers to seek hired hands elsewhere. Ultimately, in the estimation of many commercial farmers, the Spanish-speaking peon was viewed as the perfect worker; peons worked hard, were "happy" with little pay, and could return to their homeland (the term used to describe these men and women was "birds of passage") once their arduous tasks were completed. The need for such laborers helped direct the steps of hundreds of thousands of people of Mexican descent to the various states of the U.S. West.

Similar incentives brought the first substantial number of Puerto Ricans to parts of the U.S. West (Hawaii and California) in 1900. The circumstances that led members of the Hawaiian Sugar Plantation Association (HSPA) to seek labor on the Caribbean island were threefold: first, Hawaii enacted a Chinese Exclusion Act in 1886, and second, the fact that Puerto Rico became a U.S. possession in 1898 made it easier to bring workers from what was now one part of the country to another, and finally, the HSPA feared the potential labor activity among the

Japanese workers then toiling on the islands. For the Puerto Ricans, the expedition to Hawaii seemed a positive opportunity. After all, things were quite difficult at home. First, the American invasion in 1898 had aborted many Puerto Ricans' nationalist aspirations, and next a hurricane hit the island in August of 1899, which utterly ruined both the coffee and subsistence crops. By the turn of the century, conditions were such that the HSPA mounted a total of eleven labor expeditions between November of 1900 and August of 1901. After an arduous one-month journey, a trip during which some in the group abandoned the expedition in San Francisco (the genesis of the California Puerto Rican community), the first group of Puerto Ricans arrived in Honolulu on December 23, 1900.

In addition to agricultural labor, large numbers of Hispanics also worked in two other major western industries, mining and transportation (railroads). In the following sections, we will focus on the stories of *traqueros* (track workers) and *mineros* (miners) and on daily life in many different "Mexican" mining districts throughout Arizona, New Mexico, Utah, Nevada, and elsewhere. In addition, we will follow the exploits (and detail the exploitation) of track workers throughout the West, especially the Southwest. At this point, however, it is necessary to present only a brief overview of the story of these workers and their families, and scholar Ronald Takaki's *A Different Mirror: A History of Multicultural America* provides an effective synopsis.

The story of the treatment of these employees is one of repression, but also of hope. Many Mexicanos, seeking opportunity and refuge from the suffering, brutality, and bloodshed of the Mexican Revolution came to el norte seeking a better life. The illusions of improved conditions often began to fade as soon as the immigrants arrived in El Paso, Texas, home base of large numbers of *contratistas,* or *enganchistas* (literally, contractors, people who "hooked up" employers with employees). These contractors advised the recien llegados (recent arrivals) of opportunities for employment with companies in agriculture, mining, and transportation. On many occasions, the tremendous power that contratistas held over their "clients" lead to outrageous abuses. Contractors would often withhold pay, charge obscene amounts for room and board and transportation, and even charge for driving workers to Sunday mass.

The abuses of the enganchistas were not the only predicaments that the railroad workers and miners faced on their jobs. As Takaki notes, they always faced a dual wage system, limited opportunity for advancement, debt peonage, appalling living conditions (sometimes living in old railroad cars), and abysmal working circumstances. In what follows, Takaki describes one California mine:

> To bring the ore to the surface, each worker carried a two-hundred-pound pack strapped to his shoulders and forehead. Their nerves straining and muscles quivering, hundreds of these carriers ascended perpendicular steps . . . in darkness lit by candles on the walls. Emerging into the daylight at the entrance of the mine, they deposited their burdens into cars and then took time to smoke their cigarros before descending again. (Takaki, *A Different Mirror,* p. 186)

The overview presented in Takaki's materials gives us a general picture of the conditions that the newly arrived Mexicanos, as well as the Tejanos, Californios, and Nuevomexicanos, endured during the years from 1880 to 1930. Now, we turn to an examination of the dispersal of Hispanics (attracted by various industries) and provide specific examples of the types of work and circumstances faced by Spanish-speaking workers in places all over the region under study.

"DOING THE DIFFICULT JOBS": HISPANIC DISPERSAL (1900–1930)

Beginning in the late 1980s, many historians who study the experience of Mexicans in the U.S. West argued that, though it was necessary to focus upon the states with the largest Spanish-surnamed populations in the West, such as Texas and California, such narratives did not account for the totality of the Mexicano experience in the region. Clearly, there were barrios in other places, and it was necessary to scrutinize the "specific texture of American society" (Saragoza, "Recent Chicano Historiography," p. 45) (and the role of Mexicanos in them) in such locales in order to produce a fuller picture of the Mexican historical experience in the United States. Fortunately, during the past fifteen to twenty years, a number of scholars have taken up this important call and generated articles and monographs detailing life in some of the "unlikely" places where Hispanics have toiled and fought to claim their share of the American dream, supposedly easy to realize in the West.

In the following pages, we provide brief summaries of the industries that attracted *trabajadores* (workers) into places with long-standing Hispanic communities, but we also examine how and why Spanish speakers began migrating to locales that had few if any *compadres* (relatives or close friends can both be called "compadres") prior to the arrival of early twentieth-century *traqueros, mineros, betabeleros* (beet workers), and other laborers.

We turn first to the states with the largest preexisting Hispanic populations: Texas, California, Arizona, and New Mexico (including southern Colorado). Given the economic changes detailed above, what specific industries attracted additional Hispanics into these states between the years 1900 and 1930? What conditions did they face once there? Next, we branch out to discuss the genesis of Mexicano (and Puerto Rican) pockets in the following localities: Hawaii, Minnesota, Montana, Nevada, Oregon, Utah, and Wyoming. The number of states with pockets will increase as we go further into the twentieth century. One final note is necessary, however, before we begin our discussion of the "nontraditional" locales: the amount and quality of information regarding the Hispanic experience in these states varies. For some, scholars have generated books and important articles regarding the Hispanic population, and where that is the case, we will present examples of individuals and their struggles and successes; other places, however, have received limited or no scholarly attention. For these we will rely upon governmental (federal, state, and local) and other reports that provide basic statistical information, with little in the way of histories of specific individuals and communities.

TEXAS

Between 1900 and 1930, an estimated 686,000 Mexicans immigrated legally into the United States. A large number of these individuals headed to the Lone Star State, and their arrival produced much discussion regarding both the potential advantages and the drawbacks, for the state's economy and society, of this newly arrived population stream. Given the economic changes we have described, there were certain elements (particularly the large growers and their cronies) in Texas who asserted that the Mexican peon was vital to commercial expansion. David Montejano quotes one of these business leaders as saying that he and his cohorts simply could not find sufficient numbers of whites willing to perform this type of work for the wages offered: "'A lot of white men would come down from the north and set onions, but they can't do it at Mexican prices, and we can't afford to pay more at the present prices of onions'" (Montejano, *Anglos and Mexicans in the Making of Texas,* p. 183).

Neil Foley, in his work, *The White Scourge: Mexicans, Blacks and Poor Whites in Texas Cotton Culture,* makes a similar argument and notes that many cotton farmers preferred Mexicans to "poor white trash" because the former did not demand good treatment; additionally, Mexicans worked for far less than did whites or African Americans. Therefore, if "progress" was to continue, it was necessary to have relatively open borders with our neighbor to the South. Also, some businessmen intimated, Mexicans embodied certain essential qualities that made them ideal workers. As one Nueces County producer argued, "'You can't beat them as labor. I prefer the Mexican labor to the other classes of labor. It is more humble and you get more for your money. The Mexicans have a sense of duty and loyalty, and the qualities that go to make a good servant'" (Montejano, *Anglos and Mexicans in the Making of Texas,* p. 183).

Though commercial farmers considered these workers "good," in the sense that they were supposedly docile yet productive, that did not mean that elite whites were thrilled to have people that some considered "'somewhere between a burro and a human'" (Montejano, *Anglos and Mexicans in the Making of Texas,* p. 187) living among them. Still, when push came to shove, economic interests, as well as a belief that Mexicanos could be controlled, superceded most farmers' concerns about having such "others" residing in Texas. Montejano quotes one farmer who sums up this assessment succinctly by stating that he viewed Mexicans as an "'inferior race.' But principles are one thing and interests another, noted the farmer: 'My principles rule my selfishness, but I am kind of weak on that. We need them and they need us'" (Montejano, *Anglos and Mexicans in the Making of Texas,* p. 187).

Mexican laborers picking Texas cotton, 1919. Workers from Mexico became a major source of labor for this and other Texas industries beginning in the 1910s. (Bettmann/Corbis)

On the other hand, some elements of Texas society expressed major trepidation about this burgeoning group, namely, union and nonunion workers and whites with nativist concerns. Again, Montejano's and Foley's works provide overviews. Many poor whites opposed the growth of the Mexican population because they were losing their positions as tenant farmers, as landowners moved steadily to replace them with cheaper Mexican labor during the 1910s and 1920s. The sense of threat from the new arrivals was not confined to Anglo agricultural laborers. Montejano, describing the efforts of American Federation of Labor (AFL) recruiters in oil fields and elsewhere in Texas, states that organizers noted that, during the 1910s and 1920s, Mexicans were moving into other industries, such as oil field labor and construction. The reaction to this trend was nearly unanimous. "In Texas, the state chapter of the AFL refused to recognize the existence of a wage-earning class in agriculture, and its various affiliates made it clear that they would not work alongside Mexicans and that they opposed the hiring of unskilled Mexican workers" (Montejano, *Anglos and Mexicans in the Making of Texas*, p. 189).

Research by Emilio Zamora for his dissertation, "Mexican Labor Activity in Texas, 1900–1920," provides numerous instances of such attitudes and the actions associated with them. Zamora's extensive use of union archives, on both sides of the border, details both the negative feelings of American labor officials toward Mexicans, as well as how Mexicanos, therefore, "looked toward Mexico for influence and support" (Zamora, "Mexican Labor Activity in South Texas, 1900–1920," p. 11). Additionally, this study examines some of the other occupational fields (besides migrant work in agriculture) that attracted Mexican labor to Texas during 1900–1930. Zamora notes that native-born people of Mexican descent, as well as immigrants, worked in industries (both in urban and rural areas of the state) such as railroads (where they made up the majority of the work and maintenance crews that built lines in South Texas and elsewhere), land clearing, construction (such as public works and building maintenance), pecan shelling (both at home and in factories), and cigar and hat making. In regard to the specific jobs that Mexicanos and Mexican Americans performed, the patterns noted regarding Spanish-surnamed laborers elsewhere in the West are quite evident in various Texas industries:

> The better paying and more skilled jobs were reserved for Anglos. The Freeport Sulphur Works and the Freeport Chemical Works placed its Mexican workforce in laboring occupations. Mexican dock and construction workers in Galveston and oil workers in Fort Worth also worked as laborers for a lower wage. Mexican railway workers from Big Springs were largely laborers receiving low wages. In San Angelo, Mexican railway laborers earned $1.75 for a ten-hour day, while Anglos earned about $2.00 for an eight-hour day. (Zamora, "Mexican Labor Activity in South Texas, 1900–1920," pp. 43–44)

Everywhere in the Lone Star State, persons of Mexican descent endured difficult working conditions, low wages, and hostility from whites who feared for their jobs. Again, Zamora provides an effective summary of the forms that hostility took:

> Anglo workers organized public meetings and wrote letters that threatened violence if they (supervisors) hired Mexicans in the public works

systems. (Zamora, "Mexican Labor Activity in South Texas, 1900–1920," pp. 58–59)

Clearly, during these years, the ultimate goal of many white workers in the state was the expulsion of Mexican laborers, who, they felt, lowered wages and the standards for working conditions.

In addition to the labor situation, there was another major concern of many white Texans: how to deal with the large number of these worker's offspring who were entering Texas' educational institutions. Where should the *niños* (children) attend school? More importantly, how much education should they receive? Here, whether one was in favor of open or closed immigration policies, most Texans found common ground; the sons and daughters of Spanish speakers were to receive instruction that limited their knowledge, skills and, it was hoped, their aspirations for greater equality. As one Dimmit County commercial farmer put it: "'Educating the Mexicans is educating them away from the job, away from the dirt. He learns English and wants to be a boss. He doesn't want to grub'" (Montejano, *Anglos and Mexicans in the Making of Texas*, p. 193). Once again, regarding the proper education of their children (and as in the occupational realm), Mexicanos and Mexican Americans found their most strident opponents among, not the Anglo elite, but amid poorer, working-class whites:

> Unlike the confident growers and businessmen, the Anglo workers were quite conscious of having to assert their superiority over the Mexicans. The blunt statement of an American sharecropper was representative: "Why don't we let the Mexicans come to the white school? Because a damned greaser is not fit to sit side of a white girl." A Dimmit County education officer noted . . . "The lower down the white man is the more he will object to the Mexicans. The higher class American knows that going to the same school doesn't imply equality." (Montejano, *Anglos and Mexicans in the Making of Texas*, p. 194)

In sum, the overwhelming majority of Spanish-speaking people in Texas during the years 1900–1930 faced occupational and educational discrimination. They were relegated mostly to menial jobs, and their children were trapped in an educational system that provided them with only the most basic instruction. That pattern, many Anglo Texans believed, should go on in perpetuity. A recent statistical study of Mexicano life in Texas during the late nineteenth and early twentieth centuries sums up these trends by stating: "The disproportionate concentration of Tejanos in the growing unspecialized labor pool was not . . . a necessary outcome of the economic transformation." Rather, it had come about because "Anglos dominated the development of a new commercial economy and permitted Tejanos a niche only in the lowest-level service and general-labor occupations" (Stewart and De León, *Not Room Enough*, p. 97 and 100). How the Spanish-speaking population of the state (and the other states we will examine) lived with and challenged such harsh circumstances will be discussed later in this chapter.

CALIFORNIA

The literature on the arrival of Mexican immigrant laborers in California is extensive, but there are three works, in our estimation, that present among the best and most succinct outlines of this history: George J. Sánchez, *Becoming Mexican American: Ethnicity, Culture and Identity in Chicano Los Angeles, 1900–1945;* Albert Camarillo, *Chicanos in a Changing Society: From Mexican Pueblos to American Barrios in Santa Barbara and Southern California, 1848–1930,* and Douglas Monroy, *Rebirth: Mexican Los Angeles from the Great Migration to the Great Depression.* Therefore, we will use these studies as our primary guides for this portion of the chapter.

The forces that pulled Mexicanos to the Golden State were similar to those described for Texas: in California, the principal engine driving Mexican immigration was, not surprisingly, agriculture. The net effect of this development was that by 1929 "California became the largest producer of fruits and vegetables in the Southwest, a region generating 40 percent of the total United States output. Meanwhile, Mexicans rapidly replaced the Japanese as the major component of the agricultural labor force" (Sánchez, *Becoming Mexican American,* p. 19).

There were two main reasons for this changeover from one ethnic group's labor to another. First, many of the Japanese working in California agriculture showed a propensity for industriousness. This trait had both positive and negative impacts for white-Asian relations in California. While many white landowners appreciated such diligence, their industriousness, coupled with a proclivity for saving and eventually attempting to purchase land, made the Japanese, in the eyes of many whites, too aggressive and difficult to control. This trend resulted in California passing the Alien Land Law in 1913, which was designed to stop such "foreigners" from buying land in the Golden State. Still, due to increased demand for produce and their own assiduousness, some Japanese families and individuals lived out their own version of the Horatio Alger story. In other cases, including one that we will detail later, Japanese workers also displayed a fondness for joining unions, unlike Mexicans who, supposedly, were more easily guided and did their work obediently. Also, some farmers argued, the Mexicans were actually genetically programmed to do stoop labor because "'they are stronger physically than the Japanese, more tractable and more easily managed . . . they are, nevertheless, though unprogressive, intelligent enough to work fairly well under supervision. They apparently fit well on jobs not requiring any great degree of mentality, and they do not object to dirt'" (Monroy, *Mexican Los Angeles*, p. 103).

The Mexicano men, women, and children who came to California toiled in the fields picking walnuts, lemons, and other perishable food products. Their impact on the state's agricultural economy was impressive. Using the strong backs of such persons, and taking advantage of the ideal weather conditions available, commercial farmers of the state dramatically increased their offerings for America's table, as Monroy notes in his study:

> Lettuce production increased from 7.8 million crates in 1921 to 17.4 million crates by 1926; over the same period, asparagus rose from 3.3 million crates to 7.6 million crates; cantaloupes went from 11.5 million crates to 14 million. Between 1915 and 1926 the orange crop grew from 21.2 million boxes to 33.9 million boxes; lemons swelled from 880,000 boxes in 1899 to 6.6 million boxes in 1919; canned soups and fruits increased from 51.7 and 9.5 million cases, respectively, in 1914 to 101 and 25.9 million cases, respectively, in 1925. (Monroy, *Mexican Los Angeles*, p. 97)

In addition to cultivation, there were other fields that attracted Mexicano labor: railroads (both track and equipment maintenance), county and private street paving, construction, fruit packing and processing, domestic work, and clerical retail positions (mostly for women). Once again, in these varied occupational positions, Mexicanos encountered much discrimination and difficult working conditions:

> The California Immigration Commission of 1910 bluntly reported that Mexican railroad workers generally earned 25 percent less than non Mexicans. "Foremen said," according to this Bureau of Labor researcher, "that Mexicans did as much work as men of either of the other nationalities, and that the discrimination in wages was due to arbitrary orders issued from headquarters by men who had no practical knowledge of the efficiency of different kinds of workers." (Monroy, *Mexican Los Angeles,* pp. 99–100)

As in Texas, many whites in California expressed grievous concerns about the arrival of large numbers of Mexicanos in their midst. Monroy's work, like some of the studies noted in the Texas section, cites the words and attitudes of union leaders, white workers, and persons concerned about the possibility of race mixing. The issues are similar to those previously presented: Representatives of the AFL were primarily concerned with the threat posed by new competitors for jobs; social commentators expressed outrage at the possibility of Mexicans intermarrying with whites; social workers noted the lack of sanitation that, supposedly, Mexicans did not mind living with; and various voices expressed trepidation over "their" propensity for consuming alcohol and the purported violence and revolutionary tendencies that Mexicanos carried in their blood. In sum, as in the Lone Star State, Spanish speakers faced lives of relentless toil and limited economic and social prospects, hardly the stuff of opportunity associated with the legends of the West as the land of opportunity.

Before leaving the Golden State, however, it is necessary to provide a brief summary of the arrival of Puerto Ricans. As we noted above, a Hawaiian sugar consortium mounted a series of labor recruitment drives in Puerto Rico during 1900 and 1901. The boriquas who agreed to work in Hawaii were promised good travel and working conditions, but their trip was arduous indeed, and some began to doubt the veracity of the employers' claims. One scholar who has examined this voyage, Nitza C. Medina, notes that the volunteers were informed that the trip would take two weeks, whereas in reality the voyage took almost one month. Also, while riding on trains through the West, some of the Puerto Ricans managed to make contact (even though they were accompanied by armed guards) with Mexicanos or Mexican Americans who informed the travel-weary *islanderos* that similar, or even better, wages were available on the mainland. Finally, Medina suggests, "some of the migrants may not have appreciated the distance" between the islands (Medina, "Rebellion in the Bay: California's First Puerto Ricans," p. 85).

When this unfortunate group arrived in San Francisco on December 14, 1900, many of the migrants on board the trains attracted the attention of passersby and claimed that they were being taken to Hawaii as slaves. Eventually, as handlers were attempting to move them from the railroad cars to the ship that would take them to their final destination, approximately fifty-five men, women, and children escaped. Many in the San Francisco area had pity on the stranded Puerto Ricans and took groups into their homes. Eventually, most (both men and women) of working age became domestics and spread out into neighboring counties. Additionally, during the 1900s and 1910s, other groups of Puerto-rriqueños began arriving in California after working as farm laborers in Arizona. As we will detail later, by 1911 some of the islanders began constructing their own organizations in California, dedicated to maintaining a unique culture in a setting far, far away from their motherland.

ARIZONA

Whereas agriculture was the main attraction drawing Mexicanos into Texas and California during the years 1900–1930, in Arizona mining (copper, silver, and gold) was the main economic pull for Spanish speakers. Other significant sectors included railroads, working on cattle ranches, sheep herding, and later (especially during the years of World War I), the cotton crop. These segments of the Arizona economy required people willing to work hard for very little money, and as we have seen, in many places of the U.S. West during this era, people from Mexico or of Mexican descent fit this requirement nicely.

According to historian Thomas E. Sheridan, the development of Arizona's mineral wealth could not take place until the pacification of the Apaches and the completion of railroad connections linking the territory to the rest of the nation. When track laying began in Arizona in November of 1878, the Chinese made up the majority of the labor force. One census survey (in 1880) counted 853 Chinese laborers at a particular railroad camp, while Mexicanos numbered only 43 (Sheridan, *Arizona: A History,* p. 123). Still, the pattern noted by scholars who have studied the economic history of the West eventually came to Arizona, and the Mexicano peon ultimately became the preferred labor.

With railroad connections established by the early 1880s, investors from various parts of the world could then begin the process of reaping Arizona's mineral wealth. The development of mining camps in various locations of the territory attracted miners, not only from the United States, but also from China and eastern and southern Europe. Ultimately, by the early 1880s, Sheridan notes, the whites and Spanish speakers formed an alliance that drove the Chinese out of the camps.

If the miners of Mexican background believed that this allegiance had earned them the right to be treated as equals, they were sadly mistaken, as the two ethnic partners spent the next five decades in bloody conflict. As the number of Mexicanos increased (growing from roughly 14,000 to almost 30,000 between 1900 and 1910), tensions escalated. The results were not unanticipated: Mexicans were completely eliminated from some districts (such as Globe-Miami); others (such as Clifton-Morenci) allowed large numbers of Mexicans to work, but segregated employees by occupation (with the whites getting most of the supervisory positions) as well as into "Mexican" and "white" sections of the communities. In regard to pay levels, again, the Spanish speakers got short shrift: "During the 1890s the lowest wage in the Old Dominion and other Globe-Miami mines was $3.00 a day. In Clifton-Morenci, Mexicans received $1.75 to $2.00 for a ten-hour shift. The difference in wages only increased after the turn of the century" (Sheridan, *Arizona: A History,* p. 170).

By the early 1910s, with the completion of the Roosevelt Dam, commercial farmers in the Salt River Valley began cultivating hundreds of thousands of acres, producing alfalfa, wheat, and many other crops. Then the economic impact of World War I, plus a British embargo on long-staple cotton, encouraged U.S. tire companies (which used this product for tires and fabric for airplane wings) to seek new sources of this staple. By 1917 Goodyear had more than 1,500 acres of cotton under production. Further price increases before 1920 generated near land rush conditions in Arizona, which ultimately brought more than 200,000 acres under cultivation.

These farmers needed workers, and an estimated 30,000 Mexicans (including Yaqui Indians from Sonora) came to work the fields.

Not surprisingly, the men, women, and children at these work camps faced difficult circumstances: "Most pickers lived in camps unfit for animals. They slept in tents or overcrowded shacks. They drank from canals. They had no showers, no laundry facilities, and no electricity. Some camps did not even have running water or outhouses" (Sheridan, *Arizona: A History,* p. 215).

In sum, the story in Arizona is similar to that of Texas and California: When conditions warranted, the capitalists who dominated the state's most important industries called for, and often procured, enormous numbers of Mexican laborers. Once these hardworking people arrived, they were mistreated, were made to live in filthy conditions, and endured discriminatory wages.

COLORADO AND NEW MEXICO

Historical geographer William Wyckoff's recent work, *Creating Colorado: The Making of a Western American Landscape, 1860–1940*, provides an effectual summation of the thinking behind our decision to consider the story of Hispanics in these two states in one section. In his chapter on the southern periphery of the Centennial State, Wyckoff argues that "a bit of political geography" (when creating the Colorado territory in 1861) is responsible for cutting the San Luis Valley off from its ancestral ties in New Mexico. This partition generated northern and southern Spanish-speaking settlement "lobes" that retained economic and cultural linkages. It was into these segments of a regional community that Anglos and other whites brought railroad lines, commercial agriculture, and mining operations during the years 1880–1930.

The impact of this economic metamorphosis on the lives the Spanish-speaking peoples of northern New Mexico and southern Colorado has received much attention. In addition to Wyckoff, scholars such as Richard Nostrand and Sarah Deutsch have generated works that examine the daily lives and economic hardships endured by the Spanish speakers of this area. We will draw upon them in our overview.

In the San Luis Valley, Hispanics traditionally (prior to the 1860s) depended upon the cultivation of staple crops, such as corn and beans, plus sheep grazing in order to support themselves. The arrival of the Denver and Rio Grande Railroad in the valley in 1877 united the region to other parts of the state, as well as to the broader national economy. The connections attracted the attention of a variety of settlers, such as Mormons, who, by the 1880s, "lived in their farm villages and commuted daily to their nearby fields. . . . the Mormons developed agricultural surpluses that were marketed commercially elsewhere in the state" (Wycoff, *Creating Colorado,* p. 199). Later, the valley also attracted contingents of Swedish, German, French, and Dutch colonists as well.

Wyckoff argues that, at the outset, the newer elements in Conejos County brought economic and cultural diversity into the valley and that initially many "Hispano farmers and ranchers selectively profited from the more commercial agricultural economy even as they held on to many of their basic ethnic and religious values" (Wycoff, *Creating Colorado,* p. 200). But, alas, as we have seen in other cases, such benefits were not to last. With the arrival of more and more Anglos, conditions worsened. Some of the forces that brought about changes in agriculture are familiar to the reader by now and included increased expenses associated with new irrigation technology, lack of access to capital, and loss of lands (which limited the Hispanos' ability to take care of their sheep). All of these factors made it more difficult for Spanish speakers to survive and maintain their economic independence, and so many began to turn to wage labor, including toiling for farmers involved in commercial agriculture. The makeover was dramatic indeed, and by the end of the nineteenth century, much of the valley had come under the influence of capitalist cultivation, with impressive results:

> Among food crops, wheat, barley, and oats became much more significant after 1885. By 1900 more than sixty thousand valley acres were in wheat. The biggest success story was the cultivation of potatoes, which after 1895 became focused near Monte Vista and Del Norte in the western valley. Huge increases in regional and national demand came with the strong markets of the Spanish-American War in 1898 and 1899. Another surge occurred during World War I, and by 1917 more than eleven thousand acres produced an impressive 1.7 million bushels of the crop, much of it harvested by [Colorado and New Mexico native] Hispano labor (Wycoff, *Creating Colorado,* p. 204).

Although so far we have focused specifically on the San Luis Valley of Colorado, historian Sarah Deutsch's work notes similar patterns in northern New Mexico. By the early 1900s, she asserts, the possibility of independent economic survival for Spanish speakers had become quite grim, and most "Hispanic villagers had not even the choice of trying to survive and accommodate . . . [and] had to seek other modes of subsistence and expansion, other strategies" (Deutsch, *No Separate Refuge*, p. 31). These new survival tactics included, not surprisingly, an expanded reliance upon wage labor in transportation, mining, and commercial agriculture.

Deutsch notes that by 1880, when railroad tracks reached Albuquerque and Santa Fe, other lines had already cut through other parts of the Colorado and New Mexico Hispanic homeland. As we have discussed previously, most laborers on the railroads of Mexican descent were confined to maintenance work, the lowest-paying positions available. Still, "even the sectionman's wage of one dollar for a twelve-hour day or about $25 per month compared favorably to shepherd's wages" (Deutsch, *No Separate Refuge*, p. 31).

Another sector that employed laborers from such villages were coal mines in southern Colorado. Places such as Trinidad and Starkville drew Hispanos into the "epitome of turn-of-the-century industrial capitalism" (Wycoff, *Creating Colorado*, p. 215), where conditions were difficult and the pay quite low. Still, "the mines allowed Spanish-American villages to survive long after the erosion of their economic base began. . . . [As] Anglo development created wage jobs . . . Hispanics arrived to take advantage of the new opportunities" (Deutsch, *No Separate Refuge*, p. 32). Such opportunities were not limited to men, and many of these villagers' wives and daughters also found opportunities to earn cash as cooks, boardinghouse keepers, seamstresses, and domestic servants.

A final area of occupational openings in this region was beet sugar work; by the early 1900s villagers were toiling as betabeleros (beet workers) in the areas around the Arkansas River (in southern Colorado) and the South Platte River (in northern Colorado) as well as in the area west of the continental divide, known as the Western Slope. Although the work was quite difficult and the pay low, by 1910 sugar beet work did offer one major advantage: the entire family could work the field and avoid the pain of separation created by the men's departure to toil in mines or for railroads. By the early 1910s, some of these families had left their home villages and begun using Denver as winter quarters, waiting for the new planting and railroad work seasons.

The coming of World War I added yet another layer of complexity to the lives of the Spanish-speaking people of Colorado and New Mexico: the arrival of thousands of Mexican immigrants in their home states. The dramatic increase in demand for labor during the conflict, in addition to a severe drought in northern New Mexico, had pushed even more villagers into the wage labor stream. Then they were joined by many Mexicans who were also looking for work in the mines and smelters, on the railroad tracks, and in the sugar beet fields. By 1920 the Mexican-born population in both states had grown dramatically: to about 11,000 Mexicanos in Colorado and approximately 20,000 in New Mexico. Many of these Mexicans, in addition to taking jobs in rural areas, began concentrating in sections of Denver (such as North Denver and Globeville) alongside their Spanish-speaking (as well as Italian and Polish) neighbors.

The arrival of substantial numbers of recien llegados (recent arrivals) caused a great deal of concern among many Anglos who believed that now these states were being "invaded" by Mexicans. Additionally, as in South Texas and California, many of the whites saw no distinction between the native Spanish speakers and those from below the Rio Grande. Though the U.S.-born Hispano villagers sought to differentiate themselves from the Mexicans (using derisive slang terms such as *surumatos* for the newcomers, while addressing "their" people as *manitos,* short for *hermanitos,* "little brothers"), the net result of this immigration of Mexicans into the Hispano stream was to reduce the standing of native Spanish speakers even more in the view of many Anglos. Sarah Deutsch sums up this trend by stating that:

> Ironically . . . the migrant laborers . . . had a more lasting effect, changing not the villages, but the world into which the villagers could move. The effect was to narrow the boundary of possibilities that the regional community held for its Spanish American participants. Before the war it was still possible that Hispanics . . . could become integrated with Anglo communities at the local level. . . . By the end of the war, the increased scale of migration, the introduction of large numbers of Mexicans into the same jobs and patterns, the labor imperatives of new irri-

gated farming developments, and the general nativist and racist trends among Anglos conspired to ensure that such integration became a virtual impossibility. (Deutsch, *No Separate Refuge,* p. 126)

Having now completed our tour of the largest preexisting Spanish-speaking populations, we now turn briefly to the arrival of Mexican Americans, Mexicanos, and Puerto Ricans in other western states.

HAWAII

An examination of the literature dealing with Hispanics in Hawaii reveals that both Mexicanos and Puertorriqueños have long and significant histories in the state. According to Kyle Ko Francisco Shinseki's thesis, "The Mexican People of Hawai'i: Communities in Formation," there were small numbers of Spanish speakers on the islands as early as the 1830s. Most of the nineteenth-century Spanish-surnamed people living in Hawaii labored as cowboys (referred to locally as *paniolos*). The arrival of Spanish cattle and horses from Alta California in the early nineteenth century (and their prodigious procreation) convinced King Kamehameha III to seek assistance in handling livestock. Among the first to respond was a San Diego native by the name of Joaquín Armas, who arrived in Honolulu in April of 1831. By the late 1850s, Shinseki estimates, "there may have been as many as a couple of hundred, some who stayed for short periods and others who settled permanently" (Shinseki, "El Pueblo Mexicano de Hawai'i," p. 13). Most of these men married native women and "it seems that little if any Mexican culture was passed down through the generations" (Shinseki, "El Pueblo Mexicano de Hawai'i," p. 13). By the 1880s, ranching had become a significant aspect of the Hawaiian economy (in addition to the sugar industry which, as we have seen, attracted Puerto Ricans), and the paniolos worked on the islands of Oahu, Hawaii, Maui, and Kauai. Although the local cattle industry benefited greatly from the labor of Armas and others like him, this business did not generate a substantial flow of immigration from Mexico. Census records from 1930 reveal that fewer than 100 people of Mexican descent lived in Hawaii. The dramatic increase of this population did not occur until after the economic and social changes unleashed on the islands by the coming of World War II.

We have already briefly discussed how the first boriquas came to Hawaii; we now turn to a concise examination of the situation they faced once in Hawaii.

After the initial influx of December 1900, more than 5,200 men, women, and children (including 2869 men and boys over the age of 13) came to live and work in Hawaii by the end of the following year (Días, "A Puerto Rican Poet on the Sugar Plantations of Hawai'i," p. 94 and Camacho Souza, "Trabajo y Tristesa," p. 165). Upon arrival, laborers were dispersed to plantations and encountered both positive and negative circumstances. One encouraging development was the level of pay. Blasé Camacho Souza's research with HSPA records reveals that, initially, the Puerto Ricans earned "$15.00 monthly for the men, 40 cents a day for the women, 50 cents a day for the boys, and 35 cents a day for the girls. Later, for the men, pay included a bonus, usually 50 cents per week if they worked a full 26-day month" (Camacho Souza, "Trabajo y Tristesa," p. 167). In addition, employers provided living quarters and company-subsidized medical care of variable quality. Although this rate of compensation may not have been ideal, it far exceeded the rate in Puerto Rico. On the other hand, the new arrivals also confronted two major problems: first, they were simply deposited in communities were few if any spoke their language and where the "customs were incomprehensible to them" (such as the nude bathing of their Japanese coworkers, which many Puerto Ricans took as an affront to their manhood and as disrespectful of the sensibilities of their wives and children), and second, they received poor treatment from supervisory personnel (which often included field bosses coming into a worker's family quarters and dragging him out of his sickbed). Such occurrences led many boriquas to leave one plantation and seek better terms on another. Additionally, some used passive aggressive measures (such as saying "yes" when they meant "no") in order to challenge the dominance of their employers. These responses caused some in the industry to label Puerto Ricans "unreliable" and "footloose."

Still, sugar planters must have found their abilities acceptable, as by 1930 there were approximately 6,700 individuals of Puerto Rican descent in Hawaii. By then, these men, women, and children had begun constructing their own unique identity (known among their descendants as *Borinki*), which included organizations such as the Puerto Rican Civic Club (1931) and the Puerto Rican Association (1932) with ties to their homeland, while also incorporating intermarriage with Hawaiians and accepting some of their traditions.

MINNESOTA

The sugar beet industry and railroads were crucial in attracting Mexicans and Mexican Americans to Minnesota. In addition, they also found work in foundries, cement plants, and tanneries. In his recent work on barrios of St. Paul (and elsewhere in the Midwest), Dionicio Nodín Valdés notes the significant role that Spanish speakers played in this region and argues that these northerly barrios developed as a result of three separate migrations between 1900 and 1930. At first, railroad companies recruited Mexican labor from the Southwest for track maintenance and repair work. A second, more intensive, phase occurred during the years

A family of betabeleros *working in Minnesota, the far reaches of* el norte, *during the late 1930s. (Corbis)*

of World War I and brought more Spanish speakers to Minnesota and other parts of the Midwest. Finally, after the postwar depression, recruitment picked up as employers, such as the American Beet Sugar Company, attracted families.

Although initially the majority of Mexicanos who ventured to Minnesota were *solos,* by the middle of the 1920s circumstances had changed. Valdés gives the following figures:

> The resident Mexican population . . . centering on East Grand Forks and Albert Lea, was only 27 percent adult males, while the . . . sex ratio was 52 men and 48 women. Minnesota's Mexican population rose rapidly in the late 1920s in response to an increase in sugar beet acreage, which doubled in 1927 alone. . . . That year the resident Mexican population of the state was estimated at five thousand Mexicanos, which increased to seven thousand the following year, a majority residing in rural locations. (Valdés, *Barrios Norteños,* p. 53)

As we have noted, the arrival of women and children improved conditions in barrios and stimulated the purchasing of permanent homes. With such demographic changes, however, the community also faced new problems. For example, the increasing number of Mexican women endured much discrimination in trying to procure employment. Outside of beet field work, Mexicanas could only find work as domestic labor. Spanish-speaking people in the Twin Cities also faced significant difficulties in finding domiciles. Not surprisingly, "Mexicans were confined to the worst sections, often residing in basements, . . . shacks along alleys, and . . . rooms above stores and businesses" (Valdés, *Barrios Norteños,* p. 57). According to local government reports, few of these dwellings had indoor plumbing and electricity and a disproportionately large number of barrio residents suffered from pneumonia, tuberculosis, and other serious ailments.

A final concern for the parents in these developing barrios was the treatment of their children by local schools. To take one example, Valdés notes in his study that one Twin City school official asserted that it was a waste of time to educate Mexican children because they "'are like animals that work the soil. What civilization do [they] have? What business do [they] have in school?'" Such attitudes resulted in lax enforcement of mandatory attendance laws, a failure to provide books for Mexicano children, and the creation of a "special, ungraded" (Valdés, *Barrios Norteños,* pp. 73, 77, and 116) academy for such youths.

MONTANA

The information on the experience of Hispanics in the state of Montana is severely limited, with only a brief report to the state legislature produced in 1980 available. While short on specific stories, it does document a tale similar to that of other western states. The Spanish speakers who came to Montana were concentrated in two industries: beet production (in the western part of the state, specifically, the Bitterroot Valley near Billings) and copper mining in and around Butte.

As a result of increased demand after 1920, various sugar companies, such as the Great Western Sugar Company (GWSC), began focusing on Mexicanos as a potential labor pool. Employers contracted with some of the few local Spanish speakers to act as recruiters in El Paso by 1923. The jobs offered afforded families an opportunity to live in corporate-owned, worker-constructed housing. By 1924 the GWSC had paid for the building of roughly forty dwellings. Solos, on the other hand, tended to congregate at various cheap hotels located on Montana Avenue. During the off-season, many Spanish speakers toiled in nearby factories slicing beets, but others could find no remunerative work. Therefore, in order to survive the bitter Montana winters, many betabelero families took advances on wages, resulting in a kind of debt peonage that kept Mexicanos in the area.

In Butte, the primary employer of Hispanics was Anaconda, which attracted Spanish speakers from New Mexico, as well as Chile and Mexico, to the production of copper ore.

NEVADA

An 1875 census of Nevada counted a total of 311 individuals with Spanish surnames in the territory, according to M. L. Miranda in his book, *A History of Hispanics in Southern Nevada.* Among these were persons from Mexico, Chile, and other nations of Latin America. The count also noted that almost 20 percent of this group hailed from California, New Mexico, and Texas. Nevada's early Hispanics worked mostly as mule packers, miners, agricultural workers, and common laborers. As with so many of the states that we have examined, the impetus for an increase in the Spanish-speaking population of Nevada was the development of the railroad industry, as well as, later, the expansion of mining production. Although Nevada is similar in this regard to other locations in the West, dramatic economic expansion and development took a much longer period of time than elsewhere. Thus, Hispanics in Las Vegas only numbered about 2,300 at the beginning of the 1950s.

The establishment of the San Pedro, Los Angeles, and Salt Lake Railroad (completed in 1905) brought about the beginnings of the town of Las Vegas. Among the estimated 3,000 persons who witnessed this historic event were several Mexican traqueros and their families. Although they were an essential part of completing this enterprise, the Hispanics of early Las Vegas benefited little from their work, earning around $1.25 per day in wages to lay and maintain the line. The town held few occupational opportunities, and by 1910 the census counted only 122 persons of Mexican heritage in Clark County (Miranda, *A History of Hispanics in Southern Nevada,* p. 84). Of this number, there were only three nuclear families.

Although they were relatively few in numbers, the Spanish speakers of southern Nevada faced discrimination in their everyday lives. It was not only that they had little opportunity to rise above track labor; but Miranda's examination of the newspaper coverage presented of Nevada's Spanish speakers during the first decades of the 1900s reveals, not surprisingly, that many in the white population held negative stereotypes (they were considered lazy, shiftless, and dangerous) of their Mexicano neighbors. Conditions for Hispanics in the Las Vegas area did not change much until the years of the New Deal, with the construction of the Hoover Dam, and the development of Nevada's gambling industry.

OREGON

The two individuals who have done the most extensive research on the Hispanic experience in the Pacific Northwest are Richard Slatta and Erasmo Gamboa. These scholars' research reveals that, though there has been a Spanish-speaking presence in Oregon (and also Washington) since the later part of the nineteenth century, it was World War II that "was the turning point in Mexican migration" (Gamboa, "Mexican Migration into

Washington State," p. 121) to Oregon and other parts of the Pacific Northwest. The demands of American agriculture and the consequent arrival of thousands of braceros during the 1940s provided the major impetus for the growth and development of communities of Spanish speakers. Therefore, our coverage of this area in this chapter will be brief, and we will detail the expansion of this population more thoroughly in the following chapter.

Mexican vaqueros helped establish and develop the early cattle and sheep industries in Oregon. Slatta's research notes that, as early as 1872, there were mounted Mexicanos working on the P-Ranch in Harney County. Some of these men worked on this spread for "year after year, liking the location and their boss more and more" (Slatta, "Chicanos in the Pacific Northwest," p. 328). In addition, other research by Gamboa indicates that, by the turn of the twentieth century, "Oregon's proximity to California encouraged Hispanics to come to the state. . . . In the years after World War I, Hispanic families from New Mexico and Colorado lived in Nyssa and worked farms in that area of the state" (Gamboa, *Nosotros: The Hispanic People of Oregon*, p. 12). Thus, although small in numbers, Hispanics were a presence in Oregon by 1930.

UTAH

While the Mormon pioneers came to the Salt Lake Valley seeking sanctuary for their spiritual beliefs during the 1840s and 1850s, they were not able, ultimately, to keep out elements of U.S. society that wished to integrate the territory's valuable mineral deposits into the nation's capitalist economy. By the late 1890s, therefore, the Beehive State had a developing economy based on transportation, extractive industries (primarily copper mining), and commercial agriculture (most importantly, the production of sugar beets). As in other locations throughout the U.S. West, immigrants filled much of the labor needs of the various operations. At first, the majority of laborers, especially in mining, hailed from the British Isles, Sweden, Italy, and Greece, but following a 1912 strike at the Bingham Canyon mines, as noted by Jorge Iber in his book *Hispanics in the Mormon Zion 1912–1999*, employers such as Utah Copper began to import Spanish-surnamed workers from Mexico and other parts of the West.

Mexicano section gang, Rio Grande Railroad, Utah, 1940s. (Utah History Research Center)

DOMITILA RIVERA MARTINEZ AND INCARNACION VILLAREAL ESCOBEDO FLOREZ: RELIGIOUS LEADERS IN SALT LAKE CITY, UTAH

Some of the historical research mentioned in this chapter details the important roles of Mexicanas in the spiritual life of their communities. Often, the women in barrios served in nontraditional leadership roles in churches and religious organizations, as well as filling the important responsibilities of *curanderas,* providing spiritual and medical aid to families, friends, and neighbors. In researching the Hispanic community in the Salt Lake City area, Jorge Iber came across the stories of two women, Incarnacion Florez and Domitila Rivera, who filled such roles, serving as pillars to the Catholics and Mormons of the west side barrio during the 1920s and into the difficult years of the Great Depression.

The Florez family arrived in Salt Lake City in the 1910s. The patriarch of the clan, Reyes Florez, worked for the Denver and Rio Grande Line, and he and his wife Incarnacion and their children lived in an old boxcar provided by the company. Not surprisingly, conditions were difficult, and disease and death stalked the family's existence (nine of the couple's twelve children died during childhood). The family's domicile was located a mere twenty feet from the railroad tracks that Reyes helped maintain for the D and RG, and Incarnacion Florez fought a never ending battle to keep the quarters free of dirt and dust. Although the family was poor, she worked fervently to instill in her surviving children pride in their ethnic heritage, and she also provided valuable services to the less fortunate of the community. One of the couple's sons, John Florez (who is now an important political figure in Salt Lake City), recalls that, on many occasions, his mother helped persons who were in worse financial circumstances by handing out food from the family's meager resources from the door of the box car.

Another way in which Incarnacion Florez served the *comunidad* was through her talents in *curanderismo,* which has been described as "a combination of folk medicine and faith healing. To some it is all one or the other, but most curanderos/as combine a knowledge of herbal remedies with liberal doses of prayer and religious/superstitious ritual" (Benavides, "Curanderismo in Utah," pp. 373–392). Curanderismo was a very positive thing for most people in the Mexican-American community. Mrs. Florez did much to help her barrio through such efforts, and her fame eventually spread throughout Utah and into the adjoining states. She never advertised but practiced her art for a large clientele until her death in 1968. John recalls that many of his mother's clients came to her only when faced with dire circumstances, when diseases were well advanced and there was little chance for recovery. Sometimes her combination of Catholic and folk rituals and herbal remedies worked; at other times, the religious element of her work took precedence and provided some succor to both the individual approaching death and the family. Thus through her use of traditional medicine and religious ritual, Incarnacion Florez offered many Spanish speakers in the Salt Lake City area physical, emotional, and spiritual help.

The life and work of Domitila (or Tila, as she was also known) Rivera provide another example of a Mexican woman filling an important religious role. Tila Rivera was born in Chimalhuacan in 1898, and during the late 1910s, she, along with her mother and sisters (Agustina and Dolores), converted to the Church of Jesus Christ of Latter-day Saints (LDS). Tila's father did not approve of this conversion, and he constantly reminded his daughters that they would be branded as outcasts in predominantly Catholic Mexico. Though this was a concern, the clan had even greater reasons for trepidation, as, during the late 1910s, the Mexican Revolution raged around the family's residence. Amid all the chaos, Tila's parents somehow raised enough money to send their daughters to the United States; given the young women's religious affiliation, it was logical for them to move to the central location of Mormon life, Salt Lake City.

In the later years of the 1910s, Utah's sugar beet industry grew dramatically, and eventually it employed many thousands of Mexicano workers. One firm, the Utah-Idaho Sugar Company (UISC), recruited approximately 2,000 individuals to work in their fields. Shortly after Tila's arrival in the state, a church official approached the sisters and asked if they would minister to the Mexican beet workers employed by UISC in the nearby Box Elder County. During 1919 and 1920, Domitila and her siblings spread their faith among the betabeleros, and by early 1921, their efforts had helped to establish a 100-person congregation attending Spanish-language LDS services in the capital city. In 1923 the LDS hierarchy officially renamed the group the *Rama Mexicana* (the Mexican Branch).

This organization of worshippers eventually provided many services to the *Mormones* (and others) who resided in the west side barrio of Salt Lake City. The Rama was a spiritual center, as well as a hub for social activities, job information, and networking. Tila and the other Rivera sisters, for example, all met their future husbands at church-sponsored events. Within the congregation, women such as Domitila, Agustina, and Dolores all held a variety of leadership positions. For example, all three were officers in two of the most important groups within an individual LDS church (known as a *ward*); the *Sociedad de Socorro* (Relief Society) and the *Asociación de Mejoramiento Mutuo* (Mutual Improvement Association). Both of these organizations benefited the needy in the barrio and worked to attract converts to their faith. Between the early 1920s and through the early 1960s, the Rivera sisters, their husbands, their children, and other relatives and friends formed the mainstay of the Mexican Branch. This organization continues the work of the Riveras to this day (although it is now known as the Lucero (Bright Star) Ward). Domitila, after a lifetime of service to her faith and community, died in 1979.

Thus, thanks to the extensive efforts of women such as Incarnacion Florez and Domitila Rivera Martínez, the Spanish-speaking people of Salt Lake City, regardless of their religious affiliation, had help in facing the difficulties in life.

The overwhelming majority of these individuals laid track for the giant machinery that stripped the canyon in search of ore. Spanish speakers also toiled in the Cache Valley (and elsewhere), performing the difficult tasks associated with the production of sugar beets. In addition, a small community of Hispanics settled in southern Utah, working as cowboys, sheepherders, and unskilled farm laborers. Finally, the last employment sector drawing numbers of Hispanics to Utah was the railroad industry, which employed gangs of traqueros to maintain the lines that serviced the state's other industries. By 1930, such employment opportunities combined to attract a total of roughly 4,000 native-born Mexicans to Utah. Although there existed a dramatic sexual imbalance (men outnumbered women by 2 to 1) at this time, "the number of families increased dramatically (more than 1,000 of these persons were children under the age of ten)" (Iber, *Hispanics in the Mormon Zion*, p. 15). Thus, by the end of the era covered in this chapter, a discernable comunidad (community) existed on the west side of town in both Salt Lake City and Ogden (not surprisingly, near the railroad depots of each city) as well as in other locations throughout the state.

In addition to the attraction of jobs, there was another significant draw for Spanish-speaking people to the Beehive State: the presence of the Church of Jesus Christ of Latter-day Saints. The Mormons, from the early years of the twentieth century, worked diligently to convert not only Native Americans but mestizos to their faith. The reason for this trend is that the church considers them to be the descendants of Jews who migrated to the North American continent around the year AD 600 and, until the "remnants" of these people (referred to by the Mormons as Lamanites) are fully "gathered" to the church, the millennial kingdom of Christ cannot begin. Thus, by the 1920s three Mexican sisters—

Domitila, Agustina, and Dolores Rivera (from Chimalhuacan)—and three Hispanic men—Juan Ramón Martínez, Francisco Solano, and Margarito Bautista—were living in Salt Lake City and traveling to spread the gospel to beet workers in Garland, Utah, as well as southern Idaho and elsewhere. In addition, the Riveras and the other missionaries led services out of a west side (the western section of Salt Lake City was the area of greatest Mexican concentration) Mexican restaurant (owned by Martinez) with a weekly attendance of approximately 100 individuals. In 1923 the church hierarchy officially recognized this Spanish-speaking group as the *Rama Mexicana* (Mexican Branch). This branch served as one of the two centers (the other being the Catholic parish of Our Lady of Guadalupe) of Mexicano life in northern Utah until the 1960s.

WYOMING

Among the key industries that attracted Spanish-surnamed people to Wyoming were the following: sheepherding, agricultural production, transportation, mining, and oil. The story of early arrivals to this state fits perfectly within the pattern found in other areas of the West.

By the 1910s Mexicanos were recruited to work in sugar beet production in places such as Lovell and Torrington; an unspecified number of Mexicanos and New Mexicans also scratched out a living as family farmers in various parts of the state. In addition, traqueros laid track in Cheyenne, Casper, Rawlins, and Rock Springs. Many of these individuals hailed from Chihuahua, Zacatecas, and Aguascalientes and had followed the Mexican Central line to El Paso; they then found employment with the Union Pacific, which shuttled them to Wyoming. These occupational opportunities attracted many, and by 1930 the Federal Census counted approximately 7,200 persons of Mexican heritage within the state.

Again, the advantages of fairly steady work were counterbalanced by discriminatory treatment. Antonio Ríos-Bustamante, in a recent article on the genesis of the Hispanic presence in Wyoming, notes that "discrimination . . . was stronger than in neighboring states," and that at least one town (Worland) actually maintained a separate "Mexican" school at least through the 1930s (Ríos-Bustamante, "Wyoming's Mexican Hispanic History," pp. 5 and 6). In other locations, Spanish speakers confronted discriminatory treatment from retailers, movie theaters, and public facilities such as swimming pools. The Denver Mexican consulate even noted discriminatory treatment of its citizens in a Catholic Church in Lovell, with whites assigned to the front pews, while Mexicanos were forced to worship from the back rows.

COMMUNITY BUILDING, DAILY LIFE, AND GROUP IDENTITY

Having completed our succinct tour of pockets of Spanish-surnamed concentration in the U.S. West, we now turn to several aspects of daily and cultural life during the years 1880–1930. Here, we will focus on politics, religion, and a variety of community organizations. In the process, we briefly scrutinize examples of how the Spanish-speaking population worked to resist injustices in the workplace.

POLITICS

Given the dramatic decline in economic and social power experienced by people of Mexican descent throughout the West, how did they use politics in an effort to stave off total dominance by Anglo invaders? One of the most significant studies dealing with this question is *Roots of Chicano Politics, 1600–1940,* by Juan Gómez-Quiñones. Here, the author suggests that there were several key issues that stimulated political activism: denial of property rights and language rights, discrimination in the administration of justice, and religious and educational discrimination (among others). Gómez-Quiñones argues that people of Mexican descent resisted such circumstances in various ways: some chose to negotiate (far and away the most common route), others preferred legal action, and still others employed armed insurrection at various times. Although we do not have sufficient space here to examine all topics in great detail for all locales, we will present examples that typify each of these methods.

The process of political and social negotiation began, especially in places with high levels of Hispano concentration, upon the arrival of white settlers and political appointees. Due to the small number (by comparison) of Anglos in these locations, accommodations were made. For example, in Texas and California, as described by Montejano, Camarillo, Pitt, and others, the initial adjustments involved the creation of a "peace structure" that provided some protection to elite Spanish speakers. This flimsy safeguard was procured, in many cases, through the use of inter-marriages and the accommodation of whites to certain aspects of "Mexi-can" life, such as the learning of Spanish and at least nominal conversion to Catholicism. As we have described above, however, such modifications became less necessary as the Anglos perfected their control over the lands taken in the Mexican American War.

Given the new circumstances, Spanish speakers worked in order to maintain a toehold in the politics of the West. One way in which they manifested such efforts was through cooperation and negotiation with local Anglos. This process took on a variety of forms in different places. To take one example, covered in a recent study by Charles Montgomery, between the years 1880 and 1928, there was a dramatic shift in the ter-minology used to describe the Mexican-descent population in New Mex-ico. Given the numerous attempts to gain statehood by people in the ter-ritory and the negative reaction to these attempts (especially by Senator Albert Beveridge), it was necessary to reshape the identity of the Spanish-speaking population. Montgomery argues that this was accomplished partly through a rhetorical sleight of hand. The elite, and eventually even Hispanos of lower classes, accepted the moniker of "Spanish-American" in an attempt to "lighten" a significant percentage of the populace and gain greater acceptance from politicos in Washington. As Montgomery asserts, this negotiated change was designed to evoke "a proud Spanish colonial past, [and] the term also announced that *nativos* were fully pre-pared to assume the responsibilities of forward-thinking, patriotic Amer-icans" (Montgomery, "Becoming 'Spanish-American,'" p. 69). In return for such concessions of cultural identity, Nuevomexicanos were provided certain benefits, such as fuller participation in politics, the presence of cultural brokers to present grievances to Anglo elites, and even constitu-tional provisions that prohibited the exclusion or segregation of Hispanic children from public schools.

Political conditions in much of Texas were different and often pro-duced a unique arrangement: allegiance to political bosses. Gómez-Quiñones describes the situation by stating that, although Mexicanos were permitted to occupy certain offices, they "were not permitted to in-fluence state policy . . . and county and city government were the im-posed limits. Mexicans had the possibility of the vote when they were present in significant numbers and when it was in the interest of the Anglo elite for them to vote" (Gómez-Quiñones, *Roots of Chicano Politics*, pp. 333–334). Additionally, Spanish speakers in governmental positions, and beholden to bosses, could not challenge their masters too boldly, or else they would have to face serious repercussions. Again, the work of Gómez-Quiñones work is informative: "If they broke ranks with the more powerful Anglo politicians, they, as well as their kin, suffered political, economic, and physical reprisals including murder" (Gómez-Quiñones, *Roots of Chicano Politics*, pp. 338–339).

Such understandings prevailed for much of the era covered by this chapter, particularly in El Paso as well as more southern counties of the Lone Star State such as Webb, Cameron, Hidalgo, Starr, and Duval. In sum, negotiations often produced Faustian deals that provided some benefits to certain quarters of the Mexican American populace, but at a high price for most. This topic will be examined in more detail in the following chapters.

The research on the Hawaiian boriqua experience notes a major political debate regarding the group's status during the 1910s: Were the roughly 4,000 Puerto Ricans then on the islands, with the 1917 enactment of the Jones Act (which granted Puerto Ricans in general citizenship), able to participate in local elections? One community leader, Manuel Oliveri Sánchez, decided to test whether he would be permitted the opportunity to vote in Honolulu. Not surprisingly, the county clerk denied him this fundamental right, arguing that "the act did not apply to them because, having emigrated, they were no longer Puerto Ricans." Oliveri Sánchez, in conjunction with two sympathetic attorneys, took to the case to the territorial supreme court, which agreed to hear the dispute in October 1917. Ironically, Puerto Ricans in Hawaii and elsewhere were required to register for the draft only one week after the case was filed. Eventually, the court adjudicated the case in the favor of the boriquas. Although they now had full citizenship, the Puerto Rican's small numbers limited their political clout. Still, it was a positive development and "gave them some security, but it was still up to the individual to make his/her own way" (Carr, "The Puerto Ricans in Hawaii: 1900–1958," pp. 235–237). Their status also opened up the opportunity for many boriquas to work on the islands' military facilities, providing an important avenue for economic and social advancement, especially with the coming of World War II.

Another negotiating tool used by Hispanics in order to gain a certain amount of political and social acceptance was to prove their loyalty to the United States through service in the military. In a 1989 article, Carole E. Christian argues that "World War I represented a crucial stage in the assimilation of Hispanics into the political and social life of Texas and the nation" (Christian, "Joining the American Mainstream," p. 559). Christian asserts that the various parts of the Mexican American community, in Texas and elsewhere, became actively engaged in patriotic causes and supporting the war effort, and she cites numerous examples in which the Spanish-language press "urged American citizens to be patriotic and Mexican nationals to give sympathetic support to the nation that had provided exiles with a secure refuge and economic opportunities" (Christian, "Joining the American Mainstream," p. 569). Through their efforts and contributions during the conflict, many Spanish speakers believed that they had demonstrated their devotion and thus would be fully accepted as part of the nation. However, it did not turn out that way. Upon returning from overseas, the Mexican American and Mexican doughboys "felt that their sacrifices and those of their comrades were not rewarded as they deserved in the postwar era. Like black soldiers . . . [they] experienced discrimination when they returned home during a period of rising nativism and Ku Klux Klan activity" (Christian, "Joining the American Mainstream," p. 588).

Although they did not receive just rewards for their services during the 1920s, the war did have a significant impact upon the Mexican American community, and Christian notes that the "servicemen had gained increased ethnic pride and assertiveness from their wartime experience . . . [which] strengthened veterans' determination to be accepted as full members of American society" (Christian, "Joining the American Mainstream," p. 588).

It was the effort and determination of veterans that gave birth to organizations such as the order Sons of America (in 1921), the Knights of America (in 1927), and ultimately, the League of United Latin American Citizens (in 1929), which, through its myriad activities and sponsoring of lawsuits, led the charge for civil and political rights in the years after 1930.

Puerto Ricans in Hawaii also signed up for the draft, although some of the community's leaders advised them not to until the territorial supreme court clarified the issue of citizenship. Ultimately, as Norma Carr notes, "dozens were drafted . . . among them married men with children. However, no one ever went to Europe to fight" (Carr, "The Puerto Ricans in Hawaii: 1900–1958," p. 236).

Conciliation with the new political and economic order, however, was not the only tool available. On occasion, Spanish-speaking people in the West resorted to the threat of violence or to aggression in order to protect their political rights. Once again, due to limited space, it is not possible to detail all such activities here, but we will present information on two examples: the Gorras Blancas (White Caps) of New Mexico in the early 1890s and the Plan de San Diego in southern Texas in the mid-1910s.

The expansion of railroads in New Mexico, as well as the increasing power of political machines known as rings (such as Thomas B. Catron's Santa Fe Ring) did much to damage the economic and political standing of the Spanish-speaking populace. In response to the activities of such entities, especially in San Miguel County, there arose Las Gorras Blancas, a group willing to use violence, if necessary, to defend Mexican rights against the elite, to prevent the takeover of land by companies, and to fight the railroad's exploitative practices, especially its usurpation of irrigation projects (Gómez-Quiñones, *Roots of Chicano Politics*, p. 29). The Gorras used intimidation, destruction of private property (such as cutting down fencing), and an alliance with the Partido del Pueblo Unido (a political party that shared many of the Gorras' goals, composed of Hispanics disenchanted with both major parties). The Gorras reinforced their demands with night riding during the early 1890s, and both groups reached the apex of their influence during the 1890 county elections, when the Partido captured all local offices in San Miguel. By the next election, however, in 1892, constant rhetorical attacks by the Republicans, as well as the creation of a counterinsurgency organization, Los Caballeros de Ley y Orden (the Knights of Law and Order), had reduced the party's voting base. By the mid-1890s, the Partido had lost much of its influence. Still, reports from the area noted the presence of large numbers (an estimated 300 individuals) of night riders in 1903, and sporadic property destruction continued until the late 1920s (Gómez-Quiñones, *Roots of Chicano Politics*, pp. 280–283).

The Plan de San Diego, which was supposed to be implemented in February of 1915, was another example of certain Spanish-speaking people willing to use violence in order to bring about political, social, and economic change. Briefly, the plan was an attempt by certain radical elements to recapture the territories lost by Mexico during the Mexican War. In addition to the elimination of U.S. sovereignty from these areas, the plan also included a call for unity among Mexicans and other minorities in the West and especially the Southwest. Gómez-Quiñones notes that "clauses in the Plan were addressed to the Black, the Indian, and the Asian, and provisions were made for their freedom and autonomy. . . . An interim republic was to be established with perhaps an eventual reannexation . . . and Anglo and Mexican opponents would be dealt with harshly" (p. 347). The Plan's proposed uprising never materialized, although there were numerous raids in the Rio Grande Valley throughout much of 1915. Unfortunately for the Mexican American people of the area, the Texas Rangers and other vigilantes took harsh reprisals, and hundreds, if not thousands, of Spanish-speaking people were killed or driven from their homes (Gómez-Quiñones, *Roots of Chicano Politics,* pp. 347–351). A recent study by Benjamin Heber Johnson, *Revolution in Texas,* provides the most thorough coverage of this event and also makes the argument that the Plan de San Diego helped stimulate further mainstream political participation by Mexican Americans through organizations such as the League of Latin American Citizens during the 1930s.

In Hawaii, there were no cases of organized, militant resistance reported; the workers on the islands' sugar plantations did, however, resist maltreatment, not necessarily with their fists, but with their feet, as many hundreds of them left plantations in search of work in cities or towns. We will discuss this aspect of resistance more thoroughly in a subsequent section.

RELIGION

Jay P. Dolan's edited collection, *The Notre Dame History of Hispanic Catholics in the U.S.,* provides an overview of the relationship between Mexicanos and the predominant spiritual institution of this group. Although the Catholic Church was the chief religious affiliation for Spanish speakers, it did not have a monopoly upon the faith community in the

A mural on the Old Plaza Church portrays the Virgin Mary with the words "Queen of Mexico and Empress of America." Los Angeles, California. (Richard Cummins/Corbis)

barrios and *colonias,* as Spanish-speaking communities are called, throughout the West. As we will briefly detail below, numerous Protestant denominations also worked diligently to win souls to their particular beliefs.

The story of the relationship between the Catholic Church and Mexicanos in the West during the years covered in this chapter is an ambivalent one: The Church did much to help the Spanish-surnamed population, but it is also true that it did not step forward to address some of the substantial issues confronting the community. Among the positive aspects, the church opened missions and parishes and initiated schools and other institutions of learning to serve the needs of Hispanic children. In addition, such church buildings functioned as incubators of Mexican culture, housing meetings of mutual aid societies, celebrations of Mexican national holidays and feast days, and other festivities such as *jamaicas* and posadas.

On the negative side, the church often failed to provide sufficient numbers of priests to service the needs of the widely scattered faithful (for example, in 1880, there was one priest covering a 10,000-square-mile area in Arizona), also, the U.S. church replaced local clergy with French (and other European) priests, who were not familiar with or accepting of regional religious practices. Additionally, the church sometimes discriminated in its distribution of financial assistance. To take one example, in an essay in *The Notre Dame History,* Gilberto Hinojosa notes that by 1930 "the Anglo-American diocese of Dallas with 46,000 Catholics received almost as much money . . . from the Catholic Extension Society as Corpus Christi, which listed eight times as many faithful, most of whom were Mexican Americans" (Dolan, *Mexican Americans and the Catholic Church, 1900–1965,* p. 44). The church bureaucracy was also often perplexingly silent when outrages were perpetrated against Spanish speakers; for example, as Hinojosa points out, during the bloody reprisals that took place after the discovery of the Plan de San Diego, diocesan administrators "did not take a stand." Also, he argues, during the years 1880–1930, the church made "surprisingly little comment . . . about the social conditions of Mexicanos" (Dolan, *Mexican Americans and the Catholic Church, 1900–1965,* pp. 44, 61–62). This did not mean that the hierarchy completely ignored the plight of the downtrodden, but it did have to perform a delicate balancing act, pleading for better conditions, yet not antagonizing Anglo Catholics, who often owned the farms and other businesses that employed such oppressed workers. In addition, church leaders even tolerated segregation of parishioners within a church building (when a town could not afford to sustain both an Anglo and Mexican parish) on some occasions.

The church condoned similar incidents targeting Puerto Ricans in Hawaii, as many humble sugar cane cutters and their families "were criticized by other parishioners for their poor clothes and lack of shoes" (Carr, "The Puerto Ricans in Hawaii: 1900–1958," p. 208). Such episodes, in conjunction with the long distances many had to travel to attend mass, damaged the relationship between the church and boriquas. Although most remained at least nominally tied to the faith, Protestant missionaries used this rift as an opportunity for proselytizing among the Puerto Ricans of Hawaii.

During the last two decades, the church has come under criticism by historians for pushing for the Americanization of the Spanish-speaking people it served in the West. Jeffrey Burns, writing in *The Notre Dame History,* counters some of these charges. He concedes that the church did provide and fund many such programs, but, he argues, that in "an era in which Americanism went unquestioned, the goal of Americanizing the Mexicans was seen as a positive good" (Dolan, *Mexican Americans and the Catholic Church,* p. 149). Among the programs sponsored in Los Angeles, for example, were civics, home economics, and English language classes. Still, "forced Americanization was not a universal paradigm," and Burns notes examples of priests, including Irish clerics, who showed a greater "willingness to admire and preserve national traits than was the custom before." By the late 1930s, Archbishop Cantwell was lamenting that the Mexicano "children very readily accept American manners . . . adopting the worst customs which they come into contact with here." In response, by 1940, Cantwell ordered all his seminarians to "learn Spanish and obtain some knowledge of Mexican culture" (Dolan, *Mexican Americans and the Catholic Church,* pp. 149–151).

By the early part of the 1900s, various Protestant denominations began turning their attention to the growing numbers of Hispanics in the developing barrios of the West. As Hinojosa notes, Protestantism had been tolerated by many people in Mexico since the time of Benito Juárez (president 1861–1872), and during the years of the Porfiriato (the presidency of Porfirio Díaz, 1877–1880, 1884–1911), Mexico practiced a certain amount of religious tolerance. During these decades, ministers were trained and churches established in various parts of Mexico, and "the waves of immigration in the early twentieth century facilitated the Protestant evangelization of Mexicans . . . [and] they were soon to hear the gospel preached to them by [native] churchmen other than priests" (Dolan, *Mexican Americans and the Catholic Church,* p. 42). In addition, many of the sects were not only offering a new way to reach God; they also preached the American work ethic, and encouraged their charges to become increasingly Americanized. While there were not large numbers of conversions, denominations such as Mormons, Presbyterians, and Baptists, made some inroads into barrio communities.

In Hawaii, two denominations made gains with the Puerto Ricans. As early as 1906, the Salvation Army began recruiting members, and by the 1920s they had established several churches. Pentecostals (based in California) also had success in reaching out to the boriquas. One individual, Juan Lugo, who had arrived in Hawaii at the age of ten, converted, received training in San Francisco, and eventually returned to his native island, helping establish various congregations there.

ORGANIZING FOR A BETTER LIFE

Wherever people of Mexican descent settled in the West, they faced difficult conditions: most worked in low-paying, menial jobs, their children often faced discrimination in schools, and governments and other entities were routinely unresponsive to barrio needs. In this section, we will briefly examine some organizations and other entities that Mexicanos created and used in order to better daily life within their communities. We will start with mutual aid societies, then briefly discuss the Primer Congreso Mexicanista, as well as the significance of Spanish-language newspapers throughout the West. In addition, we will note the significance of Mexican American participation in business activities, as well as the importance of women in a variety of community organizations. Puerto Ricans also worked to establish similar bodies, but the information on their entities (both in California and Hawaii) is much more limited.

In order to better conditions, many in the comunidad understood that collective efforts would be necessary. Although Mexicanos established a variety of organizations in various places, there was one kind of organization they always created in order to serve their needs: all communities had *mutuales* (mutual aid societies). These groups performed three basic and important functions: (1) they celebrated the members' culture and holidays; (2) they provided (limited) financial assistance against the uncertainties of life (injury or death of a worker); and (3) they provided the community an opportunity to express pride in their culture, as well as presenting a more positive view of the comunidad to the broader public. These organizations were often named after national (Mexican) heroes, and its leaders also sought to create ties to the Anglo power structure in order to improve the treatment of Mexicanos.

One example, from the northern Utah area, will suffice to illustrate the role of mutuales throughout the West. During the mid-1920s, Jesus Avila and some colleagues who worked in the mining town of Bingham Canyon (southwest of Salt Lake City) established an organization known as *Unión y Patria* (Unity and Nation). In an oral history interview with Avila recorded in the 1970s, he noted that the group's goals included preserving Mexican traditions, teaching national history and Spanish to community youths, assisting members in dire financial circumstances, sponsoring fiestas and other cultural events, and attempting to gain better treatment from local authorities. In addition, by the 1910s, many mutual aid societies also sponsored a variety of athletic competitions for both adults and youths. According to Gómez-Quiñones, the largest network of mutual aid societies in the West was the Alianza Hispano-Americana, which started in Tucson in the 1890s and existed until the 1940s.

In a 1994 article, "Beyond Machismo, La Familia, and Ladies Auxiliaries," Cynthia E. Orozco notes that, when writing about the important contributions of mutuales and similar groups, historians "have rarely asked how gender mattered in the associations, and have rarely considered women's participation in them" (Orozco, "Beyond Machismo, La Familia and Ladies Auxiliaries," p. 38). In her essay, Orozco notes the broad range of activities (social, fundraising, and administrative) that women undertook on behalf of such societies during the late nineteenth and early twentieth centuries. In addition, Orozco notes that some of the women involved in the *mutualista* movement were, by the 1920s, pushing for greater participation in decision-making and policy-making activities.

Another significant society created by Mexican Americans was El Primer Congreso Mexicanista in Laredo, Texas, in 1911. The group, led by Nicasio Idar, sought to challenge the treatment of Mexicans and Mexican Americans in schools, workplaces, and the broader society. In addition, the Congreso worked to maintain the cultural traditions of Mexico and provide a sense of pride and unity for barrio members. Finally, the Congreso acknowledged the significant role of Spanish-speaking women as mothers, wives, and educators by establishing a Liga Femenil Mexicana (Mexican Women's League). Unfortunately, financial difficulties, as well as hostility from employers and politicians, doomed the society.

Another mechanism used to build up barrio dignity and counter Anglo oppression was the Spanish-language press. One scholar, Doris Meyer, who has studied the industry in New Mexico argues that "despite being a harbinger of a new age of mass communications, the industry was the primary vehicle for articulating and galvanizing this counterhegemonic cultural imperative" (Meyer, *Speaking for Themselves,* p. 12). Newspaper editors provided an opportunity for the comunidad to express dissatisfaction with social and economic conditions. In the pages of tabloids such as *La Voz del Pueblo, La Bandera Americana, El Regidor, La Prensa,* and many others, editors ruminated about a broad range of topics; in general they "were united in rejecting discrimination, encouraging education, [and] calling for greater political participation, and . . . they echoed the mounting dissonances for Mexicans in areas of public life" (Gómez-Quiñones, *Roots of Chicano Politics,* p. 199).

Recent studies on the role of newspapers in barrio life have also focused on the process of Mexican American identity formation. In a dissertation entitled "Voice of the People: Pablo Cruz, *El Regidor* and Mexican American Identity," Ana Luisa Martínez argues that, through an examination of the editorial pages of Spanish language papers, it is possible to uncover the goals of the Mexican American middle class. These barrio entrepreneurs saw themselves as mediators of the Americanization process and called for better (i.e., equal) treatment before the law, and an

A view of the busy workroom at La Prensa, *a San Antonio–based Spanish-language newspaper, 1916. (University of Texas, Institute of Texan Cultures at San Antonio, 083-0409)*

opportunity to prove that Spanish speakers were good Americans. Martinez notes that editors such as Cruz set themselves up as arbiters of what was acceptable and what was not in the process of redefinition. In sum, she asserts, they wanted their community to Americanize, but not to lose their sense of Mexicanness.

The editors of Spanish-language newspapers in the West were also usually the proprietors of their enterprises. Although this commercial undertaking was one of the most visible economic endeavors within the comunidades, it was by no means the only one. Until recently, historians have not paid much attention to entrepreneurs of Mexican descent and their role in barrio life. Fortunately, this trend is beginning to change, and some progress has been made in examining the significance of the social, political, and economic role of these men and women. Recently, scholars such as David Torres, Arturo González, Thomas Kreneck, and others have discussed how business owners provided goods and services to the comunidad, and how they functioned as intermediaries between the

Spanish-speaking populace and the broader community. More information on the role of entrepreneurs of Mexican descent will be provided in subsequent chapters.

The information on the formation of Puerto Rican organizations before the 1930s is sketchy (especially for groups formed in California), but it is evident that they too were active in establishing groups designed to maintain their culture, dispute mistreatment, and improve conditions. As early as 1906, some of the boriquas that refused to proceed to Hawaii in 1900 established an organization, the Club Social Puertorriqueño, or the Puerto Rican Social Club. This was followed by the Puerto Rican Club of San Francisco in 1911 and the Club Puertorriqueño de California in 1923. These organizations had as their stated goals "progressive agendas pledged to advancement and maintenance of the island's cultural heritage and values" (Sánchez-Korrol, *Teaching U.S. Puerto Rican History,* pp. 13–14).

The research of Norma Carr on Puerto Ricans in Hawaii provides a more effective examination of the limited organizational attempts by boriquas prior to 1930. Not surprisingly, some of the earliest work in this area was religious in nature. For example, the Reverend Juan Feliciano, a minister with the Salvation Army, worked diligently as pastor and social worker to improve circumstances among his flock. He also cared for orphaned children, placing them in homes and schools supported by several Protestant sects.

In addition to concerns about citizenship, there were other problems confronting boriquas in Hawaii; above all, the *haole* (white) population held very negative opinions about them, and the local newspapers expressed those opinions. Carr argues that there were several complaints about the group: their children crowded local schools, the adults were lazy, thriftless, and incorrigible thieves, and they brought exotic diseases, such as the "Porto Rican itch" and the "tropical worm." How could Puerto Ricans respond to such accusations? In addition to standing up for their rights under the Jones Act, Puertorriqueños created the Puerto Rican Welfare Association in 1921, and the group endeavored to maintain cultural identity, establish a union for sugar industry workers, and provide aid for families in financial distress. The association failed during the early 1920s and was replaced by La Unión Familial, which espoused similar goals. Unfortunately, many members found the dues too burden-some, and this organization ultimately failed. The Spanish-speaking peo-ple of Hawaii would try again to unite with the creation of the Puerto Rican Civic Club, starting in the early 1930s.

LABOR ORGANIZATIONS

Providing a brief summary of Mexican and Mexican American participa-tion in labor organizations during this period is a difficult task. Contrary to the perception of the Mexican worker's docility often perpetuated by employers of the era, trabajadores (workers) were very active over the years in seeking to improve their lot. A short listing of examples will have to serve to illustrate the resolve with which Mexicanos struggled for bet-ter working conditions.

One of the earliest strikes involving Mexican workers (betabeleros in this case) took place in Oxnard, California, in 1903 and is described in Tomás Almaguer's 1984 article "Racial Domination and Class Conflict in Capitalist Agriculture." The conditions that the workers and their fami-lies were facing are, by this point, quite familiar. The Spanish-speaking population (concentrated in an area known as Sonoratown) was segre-gated, disdained, and oppressed. Labor in Oxnard, not surprisingly, was organized along racial lines. Anglos directed and managed, while Mexi-cans and Asians did the hard work. There was, however, some level of flu-idity in this structure, and by 1902 "there were nine Japanese labor con-tractors meeting nearly all the seasonal need for farm laborers in the area" (Almaguer, "Racial Domination and Class Conflict in Capitalist Agricul-ture," p. 329).

In the spring of 1902 conditions worsened for farm employees, as local white businessmen banded together in an attempt to "end the re-liance on Japanese labor contractors"; now the workers would have to pay part of their wages to their recruiter, the employers' organization, and ac-cept a cut in pay per acre, as well as being forced to accept script instead of cash. In response to these conditions, Japanese and Mexican workers of Oxnard banded together into the Japanese-Mexican Labor Association: an entity that represented approximately 800 workers. After much strug-gle and violent confrontations, the JMLA won a contract that nearly dou-bled the pay of laborers on March 30, 1903. The success of the JMLA was hard won, but brief because it "forced the union movement to confront the issue of including agricultural workers . . . [and] forced white unions to clearly articulate their positions on the organization of Japanese and Mexican workers." Eventually, when the JMLA petitioned the American Federation of Labor for admission, Samuel Gompers insisted that the organization not permit Asian members. The Mexicanos involved refused this request, and the "AFL decision not to admit all members of the JMLA undoubtedly contributed to the union eventually passing out of existence" (Almaguer, "Racial Domination and Class Conflict in Capitalist Agriculture," 331–334, 343–345, and 347).

Historians of Mexican American history have cataloged numerous strikes throughout the West in the years before 1930. The following examples indicate the scope and variety of groups that undertook strikes: agricultural workers in Wheatland, California, in 1913; laundry workers in El Paso, Texas, in 1919; and longshoreman work stoppages in Seattle, Galveston, and San Pedro, California, during the 1910s and 1920s. There is a great deal more information regarding Mexicano participation in labor organizations during the years after 1930, and this topic, including the significant role of women in organizing union activity, will be examined in subsequent chapters.

For Puerto Ricans in Hawaii, the period before 1930 did not generate much union activity; still, workers did what they could in order to improve their situation. One of the most difficult adjustments sugar cutters endured was the level of regimentation required by the *lunas* (foremen). Norma Carr argues that many of the new arrivals, who hailed from the coffee-producing section of Puerto Rico, had never experienced such authoritarian conditions. Rather, they "were accustomed to irregular work patterns, which provided opportunity or time for the intermingling of labor and leisure" (Carr, "The Puerto Ricans in Hawaii, 1900–1958," p. 170). Lunas permitted only a brief time for lunch and demanded cutters work in the rain, and some even entered domiciles to rouse the sick from their beds. In addition to the conditions on the job, workers lived in segregated camps, bought goods from company stores, and had little access to health care; compulsory education laws were not enforced. Puertorriqueños did not submit meekly to this state of affairs. In February 1902, sixty individuals signed a complaint about conditions at the

Koloa Plantation, and a letter was mailed to a San Juan newspaper. Another common tactic used was to simply escape from sugar plantations and seek employment elsewhere. Some individuals managed to find work with coffee growers in Kona or on cattle ranches on other islands, and some found employment in cities.

A FINAL WORD

By 1930, pockets of Spanish-speaking individuals existed in most western states and in the territory of Hawaii. These men, women, and children faced difficulties at school and work that kept them from fully participating in the American dream of success and material prosperity. Still, Hispanics in the West worked diligently to maintain their culture and improve their communities, and they sought a better future for their progeny. They established churches, businesses, and self-help associations in order to achieve their aspirations. Although life was far from fair and perfect, through diligence, individual and community sacrifice and effort, many believed that their existence would continue to progress, if whites would only accept Spanish speakers as a legitimate part of the national populace. They had, between 1880 and 1930, proven themselves as dependable workers, valiant soldiers, and loyal Americans, had they not? Many of these hopes and aspirations were to be dashed in the 1930s, as the United States faced its greatest economic calamity, the Great Depression. Suddenly, the trabajadores who had helped build up so much of the wealth of the West were deemed superfluous. How would the Spanish speakers of the West deal with the economic downturn and the social changes it produced? Chapter 6 takes up that part of our story.

BIBLIOGRAPHIC ESSAY

There are many fine studies that discuss the economic changes that occurred in the West between the years 1880 and 1930. One of the most accessible, which we have found quite useful for examining important trends discussed in this and other chapters, is Richard White's massive *"It's Your Misfortune and None of My Own": A New History of the American West* (Norman: University of Oklahoma Press, 1991); the relevant chapters here are 10 through 13, which detail the commercial transformation of the region, as well as the conflicts created by the makeover of the West's social structure.

White's research, though obviously quite valuable, is sweeping and general in its coverage and can be supplemented through a reading of works with a

206 Hispanics in the American West

narrower focus. Among the most significant studies detailing the impact of the new economy upon the lives of Spanish-speaking people are David Montejano, *Anglos and Mexicans in the Making of Texas, 1836–1986* (Austin: University of Texas Press, 1987); Armando C. Alonzo, *Tejano Legacy: Rancheros and Settlers in South Texas, 1734–1900* (Albuquerque: University of New Mexico Press, 1998); Leonard Pitt, *The Decline of the Californios: A Social History of the Spanish-Speaking Californians, 1846–1900* (Berkeley: University of California Press, 1966); Lizbeth Haas, *Conquest and Historical Identities in California, 1769–1936* (Berkeley: University of California Press, 1995); Albert Camarillo, *Chicanos in a Changing Society: From Mexican Pueblos to American Barrios in Santa Barbara and Southern California, 1848–1930* (Cambridge, MA: Harvard University Press, 1979); Thomas E. Sheridan, *Arizona: A History* (Tucson: University of Arizona Press, 1995) and *Los Tucsonenses: The Mexican Community of Tucson, 1865–1941* (Tucson: University of Arizona Press, 1986); Malcolm Ebright, *Land Grants and Lawsuits in Northern New Mexico* (Albuquerque: University of New Mexico Press, 1994); and Sarah Deutsch, *No Separate Refuge: Culture, Class and Gender on an Anglo Hispanic Frontier, 1880–1940* (New York: Oxford University Press, 1987).

The works listed above focus chiefly on the way the economic changes during this fifty-year span dramatically worsened conditions for the Spanish-speaking people who had lived in the West prior to the Anglo conquest. At the same time, however, the growth and development of extractive, agricultural, and tourist industries (and others) also worked to attract substantial numbers of new Spanish speakers to the region; persons hoping to earn a share of the western version of the American dream, and many studies catalog the arrival of Mexicanos (and Puerto Ricans) in the West in search of economic improvement. Among those which we found useful in producing this work were the following: Ronald Takaki, *A Different Mirror: A History of Multicultural America* (Boston: Little, Brown, and Company, 1993); Camile Guerin-González, *Mexican Workers, American Dream: Immigration, Repatriation, and California Farm Labor, 1900–1939* (New Brunswick, NJ: Rutgers University Press, 1994); Neil Foley, *The White Scourge: Mexicans, Blacks, and Poor Whites in Texas Cotton Culture* (Berkeley: University of California Press, 1997); Gilbert G. González, *Labor and Community: Mexican Citrus Worker Villages in a Southern California County, 1900–1950* (Urbana and Chicago: University of Illinois Press, 1994); Emilio Zamora, *The World of the Mexican Worker in Texas* (College Station: Texas A&M University Press, 1993); Juan Gómez-Quiñones, *Mexican American Labor, 1790–1990* (Albuquerque: University of New Mexico Press, 1994); Norma Carr, "The Puerto Ricans in Hawaii: 1900–1958," Ph.D. dissertation, University of Hawaii, 1989; Iris López, "Introduction: Puerto Ricans in Hawai'i," in *Centro: Journal of the Center for Puerto Rican Studies* (Spring 2001); and Blasé Camacho

Souza, "'Trabajo y Tristesa,' 'Work and Sorrow': The Puerto Ricans of Hawaii, 1900–1902," *Hawaiian Journal of History* 18 (1984).

As mentioned in the text of the chapter, historians of (and other writers about) the Hispanic experience in the U.S. West (prior to the 1980s) focused their studies, and quite rightly, upon the states with the largest Mexicano populations. By the late 1980s, however, many scholars realized that such narratives did not cover the totality of the experiences of the Spanish-surnamed people of the West. The following list (by no means exhaustive) represents the major trend over the past two decades of scholarship toward articles and books detailing the life of Hispanics in unlikely places where these men, women, and children have fought to establish their communities as part of the American mosaic: Zaragoza Vargas, *Proletarians of the North: A History of Mexican Industrial Workers in Detroit and the Midwest, 1917–1933* (Berkeley: University of California Press, 1993); Erasmo Gamboa, *Mexican Labor and World War II* (Austin: University of Texas Press, 1990); Juan R. García, *Mexicans in the Midwest, 1900–1932* (Tucson: University of Arizona Press, 1996); Michael M. Smith, *The Mexicans of Oklahoma* (Norman: University of Oklahoma Press, 1980); Jorge Iber, *Hispanics in the Mormon Zion, 1912–1999* (College Station: Texas A&M University Press, 2001); Nitza C. Medina, "Rebellion in the Bay: California's First Puerto Ricans," in *Centro: Journal of the Center for Puerto Rican Studies* 13, no. 1 (spring 2001); Virginia Sánchez-Korrol, *Teaching U.S. Puerto Rican History* (Washington, DC: Publication Sales, American Historical Society, 1999); *Puerto Ricans in California* (Washington, DC: U.S. Commission on Civil Rights, 1976); Jorge Pinero, "Extended Roots: San Jose, California," in *Extended Roots: From Hawaii to New York, Migraciones Puertorriqueñas a los Estados Unidos* (New York: Centro de Estudios Puertorriqueños, Hunter College, 1984); Kyle Ko Francisco Shinseki, "El Pueblo Mexicano de Hawai'i: Comunidades en Formacion," master's thesis, University of California, Los Angeles, 1997; Iris López and David Forbes, "Borinki Identity in Hawai'i: Present and Future," *Centro: Journal of the Center for Puerto Rican Studies* 13, no. 1 (spring 2001); Dionicio Nodín Valdés, *Barrios Norteños: St. Paul and Midwestern Mexican Communities in the Twentieth Century* (Austin: University of Texas Press, 2000); Montana Department of Community Affairs, "Hispanics in Montana: A Report to the 47th Montana Legislative Assembly as Mandated by House Joint Resolution No. 19," 1980; M. L. Miranda, *A History of Hispanics in Southern Nevada* (Reno: University of Nevada Press, 1997); Erasmo Gamboa, "Mexican Migration into Washington State: A History: 1940–1950, *Pacific Northwest Quarterly* 72, no. 3 (July 1981); Richard W. Slatta, "Chicanos in the Pacific Northwest: A Historical Overview of Oregon's Chicanos," *Aztlán* 6 (fall 1975); Erasmo Gamboa and Carolyn M. Baun, eds., *Nosotros: The Hispanic People of Oregon: Essays and Recollections* (Portland: Oregon Council for the Humanities, 1995); Phillip F. Notarianni, "Utah's Ellis

Island: The Difficult 'Americanization' of Carbon County," *Utah Historical Quarterly* 47, no. 2 (spring 1979); William H. González and Genardo M. Padilla, "Monticello, the Hispanic Gateway to Utah," *Utah Historical Quarterly* 52, no. 4 (spring 1979); Antonio Ríos-Bustamante, "Wyoming's Mexican Hispanic History," *Annals of Wyoming: The Wyoming History Journal* 73, no. 2 (spring 2001).

There have been a number of fine works written on Mexican *comunidades* in nontraditional locales over the past two decades, and there have also been many recent studies that have provided increasingly sophisticated coverage of life in the more traditional areas as well (again, this listing is by no means exhaustive): Julia Kirk Blackwelder, *Women of the Depression: Caste and Culture in San Antonio, 1929–1939* (College Station: Texas A&M University Press, 1998); Roger M. Olien and Diana O. Olien, *Life in the Oil Fields* (Austin: Texas Monthly Press, 1986); George J. Sánchez, *Becoming Mexican American: Ethnicity, Culture and Identity in Chicano Los Angeles, 1900–1945* (New York: Oxford University Press, 1993); Douglas Monroy, *Rebirth: Mexican Los Angeles from the Great Migration to the Great Depression* (Berkeley: University of California Press, 1999); Vicki L. Ruiz, *Cannery Women, Cannery Lives: Mexican Women, Unionization, and the California Food Processing Industry, 1930–1950* (Albuquerque: University of New Mexico Press, 1987); Patricia Zavella, *Women's Work and Chicano Families: Cannery Workers of the Santa Clara Valley* (New York: Cornell University Press, 1987); Linda Gordon, *The Great Arizona Orphan Abduction* (Cambridge, MA: Harvard University Press, 2001); William Wyckoff, *Creating Colorado: The Making of a Western American Landscape, 1860–1940* (New Haven, CT: Yale University Press, 1999); Rebecca Ann Hunt, "Urban Pioneers: Continuity and Change in Ethnic Communities in Two Denver, Colorado, Neighborhoods, 1875–1998," Ph.D. dissertation, University of Colorado, 1999; Chris Wilson, *Santa Fe: Creating a Modern Regional Tradition* (Albuquerque: University of New Mexico Press, 1997); Richard Nostrand, *The Hispano Homeland* (Norman: University of Oklahoma Press, 1992); Jeffrey Marcos Garcilazo, "Traqueros: Mexican Railroad Workers in the United States, 1870–1930," Ph.D. dissertation, University of California, Santa Barbara, 1995.

In the final sections of the chapter, we examined some aspects of daily life in communities throughout the West; focusing specifically upon Hispanics and politics (including issues of identity), religion, and a variety of community organizations. Some of the research conducted on this topic includes the following: Juan Gómez-Quiñones, *Roots of Chicano Politics, 1600–1940* (Albuquerque: University of New Mexico Press, 1994); Charles Montgomery, "Becoming 'Spanish-American': Race and Rhetoric in New Mexico Politics, 1880–1928," *Journal of American Ethnic History* 20, no. 4 (Summer 2001); Phillip B. González, "*La Junta de Indignacion:* Hispano Repertoire of Collective Protest in New Mexico, 1884–1933," *Western Historical Quarterly* 31, no. 2 (Summer

2000); Ann M. Massmann, "Adelina 'Nina' Otero-Warren: A Spanish American Cultural Broker," *Journal of the Southwest* 42, no. 4 (Winter 2000); Evan Anders, *Boss Rule in South Texas: The Progressive Era* (Austin: University of Texas Press, 1982); Gilberto J. Quezada, *Border Boss: Manuel B. Bravo and Zapata County* (College Station: Texas A&M University Press, 1999); Carole E. Christian, "Joining the American Mainstream: Texas' Mexican Americans During World War I," *Southwestern Historical Quarterly,* number 4 (April 1989); Robert J. Rosenbaum, *Mexicano Resistance in the Southwest: "The Sacred Right of Self Preservation"* (Austin: University of Texas Press, 1981); Benjamin Heber Johnson, *Revolution in Texas: How a Forgotten Rebellion and Its Bloody Repression Turned Mexicans into Americans* (New Haven, CT: Yale University Press, 2003); *Mexican Americans and the Catholic Church,* edited by Jay P. Dolan and Gilberto Hinojosa (Notre Dame, IN: University of Notre Dame Press, 1994); David A. Badillo, "Between Alienation and Ethnicity: The Evolution of Mexican American Catholicism in San Antonio, 1910–1940," *American Ethnic History* 16, no. 4 (Summer 1997); Michael E. Engh, S.J., "A Multiplicity of Faiths': Religion's Impact on Los Angeles and the Urban West, 1890–1940." *Western Historical Quarterly* 28, no. 4 (Winter 1997); R. Douglas Breckenridge and Francisco García-Tetro, *Iglesia Presbiteriana: A History of Presbyterians and Mexican Americans in the Southwest* (San Antonio, TX: Trinity University Press, 1974); Clifton L. Holland, *The Religious Dimension in Hispanic Los Angeles: A Protestant Case Study* (South Pasadena, CA: William Carey Library, 1974); Juan Francisco Martínez, "Origins and Development of Protestantism Among Latinos in the Southwestern United States, 1863–1900," Ph.D. dissertation, Fuller Theological Seminary, Pasadena, CA, 1996; José Amaro Hernández. *Mutual Aid For Survival: The Case of the Mexican American* (Malabar, FL: Krieger, 1983); Cynthia E. Orozco, "Beyond Machismo, La Familia, and Ladies Auxiliaries: A Historiography of Mexican-Origin Women's Participation in Voluntary Association and Politics in the United States," *Renato Rosaldo Lecture Monograph Series* (Tucson: University of Arizona, 1994); Doris Meyer, *Speaking for Themselves: NeoMexicano Cultural Identity and the Spanish-Language Press, 1880–1920* (Albuquerque: University of New Mexico Press, 1996); Ana Luisa Martínez, "Voice of the People: Pablo Cruz, *El Regidor,* and Mexican American Identity," Ph.D. dissertation, Texas Tech University, 2003; David L. Torres, "Dynamics Behind the Formation of a Business Class: Tucson's Hispanic Business Elite," *Renato Rosaldo Lecture Series Monograph* (Tucson: University of Arizona, 1989); Thomas H. Kreneck, *Mexican American Odyssey: Felix Tijerina, Entrepreneur and Civic Leader, 1900–1965* (College Station: Texas A&M University Press, 2001); Tomás Almaguer, "Racial Domination and Class Conflict in Capitalist Agriculture: The Oxnard Sugar Beet Workers' Strike of 1903," *Labor History* 25, no. 3 (Summer 1984); Oscar J. Martínez, *Mexican Origin People in the United States* (Tucson: University of Arizona Press, 2001).

The materials for the biographical sketch at the end of this chapter were drawn from the following: Jorge Iber, *Hispanics in the Mormon Zion, 1912–1999* (College Station: Texas A&M University Press, 2001); Richard O. Ulibarri, "Utah's Unassimilated Minorities," in *Utah's History,* edited by Richard D. Poll (Logan: Utah State University Press, 1989); Ferol E. Benavides, "The Saint among the Saints: A Study of Curanderismo in Utah," *Utah Historical Quarterly* 41 (Autumn 1973). Also useful were the entries on both individuals in *Latinas in the United States: An Historical Encyclopedia,* edited by Vicki L. Ruiz and Virginia Sánchez-Korrol (Bloomington: Indiana University Press, 2006).

THE GREAT DEPRESSION THROUGH 1965

The half century between 1880 and 1930 was difficult for people of Mexican descent in the U.S. West. As we have detailed, the years witnessed a dramatic decline in the economic, social, and political standing of the Spanish-surnamed throughout the region. In addition, as the West became better integrated into the nation's commercial infrastructure, many Spanish speakers from New Mexico, Colorado, California, Texas, and elsewhere, as well as thousands of Mexicanos who came seeking jobs in industry and fleeing revolutionary turmoil in their homeland, became ensnared in low-paid menial jobs serving the machinery of American "progress." A similar fate befell many of the Puerto Ricans who arrived in Hawaii to work on sugar plantations starting in the early 1900s.

Although faced with challenging situations, Hispanics west of the Mississippi did not meekly tolerate difficulties in workplaces, schools, and communities. Through individual initiative and community diligence, they established churches, unions, mutual aid societies, educational facilities, businesses, and other entities designed to ameliorate situations caused by intolerance, as well as to help preserve distinctive cultures and traditions. Such entities provided a sense of belonging and opportunities for success that offered solace to men, women, and children who often were thousands of miles away from homes and families. As during the years 1880–1930, the organizations established by Spanish speakers continued working to improve circumstances of daily life during the years 1930–1965.

This chapter focuses on three key events of this era: the Great Depression, World War II, and the postconflict economic, social, and political development of the West. Within the coverage of each experience, we scrutinize various questions, including the following: (1) What attracted Hispanics to particular locales during certain years (and, in regard to the 1930s, what factors pushed individuals out of an area)? (2) What were the conditions faced in each area? (3) What organizations did Hispanics create and use in order to endure a hostile environment as well as maintain aspects of their culture? The questions are addressed through an analysis of aspects of daily life (social groups, religion, and labor organizations) and of group identity and politics. Finally, we present a snapshot summary of the state of life in the barrios and colonias in 1960, in order to provide the background that explains the appeal of a more radical version of the struggle for equality: the Chicano movement of the 1960s and 1970s (the subject of Chapter 7).

Before proceeding, it is necessary to, once again, make note of the literature available on Puerto Ricans and Cubans in the West covering the years 1930–1965. In regard to boriquas, available studies primarily focus on Hawaii (where the community now used the term "borinkis" for self-reference) and California, with some information on other locales, such as Utah. For Cuban Americans, the research mentions their arrival in two cities, Los Angeles and Las Vegas, after the Revolution of 1959 and the genesis of Cubano communities there during the early 1960s.

THE GREAT DEPRESSION

Prior to examining the impact of the Great Depression on the everyday lives of Spanish-speaking people, it is necessary to obtain an overarching sense of the calamity's influence on the West. Here, anew, we turn to Richard White, who notes that the crash of the stock market on October 24, 1929, generated some odd reactions. White notes that many regional businessmen responded in a narrow-minded and unsophisticated way to the catastrophe:

> Westerners reassured themselves that only eastern speculators . . . would suffer from the collapse of stock prices. . . . The solid things—the ore, grains, and cotton—that westerners placed their confidence in became actual liabilities in the years after 1929. (White, *"It's Your Misfortune,"* p. 463)

Given the circumstances that pummeled them during the 1930s, many thousands of previously smug and aloof western capitalists ultimately faced financial ruin. The Spanish-surnamed persons who worked for such entrepreneurs had an even more difficult time dealing with the devastation. One of the first problems confronted was the desire by some whites to rid the West of the Spanish speakers in their midst.

REPATRIATION

As westerners tackled the downward spiral of the regional and national economy, many looked for scapegoats. The "foreigners" made handy targets, and some whites accused Hispanics of taking jobs away from "real" Americans. It is estimated that during the 1930s approximately 500,000 Mexicanos (and their U.S.-born offspring) were forced, or strongly encouraged (by both U.S. and Mexican authorities), to leave the country. Several authors have written about direct efforts by local, state, and national governments, as well as private entities, to expel individuals of Mexican descent. In addition, others have noted that many left because economic conditions made it impossible for families to survive.

A study done in 2000 by Dionicio Nodín Valdés offers an excellent overview of the repatriation of Spanish speakers in St. Paul, Minnesota, and elsewhere in the Midwest. Valdés notes that by the late 1920s, "sentiment . . . intensified sharply . . . and northern politicians . . . were among the leaders in national discussions over the restriction of Mexican immigration." This was due to the "underlying fear that Mexicans were heading north and staying" (Valdés, *Barrios Norteños*, pp. 87–88). He further states that employers, such as railroad companies in Kansas, were, on certain occasions, directly encouraged by politicians (in this case, the state's governor) to lay off Spanish-surnamed workers (during 1931 and 1932) in order to provide jobs for unemployed whites. Fortunately, many companies did not cooperate with officials in running off Spanish-speaking workers, and some enterprises, such as the Santa Fe Railroad in Argentine, Kansas, which depended greatly upon Mexican labor, safeguarded employees from deportation pressures. Another reason for the exodus from the Twin Cities was the direct encouragement of the Mexican government, and Valdés argues that "Mexican consular officials were sympathetic to repatriation" (Valdés, *Barrios Norteños*, p. 99). Still, while circumstances were quite difficult in the barrios of St. Paul and elsewhere, few Mexicanos (especially after the election of Franklin Delano Roosevelt in November, 1932) left the area "due to 'less confidence in finding good adjustment in Mexico and to fewer ties with the home country.'" (Valdés, *Barrios Norteños,* p. 99)

The situation for many agricultural workers in the Rio Grande Valley of Texas mirrored such trends. In an essay on the repatriation campaigns of 1928–1931, R. Reynolds McKay discusses the panic that extradition caused and provides insight regarding the ways the interests of the government and local businesses could (and did) diverge over repatriation. The study commences with a summary of the repatriation program's genesis. After being encouraged throughout the 1920s to come and labor in Texas, the federal government began clamping down on "illegals" crossing the border and coming to toil in the Rio Grande Valley during the summer of 1928. The region's agricultural entrepreneurs complained loudly and predicted detrimental consequences for the fall harvest. A Brownsville newspaper noted that field workers "'are frightened and they will leave rapidly as soon as they have accumulated a small amount of money from work in the cotton fields'" (McKay, "The Federal Deportation Campaign in Texas," p. 96). With the collapse of the stock market, federal agents intensified efforts to keep Mexicanos out and return those already residing in the United States. Their efforts produced a dramatic response from Valley business interests. Local producers, under the auspices of the chamber of commerce, established two organizations, the Confederación Mexicana de Obreros y Campesinos (the Mexican Confederation of Workers and Farm Laborers) and the Lower Rio Grande Valley, Inc., in hopes of maintaining the availability of labor.

The entities were created for three specific purposes: to keep laborers flowing from Mexico, to encourage those in the area to remain, and to assist workers in obtaining legal residency. Unfortunately, as the downturn intensified, the groups became impossible to maintain. Although reduced in scale after the Democratic victory in 1932, deportations continued in Texas; an estimated 250,000 Mexicans left the state during the decade of the Great Depression.

Before leaving the issue of deportation in the Lone Star State, it is necessary to briefly examine the subject as it played out in the state's largest metropolis, San Antonio. Here, as Julia Kirk Blackwelder notes in her book, *Women of the Depression: Caste and Culture in San Antonio, 1929–1939,* conditions were harsh, but pressure for extradition was mitigated by the economic reality of the "city's heavy dependence on the marginal labor of Hispanics, especially women" (Blackwelder, *Women of the Depression,* p. 14). Some whites in the Alamo City still favored expulsion, but the appalling economic situation made many Mexican men and women desperate enough to take almost any job, even at below subsistence wage levels. By not forcing "Mexican" laborers out of the city, "employers could pick and choose among workers because of the abundance of labor," and many employers actually improved their bottom lines (Blackwelder, *Women of the Depression,* p. 100).

Other illustrations of repatriation programs can be gleaned from the history of both rural and urban settings in California. In an important study on Mexicano migrant workers in the Golden State, Camille Guerin-Gonzales argues that the 1930s was the first time that the "federal government sponsored and supported the mass expulsion of immigrants" (Guerin-Gonzalez, *Mexican Workers and American Dreams,* p. 77). She cites two main reasons for the desire to expel these people: fear that they would become public charges and the belief that getting rid of such individuals would open jobs for "real" Americans. Guerin-Gonzales notes that, between 1931 and 1934, almost 17,000 Mexicans were repatriated from Los Angeles County and San Bernardino alone. In addition, she estimates that roughly 40 percent of those sent "back" to Mexico were under the age of twelve and probably born in the United States.

A final example for this section comes from a state that did not have a formal repatriation program. Even without such a program, historian Jorge Iber notes in his work *Hispanics in the Mormon Zion,* Utah witnessed a dramatic falling off in the number of Mexicanos during the 1930s because of the inability of families to survive the economic hardships caused by the Depression. According to the federal census, the Beehive State had a Mexican population of approximately 4,000 people in 1930, but by 1940 that number had dropped to less than 1,100.

Much of the Spanish-surnamed populace left Utah during the 1930s because of the downturn's impact on three key industries that employed most people of Mexican descent: the railroads, agriculture, and mining.

The pay of beet workers, for example, in Idaho (many of the families who worked in southern Idaho wintered in Salt Lake City) dropped from around $28 to about $10 per acre at the start of the decade (Balderrama and Rodríguez, *A Decade of Betrayal,* pp. 16–17). Miners also fared poorly, as the price of Utah's key extractive product, cooper, dropped to below the break-even price of 12¢ per pound by 1930. This drop led to a dramatic reduction in activity in Bingham Canyon, the state's largest mining facility. Finally, with low commodity prices impacting both agriculture and mining, railroads began reducing wages and laying off track workers (the positions that most Spanish-speaking laborers filled). One person caught in this difficult circumstance was a gentleman by the name of José Mendel who was interviewed by Utah historians in the 1970s.

> [He] worked on the tracks during the 1930s and, while grateful for the opportunity to work, complained bitterly that the railroad took advantage of its employees. Mendel's supervisor warned him that he could leave if working conditions were not to his satisfaction; there were more than enough laborers willing to accept his low-paying position. . . . José recalled that during the Depression years he earned only thirty-eight cents per hour, or about fourteen dollars for two weeks of work. His family stretched his meager pay by subsisting on potatoes and gravy. (Iber, *Hispanics in the Mormon Zion,* p. 44)

Given limited employment options and the desire to repatriate "outsiders," it is not surprising that states like Utah experienced dramatic declines in the number of Spanish-surnamed people in their populations during the 1930s. Nevertheless, many familias in barrios and colonias throughout the West managed to survive, even during the most difficult economic period in U.S. history.

The Puerto Rican experience in Hawaii was somewhat different. According to Norma Carr, boriquas on the islands faced difficulties, but did not endure direct calls for repatriation. They also managed to integrate themselves more fully into island society, and they were able to improve, to a certain extent, the way whites perceived their community. Carr argues that the creation of the Puerto Rican Civic Club (in 1931) helped spur this development. While specific activities will be detailed later, now it is enough to note that the association helped improve ties between borinkis and Hawaii's politicians. Further, the PRCC enabled Puertor-riqueños to contribute to charitable causes, participate in civic endeavors, and present a more positive display of their culture and people to the broader island society.

Still, Puerto Ricans faced hostility from members of other ethnic groups (such as the Filipinos and Japanese) because the HSPA used the threat of further boriqua recruitment to reduce worker complaints during the 1930s. This trend is visible not only in ethnic newspapers but the academic literature of the time. For example, Kum Pui Lai and Caroline Lee, sociology students at the University of Hawaii, produced theses during the 1930s that presented a very negative and stereotyped image of the islands' Puerto Ricans. Within both works, diligent and conscientious borinkis were repeatedly referred to as being "dependent and lazy," and as having low morals and deficient work habits (Carr, "The Puerto Ricans in Hawaii: 1900–1958, pp. 373 and 395–410).

ORGANIZING FOR A BETTER LIFE

Given the desire among many whites to "get rid of the Mexicans" during the Great Depression, as well as the other social and economic difficulties described previously, it is not unexpected that Spanish speakers turned to various self-help groups even more strongly than they had before to sustain their communities.

Social Organizations

The most significant of such entities during the Great Depression, as before, were the mutual aid societies. We have already discussed the fact that wherever a population of Mexican descent concentrated, *mutuales* quickly became part of daily life. Their functions of celebrating Mexican culture, providing limited insurance benefits, seeking ways to present the comunidad in a more positive light to the broader public, and defending civil rights had become more important than ever. One author summarized their importance by arguing that, "In the 1920s and 1930s these societies represented the only continuous organizations life among Mexicans in which the initiative comes wholly from the Mexicans themselves. Their importance transcends the (limited) benefits given in case of illness or death" (Hernández, *Mutual Aid for Survival,* p. 6).

September 16 celebration poster, Bingham Canyon, Utah, 1942. (Utah History Research Center)

Mexican girls celebrate a quinceañera *party, Salt Lake City, Utah, 1930s. (Utah History Research Center)*

One of the earliest, and most common, examples of the work of mutuales (and other organizations), which was not discussed in Chapter 5, was the observance of *fiestas patrias* (Mexican patriotic holidays such as el Diez y Seis de Septiembre and el Cinco de Mayo). As José Alamillo notes in his study of celebrations in Corona, California, between the 1920s and 1950, the commemorations initially served as a way for the Mexican government to remind citizens living in el norte of their native land as well as to "convince emigrants to return . . . and help modernize the Mexican nation with their newfound skills and acquired savings" (Alamillo, "More than a Fiesta," p. 62). Such events, however, underwent a dramatic change with the coming of the Great Depression. Whereas during the 1920s the fetes provided remembrance, by the mid-1930s, in response to deportation campaigns and negative stereotyping of Mexicans, the Spanish speakers of Corona used the festivals to demonstrate ties to the United States. Alamillo notes that the late 1930s the celebrations featured baseball games, not only traditional Mexican dances but swing and jazz music, and floats featuring both Mexican and U.S. flags.

Mutualistas also believed it was their responsibility to help the destitute and downtrodden, and this function of course became more important

Children of the west side barrio, Salt Lake City, Utah, 1930s. (Utah History Research Center)

than ever during the Depression. One example of this work is presented in Tom Sheridan's *Los Tusconenses: The Mexican Community in Tucson, 1854–1941,* where the author notes the extensive efforts of local Mexican Americans who, through the Alianza-Hispano Americana (and other organizations) provided sustenance for poor children when little assistance entered the barrio from the Anglo community. Vicki Ruiz's study, *From Out of the Shadows: Mexican Women in Twentieth Century America,* provides further insight into such work as well as delineating the considerable role of women, more important during the Depression than ever, in the mutualistas' charitable work, stating that "Women through mutualistas, sought to help their neighbors; they worked within their communities in a public way although their labor generally remained invisible outside the barrio" (Ruiz, *Out of the Shadows,* p. 88).

Additionally, volunteer work in mutuales often stimulated women's engagement in other activities, such as direct political action; Ruiz notes, for example, that many of the mothers who had participated in California mutual aid activities helped establish the Comité de Vecinos de Lemon Grove (the Lemon Grove Neighbors Committee) which "mustered the courage to protest segregation" (Ruiz, *Out of the Shadows,* p. 89) and resulted in the groundbreaking *Alvarez v. Lemon Grove School District* decision, which prohibited the segregation of Mexicano children, in 1931.

A final area of involvement by mutuales (and similar organizations) was in recreation. Recent studies by Richard Santillán and Jose Alamillo demonstrate the value of such undertakings for both individual and barrio pride. Santillan's study focuses on baseball teams in places such as Newton, Kansas, where Spanish speakers were banned from using public parks before World War II. No matter, for industrious Mexicanos created diamonds in open pastures near the town; often using dried cow dung as bases. Similar programs existed in other towns throughout the Sunflower State, Missouri, Nebraska, and elsewhere. Alamillo discusses a similar trend in southern California, and notes that baseball *ligas* provided citrus workers and betabeleros (both men and women) with opportunities to "promote ethnic consciousness, build community solidarity . . . and sharpen . . . organizational skills" (Alamillo, *"Peloteros,"* p. 192).

The Puerto Rican Civic Club (PRCC) of Hawaii, created in 1931, performed similar duties. The initial PRCC leadership had two goals: (1) to ally itself with the Republican Party (and through this, with the HSPA) and its candidates for civic office, in order to gain certain perks for Puerto Ricans, and (2) to challenge the negative stereotyping of boriquas in area newspapers. By creating political ties, members hoped to be able to garner assistance from politicos in exchange for votes. One benefit derived was the establishment of a park to serve the needs of a Puerto Rican baseball league in the early 1930s. The club was also quite successful in forging ties with the *Star Bulletin* and the *Advertiser,* local tabloids, in order to improve the representation and treatment of the Puerto Rican community in the papers' stories and editorials.

Although the PRCC generated some benefits for the community, not all boriquas were happy with its ties to the Republican Party, which many considered an enemy of the working class. This concern stimulated the creation of a second organization, the Puerto Rican Independent Club

(PRIC) in 1932, which focused more on providing members with insurance against illness and death. Because of financial limitations, however, PRIC quickly dropped disability coverage and concentrated on death benefits. Though there were squabbles based on political differences, the two organizations cooperated on many events and ultimately merged in 1973.

EVERARDO CARLOS LERMA: ATHLETIC AND COACHING PIONEER IN SOUTH TEXAS

One of the major themes that we have discussed in this book has been the way Spanish-speaking persons in the U.S. West have struggled against discrimination and racism and sought to earn their share of the American dream. As is clear from the text, this exertion for greater equality took many forms, and in many different fields of endeavor: education, labor, politics, and so on. One of the fields that few historians had examined previously for traces of these efforts, however, was sports. Fortunately, in the last few years, individuals such as Samuel O. Regalado, Jose Alamillo, and Jorge Iber have broken new ground in the examination of Hispanic life in the West through their research on the role of sport in barrio life. The story that follows is but one example of the many diligent people of Mexican descent who have worked to open doors in new fields of endeavor, in this case as an athlete (in particular, as a football player), coach, and educator, for the Spanish-speaking people of the West during the twentieth century.

Everardo Carlos Lerma (known as E.C.) was born in the small South Texas town of Bishop in 1915. His parents had moved to the area a few years before, emigrating from Mier, Tamaulipas, Mexico. The young Lerma faced many obstacles during his youth, including being orphaned by age eight, poverty, and the low expectations of Mexican American students on the part of many of the teachers within the public school system of Kingsville, Texas. During the first decades of the 1900s, few Mexican Americans from this region graduated from high school (indeed, few completed this level of training anywhere in the state). As we have discussed, the reasons for this sad trend were varied, but included the systematic discouraging of pupils of Mexican descent by holding them back year after year and the need for these youths to help support their families, especially during the years of the Great Depression. Given the economic and familial situation of the Lerma clan, it was likely that E.C. would simply be another statistic, doomed to a lifetime of work as a field hand or day laborer who would never be able to improve his lot. Thanks to the diligent efforts of his ten older bothers and sisters, and E.C.'s own diligence in the classroom and his physical prowess, he in fact achieved many firsts through his athletic and coaching career.

As with many young men in Texas during the 1920s, E.C. was captivated by the gridiron battles that he witnessed on fall Friday nights, and as he reached his early teens, he dreamt of becoming the first Mexican American to don the jersey of the Kingsville High Brahmas. When he took the field in the early 1930s, many of his colleagues were, to put it mildly, less than thrilled, and some of his teammates actually threw him into a swimming pool. Still, through persistence and talent, E.C. won most of the players to his side, and he capped his high school gridiron career by being named to the all-district team after his senior season in 1933. His abilities attracted the attention of Texas Christian University, and the young Lerma was offered a scholarship by the Fort Worth-based institution. E.C., however, decided to stay close to home and instead accepted an opportunity to play for Texas A & I University (now renamed Texas A&M University, Kingsville).

The circumstances he faced were little different from his days at Kingsville High, as the future coach once again endured discrimination and cheap shots while playing for the freshman squad in 1934. Still, he eventually earned the respect of other members of the frosh team, and, as one of his teammates recalled, "'when we scrimmaged the varsity, we did all we could to see that E.C. got a fair shake. It took only two or three scrimmages for the varsity to realize that Lerma was here to stay, and they also developed respect'" (Iber, "Mexican Americans," p. 626). Eventually, Lerma lettered for the Javelinas, from 1935 through 1937.

Upon graduation in 1938, the young E.C., now recently married, took a job as an assistant head coach at Benavides High School in Duval County. After serving in this position, he applied for the field general position in 1940. The reaction of many in town was as expected. Did a "Mexican" have the intellectual capacity it took to guide a football program? As Lerma noted in a 1997 interview with the *McAllen Monitor,* "'People just couldn't believe that a Mexican American could do as good a job as an Anglo. Well, I think I proved them wrong'" (Iber, "Mexican Americans," p. 626).

The administration of the Benavides district was well rewarded for making Lerma one of the first head coaches of Mexican descent in the state of Texas. Between 1940 and 1955, the Eagles compiled an impressive run of football, basketball, and track glory; all under the leadership of a Mexican American head coach. In football, his record included two regional crowns (as far as a class B team could go in that era, since there was no state champion for class B Texas schools), three bi-district titles, and four district titles. After Coach Lerma left the community in 1955 to pursue opportunities at a larger school (Rio Grande City), the Benavides Eagles did not make the state playoffs in football again until 1984. By the time of his retirement from coaching in 1965, this now legendary football coach had compiled an overall football record of 154 wins, 98 losses, and 13 outright or shared crowns.

In subsequent years E.C. Lerma worked as a coordinator of physical education, as director of Migrant Education, as supervisor of Adult Basic Education (all for the McAllen school district), as principal of several schools in South Texas and Dallas, and finally, as superintendent of schools for the Benavides Independent School District in 1975–1976.

He finally retired in 1980, after breaking down barriers to Mexican American participation and leadership in education, administration, and sports. A final honor to this pioneer came in the fall of 1991, when Benavides named its football stadium in his honor. The community that in 1940 doubted whether a Mexican American had sufficient intelligence and leadership skills to pilot a football program bestowed its greatest tribute on this son of humble Mexican immigrants. Coach Lerma lived in McAllen until succumbing to complications from cancer in April of 1998 and dying at the age of 83.

One endeavor that fostered unity and cooperation between the PRCC and PRIC during the 1930s was sports. Both groups helped fund and provided competitors for the territory's Puerto Rican Baseball League. This entity provided boriquas with an opportunity to socialize, retain cultural traditions, and pit themselves against teams comprised of other ethnic groups (such as the Portuguese, Japanese, and whites). Additionally, contests often served as employment vehicles. As Norma Carr notes, when an individual player gained some fame, local firms (such as Hawaiian Electric and Mutual Telephone) would offer jobs as an enticement to play for company teams.

The Role of Religion

As detailed in the previous chapter, the Catholic Church established missions, parishes, schools, and other institutions designed to accomplish several important objectives among Spanish speakers in the West between 1900 and 1930. The goals included providing relief, preserving aspects of Mexican Catholic culture (while simultaneously pushing Americanization), and keeping members of the flock away from the influences of Protestant missionaries. Such aims remained at the center of Catholic work with Spanish speakers during the years of the Great Depression, with relief of course becoming ever more important. In the next paragraphs we note a few examples of such efforts.

In an article entitled "Between Alienation and Ethnicity: The Evolution of Mexican American Catholicism in San Antonio, 1910–1940," David A. Badillo presents readers with an overview of the church's role in the city's west side barrio and details the existence of relief efforts (both spiritual and material) by the archdiocese and individual priests. Particularly important was the work of Father Carmelo Tranchese who, after being transferred to Our Lady of Guadalupe Church in 1932, encouraged workers during the pecan shellers' strike of 1938, worked with the barrio-based School Improvement League to better educational facilities and conditions for barrio children, and lobbied for the construction of publicly funded housing projects. Tranchese also sponsored jamaicas, novenas, and commemorations of the feast of Our Lady of Guadalupe in order to sustain a sense of pride and community among his charges. In addition to such activities, the church also pushed for the Americanization of people

Our Lady of Guadalupe Parish, Salt Lake City, Utah, 1940s. (Utah History Research Center)

of Mexican descent, often tying itself to the efforts of working with middle-class reformers to establish the parameters of what it meant to be "Mexican American."

Another essay focusing on the church's relations with Mexicanos is by Roberto R. Treviño. His study offers an analysis of both the limits of and potential for social change provided by Catholic ministry. Trevino, using archdiocesan and diocesan archives, provides an overview of the myriad chores performed by nuns in Houston and San Antonio between the years 1910 and 1950. Although offering many social services to help destitute Mexicanos, Trevino argues that some sisters had "internalized the pervasive racial prejudice against Mexicans, . . . [so that] their ministry [was] greatly limited, if not [rendered] totally ineffective, by their own racial biases." He, for example, cites stories of teachers not caring about instructing Spanish-surnamed children because, after all, "it did not matter what they learned" (Treviño, "Facing Jim Crow," p. 144). Still,

Trevino's research uncovered many more instances where nuns worked for progressive causes, challenging the stereotyping of Spanish speakers and working to bring together people of all races. Overall, the efforts of such women disclose that, in the Lone Star State during the years of the Great Depression, the majority of nuns "never relinquished the ideal of a more just society" (Treviño, "Facing Jim Crow," p. 164).

As Jorge Iber notes in his research on Salt Lake City, Spanish speakers living in the metropolis' west side barrio endured grinding poverty, but benefited from the efforts of a group of nuns from the Order of Perpetual Adoration, as well as the energy and zeal of an Irish American priest named James E. Collins. Collins and *las madres,* "the mothers" (as nuns were called), sponsored baseball games, festivals, summer camps, and a Boy Scout troop, offered a meeting place for the Centro Civico Mexicano gatherings, and backed other activities to sustain daily life. Although the often cash-strapped Salt Lake Diocese could not afford to provide direct aid, the endeavors of church personnel turned the mission into a spiritual and psychic beacon where the barrio's population could "pray, gather as a community, and celebrate their heritage." The effectiveness of the efforts made by Collins and the nuns is demonstrated by the growth of the congregation during the 1930s, for "although the number of Spanish speakers in the area decreased during these years, the congregation at Guadalupe grew from 480 in 1931 to over 700 by 1939" (Iber, *Hispanics in the Mormon Zion,* pp. 35 and 48–49).

In Los Angeles, the archdiocese provided aid through nine community centers in predominantly Mexican neighborhoods by the middle of the decade. As Jeffrey Burns notes in his essay "Catholic Ministry in the Era of the 'Mexican Problem,'" these facilities offered programs like those previously noted and also supplied the needy with direct aid through the auspices of the Catholic Welfare Bureau and the St. Vincent de Paul Society. Similar efforts took place elsewhere in the metropolitan areas of the Golden State (Dolan, *Mexican Americans and the Catholic Church, 1900–1965,* pp. 157–159). While the church struggled to serve the spiritual and physical needs of Mexicanos, George J. Sánchez notes that it faced another major challenge: proselytizing by Protestants. The number of converts was never large during the 1930s, but numerous denominations made inroads. Historians of the church's relation with Mexican

Americans have noted that priests were often dismissive of converts, arguing that they transferred allegiance in hope of material advantages. Although this may have been true for some, researchers have demonstrated that conversions were not based exclusively on such expectations; many Mexicanos perceived their switch to another faith rather as an "expression of personal change, but also of acculturation" (Dolan, *Mexican Americans and the Catholic Church, 1900–1965,* p. 95). Conversion provided barrio dwellers with a sense of increased personal capacity that helped produce a core group of community leaders who often transferred their guidance, skills, and knowledge into broader activities, often political and economic.

It is necessary to mention one more point before leaving behind our discussion of Protestant proselytizing, and that is that most of the denominations stressed Americanization as part of the conversion process. Though some authors have noted and criticized efforts to root out the "Mexicanness" of converts, not all see the efforts of the Protestant missionaries in a completely negative light. One historian argues that, though such efforts were ethnocentric and often disrespectful of Mexican traditions, it is impossible to deny the benefits that conversion and Protestant organizations provided, especially during the 1930s. Vicki L. Ruiz sums up her argument for a more nuanced stand on this topic thus:

> Americanization programs have come under a lot of criticism from historians over the past two decades and numerous passages [in her research] . . . provide fodder for sarcasm among contemporary readers. Although cringing at the ethnocentrism, . . . I respect the . . . workers for their health and childcare services. Before judging . . . missionaries too harshly, it is important to keep in mind the social services they rendered over an extended period of time as well as the environment in which they lived. (Ruiz, *Out of the Shadows,* p. 40)

Labor Organizations

The Mexican-descent population of the West was quite active in labor-organizing campaigns during the 1930s. Their efforts always included the participation of both men and women, as well as community organizations, such as churches and mutual aid societies. In many cases, Spanish speakers cobbled together, if only temporarily, coalitions with other ethnic groups as well as outside entities (such as the American Civil Liberties Union) in attempts to challenge difficult circumstances and seek greater economic justice. Following are two examples from California and Texas that illustrate the struggle for increased pay and improved working conditions.

One of the most significant actions involving Mexicanos (betabeleros, in this case) during the Great Depression took place in Oxnard, California. This incident, according to historian Frank J. Barajas, the source used for what follows, is noteworthy for two principal reasons: first, it harks back to the activist ideology of the earlier Oxnard strike of 1903 (mentioned in chapter 5), and second, it "garnered a critical mass of support from inside—and from outside the community" (Barajas, "Resistance, Radicalism, and Repression on the Oxnard Plain," pp. 30 and 50).

On August 7, 1933, approximately 1,200 workers (80 percent of whom were Mexican and the remaining 20 percent Filipino) struck against the American Beet Sugar Company, demanding a wage increase and recognition. The action featured a variety of vicious tactics by the conglomerate: police intimidation, creation of a company workers' organization designed to destroy solidarity, and infringement of recruiters' civil rights. Although the union failed to achieve acknowledgment, it did generate a wage increase, as well as improving conditions; as other area firms became "anxious to avoid strikes within their orchards and packing houses . . . [other] growers preemptively increased the wage rate of their workers" (Barajas, "Resistance, Radicalism and Repression on the Oxnard Plain," p. 46). Also, the alliance created national awareness of the betabeleros' plight, attracting the attention of the American Civil Liberties Union and the International Labor Defense (among others), and bringing a strong progressive coalition into the fray. Such activities, Barajas asserts, even during the depth of the Great Depression, are illustrative of the willingness of Spanish speakers to stand up for their rights and served as "a foundation for subsequent labor conflicts . . . throughout California from the 1940s to the campaigns of the United Farm Workers during the 1960s" (Barajas, "Resistance, Radicalism and Repression on the Oxnard Plain," p. 51).

A second major strike involving Mexican Americans took place in San Antonio in 1938. This action is significant, not only because of the results it achieved, but also due to the noteworthy role of women in the union's activities. Historian Vicki L. Ruiz provides extensive coverage of this event, noting that conditions in the sweatshops were horrific (with most employees earning an average of $2 per week by 1934). Still, employers argued that they did not abuse laborers since, in addition to salaries, "shellers could eat all of the pecans they desired and chat with friends while they worked" (Ruiz, *Out of the Shadows,* pp. 79–80). Into this challenging state of affairs entered two ardent leaders, Emma Tenayuca and Luisa Moreno. The women recruited, guided, and helped sustain between 6,000 and 10,000 workers during a six-week strike, which eventually brought executives to the bargaining table and produced union recognition as well as a promise to comply with federal minimum wage statutes (twenty-five cents per hour worked). With unionization, many families could earn a living wage, and this trend helped reduce the number of children working in the industry. Unfortunately, by 1950 mechanization of pecan shelling crippled the organization, and the number of shellers employed in San Antonio declined from more than 10,000 to around 350.

One final note is necessary before finishing our discussion of Spanish speakers and union activism during the 1930s. It is not possible to provide extensive information on all actions involving the Spanish-surnamed during the 1930s; to mention only a few examples, over the past two decades historians have detailed the activities and participation of Mexicanos in 1930s strikes in El Monte, Orange County, and Madera, California, as well as in the beet-growing regions of Wyoming, Colorado, Nebraska, and Montana.

The Politics of Group Identity

In Chapter 5 we discussed issues that stimulated activism by Spanish-surnamed people during the later part of the nineteenth and the early twentieth centuries. Among their fundamental concerns were civil rights, economic grievances, and poor treatment of the community's children by school officials. During the 1920s and the Great Depression, organizations arose throughout the West to continue such battles. By the late 1930s, the most important of these, the League of United Latin American Citizens (LULAC), had produced a clearly articulated argument that called for an end to discrimination and the fuller inclusion of people of Mexican descent into mainstream American society. Before proceeding with an overview of LULAC's endeavors, however, we provide one example of the educational and economic circumstances confronting most Spanish speakers throughout the West during the Great Depression. In the years after 1930 such concerns, and the working out of ways to challenge them, lay at the heart of LULAC's activism.

Thomas Sheridan's research on Tucson, Arizona, notes that, before World War II, Mexican-heritage pupils were the largest single group within city schools. There were, however, few teachers or administrators of similar background (never more than 5 percent before 1941). Sheridan's investigation further indicates that many Anglo educators believed that Spanish speakers would never "amount to anything unless they forgot every word of their native tongue." Not surprisingly, such a state of affairs made it difficult for such children to earn diplomas. For example, one report from 1929 noted that, although the number of white and Spanish-surnamed pupils was roughly equal in elementary facilities, by the time a class reached the ninth grade, the "Mexicans" accounted for fewer than one in six high school students. The impact of such educational limitations was also evident in Tucson's occupational structure. Without the credentials necessary to compete for higher-paying jobs, most trabajadores toiled in unskilled or semiskilled posts (75 percent in 1940, while only 36 percent of whites filled such positions) (Sheridan, *Los Tusconenses,* pp. 235–236).

The League of United Latin American Citizens, which resulted from the consolidation of several mutual aid and veterans organizations, held its founding convention in Corpus Christi, Texas, in May, 1929. From its inception, LULAC positioned itself as the voice of the Mexican American middle class (the small number of doctors, lawyers, and other professionals, as well as barrio-based entrepreneurs) and sought to end discrimination as well as pushing for "American social institutions to accommodate yet another immigrant group" (Márquez, *LULAC,* p. 19). The association's leadership called for greater economic and social opportunity, but also (unfortunately) drew a clear distinction between "Mexican Americans" (people of Mexican descent born in the United States) and the newly arrived immigrants who performed menial labor throughout the West. In the decade of the 1930s, LULAC established dozens of councils in southern Texas (and subsequently in other states) taking up causes such as improving community and personal hygiene, beautifying neighborhoods, and paying poll taxes.

During the Depression, LULAC's members were busy improving numerous aspects of colonial life, but the group's main thrust was the improvement of education. In his study of Texas schools and Mexican Americans, Guadalupe San Miguel presents a long list of activities that LULACers undertook in order to increase academic success among barrio youths. The primary concern of reformers before World War II was, not surprisingly, challenging segregation.

The 1876 constitution of Texas, for example, permitted separation of blacks and whites, but it contained no such provision for children of Mexican descent. Conditions varied from locale to locale, but most local school officials funneled Spanish-surnamed students into separate classes at least during elementary grades. The two most commonly cited reasons for separation were (1) the apprehension by whites that the mere presence of "Mexicans" in classrooms limited academic progress, and (2) the belief that barrio offspring were dirty and passed on diseases to classmates. LULAC's members countered that such practices were damaging and, indeed, "the major obstacle to educational progress and to the learning of English." Initially, the organization challenged such despicable practices by filing a lawsuit (*Independent School District v. Salvatierra* in 1931). The Salvatierra challenge, funded in part by LULAC, is significant because it "was the first case in which the courts were asked to exercise . . . judicial review to determine the constitutionality of the actions of a local school district with respect to the education of Mexican Americans" (San Miguel, Jr., *"Let All of Them Take Heed,"* p. 80). The legal action was partially successful, as a Texas court ruled that Spanish-surnamed students could not be segregated purely on racial/ethnic grounds. At the same time, however, the judge asserted that children could be separated based on limited English proficiency.

Further legal challenges to the poor treatment of Spanish speakers followed in subsequent decades. The miniscule resources available to LULAC during the 1930s most often dictated a different type of strategy for bringing about educational change: moral suasion. This technique produced some limited gains during the 1930s, as the group won small victories against discriminatory practices in places such as San Antonio, Seguin, Cotulla, and Kingsville, all in Texas.

Before leaving behind the Great Depression era and LULAC's activities, it is necessary to point out two major shortcomings of the organization discussed by Benjamin Marquez. First, as we have briefly noted, middle-class LULACers tended to draw sharp distinctions between themselves and those they perceived as less worthy Mexicano brethren. The implications of this stance will be detailed later through an examination of LULAC's stance on the bracero program. Second, in its attempt to better conditions for Spanish-surnamed children in public schools (especially in Texas), LULAC often claimed that people of Mexican descent were really "white" and should be treated as such. This argument often generated hateful commentary against African Americans that made some LULACers sound just as racist as some whites. An example of such unfortunate utterances is found in a 1936 letter by association member Gregory R. Salinas, disturbed by black musicians playing at some Corpus Christi fiestas: "These musicians are now playing . . . at Mexican dances and no doubt will ply their nefarious trade on young girls of our race. Mr. Guerrero will acquaint you with the situation in detail, and will explain to you what can be done to correct it. . . . Let us tell these Negroes that we are not going to permit our manhood and womanhood to mingle with them on an equal basis" (Márquez, *LULAC,* p. 33).

Bradford Luckingham describes a similar incident, which took place in Phoenix in 1935 when the Latin American Club of Arizona (a Mexican American political and civic group) "presented a resolution to the Phoenix City Commission asking that blacks be excluded from using Southside Park . . . [in] a largely Mexican neighborhood" (Luckingham, *Minorities in Phoenix,* pp. 45 and 46).

WORLD WAR II

In order to gain a better perspective on the impact of World War II on Hispanics in the West, we note a few economic statistics presented in Richard White's study. For example, by 1943, more than 520,000 persons worked in aircraft manufacturing and shipyards in California; Seattle and other Washington communities employed roughly 250,000 laborers in similar facilities; the town of Vanport (near Portland), which did not exist before the war, grew to a population of 40,000; the government subsidized the creation of the largest magnesium plant in the world in Henderson, Nevada; and it established the massive Geneva Steel Works (which employed 14,000) near Provo, Utah (White, "*It's Your Misfortune,*" pp. 496–502). The above are illustrative of the impact of federal and private investment in response to wartime demand. In total, the national government infused over $70 billion into the West. Such enormous enterprises needed laborers, and men and women of all backgrounds headed west, searching for opportunity. Spanish-surnamed people were part of the mobilization, as thousands left rural areas for the industrializing centers of the West. White effectively sums up this migration by stating that it "was as if someone had tilted the country; (and) people, money and soldiers all spilled west" (White, "*It's Your Misfortune,*" p. 496).

The dramatic economic changes during World War II generated much social upheaval. The large numbers of newly arrived residents produced overcrowding, a lack of basic services, and increased racial tensions in many western locales. Still, the Spanish-surnamed in the region had reason to believe that the wartime economy would permit them fuller inclusion in U.S. society, primarily through the application of mechanisms such as Executive Orders 8802 and 9346 (which established and strengthened the Fair Employment Practices Committee). Historian Emilio Zamora summarizes their hopes:

> Mexicans came out of the Depression facing an unprecedented opportunity to improve their traditional position as low-wage labor and to alter the generational effects of prior occupational discrimination. The wartime rhetoric of democracy, public policy measures that prohibited discrimination by defense industries, government employers and labor unions, and, above all, dramatic job growth in high wage firms led Mexicans to believe that their time had indeed arrived. (Zamora, "The Failed Promise of Wartime Opportunity for Mexicans in the Texas Oil Industry," p. 323)

As we will consider later, this initial optimism was not fully justified, as the barriers to occupational (and social) opportunity were not completely removed. For now, however, we will present a few examples of the movement of Spanish speakers into better paying occupations, as well as the

The Salazar family's proud veteranos, Salt Lake City, Utah, 1960s. (Utah History Research Center)

impact of the era's economic and social changes on daily life in barrio communities.

A recent article from the *New Mexico Historical Review* provides valuable insights on topics such as gender roles, economic opportunity, and demographic changes in a particular comunidad: the Barelas neighborhood of Albuquerque. Carmen R. Chávez, who was a high school senior in 1942, begins her essay with an examination of the wave of patriotic fervor that swept the barrio after Pearl Harbor. Many friends and neighbors volunteered for active duty, and their resolve to serve was so fervent that, Chávez notes, "one young man from our neighborhood . . . killed himself when he was classified 4F, . . . he could not face his friends knowing he would not serve at their sides" (Chávez, "Coming of Age during the War," p. 386).

The young men from this New Mexico barrio were part of the estimated 250,000 to 500,000 Spanish-surnamed individuals who served during World War II. The quantity of historical research conducted on Hispanic participation on the battlefields of this conflict is woefully inadequate; one of the few books that explores the topic is *Among the Valiant: Mexican Americans in World War II and Korea,* by Raúl Mórin. Here, the author provides details about, to take one example, the men of the New Mexico National Guard unit that endured the Bataan Death March in the Philippines, as well as other tales of *coraje* (courage) shown by individuals with Spanish surnames who served the United States military in all theaters; including the twelve (all of Mexican descent) who earned the Medal of Honor for service above and beyond the call of duty.

The essay by Carmen R. Chávez quoted above describes the economic and social transformation in her community during the war years. She recalls, for example, that downtown Albuquerque stores began hiring men and women of Mexican descent to work counters previously staffed almost exclusively by whites. The trend eventually provided Chávez with an opportunity to move into management at Montgomery Ward. The chance to work in retailing offered her a different outlook on life as "through earning . . . wages, we had a taste of independence we hadn't known before the war." In conjunction with new economic possibilities, many of Chávez's *amigas* (female friends) met, dated, and married Anglo men, further diversifying the community's composition. The barrio confronted still other demographic changes, as "families left Barelas in search of jobs elsewhere while other ethnic groups moved into our predominantly Hispanic community." Finally, by the conflict's end, Chávez detected a dramatic, and important, transformation in the attitudes of Barelas' returning veterans, "who came back [and] seemed so different—so changed, so much older. If they had not received their diplomas before the war, they chose not to go back to high school. Many instead applied for a GED. Great numbers of returning GIs . . . took advantage of the GI Bill of Rights [to attend] colleges or trade schools" (Chávez, "Coming of Age During the War," pp. 385, 386, and 396).

Many Spanish-surnamed people who left New Mexico or southern Colorado migrated to work in the industrial and transportation web that developed in northern Utah during the war years, and, as Jorge Iber notes, thousands of beet workers, track laborers, and miners scurried to fill positions. The demand for labor afforded movement into higher-skilled and better-paying positions for some Spanish speakers employed by railroads, the copper industry, manufacturing facilities (such as the Geneva Works and Remington Small Arms Plant), and military bases and depots throughout the state.

Utah's Spanish-surnamed women benefited from the economy's vitality during the war years as well. Although most worked in "traditional" occupations (food processing and laundries, for example), some, such as Clotilda Gómez, moved into the fields of manufacturing and transportation. In a 1987 interview, Clotilda recounted how she endured sexual harassment and racial discrimination while toiling in a Salt Lake City railroad yard. She bore these burdens in order to support her children while her husband served in the military. Like Carmen Chávez, Gómez was proud of her role in the home front's economy, as well as her newfound independence: "'I think that women changed from that era. . . . [They took] this change in their lives in order to make decisions and work. Even among the Mexican families there started being a change with the women because they realized they were equal to men'" (Iber, *Hispanics in the Mormon Zion,* p. 59).

One final example of World War II's economic changes, and the improvements it provided for Spanish speakers, is found in Dionicio Nodin Valdes' study on barrios in St. Paul and other parts of the Midwest. Here, as in New Mexico, Utah, and elsewhere, Spanish-surnamed families from the Southwest and Mexico, began earning better pay while working in traditional fields such as commercial agriculture, as well as moving into "more permanent and higher-paying jobs in meatpacking, steel mills, defense plants, railroads, textile shops, and other urban industries, . . . [and] becoming an increasingly permanent segment of the region's industrial proletariat (Valdés, *Barrios Norteños,* p. 130).

In addition to laboring in factories, fields, and military installations of the West during the early 1940s, a few historians have noted the efforts undertaken by people of Mexican descent in activities that bolstered morale and in other aspects of the home front's war effort. For example, as Christine Marin explains in her article "Mexican Americans on the Home Front: Community Organizations in Arizona During World War II," barrio residents (through mutuales and similar organizations) in Phoenix were quite active in numerous vocational training programs, as volunteers in the picking and bagging of cotton and in welcoming Latin American cadets who trained at nearby installations.

Norma Carr notes that the wartime boom generated important modifications to the lives of Puerto Ricans in Hawaii (who numbered 8,296 by 1940). First, improved earnings at governmental facilities and sugar plantations permitted the establishment of a number of borinki-owned businesses, such as bars, service stations, and coffee farms. Second, the war years stimulated further integration of islanderos into the territory's social fabric. During the 1940s, Carr cites trends such as an escalating exogamous marriage rate, growing union membership, and an augmented boriqua presence at Hawaii's institutions of higher learning. Such patterns, she asserts, "raised the expectations . . . for a relationship of equals" with other Americans in the postwar years (Carr, "The Puerto Ricans in Hawaii, 1900–1958," pp. 298–301 and 305).

Commercial development also increased Puerto Rican dispersal into other Western states, such as Utah. Just as the sugar planters of Hawaii did in the early 1900s, the copper mining concerns of Bingham Canyon recruited in Puerto Rico during the 1940s. In total, several hundred came, attracted by promises of good conditions and pay. Not surprisingly, the circumstances Utah islanderos confronted were not as positive as promised. In addition to encountering a climate totally unlike that of their homeland, the men were relegated to menial labor and given little chance for promotion; they endured discrimination, not just from whites, but also from Hispanics who had begun to move into more highly skilled positions. Carlos Grimm, the Mexican consul in Salt Lake City, went as far as to equate newly arrived Spanish speakers with blacks, saying that "Spanish blood did not diffuse through Puerto Rico. During the early slave trading days, Negro blood mixed with that of the Puerto Ricans."

Jesus Arinaz, mine worker, Bingham Canyon, Utah, 1942. (Utah History Research Center)

Unfortunately, although they spoke the same language, "social, economic, and cultural differences precluded the creation of ties between the 'old' and 'new' Spanish speakers of Bingham Canyon" (Iber, *Hispanics in the Mormon Zion,* pp. 60–61).

There is substantial evidence to support the assertion that Spanish-surnamed people benefited from the West's economic transformation. Such an assessment, however, presents only part of the total historical picture. It is necessary, therefore, to consider the constraints that still shackled the progress of Spanish speakers. In order to accomplish this task, we turn to three examples: the mistreatment of Mexican workers at oil facilities in Texas; the numerous negative aspects of the bracero program; and the Sleepy Lagoon incident and Zoot-Suit Riots in California. All three of these exemplify the negative side of Hispanic life on the World War II home front.

In a 1992 article, Emilio Zamora analyzes the difficulties Mexican-born workers confronted at oil refineries along the Texas Gulf Coast and argues that their treatment reveals the limitation of Executive Orders 8802 and 9346; as well as the tenacity of Anglos in challenging the elimination of discriminatory practices. Zamora asserts that Spanish speakers toiling at Humble, Shell, Sinclair, and other plants, for example, were relegated to menial occupations and seldom promoted. The principal reason was because of the Fair Employment Practices Commission's unwillingness to force producers' adherence to a single policy of nondiscrimination throughout the industry. Additionally, Zamora states, local union leaders refused to support grievances filed by Mexicanos, fearing loss of support from whites. In sum, in this important industry, while "some improvements for minority workers resulted," during the early 1940s, the "most striking result was yet another delay in the full incorporation of Mexican workers into the Texas occupational structure" (Zamora, "The Failed Promise of Wartime Opportunity for Mexicans in the Texas Oil Industry," pp. 349–350).

A second situation that epitomizes the negative experiences of Spanish-surnamed persons in the West during the war years is the way the bracero program was implemented. As previously noted, increased opportunities in wartime production enticed many Mexican Americans to abandon rural areas to seek employment in factories and military facilities. This trend created a labor shortage that motivated western agricultural interests to lobby the federal government to permit workers from Mexico entry into the country. By August of 1942 the two nations reached an agreement designed to bring braceros (a term derived from the Spanish word for "arm") to work in fields throughout the nation. Through 1947, an estimated 220,000 individuals toiled in the United States under the auspices of this program (Gutierrez, *Walls and Mirrors,* pp. 133–134).

Laborers were promised certain benefits: they would not be drafted or face discriminatory practices; they would earn a minimum wage and have tolerable living conditions. Many employers failed to live up to such contractual obligations. In research on the Pacific Northwest, Erasmo Gamboa notes that Mexicanos taken to Washington and Oregon, to take one example, endured unsanitary conditions, substandard housing, and blatant discrimination in public spaces. Another case of such problems is found in the work on the Midwest carried out by Dionicio Nodín Valdés. Inspectors found that bracero camps often had "abysmal conditions, unsanitary housing, a lack of proper toilet, laundry and recreational facilities, spoiled and poorly prepared food, and illegal deductions from paychecks" (Valdés, *Barrios Norteños,* p. 133–134). In Idaho, the Caldwell Village Camp housed not only single, male braceros, but also migrant, Mexican American (primarily from Texas) families. Here, administrators neglected their duties by not enforcing attendance laws that required local schools to accept and educate the workers' off-spring. Stereotyping and discriminatory practices against Spanish speakers were also recorded in parts of Wyoming; with conditions in Worland and Torrington so severe that Denver's Mexican consul threatened to withdraw all braceros from the state. In Texas, strenuous protestations by farmers against the minimal guarantees stipulated in bracero contracts (the agricultural interests argued that such provisions interfered with the "free market") got the state blacklisted by the Mexican government in June 1943. Not until after the creation of the Good Neighbor Commission, established for the specific purpose of hearing complaints of discrimination by "Latin Americans" in September 1943, did the flow of braceros to Texas resume.

As David Gutiérrez notes in his work *Walls and Mirrors: Mexican Americans, Mexicans and the Politics of Ethnicity,* the reaction to this program by many members of the Mexican American middle class communicates yet another negative aspect of the wartime experience. As previously noted, during the 1930s, organizations such as LULAC worked strenuously to "emphasize the fundamental Americanness of their constituents" (Gutiérrez, *Walls and Mirrors,* pp. 134–135). By the start of the war, LULACers were not alone in this effort, and other entities, such as the Mexican American Movement (MAM, based in Los Angeles), now argued that "immigration from Mexico lay at the very heart of most of the social problems facing Mexican Americans in the Southwest" (Gutiérrez, *Walls and Mirrors,* p. 136). Instead of seeking out and assisting Mexicanos, the barrio's middle class often turned its back upon braceros and instead argued that their brethren "presented major obstacles to achieving Mexican Americans' civil rights and economic objectives" (Gutiérrez, *Walls and Mirrors,* p. 142). Further shameful exhibits of such divisions continued well into the 1950s, especially when the middle class supported the implementation of Operation Wetback, a 1954 Border Patrol campaign to round up and expel undocumented aliens.

One final example of the limitations of tolerance for the growing number of Spanish speakers in the West's metropolitan areas is illustrated by the common police practice of labeling almost all youths of Mexican descent as criminals, as demonstrated by the events surrounding the murder of José Diaz (otherwise known as the Sleepy Lagoon case) in Los Angeles in 1942 and the mistreatment of Hispanic youths during the Zoot-Suit Riots of 1943.

At this point, it is necessary to provide an overview of why Spanish-surnamed youths were perceived in this manner and the tensions extant between *pachucos* (a term used to describe Mexican American gang members, especially those who dressed in zoot-suits), police, and military personnel stationed in southern California. An important source of information on both incidents is *Murder at Sleepy Lagoon: Zoot Suits, Race, and Riot in Wartime L.A.* by Eduardo Obregón Pagán. Here, the author examines the Diaz murder and the uprisings that followed, and discusses several stresses present in wartime Los Angeles that, he argues, ultimately led to the miscarriages of justice in the Sleepy Lagoon trial and civil disturbances.

Pagán asserts that the area's growth and economic expansion during the late 1930s and early 1940s attracted thousands of Spanish-surnamed people, including zoot-suited pachucos, and that this trend generated much concern. Many whites viewed the outfits as a direct challenge to "notions of what was 'American,'" and those who wore the outlandish clothing were open to suspicion of being unpatriotic, juvenile delinquents, or both. Although the fashion (and the lifestyle associated with it) produced trepidation, the number of Mexican Americans wearing this attire never totaled more than 3 to 5 percent of the population. Nevertheless, the style was associated with minority youths, and Anglos, including police officials and many of the sailors and soldiers stationed in the Los Angeles area, assumed that most, if not all, Spanish-surnamed young men were gang members and lawbreakers.

The murder of José Diaz at Sleepy Lagoon on August 1–2, 1942 (plus the subsequent trial, conviction, and overturning of sentences), and the Zoot-Suit Riots of June 1943 have been amply documented, and therefore we will not spend time on the particular facts of the events. Instead, we argue that the episodes provide examples of the limits of acceptance by whites of the growing Spanish-surnamed populace in western cities during the years of World War II.

While thousands of barrio dwellers toiled in factories and died on the battlefields of Europe and the Pacific, what mattered most for many in the majority was not the contributions of people whose heritage was Mexican to the war effort, but rather the perceived need to keep such persons in their proper social and economic place.

Eduardo Obregón Pagán and George J. Sánchez effectively bring out the real nature of what was going on in their respective works on wartime Los Angeles. Pagán sums up the real motivation of the police roundups conducted after the Diaz murder by saying that they were used not only in the pursuit of perpetrators, but as a necessary "show of force designed to reassure the white middle class that the wartime police force was indeed capable of maintaining law and order among working class youths, who were too poor, too dark-skinned, or too aesthetically different for a mainstream Los Angeles preoccupied with wartime security and conformity to understand" (Pagán, *Murder at Sleepy Lagoon*, p. 72).

Second, it was important to remind members of the comunidad that white authorities still regarded individuals of Mexican descent as not quite worthy of equal treatment. Sánchez's recounting of one youth's experience during the riots is instructive in this regard:

> Perhaps the nature of these encounters can best be understood by looking at the experiences of Pedro García, a . . . senior at Roosevelt High School in Boyle Heights. . . . On June 7, 1943, he went to see a movie. . . . He had taken an aisle seat . . . [when] servicemen burst into the theater looking for . . . "zoot suiters." They grabbed Pedro, dragging him out. . . . [They] ripped off his clothes, kicked and beat him, and left him bleeding and unconscious. Nearby policemen witnessed the spectacle, but did not make a move.
>
> This incident and other incidents of the Zoot-Suit Riots made clear to many . . . [Mexican Americans] that much of their optimism about the future had been misguided. (Sánchez, *Becoming Mexican American*, p. 267)

In sum, while the economic and social circumstances of Spanish-surnamed people of the West did improve during the early 1940s, by war's end they had not achieved equal treatment. Now that the national emergency had passed, some whites believed that perhaps it was time to go back to "normal" (discriminatory) conditions in the workplace, schools, and neighborhoods of the region. During the 1950s and early 1960s, however, veteranos of World War II (and their families) challenged this notion in the courtroom and through direct political action.

THE POSTWAR ERA, 1946–1965

The end of hostilities in August of 1945 brought great joy to Americans; the bloodshed had ended, and the nation, they hoped, would now enjoy prosperity and peace. For westerners, however, elation was tempered by concern; how would the area be impacted by reduced levels of federal spending? According to Richard White, a recessionary phase did briefly occur: for example, between 1943 and 1946, California's industrial employment levels declined by 39 percent, and Boeing's revenues dipped from $600 to $14 million (White, "*It's Your Misfortune*," p. 513). With the coming of police action in Korea, however, and the Cold War (and corresponding investments by the federal government in western-based military and research facilities), the development of tourism (which attracted millions of Americans), and the expansion of commercial agriculture, the West's prospects soon began to brighten.

The years of conflict had generated substantial changes in the consciousness of people of Mexican descent, especially among veterans and workers who had experienced occupational improvement. Through their efforts and sacrifice, men and women of western barrios had gained a greater sense of self-worth, pride, and independence, and they were not about to return to a prewar status quo that featured poor schools, a lack of services and political access, and widespread discriminatory practices. One Salt Lake City veteran, Epifanio González, who, after earning a Silver Star at Monte Casino, was not allowed to purchase a home of his choosing, effectively summarized the determination of this generation to seek equality by asking, "How would you feel if you came (home) decorated, you fought your heart out in the war, and now you say, 'Now I am an American. I'm just as good as anybody.' And then, all of a sudden, you're just a second class citizen[?]" (Iber, *Hispanics in the Mormon Zion*, p. 66).

As before, the main focus of this section is on those of Mexican descent. Cubans and Puerto Ricans were still not playing anything like as important a role in the West, and World War II had far less impact on them, but significant changes did happen during this time period for these ethnic groups as well, and those changes will also be discussed in this section.

THE SECULAR APPROACH TO IMPROVING THE LIFE OF MEXICAN AMERICANS

In the years after World War II, people of Mexican descent dedicated to bringing about societal change joined numerous organizations in an attempt to "improve conditions in their neighborhoods and call attention to their economic, social, and political needs and concerns" (Iber, *Hispanics in the Mormon Zion,* p. 68).

Although it is not possible in the space allotted to delineate all such groups and their activities, we present brief examples of the myriad endeavors of mutuales, LULAC, American GI Forum (AGIF), Community Service Organization (CSO), Asociación Nacional Mexico-Americana (ANMA), Mexican American Political Association (MAPA), Political Association of Spanish-Speaking Organizations (PASO), and Viva Kennedy Clubs. As a collection, these diverse entities offered a variety of programs designed to enhance the social, cultural, political, and economic life of Spanish-speaking people in the West.

Mutuales continued to play a significant role in barrio life between the end of World War II and 1965. Such groups afforded members a vehicle for socialization and cultural maintenance. To take one example of the agenda of mutual aid organizations during the 1950s and early 1960s, the Centro Civico Mexicano, headquartered in the west side barrio of Utah's capital, impacted many facets of community existence. The membership worked diligently to offer a variety of services, given a limited supply of money and volunteers. Among activities sponsored by CCM were nominal life and disability insurance benefits, a ladies' auxiliary, festivities commemorating Mexican national holidays, educational offerings designed to instruct barrio children in the basics of their native language and Mexican history, a baseball league and other after-school activities, and a Spanish-language broadcast through a local radio station.

In his history of the League of United Latin American Citizens, Benjamin Márquez notes that, during World War II, numerous councils went dormant because many members enlisted in an effort to prove their loyalty to the United States. When LULACers returned home, they were filled with pride and took the notion that America had fought for democracy very much to heart. Therefore, during the late 1940s and into the 1950s, the group witnessed dramatic expansion, enlarging its numbers in Texas and establishing itself in places such as Phoenix, St. Paul, and Las Vegas. The postwar LULAC advocated goals similar to those espoused by its creators, and volunteers toiled countless hours in an effort to "pursue educational reform, conduct citizenship and English language classes, . . . [and] conduct campaigns to integrate dance halls, restaurants, swimming pools, and other public facilities" (Márquez, *LULAC,* p. 41).

During this era, LULAC's leaders supported the notion that Mexican Americans could succeed and thrive within the nation's capitalist system, and that given a fair chance, they would prove themselves worthy Americans. Thus, the group's major effort focused on improving conditions for Spanish-surnamed school children throughout the West. In this regard, organizational lawyers filed lawsuits such as the 1947 *Mendez v. Westminster School District,* which argued that segregating California *estudiantes* was contrary to the Fourteenth Amendment, and the 1948 *Delgado v. Bastrop Independent School District* case, which disputed similar conditions in Texas. In total, by "LULAC attorneys and their staff, from 1950 to 1957, approximately fifteen suits or complaints were filed against school districts throughout the Southwest" (Márquez, *LULAC,* p. 54).

In addition to filing such actions, LULAC's membership, under the direction of Houston restaurant owner Andrés Tijerina, helped establish a program, the Little School of the 400 (designed to teach Spanish-speaking children the 400 "basic" English words necessary to complete first grade) in 1958, which eventually received funding from the state of Texas and, in the words of Tijerina's biographer, "helped establish a climate conducive for implementing the bold [educational] actions that transpired during the latter half of the 1960s" (Kreneck, *Mexican American Odyssey,* p. 309).

Although LULAC did much good during the postwar era, it did have two major faults. First, the group's conservative, middle-class perspective limited its agenda. For example, as it sought to improve educational opportunities, it failed to champion the rights of braceros, actually supporting Operation Wetback, a 1954 Border Patrol campaign to round up and expel undocumented aliens. This was part of LULAC's effort to continue to assert the "whiteness" of Mexican Americans. Second, LULAC was not interested in arguing for greater social justice and a fairer distribution of income. As Marquez notes:

> Throughout the post–World War II period, the organization engaged in a self-conscious effort to divert discontent generated by poverty and racial discrimination into socially approved channels. How the individual would fit into the economic hierarchy was a matter to be determined by the individual's talent, energy, and achievements—factors beyond the scope of group politics. (Márquez, *LULAC*, pp. 59–60)

Clearly, LULAC did not wish to raise such contentious issues, but a future generation of Mexican Americans would.

The American GI Forum (AGIF) was started in Corpus Christi in 1948 by Dr. Hector P. García and in many ways shared LULAC's goals. Writers such as Patrick J. Carroll, Ignacio M. García, and Henry A. J. Ramos have explored how the veterans involved in this organization sought to improve schools, participated in poll tax drives, raised money for scholarships, challenged political machines that controlled Mexican American voters (primarily in South Texas), and worked to reduce discriminatory practices. Efforts were initially focused in Texas, although the AGIF eventually spread to states such as Arizona, Colorado, Minnesota, New Mexico, and Utah.

The initial impetus for the association's founding was a disgraceful episode that occurred in Three Rivers, Texas, when the local mortuary refused to hold a wake for a Mexican American soldier killed in the Philippines. Dr. Hector García (himself an army veteran), who had provided medical care for barrio residents of Corpus Christi and challenged discriminatory practices at local hospitals, was contacted by Longoria's widow in January 1949. Garcia's reaction to the outrage was to mobilize fellow veteranos. Out of the efforts associated with the Longoria affair arose the AGIF. The group (and especially Dr. García) advocated direct community action to bring about social change, and during the 1950s and 1960s, it cultivated important political ties, especially with Texan Lyndon Baines Johnson.

AMERICAN GI FORUM OF THE U. S.

MISS OLIVIA ANN MARTINEZ
1968 - 1969 NATIONAL QUEEN

American GI Forum National Queen, 1968. (Utah History Research Center)

Recent research on the AGIF notes that, though there were similarities to LULAC, there were differences as well. For example, Jorge Iber argues that branches in Salt Lake City and Ogden did much to improve conditions in the state's barrios. Still, however, the association's actions were limited due to a fear of being labeled as radicals. Therefore, as with LULAC, the AGIF's efforts and rhetoric were often curbed, as they "attempted to fight discrimination while not being overly critical of a bigoted society" (Iber, *Hispanics in the Mormon Zion,* p. 81). Rather than arguing for the whiteness of Mexican Americans, AGIF simply assumed that "their whiteness was a given. As a result, the post–World War II generation looked beyond this claim, and more clearly tried to define Mexican Americans' place as an ethnic group within white U.S. society (Carroll, *Felix Longoria's Wake,* pp. 128 and 239).

Information on the next three organizations, CSO, ANMA, and MAPA, is found in the works of Mario T. García, especially in his "oppositional history" study, *Memories of Chicano History,* the source used in what follows. This book, a narrative of the life and times of labor and civil rights leader Bert Corona, demonstrates the existence of Mexican Americans with a more aggressive agenda than those of LULAC and AGIF.

The CSO began operation in 1947, in part as a response to the injustices associated with the Sleepy Lagoon case and the Zoot-Suit Riots. One of its goals was to increase voter registration and political participation among barrio dwellers, and in fact the group helped elect Edward Roybal to the Los Angeles City Council in 1949. The CSO, according to Corona, also brought together community activists with concerned individuals from the hierarchy of the Catholic Church and Protestant groups.

Organized in Phoenix in 1949, ANMA took a vigorous stand for the civil, political, and economic rights of Mexican Americans. In addition, unlike LULAC, ANMA acknowledged direct ties between Mexicanos on both sides of the Rio Grande, as well as shared interests. The group had linkages with labor associations such as the Mine, Mill and Smelter Workers and the Longshoremen's Union. One goal was to improve familias' finances by attacking the pattern of wage discrimination against Mexican workers prevalent throughout the West during the 1950s. ANMA's directors believed this could best be accomplished by means of collective bargaining. The leadership's desire to expand union membership even included recruitment of braceros. Finally, again unlike LULAC, ANMA sponsored and participated in protest activities against the government's Operation Wetback, which deported more than one million Mexicanos during 1954.

Bert Corona and other organizers established MAPA in April of 1960 in Fresno. They created the group mostly in response to a lack of direct support by the Democratic Party for Mexican American candidates running in California statewide races in 1954 and 1958. MAPA's primary goal was simple; to organize Spanish speakers, as well as poor whites and African Americans, into a block that could "effectively deliver a sizeable vote" for individual candidates. But this was not its only ambition. Corona hoped to use MAPA to push for grassroots social change, so that the entity "would be an organization based on the needs of the community and not the electoral needs of the Democratic Party." Unfortunately, there were internal struggles, and by 1964 the directors faced a dilemma: many early members of MAPA were government employees who owed their jobs to the party; if there were disputes with Democrats, would such individuals be loyal to MAPA or the party? Eventually, through diligent effort, the more progressive members managed to steer MAPA in their direction. According to Corona, "those who had joined MAPA to engage strictly in electoral politics had fallen by the wayside. These types were simply not willing to invest time and energy on civil rights issues" (García, *Memories of Chicano History,* pp. 169–186). In the second half of the 1960s, MAPA came to play an important role in the Chicano movement and other struggles for social justice.

During the AGIF convention in the summer of 1960, group members were approached by a Kennedy campaign aide who suggested that Mexican Americans should establish Viva Kennedy clubs. By late August the first such entity was established in Hidalgo County, Texas. According to historian Ignacio García, organization leaders throughout the West shared some basic aspirations for Mexican Americans, including a fuller inclusion in the American mainstream, greater economic power, and more political access, and "these goals were believed to be possible in a Kennedy administration that would . . . appoint Mexican Americans to important government posts, and recognize its political debt to Viva Kennedy support" (García, *Viva Kennedy,* p. 74).

By early 1961, García argues, the directors felt slighted because the administration did not offer the comunidad sufficient jobs or reform legislation in return for electoral efforts. This affront necessitated the creation of a more permanent entity, and community leaders gathered at a MAPA meeting in Phoenix with hopes of establishing a permanent association; this gathering was the genesis of the Political Association of Spanish-Speaking Organizations (PASO). Unfortunately, divisions were evident from the beginning, as California-based MAPA members wanted to emphasize the group's Mexicanness, while the Texan contingents argued for referring to members as "Americans," so that "they could then be seen as equals and permitted access to all aspects of American society" (García, *Viva Kennedy*, p. 128). The divisions negated the possibility of unity and helped bring about the group's demise during the years of the Chicano movement.

THE RELIGIOUS APPROACH TO IMPROVING THE LIVES OF MEXICAN AMERICANS

In the years between 1945 and 1965, the Catholic Church and various Protestant denominations increased their level of activity in addressing the needs of the people of Mexican descent in the West. Although it is not possible to discuss all individuals, activities, and programs, the next paragraphs provide a sense of the expanding role of such institutions in improving the daily and spiritual lives of the Spanish-surnamed men, women, and children of the region. The principal work used to develop this section was the collection edited by Jay Dolan entitled *The Notre Dame History of Hispanic Catholics in the U.S.*

In *Mediator Dei,* a 1947 encyclical by Pope Pius XIII, Catholic clergy were encouraged to take on greater roles in challenging social injustice, and as a result, priests, nuns, and other clergy throughout the West became more active in a variety of social causes. During the 1950s and early 1960s, the church made concerted efforts to improve the daily lives of people in the barrio; the institutional hierarchy placed special emphasis on working with the comunidad's teenagers, increasing the participation of men in religious activities, and bettering the circumstances for migrant workers.

It is not surprising, given the effect of the Sleepy Lagoon case and the Zoot-Suit Riots, that one of the most extensive Catholic-sponsored youth services programs existed in Los Angeles. In the postwar years, the Catholic Church in southern California faced two principal challenges: how to keep adolescents out of trouble with the law, and how to retain second and third generation Mexicanos' interest in church teachings.

Beginning in the 1930s, the archdiocese constituted a series of popular groups designed to appeal directly to this target audience. Among the most important were the Young Christian Workers/Young Christian Students (YCW/YCS) and the Catholic Youth Organization (CYO). Members taught church doctrine in Mexicano parishes and provided access to athletic competition, casual meeting places where young men and women could interact under the watchful eyes of chaperones, and drama, art, and dance classes. The CYO even sponsored two East Los Angeles-based car clubs, the Road Knights and the Starlighters, in an effort to reach youths. In many instances, counselors at church-run facilities were former gang members, actively recruited by the CYO in hope of developing community leaders. Some of the group's social goals were to turn around the lives of pachucos, to improve relations with police, and to create a more positive image of barrio teenagers in the broader society.

A second Catholic approach to both increasing spirituality and confronting social injustice was the Cursillo movement. This intense program of personal self-reflection started in Texas in 1958 and soon spread to California and elsewhere in the West. The goal of the "little courses" (*cursillos*) it offered was to ignite (or reignite) in men a passion for Christ, the Gospel, and social service; men constituted a segment of the comunidad that seldom joined in Church activities. In addition, many participants gained a greater sense of self-worth and responsibility for their families and community. A quintessential example of such teachings in action is the career of *cursillista* César Chávez, whom we will discuss in the following chapter.

The many local groups called *Guadalupanas* constituted a movement that was in many ways the female counterpart of the Cursillo movement. These groups, which initially focused on commemorating the feast day of Our Lady of Guadalupe (December 12), eventually expanded into a potent force for social action. An example of the power of such efforts is visible in the establishment of a community action group in Salt Lake City. In 1962 a number of barrio women began meeting with their priest to discuss neighborhood issues and how to address them. The result was the creation of the Guadalupe Center, which initially served as a meeting place, but ultimately led to the genesis of numerous projects, including a Catholic credit union, a cooperative food market, and an *escuela* (school) for adult literacy classes.

In the years immediately after World War II, the CYO, the Cursillos, the Guadalupanas, and similar programs did much to help urban barrio dwellers, but an entire population of Catholics, made up of migrant workers and braceros, often remained beyond effective reach. This situation changed during the 1950s as the church implemented efforts to better serve agricultural workers.

Beginning in the late 1940s, specific dioceses or archdioceses assigned personnel to visit bracero and migrant camps in order to say mass. While there, the priests would hear confession, pray the rosary, and hand out medals and scapulars. As a result, many clergymen became concerned about the impact of the bracero program on the spiritual and physical well-being of the people they visited. Most early complaints centered on a lack of access to church services, poor sanitary conditions in the camps, and the temptations (such as prostitution) that the men confronted. With the establishment of the Spanish Mission Band (within the Archdiocese of San Francisco), some ministers began to convey complaints of a more political nature.

In 1950, four newly ordained clerics took on the responsibility of ministering to agricultural laborers in Contra Costa County, Alameda, Santa Clara, and San Joaquin. At the outset, their charge was similar to earlier church endeavors, but the group quickly branched out into more confrontational activities, such as calling for improved housing and helping establish banking facilities.

Eventually, the Spanish Mission Band became involved in unionization efforts. Initially, members were advised to simply attend meetings "'to explain the teachings of the church on management-labor cooperation'" (Dolan, *Mexican Americans and the Catholic Church, 1900–1965*, pp. 209–221). In fact, however, their efforts went well beyond this appeal. Discouraged by what they perceived as a lack of concern for migrants by the AFL-CIO, Fathers Thomas McCullough and Donald McDonnell established the Agricultural Workers Association, with the assistance of Dolores Huerta, in 1958. This action generated much consternation among other priests, especially those who ministered to Catholic farmers and employers in the area. By 1961, following the death of Archbishop John J. Mitty (who had supported the Band), the Archdiocese of San Francisco's hierarchy disbanded the Spanish Mission Band. Although this was a setback to unionization and the church's social service efforts, the Band turned out to be just the beginning of the relationship of the Catholic Church and the migrant worker labor movement.

Protestant denominations were also active in challenging the social ills confronting Spanish speakers in the postwar decades, although many campaigns still included goodly doses of 1920s-style Americanization. Historian Vicki Ruiz noted the trend in her research on the Houchen Settlement, sponsored by the Methodist Church in El Paso's El Segundo barrio. While acknowledging that center personnel provided important programs such as medical services, child care, instruction in arts and crafts, and even a meeting place for LULAC, she points out that the entity's principal thrust throughout the 1940s and 1950s continued to be conversion and increased Americanization. As she puts it, it "is important to remember that Houchen provided a bilingual environment, not a bicultural one." She also states, however, that by 1959 there was a reevaluation of the house's mission, dropping the focus on altering beliefs and instead seeking to "'establish a Christian democratic framework for individual development, family solidarity, and neighborhood welfare'" (Ruiz, *From Out of the Shadows*, pp. 46–48).

CUBAN AMERICANS AND PUERTO RICANS IN THE POSTWAR WEST

Cuban Americans

An essay on Cuban Americans by Thomas D. Boswell in Jesse O. McKee's *Ethnicity in Contemporary America* notes that during the early 1960s there were three major stimuli that attracted pockets of Cubanos to Las Vegas and Los Angeles. The first impetus was, unfortunately, the success of the 1959 Revolution; between Fidel Castro's triumphant entry into Havana and 1962, more than 215,000 Cubans left the developing island gulag. The second factor was the desire on the part of the federal government and other authorities, to seek a more even distribution throughout the nation of arriving Cubanos; one of the choices offered refugees as a final destination for resettlement was Los Angeles. Finally, some of the immigrants selected a city based upon their occupational skills, seeking to be able to remain in a specific field of endeavor; this desire accounts for much of the appeal of Nevada's largest city to newly arrived Cubans who had worked in the gaming industry in Cuba.

According to the federal census of Las Vegas, there were 245 Cubans living in the city by 1960; not surprisingly, the majority were employed by casinos. Once the dictatorial revolutionary government had shut down such facilities on the island, Cubanos migrated first to the United States and then west, to Las Vegas, where other Cubanos were already working in the gaming industry. Former baccarat and roulette dealers from Havana (many of whom already spoke English) were able to get positions that "paid relatively well and served as a vehicle for rapid advancement into the middle class" (Clayson, "Cubans in Las Vegas," p. 3). The combination of admittance to decent paying jobs, a high level of labor participation by women, access to a fairly extensive initial program of governmental assistance, and a diligent work ethic produced positive economic results for Las Vegas' Cuban populace; by 1980, their median income stood at $15,982, surpassing that of Mexican Americans, which was $12,538.

By 1970, there were approximately 1,500 Cubanos in the city, and the comunidad was prosperous and stable enough to establish an ethnic organization, El Circulo Cubano (the Cuban Circle), which staged traditional events such as domino tournaments, dances, and commemoration of national holidays and other fetes. Key individuals within the Circulo's membership roll served as the leadership cadre of another important Hispanic group in Las Vegas, the Latin Chamber of Commerce, which opened in 1976 (Clayson, "Cubans in Las Vegas," pp. 4 and 7).

Like the oasis in the Nevada desert, the city of Los Angeles had a Cuban population of a few hundred individuals prior to the post-1959 exodus. According to researcher Vincent Edward Gil, the resettlement efforts of the 1960s attracted approximately 25,000 Cubanos to the area during the decade. Many of the earliest refugee arrival had ties to individuals who had lived in the area since the 1920s. For the majority of the resettled, however, the attraction of southern California was the existence of an extensive support network provided by Catholic Community Services and other denominational organizations. This safety net, according to Gil, made the move west relatively unproblematic and provided Cubans, many of whom had been well educated in their home country, with an opportunity for a new economic and social start. By the 1970s, this group displayed "a progressive occupational history . . . and a fair percentage of individuals being able to re-establish themselves in similar occupational levels" to what they held in Cuba (Gil, "The Personal Adjustment and Acculturation of Cuban Immigrants in Los Angeles," pp. 59–63, 135, 143, and 153).

Puerto Ricans

The boriquas of Hawaii further consolidated their place in island society during the postwar years; although they still often confronted a degree of stereotyping by the broader society, particularly from social scientists and other academicians doing research on the community.

During the 1950s, islanderos continued to participate in activities of the PRCC and the PRIC. Both clubs, working together and separately, staged events designed to reinforce cultural pride, to participate in the Puerto Rican Athletic League, and to further connect the comunidad's population with haoles and other ethnic groups of the territory. The most important of all such undertakings took place in 1950, with the commemoration of the fiftieth anniversary of the arrival of the first group of their forbears on the island in 1900. Other positive developments included an increasing number of children completing high school (and even attending college) and more individuals moving into more highly skilled trades and occupations.

By the late 1950s, the second and third generation of the group were exhibiting some "American" traits, and some were concerned that part of the boriqua culture was being lost. For example, in June of 1958 the two major ethnic associations worked to establish a Spanish-language school in Honolulu, in hopes of encouraging adolescents to attend and learn their "native" tongue. Unfortunately, the school was not very successful in attracting students; and ironically, some public ceremonies for the academy were held in English.

A final aspect of Puerto Rican life in Hawaii during the postwar era is found in a series of theses and dissertations that appeared during the 1940s and 1950s. Regrettably, the various studies demonstrated continued stereotyping of the boriqua populace. In the same way, a 1948 study by sociologist Dr. Lee M. Brooks (and other studies during the 1950s) emphasized the same issues as earlier works: Puerto Ricans were lazy, did not value education, and doggedly resisted Americanization, holding on, instead to a "backward" culture.

The other major pocket of Puerto Rican concentration in the West by 1965 was in California. Regrettably, not much historical research has been done on this population, making it necessary to rely on basic statistics and other information presented in a 1980 U.S. Commission on Civil Rights study. This publication notes that Puerto Ricans began arriving in the Golden State in substantial numbers during the 1940s, due to employment opportunities in military and other federal facilities established during the war. Further scattered migration occurred from the declining industrial areas of the Northeast and Midwest during the 1950s and 1960s. By 1970, the federal census reported approximately 47,000 boriquas in California, with the Los Angeles–Long Beach and San Francisco metropolitan areas accounting for roughly 70 percent of the statewide counts.

RESULTS OF THE STRUGGLE

The Spanish-speaking people of the U.S. West struggled diligently to better their individual and community lives and claim their rightful place as Americans during the years 1930–1965. Clearly, despite the setbacks of the Great Depression years, progress was made during World War II and the postwar years in terms of economic and social standing. Still, a cursory examination of statistics from the 1960 census, and other materials as well, reveals that men, women, and children of Mexican descent still lagged well behind in a variety of social indicators.

The levels of education and income for the Hispanic people of the West were dramatically below that of whites. For example, in a research project on Arizona, California, Colorado, New Mexico, and Texas, Walter Fogel noted that, in 1960, the median educational attainment of

Spanish-surnamed individuals was 7.2 years, versus 11.7 for whites (Fogel, "Mexican American Study Project: Education and Income," p. 8). In regard to earnings, a similar trend existed. In 1950 and 1960, in urban areas of the states surveyed, median income for all persons was $2,093 and $3,226, respectively. For the Spanish-surnamed, the amounts totaled only $1,385 (66 percent of the median for all persons) and $2,317 (72 percent) (Mittlebach and Marshall, "Mexican American Study Project: The Burden of Poverty," p. 12). Finally, in order to gain some perspective on group health, we note that, according to A. Taher Moustafa and Gertrud Weiss's "Mexican American Study Project: Health Status and Practices of Mexican Americans," in San Antonio between 1954 and 1963, the neonatal death rate (per 1,000 live births) in the city was 34.2 for Spanish-surnamed families, 20.7 for whites (Moustafa and Weiss, "Mexican American Study Project: Health Status and Practices, p. 11).

By the early 1960s members of the "Mexican American generation," as it has been called, could point with pride at the enormous "progress" made since the 1930s through their "cooperative" approach. Still, however, stubborn obstructions remained on the path to social equality. The next generation of Spanish speakers in the West, a group with much higher expectations of themselves and society, were not as tolerant or patient, and their goal was not necessarily to get along, but rather to foster rapid and even (in some cases) radical change, in the realms of economics, education, culture, and beyond.

BIBLIOGRAPHIC ESSAY

This chapter covers years during which two major events, the Great Depression and World War II, as well as postwar economic and social changes, impacted the daily lives of Spanish-speaking peoples in the West. Once again, we found Richard White's *"It's Your Misfortune and None of My Own": A New History of the American West* (Norman: University of Oklahoma Press, 1991) an invaluable resource for an overview of important trends. In particular, chapters 16–18 of his work proffer much information regarding the Depression's impact on the western economic scene, the New Deal's efforts in the region, the surge in industrial development during the war years, and the results of geographic redistribution, the Cold War, and the expansion of tourism on the West after 1945.

In the first section of the chapter, we examined the influence of the economic downturn upon the lives of Mexicanos in the West. One of the most significant pressures on the lives of comunidades throughout the region during these years was the fear of repatriation back to Mexico. Several works have detailed the drive to send "foreigners" back "where they belong," and to safeguard jobs for "real" Americans. Some of the works consulted in writing this portion include the following: R. Reynolds McKay, "The Federal Deportation Campaign in Texas: Mexican Deportation from the Lower Rio Grande Valley during the Great Depression," *Borderlands Journal* 5, no. 1 (fall 1981); Francisco È. Balderrama and Raymond Rodríguez, *A Decade of Betrayal: Mexican Repatriation in the 1930s* (Albuquerque: University of New Mexico Press, 1995); and Abraham Hoffman, *Unwanted Mexicans in the Great Depression: Repatriation Pressures, 1929–1939* (Tucson: University of Arizona Press, 1974).

Other works that detail the repatriation process in a variety of locales include the following: Dionicio Nodín Valdés, *Barrios Norteños: St. Paul and Midwestern Mexican Communities in the Twentieth Century* (Austin: University of Texas Press, 2000); Julie Kirk Blackwelder, *Women of the Depression: Caste and Culture in San Antonio, 1929–1939* (College Station: Texas A&M University Press, 1998); Douglas Monroy, *Rebirth: Mexican Los Angeles from the Great Migration to the Great Depression* (Berkeley: University of California Press, 1999); Camile Guerin-Gonzales, *Mexican Workers and American Dreams: Immigration, Repatriation, and California Farm Labor, 1900–1939* (New Brunswick, NJ: Rutgers University Press, 1996); and Lisbeth Haas, "San Juan Capistrano: A Rural Society in Transition to Citrus," *California History* 74, no. 1 (Spring 1995).

In other places, such as Utah, the state and federal governments did not have a formal repatriation program; however, the terrible economic conditions extant caused the migration of many thousands of familias. See Jorge Iber, *Hispanics in the Mormon Zion, 1912–1999* (College Station: Texas A&M University, 2001).

The Puerto Ricans of Hawaii also did not confront direct attempts at deportation during the 1930s; they did face mounting tensions in their relations with other island peoples (such as Filipinos and Japanese), who became hostile because employers used the threat of renewed recruitment in Puerto Rico as a way to stifle worker complaints. See Norma Carr, "The Puerto Ricans of Hawaii: 1900–1958," Ph.D. dissertation, University of Hawaii, 1989.

The difficult circumstances confronted by Spanish speakers during the 1930s were not met with meek resignation; rather, many western Mexicanos challenged maltreatment through the use of grass roots, civic, proeducation, and religious organizations. See Jose Alamillo, "More Than A Fiesta: Ethnic Identity, Cultural Politics, and Cinco de Mayo Festivals in Corona, California, 1930–1950," *Aztlán* 28, no. 2 (fall 2003); Vicki L. Ruiz, *From out of the Shadows: Mexican Women in Twentieth Century America* (New York: Oxford University Press, 1998); Jose Alamillo, *"Peloteros* in Paradise: Mexican American Baseball and Oppositional Politics in Southern California, 1930–1950," *Western Historical Quarterly* 34, no. 2 (Summer 2003); Gilberto M. Hinojosa, "The Mexican American Church, 1930–1965," in *Mexican Americans and the Catholic*

Church, 1900–1965, edited by Jay P. Dolan and Gilberto Hinojosa (Notre Dame, IN: Notre Dame University Press, 1994); Roberto R. Treviño, "Facing Jim Crow: Catholic Sisters and the 'Mexican Problem' in Texas," *Western Historical Quarterly* 34, no. 2 (Summer 2003); Frank P. Barajas, "Resistance, Radicalism, and Repression on the Oxnard Plain: The Social Context of the *Betabelero* Strike of 1933," *Western Historical Quarterly* 35, no. 1 (Spring 2004); Suzanne Forrest, *The Preservation of the Village: New Mexico's Hispanics and the New Deal* (Albuquerque: University of New Mexico Press, 1998); Gilbert G. González, "The Mexican Citrus Picker Union, The Mexican Consulate and the Orange County Strike of 1936," *Labor History* 35 (Winter 1994); Benjamin Márquez, *LULAC: The Evolution of a Mexican American Political Organization* (Austin: University of Texas Press, 1993); Guadalupe San Miguel Jr., *"Let Them All Take Heed": Mexican Americans and the Campaign for Educational Equity in Texas, 1910–1981* (Austin: University of Texas Press, 1987); Bradford Luckingham, *Minorities in Phoenix: A Profile of Mexican American, Chinese American, and African American Communities, 1880–1992* (Tucson: University of Arizona Press, 1994).

Many historians, in examining the years of World War II, have argued that this event provided opportunity for Mexican Americans to improve their economic and social lot. In recent years, however, others have argued that, even with the dramatic improvements in the western economy during the era of conflict, the circumstances of Mexicanos and Mexican Americans did not progress as much as previously thought and that 1940s American society continued to limit both job opportunities and cultural expression (as seen, for example, the zoot-suit riots) of Spanish speakers. In an effort to provide a balanced presentation of this era, we consulted works that presented both arguments: Emilio Zamora, "The Failed Promise of Wartime Opportunity for Mexicans in the Texas Oil Industry," *Southwestern Historical Quarterly* 45, no. 3 (January 1992); Carmen R. Sánchez, "Coming of Age During the War: Reminiscences of an Albuquerque Hispana," *New Mexico Historical Review* 70, no. 4 (October 1995); Raul Morin, *Among the Valiant: Mexican Americans in WWII and Korea* (Alhambra, CA: Borden Publishing, 1966); David Gutiérrez, *Walls and Mirrors: Mexican Americans, Mexicans and the Politics of Ethnicity* (Berkeley: University of California Press, 1995); Erasmo Gamboa, *Mexican Labor and World War II: Braceros in the Pacific Northwest, 1942–1947* (Austin: University of Texas Press, 1990); Raymona Maddy, "Farmway Village—A Place to Call Home: History of the Farm Labor Camp in Caldwell, Idaho, 1939–1997," in *The Hispanic Experience in Idaho: Papers Written for a Research Seminar at Boise State University,* edited by Errol D. Jones and Kathleen Rubinow Hodges (Boise, ID: Boise State University, 1998); Christine Marin, "Mexican Americans on the Home Front: Community Organizations in Arizona During World War II," *Perspectives in Mexican American Studies* 4 (1994); Eduardo Obregón Pagán, *Murder at the Sleepy Lagoon: Zoot*

Suits, Race, and Riot in Wartime Los Angeles (Chapel Hill: University of North Carolina, 2003); Mauricio Mazón, *The Zoot Suit Riots: The Psychology of Symbolic Annihilation* (Austin: University of Texas Press, 1984); Edward J. Escobar, *Race, Police and the Making of a Political Identity: Mexican Americans and the Los Angeles Police Department* (Berkeley: University of California Press, 1999); Mario Barrera, *Race and Class in the Southwest: A Theory of Racial Inequality* (Notre Dame, IN: Notre Dame University Press, 1979); and Juan Ramón García, *Operation Wetback: The Mass Deportation of Undocumented Mexican Workers in 1954* (Westport, CT: Greenwood Press, 1980).

Although the social and economic trends of the World War II era did not break down all obstacles that stood in the way of Hispanic progress, the war and concurrent activity on the home front did much to change the consciousness of people of Mexican descent. In the years after the conflict, civic, political, religious, labor, and grass roots organizations (especially those involving veteranos) worked diligently to solidify and improve upon the gains of the first half of the 1940s. For more information on these topics, please see Thomas H. Kreneck, *Mexican American Odyssey: Felix Tijerina, Entrepreneur and Civic Leader, 1905–1965* (College Station: Texas A&M University Press, 2001); Benjamin Márquez, *LULAC: The Evolution of a Mexican American Political Organization* (Austin: University of Texas Press, 1993); Patrick J. Carroll, *Felix Longoria's Wake: Bereavement, Racism, and the Rise of Mexican American Activism* (Austin: University of Texas Press, 2003); Ignacio M. García, *Hector P. García: In Relentless Pursuit of Justice* (Houston, TX: Arte Público Press, 2002); Henry A. J. Ramos, *The American GI Forum: In Pursuit of a Dream, 1948–1983* (Houston, TX: Arte Público Press, 1998); Mario T. García, *Memories of Chicano History: The Life and Narrative of Bert Corona* (Berkeley: University of California Press, 1995); Ignacio M. García, *Viva Kennedy: Mexican Americans in Search of Camelot* (College Station: Texas A&M University Press, 2000); Jeffrey M. Burns, "A New Era: World War II and After" and "Migrants and Braceros," both in *Mexican Americans and the Catholic Church, 1900–1965,* edited by Jay P. Dolan and Gilbert Hinojosa (Notre Dame, IN: Notre Dame University Press, 1994). For more information on the role of women in post-1945 organizations, see Vicki L. Ruiz, *From Out of the Shadows: Mexican Women in Twentieth Century America* (New York: Oxford University Press, 1998).

Beginning in the 1970s, some scholars began to take notice of the Cuban American population that had developed in two western locales (Las Vegas and Los Angeles) following the 1959 Castro revolution. The earliest study we found dealing with this group is Vincent Edward Gil, "The Personal Adjustment and Acculturation of Cuban Immigrants to Los Angeles," Ph.D. dissertation, UCLA, 1976. In addition, during the 1990s, both M. L. Miranda's *A History of Hispanics in Southern Nevada* (Reno: University of Nevada Press, 1997) and William Clayson's "Cubans in Las Vegas: Ethnic Identity, Success, and Urban Life in the

Late Twentieth Century," *Nevada Historical Society Quarterly* 38 (Spring 1995) detailed the arrival and establishment of a number of Cuban Americans (initially working almost exclusively in casinos) in the Las Vegas area commencing in the early 1960s.

In this chapter we continued to base most of our writing on Puerto Ricans in Hawaii on Norma Carr's 1989 dissertation.

In the last portion of this chapter, we provided a "snapshot" of conditions among Mexican Americans of the West by relying upon studies of educational, income, health, and other such social indicators based on 1960 federal census and other research data. We garnered these materials from the following sources: Walter Fogel, "Mexican American Study Project: Education and Income of Mexican Americans in the Southwest," (Los Angeles: Division of Research, Graduate School of Business Administration, UCLA, 1966); Frank G. Mittlebach and Grace Marshall, "Mexican American Study Project: The Burden of Poverty" (Los Angeles: Division of Research, Graduate School of Business Administration, UCLA, 1965); and A. Taher Moustafa and Gertrud Weiss, "Mexican American Study Project: Health Status and Practices of Mexican Americans" (Los Angeles: Division of Research, Graduate School of Business Administration, UCLA, 1968). Other sources of information on the lives of Puerto Ricans in the US West during the 1960s and 1970s include: US Civil Rights Commission, "Puerto Ricans in the Continental United States: An Uncertain Future," (Washington, DC, 1976) and "Puerto Ricans in California," (Washington, DC, 1980).

Finally, the materials for the biographical sketch at the end of this chapter are drawn from Jorge Iber's article "Mexican Americans of South Texas Football: The Athletic and Coaching Careers of E. C. Lerma and Bobby Cavazos, 1932–1965," which appeared in the *Southwestern Historical Quarterly* 55, no. 4 (April 2002). For more information regarding the topic of Mexican Americans and sport, please see the following: Jorge Iber, "On-Field Foes and Racial Misconceptions: The 1961 Donna Redskins and Their Drive to the Texas State Football Championship," *International Journal of the History of Sport* 21, no. 2 (March 2004); Jose M. Alamillo, "Peloteros in Paradise: Mexican American Baseball and Oppositional Politics in Southern California, 1930–1950," *Western Historical Quarterly* 34, no. 2 (Summer 2003); Richard Santillán, "Mexican Baseball Teams in the Midwest, 1916–1965: The Politics of Cultural Survival and Civil Rights," *Perspectives in Mexican American Studies* (2000); and Samuel O. Regalado, "Baseball in the Barrios: The Scene in East Los Angeles Since World War II," *Baseball History* 1, no. 1 (Summer 1996).

CHAPTER SEVEN

THE ERA OF
THE CHICANO/A MOVEMENT,
1965–1980

B etween 1930 and 1965 the predominant philosophical and political
initiatives of barrio leaders throughout the West sought to accomplish two main tasks: (1) to engage in dialogue and compromise with the majority populace in hope of engendering greater equality, and (2) to bring about recognition of Spanish-surnamed people as part of the nation's "white" population. The power of the push to achieve these goals is evidenced by the substantial number of Spanish speakers who fought during World War II and the Korean police action in an effort to prove their worthiness as Americans. Surely, members of the Mexican American and GI generations argued, if our boys were good enough to shed blood for the United States in foreign conflicts (and other members of our community were qualified to work in vital home front industries), then our people are worthy of equal status and opportunities in the postwar era.

During the years after 1945, clear progress occurred in a variety of areas, and there was a certain amount of economic improvement during the wartime boom. Also, the postwar era witnessed the expansion of LULAC, the birth of the AGIF, and the activity of numerous other organizations dedicated to asserting civil rights and bettering economic, educational, and political circumstances in western comunidades. The concerted efforts of such entities helped to break down some barriers to schooling, housing, and participation in juries, and to end other discriminatory practices that had debased the daily existence of most Mexican Americans.

However, as revealed by an examination of critical social statistics found in the 1960 Federal Census, major obstacles to equality still remained. In general, people of Mexican descent earned less money, had lower educational levels, and lived shorter lives than did the white population. Aware of the relatively slow pace of change since the 1930s and witnessing the dramatic impact of the African Americans' civil rights struggle of the 1960s, many barrio dwellers argued that getting their fair share of the economic and societal pie required more aggressive and confrontational tactics than those used by earlier generations of Spanish-surnamed activists. Additionally, some in the barrios, influenced by radical theories and events (such as the Cuban Revolution of 1959), began calling for an overthrow of what they viewed as the inherently flawed and unjust economic and civil systems of the United States.

This chapter, then, focuses on the rise of a mass movement, as well as detailing some of the principal individuals, organizations, events, and trends of the Mexican American struggle for civil rights, otherwise known as the Chicano/a movement, or the *movimiento.* Within our coverage, we consider some of the specific goals of leaders and groups during the years of the movimiento, as well as the divisions that existed both within the movement and within individual comunidades. Finally, we present a snapshot summary of the state of life in 1980 in order to assess the extent and breadth of the transformation unleashed by such efforts, and thus to judge whether the movimiento was successful.

At this point, it is necessary to present the reasons for our decision to end this chapter in 1980. First, the election of Ronald Reagan and the ascension of Pope John Paul II (in 1978) to positions of leadership had a dramatic impact upon the lives of Spanish-speaking people. Both men, it is safe to say, had more conservative visions of their institutions than their predecessors and worked diligently to change the way they functioned. President Reagan, for example, focused on cutting taxes and defeating the Soviet Union, rather than furthering Great Society social programs, many of which had been quite beneficial to Spanish-surnamed families. Pope John Paul II, similarly, worked to rein in the actions of Catholic clergy who, influenced by *Mediator Dei,* Vatican II, and Liberation Theology, had sought to dramatically increase (and even radicalize) the activities of the church regarding issues of social justice. Such trends had important consequences for the lives of Hispanics in the West.

Second, many government and business leaders hailed the 1980s as the "Decade of the Hispanic," during which, it was assumed, the

Spanish-surnamed populace of the United States would come into its own economically, socially, and politically. By cutting off the movimiento chapter at 1980, we are able to focus our analysis on the impact of Chicano/a efforts for change during the 1960s and 1970s, and thus to provide a few educational and economic benchmarks with which to examine events of the 1980s and beyond in chapter 8.

Before proceeding, it is necessary to, once again, make note of the literature available on Puerto Ricans and Cubans in the West covering the years 1965–1980. In this chapter, we will again look at the experience of Puerto Ricans and Cubans in the West, and during this time period their story turns out to be more intimately intertwined with that of Hispanics of Mexican descent. In regard to Cuban Americans, we continue our focus on the Los Angeles and Las Vegas pockets. Additionally, we will spend some time discussing how Cuban Americans, with their conservative (anticommunist) political views, often acted as a counter to the more radical pronouncements by some Chicano/a leaders (many of whom went to the island and praised the policies of dictator Fidel Castro). For Puerto Ricans, the research expands upon previously detailed experiences in Hawaii, and also briefly describes their participation in the civil rights movement (frequently tied to the Chicano/a movement) in California.

THE GENESIS OF A MOVEMENT

Before focusing upon specific individuals and events associated with the movimiento, it is necessary to scrutinize some reasons for its origins among those of Mexican descent in the West. Here, anew, we turn to Richard White, who summarizes the important political changes which took place in the region in the postwar years by noting the "rise in conservative individualist philosophies among many western whites paralleled [by] a rise among minority westerners of demands for government action of their collective grievances" (White, *It's Your Misfortune,* 577).

During the early 1960s, the Spanish speakers, African Americans, and Native Americans in the West, all of whom had endured varying conditions of de facto segregation, as well as other discriminatory practices, began to be inspired by the 1954 Brown decision, the civil rights struggle in the south, and black empowerment movements in the north (and elsewhere) to challenge the western social and economic status quo. This trend, in conjunction with the antipoverty programs established by the Great Society, helped stimulate a desire to validate each group's individual cultural legacies, rather than simply accepting the aspirations and standards of white middle-class Americans.

One major sign of the new trend was that the pejorative term *Chicano/a* for a person of Mexican descent began to be widely used by the very people who had previously resented it. The word served as a rallying cry for many (especially young) men and women in the barrios since it "submerged all the complicated . . . class, and social divisions of the Mexican and Mexican American community under one term" (White, *"It's Your Misfortune"*, p. 593). In sum, by the middle of the 1960s, many of the arguments put forth by earlier generations of Mexican American activists who had sought cooperation with whites and assimilation were being discounted, and even ridiculed, by some leaders associated with the movimiento. Although not everyone involved with the Chicano/a movement sought to bring about revolution, most were much more strident in their demands for social, economic, and political change in the western United States.

KEY INDIVIDUALS AND LEADERS OF THE CHICANO/A MOVEMENT

The Chicano/a struggle was not a unified, cohesive mass mobilization. From the start, different organizations existed, pushing for a multiplicity of initiatives in cities and towns throughout the West. Thus the sundry principals of the movement espoused diverse causes before local, regional, and national audiences. In order to appreciate this mixture, we will, in the next few pages, provide an overview of the activities of the most significant national Chicano/a leaders; César Chávez and Dolores Huerta, Reies López Tijerina, Corky Gonzales, and José Angel Gutiérrez.

CÉSAR CHÁVEZ

For millions of ordinary Americans, mostly oblivious to the terrible plight of migrant workers, the activities and efforts of the late César Chávez (and, ultimately, those of the United Farm Workers, the UFW) served as an introduction to the Chicano/a movement. The majority of the information in this section of the chapter comes from Richard Griswold del Castillo and Richard Garcia's recent biography, *César Chávez: A Triumph of the Spirit*. Chávez was born in 1927 into a Yuma, Arizona, migrant familia that worked throughout the West. In many ways, his childhood experiences were typical of Mexican Americans who "followed the crops," and his education was severely compromised due to constant traveling; indeed, he attended sixty-five different schools and reached only the seventh grade. Chávez's father suffered a debilitating injury in 1942, and the incident effectively ended César's formal academic endeavors (although he certainly continued to educate himself beyond this point). In 1944 the young Chávez joined the Navy and received a discharge in 1946. In 1952 he began working with Father Donald McDonnell and the Community Service Organization (CSO) (discussed in chapter 6), providing services for farm laborers and braceros in the Oxnard, California, area.

One of Chávez's important ambitions was a desire to establish a migrant workers' union. Chávez argued that one of the most significant impediments to this goal was the use of braceros by commercial farmers throughout the West. Until this pool of labor dried up, he reasoned, circumstances for Mexican Americans who followed the crops would remain arduous. The CSO's leadership did not wish to focus on labor organizing and this disagreement led to Chávez's resignation from the organization in 1962. He promptly set out (with the assistance of Dolores Huerta) to create the National Farm Workers Association (NFWA), which commenced operations in Fresno, California, on September 30, 1962. In September of 1965 the NFWA joined forces with another group, the Agricultural Workers Organizing Committee (the AWOC, a Filipino organization associated with the AFL-CIO) in a strike against grape growers in the city of Delano. The events surrounding this labor action eventually brought César Chávez to the forefront of the Chicano/a movement and into national consciousness.

The demands of Delano workers were not at all unusual or radical: improved pay, a better working situation, and union recognition. Chávez, greatly influenced by the writings of Gandhi and Martin Luther King Jr., espoused a nonviolent philosophy for his efforts and sought to appeal to the conscience of the average American. The NFWA used a myriad of tactics to achieve this end, including *huelgas* (strikes), consumer boycotts, marches, and the use of religious imagery. By 1966 Chávez's endeavors had proved successful, and the first labor agreement with a grape grower (Schenley Wine Company) went into effect. The NFWA then became the United Farm Workers (UFW), and the new union associated with the AFL-CIO.

A second round of boycotts began in 1968 in order to gain contracts from other producers. This campaign eventually brought success, and twenty-seven more labor agreements by 1970. In addition, by the early 1970s, the UFW incorporated other demands into its bargaining positions, including the elimination of certain pesticides from the fields, as well the outlawing of a small hoe known as *el cortito* (the short one). This hoe was particularly disliked by migrant workers because its short size meant that the worker would have to stoop in order to use it, sometimes for hours. This effort culminated when California Governor Jerry Brown signed the Agricultural Labor Relations Act in 1975. At this point, the union had an estimated 70,000 members, and it appeared that it had overcome the challenges of unionizing a highly mobile worker population. Unfortunately, such accomplishments did not last, and the UFW was slowly debilitated by challenges from other unions (such as the Teamsters), mechanization, and the rising tide of conservatism during the later part of the 1970s and the early 1980s. By the time of César Chávez's death in 1993, he was an icon of the movimiento for most Americans (his funeral was attended by more than 35,000 mourners); the union he led, however, had dwindled to less than 26,000 members (out of a total of 1.6 million farm workers in the United States) (Gonzalez, *Mexicanos*, pp. 200–201).

DOLORES HUERTA

Various scholars have written biographies of César Chávez, but his principal ally and collaborator in the creation of the UFW, Dolores Huerta, has not received much academic attention. Still, it is evident, that without the assistance of this remarkable woman, Chávez's projects would not have been as successful as they were. The majority of the information for this section was drawn from the UFW Web site, as well as from journal articles by Margaret Rose and Richard A. Garcia.

Vice President of United Farm Workers Union Dolores Huerta sitting on stage at "Robert F. Kennedy Remembered" symposium at Loyola Marymount University. (Time Life Pictures/Getty Images)

Dolores Huerta was born in Dawson, New Mexico, in 1930. Her father, Juan Fernández, was a miner, field worker, and labor recruiter. Huerta's mother, Alicia Chávez, divorced Juan when Dolores was only three. Through determination and diligence, Alicia raised her three daughters and two sons in Stockton, California, and eventually became an entrepreneur (she owned a hotel and restaurant). With her family's assistance, Huerta completed high school (she married right after graduation) and earned a teaching degree from Delta Community College. By the mid-1950s, however, she felt unfulfilled in both her job and marriage and decided that she needed to do more to improve the lives of the poor. This decision eventually led her to join the CSO, where she met César Chávez.

Huerta's role in the UFW was just as momentous as that of her more famous collaborator. She participated in a myriad of activities, including leading the negotiations with Schenley Wine in 1966, supervising the endeavors of forty-three boycott coordinators (located throughout the United States and Canada during the years 1968 through 1970), and leading the project in the nation's largest media market, New York City. Additionally, Huerta's work as a lobbyist for the UFW helped bring about passage of legislation such as the Agricultural Labor Relations Act of 1975 (which, in addition to eliminating the hated *el cortito* granted farm workers the right to collective bargaining) and the Immigration Act of 1986 (which granted amnesty to millions of undocumented workers). Dolores Huerta did much to energize key aspects of the Chicano/a movement agenda. She fought for better conditions for migrant (and other) workers, while at the same time expanding the role of women in the leadership of a major labor organization and serving as a role model for other Chicanas of the movimiento.

REIES LÓPEZ TIJERINA

Although Chávez's use of the nonviolent techniques of King and Gandhi, with their emphasis on religious elements and marches used to gain attention and sympathy, was applauded by elements of the movimiento, other individuals (and groups) embraced different schemes; with the career and activities of Reies López Tijerina ("El Tigre") serving as a prime example of the use of violence in attempts to generate social and economic change. The majority of the information for this section of the chapter comes from a recent autobiography (translated by José Angel Gutiérrez), *They Call Me King Tiger: My Struggle for the Land and Our Rights* and the writings of scholars such as F. Arturo Rosales, Julian Samora, and Patricia Vandel Simon.

In many ways, Tijerina's early life paralleled that of Chávez. He was born in September of 1926 in Falls City, Texas, to a family of farm workers. He traveled with his parents and worked the fields until age six, when his mother died and the clan moved to Michigan. Although Tijerina's formal education was limited (he was mostly self-taught), at the age of eighteen he entered the Assembly of God Bible Institute in Ysleta, Texas. Upon graduation, he, along with his wife Mary Escobar, began a career as an evangelical preacher. In 1956, Tijerina left behind Christian evangelization and focused on more temporal concerns, helping to establish the Valley of Peace commune (along with seventeen other families) in Arizona.

Relations with the group's Anglo neighbors were strained, and by the early 1960s Tijerina had moved to New Mexico, where he became interested in the history of land grants. It was his concern over the scandalous mistreatment of Spanish speakers' property rights that led to the establishment of the Alianza Federal de Mercedes (Federal Alliance of Land Grants) in 1963; as Juan Gómez-Quiñones notes in his work, *Chicano Politics: Reality and Promise, 1940–1990,* this movement struck a bold call for social justice by "emphasizing land and language . . . [and] did much to shape the character of cultural nationalism" (Gomez-Quinones, *Chicano Politics,* p. 115).

Alianza members took direct, and sometimes violent, actions in order to assert their claims. In October of 1966, for example, Alianzistas "took over" the Echo Amphitheater (on what had been mercedes [land grant] lands, now located within the boundaries of the Kit Carson National Forest) and declared the birth of a free and independent state. Additionally, two park rangers were arrested for "trespassing," convicted, and, by the "people's" mercy, given suspended sentences. This incident brought attention to the Alianza's claims, but ultimately resulted in Tijerina's conviction on two counts of assault. He was sentenced to two years of incarceration and five years probation. Before this conviction, however, Tijerina was directly involved in an even more noteworthy and intense incident, the Tierra Amarilla county courthouse raid of June 5, 1967.

On June 1, Alianza members were scheduled to meet in the town of Coyote. The local district attorney, Alfonso Sánchez, determined to halt the gathering, had local peace officers arrest Tijerina' allies upon their arrival in the county. The eight individuals imprisoned were scheduled for arraignment on June 7. On June 5, however, about twenty Alianzistas raided the courthouse, shooting and injuring several local officials. One of the wounded men, Eulogio Salazar, survived the attack, but was later beaten to death; the perpetrators of this dastardly deed were never found. In response, the governor of New Mexico called out the National Guard to restore order. Tijerina was found in Albuquerque two weeks later and arrested for his alleged role in the events. He was tried in Albuquerque the following year. Tijerina, who served as his own attorney, used the court case to put the U.S. government's adherence to the Treaty of Guadalupe Hidalgo on trial. He was acquitted of all charges for the Tierra Amarilla raid.

Authorities, however, continued to look for a way to silence Tijerina, who was ultimately convicted of charges relating to the Echo Amphitheater and other incidents. He served two years in federal prison, and during that time the Alianza lost most of its momentum, failing to resolve both internal ideological differences and being unable to replace its charismatic leader. After his release, Tijerina "spoke now of 'brotherhood and love' rather than confrontations. He found himself more and more in contradiction with former followers" (Gómez-Quiñones, *Chicano Politics*, p. 118) and other, newer and more radical Chicano/a organizations. Although his movement failed to achieve its goals, the Alianza provided an intense spark for the Chicano/a movement. Reies López Tijerina's time in the spotlight was brief, but fiery and inspirational.

Rodolfo "Corky" Gonzales

The efforts of César Chávez, Dolores Huerta, and Reies López Tijerina generated attention to the circumstances confronting migrant workers and rural Spanish speakers, and such undertakings served as fundamental underpinnings for the broader Chicano/a struggle for social justice. By the 1960s, however, the majority of people of Mexican descent in the West lived, not in countryside, but in urban barrios. Certainly, the endeavors of the UFW and the Alianza created awareness of the plight of

Chicano organization leader Rodolfo "Corky" Gonzales, speaking at the Colorado State Penitentiary during a Chicano Conference. (Bettman/Corbis)

campesinos and land grant heirs, but they did not provide direct succor and aid to the men, women, and children who endured poor schools, political neglect, limited advancement opportunities, crime, and many other maladies within cities. Beginning in the mid-1960s, however, Rodolfo "Corky" Gonzales took on the task of rallying disaffected people of Mexican descent (primarily youths) living in the West's urban areas to the call of civil rights and a militant Chicano/a nationalism. The majority of the materials for this section are drawn from the works of scholars such as Tom I. Romero and Ernesto Vigil.

Corky Gonzales, born in 1928, is the son of migrant workers. His birth in Denver was a mere coincidence, Gonzales has claimed, for he should have been born in nearby Keenesburg. His parents had had to travel to Colorado's capital city because local medical personnel refused to serve the needs of Mexicano beet workers.

During his youth, Gonzales used boxing as a vehicle to gain acceptance and won Golden Gloves competitions in 1946 and 1947, as well as being national American Athletic Union (AAU) bantamweight champion in 1947. A recent article by Tom I. Romero notes that Gonzales's success in the ring helped him achieve both recognition and a positive reputation among Denver's sports writers and, subsequently, local Democratic Party officials. After a brief pro career (1948–1952), Gonzales began operating his own restaurant and later on, bail bonds service in the east-side barrio of Denver.

Gonzales worked with the local Viva Kennedy club during the 1960 election. Expanded ties with the party's machinery followed, although, as Romero asserts, Gonzales was never afraid to criticize party politicians if necessary. Ultimately, under the administration of Mayor Tom Currigan, the former pugilist was appointed to serve as the director of the Denver Neighborhood Youth Corps in 1965. This position lasted only one year, as Gonzales became disillusioned with what he felt was the Democrats' condescending attitude toward the city's Mexican Americans. In 1966 Gonzales, along with other members of a group called Los Voluntarios (the volunteers), bolted the party and established their own organization, designed to meet the needs of barrio dwellers.

The Crusade for Justice (CFJ) undertook a wide variety of local activities designed to promote civil rights and social justice for the Spanish-surnamed population. Gonzales' group participated in many undertakings, including publication of a barrio newspaper called *El Gallo* (the rooster), establishment of a community center and a school (Escuela Tlatelolco) designed to offer barrio children lessons in Chicano/a history and bilingual classes, and a campaign to desegregate recreational facilities (such as public swimming pools).

Many of the CFJ's efforts focused upon bettering the Denver community, but there was also a national thrust to the group's endeavors. For example, the CFJ participated in the Poor People's March (along with Martin Luther King) in 1968, sponsored the Chicano Youth Liberation Conference in March of 1969, and participated in the La Raza Unida Party's 1972 national convention. At the 1969 gathering, which had as its goal to "unite the various elements of Chicano communities and their allies throughout the Southwest," Gonzales disseminated his 1967 poem, *I Am Joaquín,* as well as the revolutionary and sweeping *Plan Espiritual de Aztlán,* which called for economic, social, and political sovereignty of the West by people of Mexican descent. This event (which we will describe in more detail later) signaled an increased radicalization and militancy of certain elements of the movimiento.

Although the CFJ did much to help people in the barrio, the organization was also implicated in several violent incidents during the 1970s. For example, in March of 1973, as police attempted to arrest a man in front of the group's offices, CFJ members (and others from the barrio) protested the officers' actions. The incident escalated into a riot, and featured both gunplay and an explosion at a CFJ-owned apartment building. A total of seventeen individuals were injured, and one person was killed during the melee. A second episode (in 1975) involved group member Juan Haro's attempt to transport an explosive device, supposedly intended to destroy a city police facility. Although Haro was acquitted, his involvement in the incident did not shed a positive light on the CFJ. Events such as these, in addition to the rising conservative tide during the later part of the decade, helped reduce the CFJ's and Gonzales's influence. The organization officially folded operations in 1983, and Gonzales suffered a debilitating injury as a result of a 1987 automobile accident. Although the Crusade for Justice did not survive the Reagan era, its legacy lives on. The Escuela Tlatelolco still operates, and as Nita Gonzales, one of Gonzales's daughters, notes, the group's most positive bequest to subsequent generations of Spanish-surnamed people is his legacy of fighting for the rights of his people. Corky Gonzales passed away in April of 2005.

JOSÉ ANGEL GUTIÉRREZ

The activities of José Angel Gutiérrez have been fairly well documented by scholars such as Juan Gómez-Quiñones, Ignacio García, Armando Navarro, and Mario T. Garcia. In addition, Gutiérrez recently published an autobiography entitled *The Making of a Chicano Militant: Lessons from Cristal.* These works served as the primary sources for the material in this section.

José Angel Gutiérrez was born in Crystal City, Texas, on October 25, 1944. Unlike the other members of the national Chicano/a leadership cadre, Gutiérrez, the son of a medical doctor who served the area's Mexican American community, never worked in the fields. This greater material prosperity, however, did not insulate him from the difficulties Spanish speakers endured during the 1950s. Though Gutiérrez completed his education (he graduated from Crystal City High School, Texas A&I University (now Texas A&M, Kingsville), attended graduate school at St. Mary's in San Antonio, and ultimately earned a law degree from the University of Houston), he early on recognized the great disparities that separated whites from people of Mexican descent in his hometown:

> There was a fifth-year grade-one class, a fifth year grade-two class and a fifth year grade-three class; the "one" class was all Anglo, the "two" mostly Mexican students with a few Anglos, and the "three" was all Mexican. . . . At the end of the day . . . the Anglos went to their side of town. . . . In fact, it was illegal for a Mexican to join the Crystal City Country Club, to swim at the city pool on Anglo swim days, to be buried in the Anglo cemetery, to join in the service clubs like the Lions Club or Chamber of Commerce, or to join an Anglo boy scout troop. (Gutiérrez, *Making of a Chicano Radical*, p. 24)

Such circumstances spurred Gutiérrez into political action.

In the summer of 1962, after graduating from high school, Gutiérrez became involved with the Crystal City chapter of the Political Association of Spanish-Speaking Organizations (PASO) (see chapter 6), which, under the influence of activists from San Antonio, had begun recruiting individuals to run for commissionerships in the upcoming 1963 city election. This was a bold step for Crystal City Mexican Americans, for although they outnumbered whites by a ratio of 4 to 1, there had never been an organized campaign to run a slate of Spanish-surnamed aspirants for local office. Gutiérrez contributed by going door-to-door to register voters. Although Texas Rangers and local officials attempted to intimidate the Mexican American populace in order to lessen their enthusiasm and effort on behalf of *los cinco candidatos,* PASO's and Gutiérrez's efforts produced a stunning victory in April of 1963.

Once elected, however, the group of naive politicos quickly fell into petty squabbling over patronage and power and proved unable to withstand an effective counterattack orchestrated by whites. Not surprisingly, during the next round of elections, none managed to hold on to their positions. For the teenaged Gutiérrez, however, the 1963 campaign proved heady and provided him with the knowledge and tactics he used in future civil rights undertakings, including the founding of important movimiento groups such as the Mexican American Youth Organization (MAYO) and La Raza Unida (The United Race) Party (LRUP). It was these two groups and their activities on behalf of Spanish-surnamed (and poor) people of the West that brought this South Texas native national and international acclaim.

During the 1960s and 1970s, leaders such as César Chávez, Dolores Huerta, Reies López Tijerina, Rodolfo "Corky" Gonzales, and José Angel Gutiérrez pricked the conscience of the nation. They pointed out and challenged the many daily injustices inflicted upon people of Mexican descent and made apparent to an uninformed national populace the wretched status of men, women, and children who earned less, attended (but rarely graduated from) inferior institutions of learning, endured difficult and dangerous working conditions, had limited access to economic assets (such as land) and advancement, and lacked political influence commensurate with their numbers. In the next section, we provide a more detailed overview of the goals of their various organizations (and others established by less well-known activists), as well as describing some of the changes that occurred within older and more conservative Mexican American civil rights organizations, such as LULAC and AGIF (see chapters 5 and 6).

SOME KEY ORGANIZATIONS OF THE CHICANO/A MOVEMENT

The efforts of the five national organizers mentioned in the previous section helped stimulate the genesis of numerous associations conceived to enhance the schooling, working conditions, and economic and political circumstances of people of Mexican descent. We now focus on providing brief sketches of the goals, activities, and accomplishments of some of the organizations in various cities and towns throughout the West. Although it is not possible in the space allotted to cover all groups and endeavors, we expound upon some undertakings of the UFW, Crusade for Justice (CFJ), Movimiento Estudiantil Chicano de Aztlán (MEChA), MAYO, LRUP, Brown Berets, Centers for Autonomous Social Action (CASA), Mexican American Legal Defense Fund (MALDEF), Southwest Voter Registration and Education Project (SVERP), and National Council of La Raza (NCLR), as well as noting the impact of increased militancy during the 1960s and 1970s on the rhetoric and objectives of LULAC. Additionally, we present information on lesser-known organizations in places such as Utah, which fought for Chicanos/as in locales with much smaller Spanish-surnamed populations.

UNITED FARM WORKERS (UFW)

As noted in our discussion on César Chávez and Dolores Huerta, the United Farm Workers, through the use of nonviolent protest methods, secured a series of impressive victories during the years 1965 through 1970. Clearly, by the start of the new decade, the union had energized thousands of workers and outside sympathizers. However, at the very moment of these significant accomplishments, two key problems became perceptible. First, there was the UFW's inability to sustain the initial bread-and-butter gains of the late 1960s, and second, there was the union's growing philosophical disconnection from the goals of other, more militant key groups of the Chicano/a movement, particularly on the issue of undocumented immigrants.

After the success of the Delano strike, Chávez and Huerta sought to export their methods and recruitment tactics nationwide. The UFW, for example, helped start a strike in the fruit fields of Starr County, Texas (in 1966), as well as other job actions in the Midwest and western states during the early 1970s; starting in 1973, however, a series of setbacks worked to undermine the association's viability.

The initial reverses occurred in California, as the preliminary contracts negotiated in the 1966 through 1970 period expired, and numerous corporations signed sweetheart contracts for migrant labor, not with the UFW, but with the Jimmy Hoffa–led Teamsters. Concurrent with having to fight a rearguard action against another labor organization, as historian Juan Gómez-Quiñones notes, numerous "signs of faulty administration, poor decision making and non democratic tendencies" further weakened the union (Gómez-Quiñones, *Chicano Politics,* p. 107). The growing strength of the conservative message and the Republican ascendancy of the early 1980s also reduced the effectiveness of Chávez (who had tied the UFW directly to the more "progressive" elements within the Democratic Party) and the UFW. In sum, "by the late seventies and eighties the UFW faced, major problems, some of which were concurrent with its overt and partisan participation in electoral politics" (Gómez-Quiñones, *Chicano Politics,* p. 107).

Simultaneous with the predicaments outlined, the UFW fell out of step with more belligerent and radical components of the Chicano/a movement on the issue of immigration. From the UFW's inception, Chávez had argued for an end to the bracero program (see chapter 6), as well as for strict regulation of the U.S.-Mexican border. This stance, based on a belief that undocumented workers deprived Mexican Americans of jobs, created rifts with other movimiento leaders. MAPA stalwart Bert Corona, for example, put it this way: "'I did have an important difference with César. This involved his . . . position on the need to apprehend and deport undocumented Mexican immigrants . . . used as scabs by the growers. . . . We did not support deportation of people'" (García, *Memories of Chicano History,* p. 249). By 1974, other organizations involved in the Chicano/a struggle (even the usually more conformist LULAC and AGIF) began speaking out against the UFW's position. In order to save face, Chávez reconsidered his union's perspective, although the schism further undermined the group's base of support. With all of these obstacles facing them, by the start of the 1980s the UFW began a period of steady and continued decline.

THE CRUSADE FOR JUSTICE (CFJ)

As both Gómez-Quiñones and Vigil note in their studies, shortly after his termination from the post of director of the Denver Youth Corps in 1966, Corky Gonzales held a rally during which the now unemployed administrator denounced both the city's administration and the Democratic Party apparatus. This break with mainstream politics served as the genesis for a "'crusade for justice which we are going to carry into every city in Colorado'" (Vigil, *Crusade for Justice,* pp. 26–27). As one historian of Chicano/a politics has noted, this effort was kindled by forces such as "urban inequalities, exclusionary Democratic Party politics, and the disillusionment with poverty programs" (Gómez-Quiñones, *Chicano Politics,* p. 112).

Between 1966 and the early 1980s, the CFJ participated in a wide variety of undertakings designed to improve circumstances in Denver's barrio as well as inspire ethnic pride and solidarity. In addition to the efforts mentioned in our discussion of Corky Gonzales, the CFJ participated in anti-Vietnam war rallies, worked to reduce gang violence, protested for improved conditions in area schools, and pursued policies to stimulate economic empowerment and independence for Spanish-surnamed people. Among the myriad entities established under the CFJ umbrella were a federal credit union, the Colorado Prisoners Rights Organization (CPRO), the Ballet Chicano de Aztlán dance troupe, and the Colorado Recreation and Boxing Coaches Association (CRBCA). These various entities labored to serve the comunidad and improve the daily lives of men, women, and children of north Denver and Colorado.

Unfortunately, this heady period of activity did not persist. Through the sustained efforts of law enforcement authorities (such as FBI and local police surveillance), legal problems of key personnel, and a declining interest by the CFJ's constituent base, the organization entered a period of deterioration by the early 1980s. As one member recalls, the descent was a lethargic process which "no one incident, date or information source [can] fully account for" (Vigil, *Crusade for Justice,* p. 365). By the time of Corky Gonzales's tragic 1987 automobile accident, what remained of the CFJ was but a shell of its former militant incarnation. In fact, the group's primary objective now is the operation of the Escuela Tlatelolco. Corky Gonzales passed away in April of 2005 at the age of 76.

MOVIMIENTO ESTUDIANTIL CHICANO DE AZTLÁN (MECHA)

The start of the 1960s, according to activist and scholar Armando Navarro, was "the calm before the storm," as the number of Mexican Americans attending western colleges and universities increased slightly. It is not surprising, given the discriminatory practices they had experienced in their own communities, that some of these students became associated with the African American struggle for civil rights. Individuals such as Maria Varela and Elizabeth Sutherland Martínez, for example, participated in the efforts of campus organizations such as the Student Non-Violent Coordinating Committee (SNCC) and Students for a Democratic Society (SDS) (Navarro, *Mexican American Youth Organization,* p. 51). Others, particularly Luis Valdez and Roberto Rubalcava, helped to bring about the earliest manifestations of Chicano/a protests; being inspired, in part, by involvement with the Progressive Labor Party

(PLP) at San Jose State. Upon returning from a trip to witness the supposed benefits of the Cuban Revolution, the two penned a manifesto that argued that the Spanish-surnamed people in the West should agitate for similar revolutionary measures.

Additionally, the budding radicals forcefully criticized the more moderate measures utilized by an earlier generation of Mexican American activists, stating that "Spanish-speaking leaders are not leaders at all; Americanized beyond recall, they neither understand nor care about the basic (Chicano) population, which has an identity of its own. . . . Having no leaders of our own, we accept Fidel Castro" (Navarro, *Mexican American Youth Organization,* p. 51).

By the later part of the 1960s, there existed other entities at California universities and colleges that espoused similar goals, including the Mexican American Student Association (MASA) at East Los Angeles Community College, United Mexican American Students (UMAS) at Loyola University, the Mexican American Youth Association (MAYA) at the University of San Diego, and the Mexican American Student Confederation (MASC), with branches at San Jose State, Fresno State, and California State Hayward and Sacramento. Although the majority of the membership was comprised of Chicanos/as, the Puerto Rican population living in northern California also became involved with the operations of some branches. In 1967, a like-minded group, the Mexican American Youth Organization (MAYO), became active in Kingsville, Texas, on the campus of Texas A&I University (which would later become known as Texas A&M University, Kingsville).

In March 1969, representatives from several California Chicano/a student organizations attended the Youth Liberation Conference in Denver. Inspired by the rhetoric of Gonzales's El Plan Espiritual de Aztlán, UMAS leader Carlos Muñoz (and others) called for a gathering to discuss the many difficulties confronted by estudiantes at the state's institutions of higher learning. This Santa Barbara-based assembly also sought to integrate the protest and barrio-based activities of youth groups. Among the results of this key encounter were the publication of El Plan de Santa Barbara and the unification of the separate groups under the Movimiento Estudiantil Chicano de Aztlán (MEChA) banner. The name change was not of minor significance, as Carlos Muñoz noted in his work, *Youth, Identity and Power: The Chicano Movement:* "The adoption of the new name and acronym, MEChA, signaled a new level of political consciousness among student activists. It was the final stage in the transformation of what had been loosely organized, local student groups into a single, structured and unified student movement" (Muñoz, *Youth, Identity, and Power,* p. 80).

El Plan de Santa Barbara called for a dramatic transformation in the curriculum of educational programs for students of Mexican descent. Instead of stressing assimilation into American cultural practices and beliefs, MEChA demanded an academic course that would challenge the dire economic and political circumstances extant in many western barrios, while simultaneously conveying to Chicano/a youth the glory of Aztec civilization, as well as noting positive elements of Mexican American life (Muñoz, *Youth, Identity, and Power,* p. 139).

During the 1970s MEChA members worked to accomplish many of these goals and achieved many successes. For example, Chicano Studies Programs became common at universities throughout the United States; important Chicano/a journals (such as *El Grito, Aztlán,* and *Journal of Mexican American History*) served as vehicles for academic debate regarding facets of barrio life; institutions of higher learning and private foundations funded the works of playwrights, artists, and writers, who generated important projects on the Chicano/a experience; and finally, many activists participated in political campaigns (especially school board elections) throughout the West, always emphasizing the needs, problems, and desires of the comunidad.

While much was accomplished, by the late 1970s MEChA's militancy had started to decline. As Navarro notes, by the start of the 1980s the movimiento had petered out, and "the climate . . . was no longer actuated and dominated by the radical politics of the era of protest." Carlos Muñoz concurs, and he argues that during the Reagan years Chicano/a studies became "mainstreamed," and many estudiantes, in his estimation, had returned to the pro-assimilation model (Muñoz, *Youth, Identity, and Power,* pp. 158, 175, and 177).

BROWN BERETS

The CFJ and other movimiento groups sometimes utilized militant tactics and secessionist and nationalistic rhetoric to achieve stated ends, but according to activist-scholar Armando Navarro, it was the Brown Berets that functioned as the "militant arm of the Chicano Movement" (Navarro, *Mexican American Youth Organization,* p. 63).

The Brown Berets, founded in Los Angeles in 1967, based on the efforts of David Sánchez and Carlos Montes and their endeavors to defuse gang activity and violence, as well to unify the barrio's population into a coherent, confrontational, and revolutionary body. Although the group "never developed a clear ideology, . . . [it was] antithetical to capitalism [and] was predicated on cultural nationalism." The membership rejected assimilation, was suspicious of middle-class Mexican American reformers, and sought to bring about the establishment of the "nation" of Aztlán within the borders of the U.S. West. At its apex, it had an estimated 5,000 male and female members, with ninety chapters throughout the nation (Navarro, *Mexican American Youth Organization,* pp. 63–64).

Brown Berets, decked out in striking quasi-military outfits, often served as security details for pro-Chicano/a rallies and functions throughout the West. The organization participated in many of the key events of the movimiento, including the Poor People's March and the school blowouts (planned protests by Chicano/a students against conditions in their schools; at a designated time, students would simply leave their campuses in order to form picket lines to protest unjust conditions) of 1968, the Chicano Youth Liberation Conference in 1969, the Chicano Moratorium Committee's efforts against the Vietnam War in 1970, and the symbolic invasion of Catalina Island (to highlight concerns regarding the interpretation of the Treaty of Guadalupe-Hidalgo) in 1972.

Not surprisingly, such activities, as well as the belligerent oratory of the group's leaders, aroused the suspicions of police and the FBI. Shortly after the Catalina Island "invasion," Sánchez announced that the association was disbanding, due to both internal dissonance as well as "severe harassment by law-enforcement agencies" (Navarro, *Mexican American Youth Organization,* p. 66).

Although the militaristic posturing of the Brown Berets lent itself to making the organization a hotbed of machismo, new research reveals the significant role played by female members. A recent article by Dionne Espinoza, for example, presents an analysis of the contributions of numerous "revolutionary sisters" who struggled alongside male Brown Berets in order to improve conditions in their comunidad.

Gloria Arellanes was one such individual, serving in the capacity of minister of finance and correspondence for the East Los Angeles chapter. Arellanes and other barrio *mujeres* (women) became interested in the organization because of its call for radical social change. As Espinoza notes, the Brown Berets appealed to Chicanas because it "affirmed . . . their commitment to recovering the indigenous, which was a strong current in the revaluing of racial-ethnic identity." In addition, women were to be included in other undertakings such as "drilling, rapping and planning group events" (Espinoza, "Revolutionary Sisters," pp. 27 and 30).

Although mujeres did participate in such tasks, the leadership too often reverted to a stereotyped notion of women's roles, thereby helping to alienate the majority of the female members. Arellanes, for example, received no credit for her organizational skills and diligent work in the establishment of a free clinic. When photographs of the grand opening of the facility were published in the Brown Berets' newspaper (*La Causa*), only "photos of the three male ministers were printed. . . . In effect, Arellanes was rendered invisible in the organization's public self-presentation" (Espinoza, "Revolutionary Sisters," p. 35). In February of 1970, Arellanas resigned in protest. Other instances of the stereotyping and maltreatment mentioned by Espinoza included Brown Berets asking Chicanas to dance for Reies López Tijerina at the Chicano Youth Liberation Conference and the assumption by the male hierarchy of the East Los Angeles branch that women would do the cooking and cleaning at all chapter events.

MAYO AND LRUP

José Angel Gutiérrez, along with Willie C. Velásquez, Mario Compean, Ignacio Perez, and Juan Patlan, founded the Mexican American Youth Organization in 1967 while students at St. Mary's University in San Antonio. The principal source for the materials for this section of the chapter come from Ignacio Garcia's work, *United We Win: The Rise and Fall of La Raza Unida Party,* as well as from the LRUP Web site. From its inception, MAYO was committed to several goals, including a grassroots strategy for mobilizing the Mexican descent population (in keeping with some of the successes that Gutiérrez experienced during the campaign of 1963), Chicano/a nationalism for the benefit of *la raza* ("the race," as Mexican Americans have traditionally referred to themselves); and "to redirect political, social, and economic resources . . . to benefit . . . and ultimately maximize Mexican political representation" in Texas and elsewhere (Gómez-Quiñones, *Chicano Politics,* p. 129).

The response by many Mexican American youths to the organization was positive, and by 1968 chapters existed in various parts of the Lone Star State, especially in the Rio Grande Valley and other areas of southern Texas. Unfortunately, the reaction to the rhetoric and confrontational tactics of MAYO by the parents of these young men and women was far less enthusiastic. This divide was evidenced in the rejoinders of important mainstream Spanish-surnamed politicians (such as Democratic representative Henry B. González), who believed that MAYO leaders such as Gutiérrez (who, in a 1969 speech suggested that "killing gringos" might be a last resort to generate change), were far too radical and divisive to bring about social transformation. Given this generational rift, it is not surprising that scholars like Armando Navarro argue that it was the Chicano/a youth that acted as the driving force of the movimiento, not older and more conservative reformers.

Between 1967 and 1970, MAYO pushed for a variety of reforms and assistance programs; but their main concern was the improvement of educational facilities and opportunities for Chicano/a students. During these years, it organized and helped stage thirty-nine boycotts in locales such as Edcouch-Elsa, Kingsville, Crystal City, and elsewhere in Texas, as well as in California and Colorado. In addition to educational improvements, MAYO pushed to enhance conditions in barrios, partnering with entities such as Volunteers in Service to America (VISTA) and the Ford Foundation to establish antipoverty, community upgrading, and economic development efforts. Unfortunately, as Navarro notes, such relationships came with a steep price: the limiting of MAYO's ability to act independently and the ultimate decline of the group's ability to produce more radical social change: "A movement-oriented organization must possess sufficient resources of its own to develop a capacity for mobilization and to carry out its organizing and advocacy activities. Such was not the case with MAYO. . . . The result was that MAYO was caught in the web of financial dependency" (Navarro, *Mexican American Youth Organization*, p. 160). Although this problem proved to be the organization's Achilles heel, the late 1960s were still heady days for MAYO's leadership. In 1968 some within organization even argued that, after working so diligently in the San Antonio barrio, perhaps it was time for the organization to begin flexing its political muscles.

Beginning in late 1968, MAYO leaders organized a campaign with the goal of fielding a slate of candidates for city offices in San Antonio for the April 1969 election. The organization consolidated its effort under the banner of the Committee for Barrio Betterment (CBB) which featured a run for office and conducted a campaign "predicated on a 'Chicano power' strategy that sought community control of the city's political institutions" (Navarro, *Mexican American Youth Organization*, p. 187). The CBB stressed a commitment to improving the terrible social and economic conditions that plagued the West Side of the Alamo City. Even though MAYO was greatly outspent by the ruling political machine, the CBB candidate for mayor, Mario Compean, came within fewer than 400 votes of forcing the current mayor into a runoff. Although Gutiérrez experienced some trepidation before launching this campaign, the "elections proved the inherent strength of bloc voting, . . . [and] Gutiérrez [was] more convinced than ever . . . that a Chicano political party in South Texas could mean the beginning of a new political era for Chicanos, an epoch where the Chicano was not the powerless but the powerful" (Navarro, *Mexican American Youth Organization*, p. 190). Confident after CBB's positive showing, MAYO turned to birthing yet another revolutionary idea, the establishment of a Chicano/a-based political party, the La Raza Unida Party.

The LRUP began operation in January 1970, filing for party status in various South Texas counties and seeking to expand on the temporary gains accomplished by los cinco candidatos in 1963. In both the 1970 and 1972 cycles, LRUP scored victories in towns such as Crystal City and Cotulla.

Buttressed by its early successes, LRUP staged a state convention in October of 1971, choosing a young attorney, Ramsey Muñiz, as candidate for governor of Texas. Not surprisingly, Muñiz ran well in the border region, claiming an impressive 6 percent of the votes cast and causing

Dolph Briscoe to suffer the ignominious fate of being the first twentieth-century Democratic gubernatorial candidate not elected with a majority. By the start of 1973, it seemed as if the LRUP could become an important player in the politics of Texas. But it was not to be, and by 1978 the party had lost control of its Zavala County base as well as its party status throughout Texas. In part, this failure was caused by the LRUP's attempt to become a national party and its continuing inability to appeal to older, more moderate Mexican Americans (Navarro, *Mexican American Youth Organization,* pp. 212–236).

From the LRUP's inception, individuals in states such as Arizona, California, New Mexico, Colorado, and elsewhere worked to establish chapters, and by late 1971 Corky Gonzales, head of the Colorado branch, issued a call for a national convention, to be staged in El Paso on September 1, 1972. From the meeting's commencement, important philosophical and operational issues split LRUP into belligerent camps, one nationalistic (the Colorado faction), the other more cautious and pragmatic (representing the Texas LRUP).

As noted by historian Ignacio García, during a raucous four days, Corky Gonzales guided the more militant splinter group, which was dedicated to the establishment of a Chicano/a homeland, as well as rejecting compromise with those who did not agree with the third-party option. Dishearteningly, this led the Coloradans to not invite César Chávez, who was strongly tied to the progressive wing of the Democrats, to the congress. José Angel Gutiérrez's supporters represented the opposition to the nationalistic stance. As the LRUP worked to solidify its base in the Lone Star State, Gutiérrez eventually realized that, to achieve broader appeal, the party would have to attract Mexican American voters usually tied to the Democrats. This led him to curb his more militant pronouncements and to reject "counterculture antics . . . [and] Marxist rhetoric that could confuse the people" (Garcia, *United We Win,* pp. 53–55). Rather, Gutiérrez called for party unity in order to win political races and elect members to school boards and local governments. Ultimately, this viewpoint prevailed, and the gathering elected Gutiérrez party chairman. Unfortunately, the seeds of division were sown at the El Paso convention, and as F. Arturo Rosales notes, "no one who left the convention was committed to continue building the national organization; instead they returned to their more provincial spaces of activism." Further, as some party activists (especially from California and Colorado) drifted more and more to Marxism, "the national infrastructure that had been established . . . began to crumble and, by 1979, the few remaining members decided to hold their last meeting" (Rosales, *Chicano,* p. 242).

CENTER FOR AUTONOMOUS SOCIAL ACTION (CASA)

The tumult of the Chicano/a era increased attention to the economic and political circumstances of Mexican Americans in the West. The movimiento also generated renewed interest in the fate and condition of another group, undocumented workers toiling in the region's agricultural concerns. The association that focused most upon such concerns during the movement era was the Center for Autonomous Social Action (CASA), started by Bert Corona and Chole Alatorre in 1968. The principal sources for this section of the chapter are works by Mario T. García, David G. Gutiérrez, and Vicki L. Ruiz. The entity's stated goal was to function in a way similar to a mutual aid society, but to specifically concentrate upon providing "services including immigration counseling, notary, and legal services" (Gutiérrez, "Sin Fronteras," p. 17).

The organization spread rapidly and by 1970 had partnered with groups throughout California, Texas, and other western states. In addition to its offering of direct assistance, CASA pushed to change the perception among many Mexican Americans that their brothers and sisters from across the border were a threat to their social, occupational, and economic standing.

Under the slogan *Somos Un Pueblo Sin Fronteras* (We Are One People without Borders), Corona and his colleagues battled to gain recognition from moderates (such as LULACers) that "the basic guarantees of American law represented only the bare minimum to which undocumented workers were entitled. CASA proposed, therefore, that the undocumented be granted . . . a statute of limitations of one year on deportations, eligibility for citizenship after one year's residence, and the right 'to be offered employment on equal terms with workers native to the host country'" (Gutiérrez, "Sin Fronteras," p. 18).

CASA was successful in achieving this objective, partly through forging alliances with student activists based on their call for working class unity. The organization also found allies within the California LRUP and the Colorado-based CFJ against proposed federal legislation designed to make it more difficult for *indocumentados* (those without immigration documents) to work. By the early 1970s a coalition of Mexican American and Chicano/a organizations claimed that if the proposed law (authored by New Jersey Democrat Peter Rodino) passed, "'all Latinos, Chicanos [and] Mejicanos will be obligated to produce identity papers, and many applicants for jobs will be denied a chance for employment . . . on the fact that we may 'appear' alien'" (Gutiérrez, "Sin Fronteras," p. 19).

CASA's success was even more impressive because it was able to help shift the position of more traditional organizations such as LULAC, which, when President Carter announced his version of the Rodino proposals in October 1977, stated that the new regulation would create "'a dual system of employment [in which] hiring will be based largely on a prospective employee's pigmentation and English-speaking ability'" (Gutiérrez, "Sin Fronteras," p. 26). AGIF, MAPA, and other organizations followed with similar statements.

By the late 1970s, CASA helped orchestrate a dramatic transformation in the way older Mexican American civil rights organizations understood the issue of immigration; yet by 1978 CASA had ceased operations due to internal quarrels, primarily between younger and older members. In Mario T. Garcia's 1994 biography of Bert Corona, the leader's recollection of CASA's downfall centers upon the unwillingness of the "young turks" to spend the time necessary to recruit and mold the familias of indocumentados into a political base. Instead, they "'thought the people would be attracted by the political line, by the rhetoric, or by the glamour'" (Garcia, *Memories of Chicano History*, pp. 308–315).

MALDEF, SVREP, AND NCLR

The Mexican American Legal Defense and Educational Fund (MALDEF), Southwest Voters Registration and Education Project (SVERP), and the National Council of La Raza (NCLR) all came into existence during the late 1960s and early 1970s. Unlike MAYO and LRUP, these organizations focused upon using the power of the ballot (and community organizing and entrepreneurial activities as well) within the traditional two-party structure to improve circumstances for the Chicano/a population. The Web sites for these various groups served as the primary sources for the materials for this section of the chapter.

The individual most directly involved in the conception and early operation of MALDEF was Laredo native Pete Tijerina. In many ways, his decision to become an activist was based on the same motives as advocates of the Mexican American generation. Tijerina's father was an independent truck driver, and he passed on to his son a strong desire for self-improvement. In December 1945, after Tijerina's discharge from the Air Force, the young man offered to invest his life savings in the family business. Not surprisingly, the elder Tijerina turned him down and advised Pete to seek a college education. After much struggle to complete not only college but law school, he began practice in January 1952.

As a trial lawyer, Tijerina was exposed to the discriminatory practices foisted upon Mexican Americans in Texas. "No Mexicans Allowed" signs, a lack of representation on juries, and other injustices led Tijerina to become part of LULAC's "flying squad," a group that went from town to town to protest, and hopefully eliminate, maltreatment of Spanish-surnamed persons. Unfortunately, this effort, though valiant, was too scattered to be truly effective and required both time and money, neither of which a young attorney had in abundance. As a result of Tijerina's efforts, however, he was invited to a 1966 conference where he met Jack Greenberg (who directed the National Association for the Advancement of Colored People's Legal Defense Fund, NAACP-LDF). Through Greenberg's intervention, Tijerina approached the Ford Foundation, which in 1968 provided over $2 million to fund the initial operation of MALDEF.

During the 1970s and 1980s, MALDEF filed numerous friend-of-the-court briefs, often working with the NAACP and other organizations to fight for the civil rights of minorities. The results were impressive, as MALDEF participated in or initiated several important cases. *White et al. v. Regester et al.* (1973) forced the state to bring its practices into line with the Voting Rights Act of 1965. *Edgewood ISD v. State of Texas* (1984) overturned the Lone Star State's antiquated and unfair method of public educational finance, establishing the Robin Hood plan to help poorer school districts. Finally, *Plyler v. Doe* (1982) made it possible for children of undocumented workers to attend school and receive a public education.

A second organization focused on improving levels of representation among Spanish speakers was SVREP, which began operations in San Antonio in 1974 (using funding from the Ford Foundation). Under the leadership of MAYO stalwart Willie Velásquez, the SVERP, in conjunction with MALDEF, LULAC, the NAACP, and others, staged registration drives (using tactics similar to those used in the South during the 1960s) throughout the West. After a decade of effort, SVERP's efforts produced a dramatic increase in both the total of registered Mexican American voters (increasing in Texas from 400,000 to more than 1.2 million by 1988) as well as the number of Spanish-surnamed holders of public office (increasing from less than 600 in 1973 to almost 1,600 by 1988). During the 1980s, SVERP also established a litigation and research institute.

BIDAL AGUERO, CHICANO ACTIVIST AND ENTREPRENEUR IN LUBBOCK, TEXAS

In a 1991 essay entitled "Small Business in America: A Historiographic Survey," Mansel G. Blackford reviewed the role of small firms in the American economy and noted that, rather than fading away, such businesses have endured and remain a vital aspect of the American economy for many industries and regions of our country. Works by Professor Blackford and others have done much to reveal the history and importance of small business, but there remain important gaps in this field.

Above all, the contributions of minority entrepreneurs, specifically Hispanics who are self-employed, have not received much coverage in the academic historical literature. Therefore, the story that follows is offered as one example of what we believe is the important role of Hispanic businesspeople in the social, political, and economic history of the Spanish-speaking population of the U.S. West. Like his colleagues elsewhere, the concerted efforts of individuals such as Mr. Bidal Aguero have improved the economic, educational, and professional opportunities of barrio residents throughout the region over the past three decades.

Bidal Aguero was born on July 23, 1949, in Lubbock, Texas, the son of a poor farm laborer and his wife. He grew up on the city's impoverished north side and, like so many of his generation, faced much discrimination in area schools. In various interviews during the past twenty years he has noted that the Anglo teachers in the public schools did little to reach out and motivate Mexican American students. The facilities for these children were minimal, he recalls, and there was little emphasis on teaching estudiantes (students) much beyond the basics of reading, writing, and arithmetic. After all, most teachers reasoned, these children were destined for the fields, not for higher learning.

In addition to facing the problem of low expectations, most children from Bidal's neighborhood also worked picking cotton or cleaning houses after school to help their families' meager finances. Due to such circumstances, the possibility of barrio youths attending the local institution of higher learning, Texas Tech University, was nearly zero. Although he admits that he did not do well academically in his final year at Lubbock High School, Bidal did enough to gain acceptance by his hometown university, beginning classes there in September of 1967.

Not surprisingly, there were few other Chicanos/as on campus at that time. Bidal became active in the local La Raza Unida Party, ACLU, and MEChA. By 1972 he had completed his degree, and he went on to do graduate work at the University of Wisconsin-Whitewater; graduating with a master's degree in special education in 1974. This background helped him land a position with the South Plains Association of Governments, a social service agency, upon his return to Lubbock. In March of 1977 he quit this employment, disillusioned when he did not receive a promotion, he felt, because of his ethnicity.

Some scholars who have examined the genesis of minority businesses have argued that racially charged events can often act as catalyst for the start of entrepreneurial activities. By the middle of 1977 Bidal Aguero had reached a crossroads: should he continue in social work or use his talents in other areas? Having worked in publishing during his time at Texas Tech University, Aguero became convinced that a Lubbock-based newspaper geared to providing national news, community information, and commentary for Spanish speakers could succeed.

In early 1977 Aguero used $1,500 of his savings, borrowed from family and friends, and used advance advertising sales to launch the first issue of his circular, *El Editor*. He did not approach local financial institutions because he believed that they would not be interested in investing in a minority-owned enterprise. The paper was, initially, a one-person operation. Bidal wrote editorials, solicited ads, distributed the paper, and started two other entities, a pest control company and a consulting firm. Through a tremendous amount of hard work, *El Editor* grew slowly and steadily. By 1981 the circulation had increased from 2,000 to 10,000 copies per issue. With at least a level of profitability insured, Aguero returned full force to his other passion, serving his community.

Since the late 1970s, Bidal's commitment to improving social conditions confronting his neighbors has involved him in activities such as political campaigns, lawsuits, social services for the poor and downtrodden, and efforts at barrio economic development. He has run for public office, participated in a lawsuit that led to the establishment of single-member districts (allowing areas of a city to elect representatives from their own district, as opposed to "at-large" elections where all commissioners are elected by all voters in a city, making it easier for minorities to elect representatives from their communities) for the Lubbock Independent School District, established a center, the Lubbock Centro Aztlán (still in existence), that provides a wide array of services to barrio residents, helped improve conditions for area migrant workers, and assisted in the establishment of a food bank.

A final sector of community work for this entrepreneur has been to help other Spanish speakers to fit into (and benefit from) the market system by starting their own commercial enterprises. During the late 1970s, he contacted other local *comerciantes* (merchants) and convinced them to establish an association that would help them network, operate their firms more effectively and professionally, and bid for local and state government contracts. The result of these labors was the birth of Comerciantes Organizados Mexicano-Americanos (Organized Mexican American Merchants), or COMA. In conjunction with improving the operation and profitability of Chicano/a-owned enterprises, COMA, like its founder, worked to improve the barrio community. Members served in various citywide committees and sponsored conferences and other

events designed to improve educational opportunities for
Spanish-surnamed youths and increase the number of minority
female business owners.

By the late 1990s, Bidal Aguero had retired from daily
operation of *El Editor* (which is now operated by a daughter).
Looking back on his extensive career and activities in a 1998
interview, he was both proud of what he had accomplished,
and disgusted by many aspects of life in conservative West
Texas. On the one hand, he had helped increase the number
of Hispanic entrepreneurs in the area. On the other hand, he
was upset that COMA had morphed into the Lubbock
Hispanic Chamber of Commerce, which he considered to be
too conservative and tied to the Anglo power structure.

In regard to education, Aguero criticized the lack of action
by local school officials to reduce the high rate of dropouts
among barrio schoolchildren. In terms of economic
development, he railed against the way the southwestern
section of the city of Lubbock had grown while the north side
(mostly Mexican American) and the east side (mostly African
American) remained economically stagnant and faced the
closing of elementary and junior high schools during the late
1990s. Finally, Aguero continues to cry out for increased
representation for minorities in city government.

It is evident that, in 2005, this Chicano activist is still
fighting for the progressive causes he has championed for
decades. Although some things have improved in Lubbock,
Texas, Bidal Aguero argues that much still remains to be done
in order to achieve the goals of the idealistic Chicano/a
activists and white liberals of the 1960s and 1970s.

Finally, the NCLR (also dependent on Ford Foundation money for
its start) began operations in Phoenix, Arizona, and Washington, D.C.,
in 1972, seeking to serve as a national organization for "the integration of
Chicano interests into all major facets of society and for providing . . .
clearinghouse activities as well as dissemination of information" (Gómez-
Quiñones, *Chicano Politics*, p. 110). The NCLR's principal goal, under
the leadership of Raúl Yzaquirre, was to provide knowledge, contacts, and
tactics for groups working locally. The NCLR also functioned as a lobbying organization (putting out position statements on issues affecting the

comunidad), as well as working to increase the percentage of minority vendors and entrepreneurs doing business with Fortune 500 and other large corporations. Clearly, by the start of the Reagan era, organizations such as NCLR had very different aspirations and tactics from those of the "Chicano nationalism" years of the 1960s and early 1970s.

SPANISH-SPEAKING ORGANIZATION FOR COMMUNITY, INTEGRITY, AND OPPORTUNITY (SOCIO)

The majority of organizations mentioned in this section operated in territories with substantial numbers of Chicanos/as (such as California, Texas, and Arizona). Such states were not, however, the only places where Spanish speakers fought to better conditions during the movimiento years. Although space limitations do not permit a discussion of the activities of Chicano/a associations in Nevada, Idaho, Wyoming, Minnesota, Oregon, and elsewhere, recent works (discussed in the Bibliographical Essay) provide useful summaries of the myriad activities designed to better the lives of migrants, improve the education of Mexican American students, and boost economic and political development of barrio dwellers throughout the West.

One example of the many organizations doing this work will have to serve: the Spanish-speaking Organization for Community, Integrity, and Opportunity (SOCIO), based in Salt Lake City from 1968 through 1986. Historian Jorge Iber notes that this group, founded by a Catholic priest and a Mormon bishop, sought to better the educational, economic, and political life of Spanish speakers throughout Utah, although SOCIO's main efforts took place in the more urbanized areas of the state. During its early existence, SOCIO's volunteer base worked tirelessly with government officials, public school educators, University of Utah professors and administrators, and religious denominations to increase the availability of affordable housing, reduce criminality among barrio youths, increase graduation rates, improve Mexican American representation at state colleges and universities, and improve occupational training.

SOCIO was fairly successful in achieving many of its goals, and by the late 1970s the group had become a well-connected (and fairly powerful) influence on state government, while also having direct ties to Utah's Mormon leaders. One of the group's founders, Dr. Orlando Rivera, recently argued that perhaps SOCIO was too successful, and that this led, in part, to the organization's death. By the late 1980s, this University of Utah education professor had noted a dramatic transformation in the daily lives of many of the Spanish-surnamed people living in the Beehive State.

THE CHICANO/A MOVEMENT'S IMPACT ON THE VIETNAM WAR, THE ARTS, AND RELIGION

THE VIETNAM WAR

As we have noted, individuals of Mexican descent have participated in various U.S. military conflicts, and youths from many comunidades have paid the ultimate price to defend their country. Earlier studies (discussed in chapter 6) attested to the valor of Spanish-surnamed soldiers and, particularly after World War II and Korea, participation in homeland defense convinced many veteranos that "wartime service was a way to gain equality . . . [and] Mexican Americans were eager for others to know that, considering their fighting capacity . . . they were more than deserving of fair treatment" (Oropeza, "Making History," p. 3). The principal sources for this section of the chapter are works by Lea Ybarra, Juan Ramírez, and George Mariscal.

In Lea Ybarra's recent work, *Vietnam Veteranos: Chicanos Recall the War,* she quotes a former 101st Airborne Division sergeant, whose words provide readers with a succinct précis of the importance of military service to the Mexican American community: "'When I was a kid, all I wanted to be was a damn paratrooper. I was going to be a man's man and there was no restriction from it. It's could I run five miles in the morning and could I jump out of a damn airplane, and it was the first time that there was equal opportunity to compete and you're damn right I competed. For once in my life, I felt like I was a man. It didn't matter what color I was'" (Ybarra, *Vietnam Veteranos,* p. 151). The antiwar protests of the Chicano/a movement obviously represent a real change in attitude toward serving in the military, one that was made more widespread by the actual experiences of those who did serve.

One movimiento era group closely associated with antiwar demonstrations was the Brown Berets, which, with the assistance of Mario Compean of MAYO, established roughly one dozen "Chicano Moratorium" committees throughout the West by the spring of 1970. In addition to mobilizing barrio populations to call for U.S. withdrawal from Vietnam, some Chicano/a leaders hoped to strengthen their own movement by shifting the nation's focus away from overseas adventures to problems of poverty and discrimination within the United States. As one moratorium leader, Ramses Noriega, argued, "If people were willing to talk about the war and deal with the war, maybe they would also start talking about and dealing with issues closer to home" (Oropeza, "Making History," p. 6).

In order to achieve this goal, it was necessary to overcome deeply imbedded notions of machismo. In her recent article on this topic, Lorena Oropeza notes the role that some Chicanas played in mobilizing the barrio-based antiwar movement:

> A writer for *El Alacran,* the Chicano student newspaper at California State Long Beach, placed a special burden upon Chicanas to recognize that machismo began at home. Because of their "cultural upbringing," Chicanas valued manly acts of courage and so, indirectly, put pressure upon Mexican American men to go to war. . . . She implored Chicanas to "become educated on the total Vietnam War" and to recognize that "manliness is a beautiful cultural concept that should be utilized for the betterment of our people, and not for the destruction of other people." (Oropeza, "Making History," p. 8)

These efforts culminated in the National Chicano Moratorium Committee march, which took place on August 29, 1970 at Laguna Park in Los Angeles and attracted support from organizations such as CFJ and various Mexican American student groups, as well as more radical, pro-Marxist organizations.

On that day, approximately 25,000 people marched down Whittier Avenue to show their disapproval of the war and the disproportionate number of casualties suffered by Spanish-surnamed soldiers. The march, according to one participant, was "united" in using the slogan, "Raza si, Guerra no!" More radical elements, however, unfurled banners calling for "Raza si, Guerra aqui!" (Race yes, revolutionary war here!), and this caused some dissension among the ranks. Ultimately, the Los Angeles police turned upon the demonstrators, and the resulting melee resulted in extensive property damage and the deaths of three individuals, including *Los Angeles Times* reporter Rubén Salazar. The Moratorium and Salazar's

Domingo Nick Reyes (left), *Executive Director of the National Mexican-American Anti-Defamation Committee, told a press conference that Mexican-Americans had "very few alternatives" left other than violence but that his organization did not advocate violence. Another committee member, Armando Rendon* (right), *said a key complaint of Chicano youths was that Mexican Americans were dying in Vietnam "at a higher rate, highly disproportionate to their numbers in the total population of the United States." He holds a chart to illustrate his point. Washington, D.C., August 1970. (Bettman/Corbis)*

death combined to radically alter the perception of the war among many in the West's barrios. While many youths of Mexican heritage continued to fight (and die), by the late 1960s and early 1970s there were many within the community (as well as some serving in Vietnam) who developed serious doubts both about the war and also regarding the "value" of military service for barrio youths.

In the last decade, a few authors have examined the impact of Vietnam on returning Chicano/a veterans. In general, the tone of the works has been negative. The writers (many of whom are veterans) provide a sense of why they joined (usually for a combination of patriotic, economic, and machismo reasons), then move on to discuss their experiences overseas. Highlighted in the "in country" aspects are discussions of racial discrimination against minority soldiers and of the increased sense of disillusionment regarding the war effort. Although this may not be the totality of the experience, it is certainly the most emphasized aspect. To take one striking example, Ybarra quotes an Army veteran, who summarizes his experience thus:

> "Before, I was politically naïve. . . . I was very patriotic. . . . I was a flag waver. . . . I felt a real sense of calling to duty . . . [and] I had to validate myself, that I was in fact American, that I was a citizen. I was detached . . . in '68. . . . By that time I was definitely against the war. I would tell all those little Chicanitos that have a bent toward becoming military people to seriously reconsider those impulses and to struggle in getting a good, solid education, to not be fooled by the marketing techniques that the military's come up with nowadays." (Ybarra, *Vietnam Veteranos,* pp. 26–27)

THE ARTS

It is not surprising that the Chicano/a Movement had a dramatic impact on artistic expression. Increased emphasis on cultural pride and the rising tide against assimilation left clear imprint in fields such as music, theater, film, art, and literature (academic and popular). In the following paragraphs we present a brief account of important individuals and works in each of these categories.

Music

In *Land of a Thousand Dances: Chicano Rock 'n' Roll from Southern California,* authors David Reyes and Tom Waldman offer readers an overview of the history of Mexican Americans and modern music in the Los Angeles area. During the 1950s, they argue, it was common for Spanish-surnamed youths to use rock and roll as a way to fit in with Anglo society and differentiate themselves from their parents' generation. An example of the assimilationist tendency was the career of Ritchie Valenzuela, who Anglicized his name to Ritchie Valens at the request of his promoter. After Valenzuela's tragic death in 1959 (along with Buddy Holly and "Big Bopper" Richardson), his influence declined, and at least one writer argues that it is "difficult to trace any measurable influence that

Valens had on the development of Chicano rock and roll in the 1960s and 1970s" (Tatum, *Chicano Popular Culture,* p. 35).

The Chicano/a era certainly brought about a transformation of rock and roll. Reyes and Waldman note two influences that moved barrio rock from sentimental tunes such as Valens's "Come On, Let's Go!" to something more substantial and progressive. The first inspiration was the rhetoric of movement leaders, especially Corky Gonzales. The nationalistic and militant tones emanating from Denver and elsewhere in the West "left bands in a quandary. . . . Their models had always been black and white performers" (Tatum, *Chicano Popular Culture,* p. 38). The second motivation was personal and could be market driven or driven by genuine conviction. Reyes and Waldman assert that "Chicano bands were not oblivious to industry trends," and some groups recorded songs that dealt with movimiento issues, such as Eddie Torres's "Chicano Power" and The Midniters' "Ballad of César Chávez," in hope of making a profit. Others, like Ruben Guevara, "took to calling himself J. Guevara, a tribute to Castro's revolutionary comrade, Che Guevara." Other bands influenced by Chicano/a thought and active in university and barrio politics included El Chicano and Tierra (Reyes and Waldman, *Chicano Rock 'n' Roll,* p. 105).

Theater

Theater was an essential component of the efforts of the UFW, and no one was more important to this area of Chicanismo than Luis Valdez and El Teatro Campesino. As noted previously, Valdez, while a student at San Jose State, was greatly influenced by the Cuban Revolution as well as the Plan Espiritual de Aztlan. The two inspirations, along with his training in drama, stimulated the birth of a theater company tied to the farm workers' struggle. Between 1967 and the late 1970s, the Teatro focused its plays on social and economic issues impacting the Spanish-speaking people of the West, including works on employment conditions, discrimination (such as the play *Zoot Suit,* which was made into a movie in 1981), and the Vietnam War. In the years since the demise of the Teatro, other troupes, such as El Teatro del Piojo (The Flea Theater) and El Teatro Aztlán have continued this progressive brand of political theater and satire.

Scene still from Salt of the Earth, *1954. Directed by Herbert Biberman. (International Union of Mine, Mill and Smelter Workers/Kobal Collection)*

Film

Tatum also discusses the important role that movies played in the civil rights struggle of the Spanish-surnamed people. Two of the most important, *The Lawless* (1950) and *Salt of the Earth* (1954), examined the difficult working conditions of Mexicano agricultural workers and miners during the 1950s and directly challenged mainstream films' depictions of all Mexican Americans as criminals or "as helpless children often rescued by brave and altruistic Anglo heroes" (Tatum, *Chicano Popular Culture*, p. 57).

The movimiento stimulated the development and production of various films during the 1970s and early 1980s that dealt with issues such as ethnic identity, illegal immigration, and resistance to white tyranny. In his recent work on Mexican American popular culture, Charles M. Tatum discusses what he considers two of the most significant Chicano/a-themed (and Chicano/a-produced) movies of this era. *Raices de Sangre* (Roots of Blood), which deals with a young Mexican American lawyer who has to decide whether to assist the Chicano/a poor or continue living with "his middle-class assumptions and assimilationist tendencies" (Tatum, *Chicano Popular Culture,* pp. 62–65). *The Ballad of Gregorio Cortez* (1982; based on Américo Paredes's classic study of a Tejano ballad, *With a Pistol in His Hand)* starring Edward James Olmos, portrays an unjustly accused South Texas Mexicano rancher "as both victim and heroic figure. Through his actions he represents the resistance of his people against Anglo tyranny and oppression so prevalent in Texas during the historical period that serves as the setting of the film. . . . The film shows how Mexican Americans of the border region . . . attribute to Cortez the qualities of an epic hero who embodies their deepest sentiments of fear, defiance, and hope for a better life free of injustice" (Tatum, *Chicano Popular Culture,* p. 69).

Art

Tatum's study also examines the impact of the Chicano/a movement upon art. One of the foremost undertakings of Chicano/a artists during the 1960s and 1970s was the painting of murals on the sides of buildings (and other open spaces) in barrios throughout the West. Many *artistas* were inspired by the works of Mexican muralists such as Diego Rivera and José Clemente Orozco, whose efforts focused upon "the exaltation of Mexico's indigenous cultures and the history of oppression that these cultures had suffered under the yoke of . . . conquerors" (Tatum, *Chicano Popular Culture,* p. 164). It is not surprising, therefore, that nationalistic and militant youths were attracted to such painters; many also drew inspiration from the Cuban Revolution. Among the major contributors to this field were groups like the Royal Chicano Air Force, an artist cooperative founded in 1969.

Other important methods of expression during the movement included performance art. Among the most significant contributors to what Tatum refers to as guerilla theater was the early 1970s group known as ASCO (the Spanish term for nausea). Members, among them Harry Gamboa, staged outrageous events in locales such as Whittier Boulevard, events designed to criticize American consumer culture, discriminatory practices against minorities, and the Vietnam War.

Literature

The philosophical, political, and personal tumult unleashed by the movimiento found intense and effectual articulation in the fictional writings of authors such as the late Tomás Rivera (in . . . *y no se lo tragó la tierra,* 1970), Rudolfo Anaya (particularly in *Bless Me, Ultima,* 1972), and Rolando Hinojosa (in *The Valley,* 1983). All of these pieces portrayed the Mexican American experience in richer and more complex ways than previously. Instead of presenting the Spanish-speaking people of the West in simplistic form, the works revealed Chicanos/as as multifaceted people with myriad emotions, desires, goals, and motivations. As Tatum says, all three novelists draw "heavily upon the lives of the people . . . while at the same time elevating their fears, struggles, and beliefs beyond the level of social protest. This is not to say [they] ignore the causes, . . . rather [they] give their cause greater force and credibility by creating characters who are multidimensional, . . .[rejecting] the stock sociological or historical characters of inferior pulp fiction" (Tatum, *Chicano Popular Culture,* p. 135).

The turbulence discernible in barrios found additional expression in the writings of historians and other academicians. The struggles of Mexican Americans had been presented during the 1930s–1950s by scholars and activists such as George I. Sanchez, Carlos Eduardo Castañeda, Carey McWilliams, Ernesto Galarza, and others. Such efforts were progressive (for their era) because they presented Mexican Americans as multifaceted beings, while also calling for social justice, improved working conditions, and enhanced educational opportunities. All of these progressive tomes, however, called for working within the American political and economic "system." By the late 1960s and early 1970s, many Chicano/a writers were willing to call for much more radical social change.

The movimiento had a dramatic influence on the scholarly work of Mexican Americans, especially those who studied the movement itself. By far the most important work of historical scholarship to appear during the era was Rodolfo Acuña's 1972 tome, *Occupied America: The Chicanos' Struggle toward Liberation.* As Alex M. Saragoza noted in his important

1990 essay, "Recent Chicano Historiography: An Interpretive Essay," this work reflected some of the central tendencies (and limitations) of the more militant sectors of the movement, including a strong nationalistic, anti-assimilationist bent, the concept of racial conflict, little recognition of the comunidad's internal differences, a tendency to focus upon only a few locales (mostly California, Texas, and New Mexico), and little attention to gender issues. By the late 1970s, while praising Acuña for his effort and passion, some historians were criticizing the first edition as being too simplistic and not a full rendition of historical reality.

In reaction to *Occupied America*'s limitations, a group of young scholars produced more sophisticated historical and sociological analyses that refined and polished many of Acuña's assertions. For example, Albert Camarillo, Richard Griswold del Castillo, Ricardo Romo, Mario T. García, and Arnoldo De León all revealed a more complex economic, social, gender, and religious existence within the region's barrios. Additionally, Vicki L. Ruiz, Cherie Moraga, Gloria Anzaldúa, and others provided readers with an overview of the lives, contributions, and tribulations of Chicanas.

RELIGION

In the years between 1965 and 1980, the Catholic Church and the various Protestant denominations showed increased activity in addressing the spiritual needs of people of Mexican descent. Additionally, church groups, especially those influenced by the movimiento, focused more upon issues of ethnic identity and awareness, as well as social justice, within their ministries. Although it is not possible to discuss all individuals, activities, and programs, the following paragraphs impart a sense of the expanding role of such entities in bettering the lives of the Spanish-surnamed people of the West. In addition to the work by Dolan which we have mentioned previously, the key sources for this section of the chapter include works by scholars such as Ana Maria Díaz-Stevens, Anthony M. Stevens-Arroyo, Jorge Iber, R. Douglas Brackenridge, Francisco O. García-Treto, and Erasmo Gamboa.

Building upon the encyclical *Mediator Dei* (issued in 1947), progressive elements within the Catholic hierarchy welcomed the outcomes of Vatican II (which called for the church to push for greater social justice) and used this appeal as a call to action, often forging direct linkages with Chicano/a associations. During the late 1960s and early 1970s, it was common to see cursillistas and clergy participate in meetings and rallies of Chicano/a organizations such as the UFW, Communities Organized for Public Service (COPS), and groups working to improve the lives of undocumented immigrants. In addition, members of the clergy established their own organizations for community involvement, including Las Hermanas (an association of religious women) and PADRES, a group of priests specifically dedicated to ministry among Mexican Americans. Clearly, by the late 1970s, as Ana Maria Diaz-Stevens and Anthony M. Stevens-Arroyo note, "the radical demands of Latino student militants, the resources of the Catholic and Protestant churches, and the piety of Latino cursillistas had come into syzygy" (Díaz-Stevens and Stevens-Arroyo, *The Emmaus Paradigm,* pp. 17, 125, and 144).

One specific example of the myriad of works performed by such entities can be seen in the combined efforts of the Salt Lake Diocese and SOCIO in the state of Utah, as noted by Jorge Iber. In 1972 Bishop Joseph Lennox Federal established a Diocesan Office of the Spanish-Speaking and named a member of SOCIO, Ruben Jiménez, to direct the operation. During his nine-year tenure, Jiménez utilized both Church and SOCIO connections to expand the Guadalupe Community Center, as well as to help establish the Utah Immigration Project (UIP), an office dedicated to assisting immigrants prepare residency applications. Further, the coalition lobbied for increased funding for affordable housing in Salt Lake City, established rehabilitation and vocational programs for barrio youths, helped fund the operation of the Utah Migrant Council, and dramatically expanded the number of Spanish-language masses throughout the state.

Protestant denominations were also active in working with the Spanish-surnamed population of the West during the Chicano/a era. Among the many examples of such connections are the following two examples: (1) the role of Baptist ministers in Los Angeles during the blowouts at local high schools during 1968, and (2) the participation of the Oregon Council of Churches in the founding and funding of efforts to better the lives of migrant workers (Gamboa and Buan, *The Hispanic People of Oregon,* p. 48, and Rosales, *Chicano,* p. 191).

Unfortunately, as the movement lost momentum during the late 1970s, so did many of the more progressive church groups. In particular, as Diaz-Stevens and Stevens-Arroyo argue, the election of Ronald Reagan and the start of John Paul II's reign as pope signaled the start of a more conservative era for the Catholic Church (and for Protestant denominations as well). An example of this trend is visible by the early 1980s, with the decline of groups such as PADRES and Las Hermanas that at one time "had made common cause with militant Chicanos . . . [but] now retracted to an agenda focused upon internal Church reforms . . . [and not] upon radical subversion of ecclesiastical structures" (Díaz-Stevens and Stevens-Arroyo, *The Emmaus Paradigm*, p. 179; Dolan, *Hispanic Catholic Culture in the U.S.*, p. 114).

CONNECTIONS AND DISSENSIONS: THE CHICANO/A MOVEMENT, CUBAN AMERICANS, AND PUERTO RICANS

CUBAN AMERICANS

The number of Cuban Americans in the two major pockets of western concentration, Las Vegas and Los Angeles, grew moderately between 1965 and 1980. In Nevada, the number of immigrants moving to the city during the 1970s was estimated at fewer than 700, bringing the Cuban population of Clarke County to an estimated 3,000 by 1980. Federal census records tabulated the number of Cubanos in California in 1970 at approximately 47,500 (although community activists claimed the correct figure was closer to 60,000), with over 80 percent residing in the Los Angeles Standard Metro Statistical Area.

In both cases, the move to the U.S. West had produced many positive results for the group. Two studies, conducted by William Clayson and Vincent Edward Gil, present similar arguments and conclusions: in general, Cuban Americans in the West had adjusted well to their new surroundings; were earning higher median (family) incomes than did Mexican Americans; believed that life in the United States was positive, even for minorities; and argued that what was needed to get ahead in the United States was a good work ethic, not government assistance. Although such assertions were clearly not realistic, they were very much a part of the Cubano experience and worldview (in both Florida and the

West) during the 1970s. This belief system put Cubans in direct philosophical and political conflict with the Chicanos/as in their communities.

Yet another reason for the Cubano-Chicano divide lay in the glowing terms used by movimiento leaders to describe the Cuban Revolution and its dictatorial leader, Fidel Castro. The animosity over this topic often spilled into the rhetoric of movement organizers. Certainly, this attitude did not resonate with the thousands who had just fled from Castro's island gulag.

LRUP founder José Angel Gutiérrez was even more direct in his support for the Cuban Revolution. In his recent autobiography, Gutiérrez speaks glowingly of what he saw during his 1975 trip to the island: "While we were there the Cuban experiment with socialism was most attractive to many of us, particularly in the area of health, education, housing, and agriculture. Poor people had access to all the essentials that make for a quality life. The Cuban models of development . . . were fascinating. I, for one, thought then that we had a lot to learn from Cuba, particularly in these fields" (Gutiérrez, *The Making of a Chicano Radical*, p. 239). In addition, he pulls no punches in expressing his view of the majority of the Cuban American population: "Cubans seldom support our efforts, but always look for support from us. . . . Any person who is perceived to be a . . . socialist . . . is deemed a pro-Castro communist sympathizer by these Cuban bigots. It is very hard to work with Cubans who have such a closed mindset and narrow view of the world; mostly you cannot" (Gutiérrez, *The Making of a Chicano Radical*, p. 286).

We do not imply that all fault for this rift lies at the feet of Chicano/a leaders, as we will note in the next chapter, many Cuban Americans have had and continue to have an air of superiority regarding the plight of Mexican Americans. At the same time, however, it is certainly reckless to ignore the impact of the Revolution upon the lives of those who fled the island. Praising the benefits of an individual and political system that has caused misery and death for many thousands of Cubans is not the most effective way to build bridges among Hispanic groups in the West.

PUERTO RICANS
Unlike Cuban Americans, the Puerto Rican populace in California believed it had much in common with Mexicanos and often worked

cooperatively with Chicano/a organizations. In a recent study of the CFJ, for example, Ernesto B. Vigil notes that boriquas participated in such Chicano/a events as the National Youth Liberation Conference in 1969 and the Poor People's March in 1968, as well as collaborating with Chicano and Native American groups during the takeover of Wounded Knee in 1973. The CFJ reciprocated this support by standing with Puerto Rican nationalists in their attempt to achieve independence from the United States during the 1970s.

As we noted previously, the Puerto Rican population of the Golden State was approximately 47,000 by 1970 (although some activists claimed the correct figure was closer to 200,000); much of the migration driven by the decline of heavy industry in the Northeast and Midwest. Boriquas faced challenges similar to those confronting other Spanish speakers upon arriving in California. A 1980 federal study on this population revealed a long litany community ills: for example, only about 6 percent of the group had college degrees; about half had a high school diploma; the unemployment rate for Puerto Ricans was higher than of white Californians; and few (about 2 percent) held managerial or professional occupations. Puerto Ricans responded to difficult circumstances in a manner similar to Chicanos, by forming a Puerto Rican Student Association to help increase access to higher education and establishing the Western Region Puerto Rican Council in 1973 to fight for increased representation, better schools, cultural maintenance, and assistance for newly arrived persons of limited English proficiency.

Norma Carr's 1989 dissertation provided readers with a wealth of information on Puerto Rican life in Hawaii through 1958, but the subsequent decades of this story have not been the subject of as much research. Among the few essays on this topic is "Borinki Identity in Hawai'i: Present and Future," by Iris López and David Forbes, which appeared in 2001. Here, the authors focus upon a crucial question: are the boriquas on the islands still ethnically Puerto Ricans? The results of the López and Forbes research are mixed. Among the disturbing trends for group identity they found high percentages of intermarriage, low rates of participation in Puerto Rican ethnic associations, and few third- or fourth-generation individuals who spoke Spanish. Simultaneously, there were some positive trends: the United Puerto Rican Association of Hawai'i (the combination of the Puerto Rican Civic Club and the Puerto Rican Independent Association) had existed since 1973 and continued to operate, a Puerto Rican Heritage Society commenced business in 1983, and a substantial number of local bands (such as one called Alma Latina, "Latin Soul") continued to play traditional music to large audiences throughout the islands.

CONCLUSION

At the start of the final chapter of *Chicano: The History of the Mexican American Civil Rights Movement,* author F. Arturo Rosales poses a poignant question about the movement that had so great an impact on the tumultuous era described in this chapter: quite simply, "Did it succeed?" (Rosales, *Chicano,* p. 250). Unfortunately, there is no straightforward answer to this query. What exactly does "succeed" mean? Does it imply that all social, economic, and political problems that people of Mexican descent faced in the United States were solved? Clearly, using this understanding of the term, the sound and fury of the Chicano/a movement was not successful. If, on the other hand, the word can be used to characterize the achievements of a social movement that not only generated a modicum of civic improvements and some new opportunities, but also produced a fundamental shift in the way that Mexican American viewed themselves and their nation, then it is possible, indeed historically accurate, to argue that the movimiento was a triumph.

As revealed in the 1980 Federal Census, the levels of education and income for Spanish-surnamed people of the West remained well below that of whites. For example, in Texas, the federal census disclosed that, even with the activities of MAYO, LRUP, and school blowouts, only 37.2 percent of all Hispanics twenty-five and older had earned high school diplomas; compared to a figure of 68.5 percent for whites. Not surprisingly, educational disparities helped generate dramatic inequality in a variety of income categories. For example, for "Spanish origin" males fifteen years and older, the median income in 1979 was $8,279, compared to $13,227 (62.6 percent) for persons "not of Spanish origin." For females, the same figures were $3,933 versus $5,531 (71.1 percent) (Bureau of the Census, *1980 Census of Population, General Social and Economic Characteristics, Texas, Section 1,* tables 76, 86, 91, and 92 on pp. 126, 143, 148, and 149).

The numbers in California, while not quite as negative as those for the Lone Star State, also exhibited a wide gap. The percentage for Spanish-surnamed people twenty-five and older with a high school diploma was only 43.6, while the same number for whites was 76.6. For "Spanish origin" males fifteen years and older, the median income in 1979 was $9,354, compared to $13,925 (67.2 percent) for persons "not of Spanish origin." For females, the same figures were $5,119 versus $6,282 (81.5 percent) (Bureau of the Census, *1980 Census of Population, General Social and Economic Characteristics, California, Section 1,* tables 76, 86, 91, and 92, on pp. 122, 139, 144, and 145).

The figures listed in these two paragraphs are just one example of the results visible in other western states. Undoubtedly, the Chicano/a movement had helped change parts of the social reality of barrio life, but it had failed to remove all barriers to the goal of educational and economic equality for persons of Mexican descent. There was still a long way to go to reach the utopian vision of many movement leaders.

The era did not bring about radical transformation (on the model of the 1959 Cuban uprising), but it did generate much change. In his important 1997 work, *Chicanismo: The Forging of a Militant Ethos among Mexican Americans,* Ignacio García presents readers with a more optimistic overview of the results of the Chicano/a years. García argues that the movimiento ushered in a new era, one in which people of Mexican descent saw themselves differently, and that it altered the manner in which they accommodated to Anglo American society. His main contentions are that, as a result of the movement, Mexican Americans reinterpreted their past, took increased pride in their group history, and were better able to empower comunidades for social action and change. Clearly, as is visible in the myriad of examples presented in this chapter of community and personal empowerment, in the continued existence and expansion of Chicano studies programs throughout the nation, and in the extensive outreach by both major political parties to Mexican Americans, the Spanish-surnamed people of the West were by 1980 living in a new era, one which, although not utopian by any stretch of the imagination, was certainly better than the days of "No Mexicans Allowed" signs and unabashed discriminatory practices. Although this progress may not be enough to satisfy the most rabidly "progressive" elements in the community and academia, life was better for a great percentage of Spanish speakers in 1980 than in 1930.

A visiting speaker at a 1970 guest lecture at the University of Utah, Dr. Rudolpho Martínez, foretold the nature of the triumph of the Chicano/a era, stating that "there is going to be no revolution, but rather an evolutionary change," that ultimately improved the lives of people in the barrios (quoted in Iber, *Hispanics in the Mormon Zion,* p. 105). In our next chapter we explore whether the evolution has continued and the promise has been fulfilled, or whether new problems and obstacles arose in the 1980s and 1990s, which continue to impede the social and economic development of the Spanish-surnamed people of the West.

BIBLIOGRAPHIC ESSAY

As in previous chapters, we relied upon Richard White's *"It's Your Misfortune and None of My Own": A New History of the American West* (Norman: University of Oklahoma Press, 1991) for a broad overview of the economic and social circumstances in the West that helped stimulate the genesis of the Chicano/a movement. Although the White text offered an appropriate overview for a general work, anyone interested in studying the specifics of the movimiento needs to begin their reading with F. Arturo Rosales's wonderful synopsis of the era, *Chicano: The History of the Mexican American Civil Struggle* (Houston, TX: Arte Público Press, 1997).

While the Rosales work provides impressive coverage, it suffers from the drawbacks that affect most textbooks: a lack of space to present extensive treatment of the historical specifics at a large number of locations. Although Rosales' work is excellent scaffolding, we wanted to provide as many examples as possible of the broad range of experiences that made up the movimiento. Were the demands and action strategies of Chicanos/as in Los Angeles and Salt Lake City, for example, exactly the same? Not quite. Therefore, we believed it imperative to provide as much discussion of events, peoples, and organizations, from as many different locations, as possible. In order to achieve this, we consulted a substantial number of works that describe events, trends, and specifics of the era from a large number of cities and towns throughout the West; including places where the Spanish-speaking population was not very large (in comparison with Texas, New Mexico, and California, for example).

Before commencing an examination of the movement's impact on the West, it seemed to us important to introduce the leadership cadre (at least at the national level) of the Chicano/a era. Fortunately, there have been a few excellent studies on some of these individuals. We consulted the following sources for the production of the section on César Chávez: Richard Griswold del Castillo and

Richard García, *César Chávez: A Triumph of the Spirit* (Norman: University of Oklahoma Press, 1995); Laura Pulido, *Enviromentalism and Economic Justice: Two Chicano Struggles in the Southwest* (Tucson: University of Arizona Press, 1996); and Manuel G. González, *Mexicanos: A History of Mexicans in the United States* (Bloomington: Indiana University Press, 1999).

There are few scholarly works that deal with the career and life of Dolores Huerta, and therefore much of the material on her was drawn from the United Farm Workers Web site, from an anonymous entry entitled "Dolores Huerta Biography" (http//:www.ufw.org/dh.htm). We did find, however, two excellent articles by academicians: Margaret Rose, "'Woman Power Will Stop Those Grapes': Chicana Organizers and Middle Class Female Supporters in the Farm Workers' Grape Boycott in Philadelphia," *Journal of Women's History* 7 (Winter 1995) and Richard A. García, "Dolores Huerta: Woman, Organizer, and Symbol," *California History* 72, no. 1 (Spring 1993).

The information for the section on Reies Lopez Tijerina was drawn from the following sources: Reies López Tijerina and José Angel Gutiérrez (translator), *They Call Me "King Tiger": My Struggle for the Land and Our Rights* (Houston: Arte Público Press, 2000); Juan Gómez-Quiñones, *Chicano Politics: Reality and Promise, 1940–1990* (Albuquerque: University of New Mexico Press, 1990). For an overview of land grants and similar issues, see Malcolm Ebright, *Land Grants and Lawsuits in Northern New Mexico* (Albuquerque: University of New Mexico Press, 1993). See also the following Internet sources: Kevin Klein, "'Viva La Alianza': Thirty Years After the Tierra Amarilla Courthouse Raid," *Weekly Wire,* June 13, 1997, http://www.weeklywire.com/ww/06–13–97/alibi_feat1.html; Rees Lloyd, "'King Tiger': Reies Lopez Tijerina Still Roars for Justice on 'Cinco de Junio,'" *Welsh American,* June 5, 2003, http://www.welshamerican.com/Rees/tiger.htm.

The information on Rodolfo "Corky" Gonzales was drawn from the following: Tom I. Romero, "Wearing the Red, White, and Blue Trunks of Aztlán: Rodolfo 'Corky' Gonzalez and the Convergence of American and Chicano Nationalism," *Aztlán* (Fall 2004); Ernesto Vigil, *Crusade for Justice: Chicano Militancy and the Government's War on Dissent* (Madison: University of Wisconsin Press, 1999); and John C. Ensslin, "Chicano Movement was a Turning Point for Denver," Denver *Rocky Mountain News* (September 21, 1999).

Finally, for the section on the leaders of the Chicano/a movement, the information on José Angel Gutiérrez was drawn from the following: José Angel Gutiérrez, "La Raza and Revolution: The Empirical Conditions of Revolution in Four South Texas Counties," master's thesis, St. Mary's University, 1968; Armando Navarro, *Mexican American Youth Organization: Avant Garde of the Chicano Movement in Texas* (Austin: University of Texas Press, 1995); Armando Navarro, *The Cristal Experiment: A Chicano Struggle for Community Control*

(Madison: University of Wisconsin Press, 1998); José Angel Gutiérrez, *The Making of a Chicano Militant: Lessons From Cristal* (Madison: University of Wisconsin Press, 1998); Ignacio M. García, *Viva Kennedy: Mexican Americans in Search of Camelot* (College Station: Texas A&M University Press, 2000); Ignacio M. García, *Chicanismo: The Forging of a Militant Ethos Among Mexican Americans* (Tucson: University of Arizona Press, 1997); Ignacio M. García, *United We Win: The Rise and Fall of La Raza Unida Party* (Tucson: University of Arizona Press, 1989); Juan Gómez-Quiñones, *Chicano Politics: Reality and Promise, 1940–1990* (Albuquerque: University of New Mexico Press, 1990); and Mario T. García, *Memories of Chicano History: The Life and Narrative of Bert Corona* (Berkeley: University of California Press, 1994).

The following section of the chapter examined some of the important organizations that fought to improve circumstances for Chicanos/as throughout the West during the years of the movement. Among the works available that detail the goals, activities, and successes of these groups are the following: Mario T. García, *Memories of Chicano History: The Life and Narrative of Bert Corona* (Berkeley: University of California Press, 1994); Ernesto Vigil, *Crusade for Justice: Chicano Militancy and the Government's War on Dissent* (Madison: University of Wisconsin Press, 1999); Armando Navarro, *Mexican American Youth Organization: Avant Garde of the Chicano Movement in Texas* (Austin: University of Texas Press, 1995); Carlos Muñoz, *Youth, Identity and Power: The Chicano Movement* (New York: Verso, 1989); Aurelio Salazar Jr., "History of M.E.Ch.A.," http://www.angelfire.com/sd/mcdsd/HistoryOfMEChA.html; Dionne Espinoza, "'Revolutionary Sisters': Women's Solidarity and Collective Identification Among Chicana Brown Berets in East Los Angeles," *Aztlán* 26, no. 1 (Spring 2001); "The Brown Berets: Young Chicano Revolutionaries," an interview with cofounder Carlos Montes, in *Fight Back! Luche y Resiste,* Winter 2003, http://www.fightbacknews.org/2003winter/brownberets.htm; Ignacio M. García, *United We Win: The Rise and Fall of La Raza Unida Party* (Tucson: University of Arizona Press, 1989); Teresa Palomo Acosta, "Raza Unida Party," *The Handbook of Texas Online,* http://www.tsha.utexas.edu/handbook/online/articles/view/RR/war1.html, and "Mexican American Youth Organization," *The Handbook of Texas Online,* http://www.tsha.utexas.edu/handbook/online/articles/view/MM/wem1/html; Vicki L. Ruiz, *From Out of the Shadows: Mexican Women in Twentieth Century America* (New York: Oxford University Press, 1999); David G. Gutiérrez, "'Sin Fronteras': Mexican Americans and the Emergence of the Contemporary Mexican Immigration Debate," *Journal of American Ethnic History* 10, no. 4 (Summer 1991); Partido Nacional de La Raza Unida, "A Brief History of La Raza Unida," http://members.tripod.com/~larazaunida/hist.htm; MALDEF: Mexican American Legal Defense and Educational Fund, "The Founding of MALDEF," http://www.maldef.org/about/founding.htm; Teresa

Palomo Acosta, "Southwest Voter Registration Education Project," *The Handbook of Texas Online,* http://www.tsha.utexas.edu/handbook/online/articles/view/SS/wcs1.html; National Council of La Raza, "About NCLR," http://www.nclr.org/section/about.

For some materials on Chicano/a organizations in locations outside Texas, California, and New Mexico, please see the following: M. L. Miranda, *A History of Hispanics in Southern Nevada* (Reno: University of Nevada Press, 1997); Jorge Iber, *Hispanics in the Mormon Zion: 1912–1999* (College Station: Texas A&M University); Dionicio Nodín Valdés, *Barrios Norteños: St. Paul and Midwestern Mexican Communities in the Twentieth Century* (Austin: University of Texas Press, 2000); Juan Coronado, "Chicanos in Rawlins, Wyoming," and Jesse Vialpando, "The La Cultura Oral History Project: Mexicano/Hispanic History in Wyoming," both in *Annals of Wyoming History: The Wyoming History Journal* 73, no. 2 (Spring 2001); *Nosotros: The Hispanic People of Oregon, Essays and Recollections,* edited by Erasmo Gamboa and Carolyn M. Buan (Portland: Oregon Council of the Humanities, 1995).

In recent years, several scholars have published works dealing with the Chicano/a experience in Vietnam and after returning to the "real world": *Vietnam Veteranos: Chicanos Recall the War,* edited by Lea Ybarra (Austin: University of Texas Press, 2004); Juan Ramírez, *A Patriot After All: The Story of a Chicano Vietnam Vet* (Albuquerque: University of New Mexico Press, 1999); *Aztlán and Vietnam: Chicano and Chicana Experiences of the War,* edited by George Mariscal (Berkeley: University of California Press, 1999); Manuel García, *An Accidental Soldier: Memoirs of a Mestizo in Vietnam* (Albuquerque: University of New Mexico Press, 2003); "The Chicano Moratorium 30 Years Ago . . . And the Struggle Today," Part 1 *Revolutionary Worker Online,* August 27, 2000, http://www.angelfire.com/rebellion2/chicanosporevolucion/chicanomoratorium301.html.

Information for the section on the arts and the Chicano movement was gleaned from the following: Charles M. Tatum, *Chicano Popular Culture: "Que Hable el Pueblo"* (Tucson: University of Arizona Press, 2001); Yolanda Broyles-González, *El Teatro Campesino: Theater in the Chicano Movement* (Austin: University of Texas Press, 1994); *Hispanic Theater in the United States,* edited by Nicolas Kanellos (Houston, TX: Arte Público Press, 1984); David Reyes and Tom Waldman, *Land of a Thousand Dances: Chicano Rock 'n' Roll from Southern California* (Albuquerque: University of New Mexico Press, 1998).

The most significant contribution to Chicano historical study during the early 1970s was *Occupied America: The Chicanos' Struggle toward Liberation* (San Francisco: Canfield Press, 1972) by Rodolfo Acuña. For an excellent overview of the more recent historiography of Mexican Americans, please see Alex M. Saragoza, "Recent Chicano Historiography: An Interpretive Essay," *Aztlán* 19, no. 1 (Spring 1988–1990). For an example of the scholars who moved Mexican

American history beyond the more simplistic interpretation of Acuña in his 1972 work, please see the following: Albert Camarillo, *Chicanos in a Changing Society: From Mexican Pueblos to American Barrios in Santa Barbara and Southern California* (Cambridge, MA: Harvard University Press, 1979); Richard Griswold del Castillo, *The Los Angeles Barrio: A Social History* (Berkeley: University of California Press, 1979); Ricardo Romo, *History of a Barrio: East Los Angeles* (Austin: University of Texas Press, 1983); Mario T. García, *Desert Immigrants: The Mexicans of El Paso, 1880–1920* (New Haven, CT: Yale University Press, 1981); Arnoldo De León, *They Called Them Greasers: Anglo Attitudes toward Mexicans in Texas, 1821–1900* (Austin: University of Texas Press, 1983); Vicki L. Ruiz, *Cannery Women, Cannery Lives: Mexican Women, Unionization, and the California Food Processing Industry* (Albuquerque: University of New Mexico Press, 1987); *This Bridge Called My Back: Writings by Radical Women of Color,* edited by Cherie Moraga and Gloria Anzaldúa (New York: Kitchen Table Women of Color Press, 1983).

For an overview of the role of various religious denominations during the Chicano/a era, please see the following: Anthony M. Stevens-Arroyo, "The Emergence of Social Identity among Latino Catholics: An Appraisal," in *Hispanic Catholic Culture in the U.S.: Issues and Concerns,* edited by Jay P. Dolan and Allan Figueroa Deck, S.J. (Notre Dame, IN: University of Notre Dame Press, 1994); Ana María Díaz-Stevens and Anthony M. Stevens-Arroyo, *Recognizing the Latino Resurgence in U.S. Religion: The Emmaus Paradigm* (Boulder, CO: Westview Press, 1998); Jorge Iber, *Hispanics in the Mormon Zion, 1912–1999* (College Station: Texas A&M University Press, 2001); R. Douglas Brackenridge and Francisco O. García-Treto, *Presbiteriana: A History of Presbyterians and Mexican Americans in the Southwest* (San Antonio, TX: Trinity University Press, 1974).

Materials on the experiences of Cuban Americans in several western cities include the following: William Clayson, "Cubans in Las Vegas: Ethnic Identity, Success, and Urban Life in the Late Twentieth Century," *Nevada Historical Society Quarterly* 38, no. 1 (Spring 1995); Vincent Edward Gil, "The Personal Adjustment and Acculturation of Cuban Immigrants in Los Angeles," Ph.D. dissertation, UCLA, 1976; Richard Ferro, "Perceptions of Discrimination: Cubans in the Pacific Northwest," Ph.D. dissertation, University of Washington, 1996.

Materials on the experiences of Puerto Ricans in California and Hawaii include the following: U.S. Commission of Civil Rights, "Puerto Ricans in California: A Staff Report of the Western Regional Office, United States Commission on Civil Rights," (Washington, DC: Bureau of the Census, 1980); Jorge Pinero, "Extended Roots: San Jose, California," in *Extended Roots: From Hawaii to New York: Migraciones Puertorriqueñas a los Estados Unidos* (New York: Hunter College); and Iris López and David Forbes, "Borinki Identity in Hawai'i: Present and Future," *Centro: Journal of Puerto Rican Studies* 13, no. 1 (Spring 2001).

The materials for the Bidal Aguero biographical sketch were collected from the following sources: Jorge Iber, "Bidal Aguero and *El Editor* Newspaper: The Varied Roles of a Spanish-Surnamed Entrepreneur in a Lubbock, Texas, Barrio, 1977–1999," *West Texas Historical Association Yearbook* 74 (1999); Andres Tijerina, *History of Mexican Americans in Lubbock County, Texas* (Lubbock: Graduate Studies, Texas Tech University, 1979); Mansel G. Blackford, "Small Business in America: A Historiographic Review," *Business History Review* 65 (Spring 1991); and Michael D. Woodward, *Black Entrepreneurship in the United States: Stories of Struggles and Success* (New Brunswick, NJ: Rutgers University Press, 1996).

CHAPTER EIGHT

PROMISES FULFILLED AND DELAYED, 1980–2004

A recent article in the *Washington Times* (by Valerie Richardson) informed readers about a controversy concerning the placing of a Mexican flag within a Denver high school. The story, with "Denver, Mexico?" as its headline, noted the hullabaloo caused by the positioning of a foreign standard at the same level as Old Glory in a specific classroom. On one side of the argument were KOA-AM conservative talk show host Mike Rosen, and the majority of his audience, who adamantly maintained that "no other country should have its flag displayed with equal prominence. . . . This is not a Mexican-American school. This is not a colony of Mexico—it's part of Colorado, which is part of the United States" (August 24, 2004). A spokesperson for the city's educational bureaucracy disputed such sentiments and stated that administrators "intend to put the flag back up," because, by placing the symbol in a prominent place, the institution promoted "respecting equality, human rights, human dignity, and safety" (Richardson, *Washington Times).*

It is not our purpose here to argue for or against the positions of any individuals or organizations in regard to this particular debate. Rather, the story serves as an introduction to one of the most contentious issues of Hispanic existence in the West during the last three decades: the dramatic increase in immigration (both documented and undocumented) into the region, and the heated dispute about this trend's beneficial and negative effects.

As stated previously, the movimiento ushered in major transformations in the life of western barrios during the years 1965–1980. Though the Castroesque revolution many "progressive" elements sought failed

As a result of the Chicano/a movement, the barriers to certain areas of employment for Spanish speakers decreased during the late 1960s and early 1970s. Here Porfirio de Leon patrols the streets of Lubbock, Texas, during the early 1970s. (Bidal Aguerro Photgraph Collection E22 #21, Southwest Collection/Special Collections Library, Texas Tech University, Lubbock, Texas)

(fortunately) to materialize, and though numerous obstacles to social and economic parity remained, it is clear that by the start of the Reagan administration, circumstances for Spanish speakers in the region had improved.

Whereas some community activists of the 1930s had called for the recognition of Mexican Americans as "whites," by the end of the Chicano/a era, the government and most Americans recognized that the group was indeed, "brown," not "white." There were increased opportunities for the comunidades' offspring to pursue educational attainments and professional occupations that had been off-limits or unattainable in their grandparents' and parents' generations. Moreover, the movement instilled an increased sense of pride in being of Mexican descent. No longer would the members of this group have to reject their culture and traditions outright in order to gain acceptance into the American mainstream. In fact, many prominent individuals in government, academia, and business optimistically asserted that the 1980s would be the "Decade of the Hispanic," during which this population would realize further improvements in their social, educational, financial, and political status.

This chapter, then, focuses on some of the important trends that have shaped the lives of Spanish-surnamed men, women, and children in the U.S. West during the post-Chicano/a era. Our coverage attempts to answer two critical questions: (1) How have the circumstances (economic, educational, political, and social) of the region's Spanish-speaking people changed over the last two and a half decades? (2) In which areas of community life have the goals of earlier reformers been realized, and where does work still need to be done?

In order to summarize the past quarter century, we will use a different format than previously; rather than focusing on specific persons, groups, or organizations, this chapter features a series of brief discussions of important statistical trends pertaining to the individual and collective lives of Spanish-speaking people in the region. The areas are education, economic development, medical care, politics, and immigration. We examine the nuts and bolts of such developments through the use of census records and the analysis of social scientists and economists. A somewhat fuller treatment of the debates that have been stirred up by these trends will be part of chapter 9, as we provide a basis for suggestions about the future of the study of Hispanics in the West.

In regard to Cuban Americans, we will once again discuss life in the largest pockets of concentration; Las Vegas and Los Angeles, but also introduce materials on Cubanos in Seattle as well. Additionally, we summarize some materials that reveal the plight of Marielitos (Cubans who arrived in the United States as a result of the 1980 Mariel boatlift) who have made their way west. Unfortunately, the more recent arrivals have not achieved anywhere near the same level of economic and social success as many of those who moved to the area during the 1960s or 1970s. The literature for Puerto Ricans is not extensive, and we continue our focus upon experiences in Hawaii and California.

A new element is added to the story of Spanish-speaking people in the U.S. West during this period, with the arrival of many who fall under the census category of "Other Hispanics," specifically, considerable numbers of Guatemalans and El Salvadorans. Men, women, and children of both nationalities began arriving during the late 1970s and early 1980s, most seeking greater economic opportunity, others fleeing to escape violence and brutal political repression in troubled homelands. Later, as some individuals settled in places such as Houston and Los Angeles, and became *mas establecido* (more established), many began advising family members and other compatriots to come to the United States (either legally or illegally).

Recently, as one example of this migratory *cadena* (chain), journalist Roberto Suro, in his important work, *Strangers among Us: Latino Lives in a Changing America,* noted the story of Juan L. Chanax, a weaver from the Guatemalan highland of Totonicapan who, during his adolescence in the 1970s heard

> Talk . . . of people who had gone to the United States and found jobs that paid a lot of money. . . . In 1978, he decided to go north, traveling alone. He was not alone for long. His hometown, San Cristobal, and the villages that surround it had a population of about four thousand people when he left. Within fifteen years, some two thousand of them had joined him in Texas.
>
> "First my relatives came," said Juan, "and then my friends came, and then the friends of my relatives and then the friends of my friends' relatives came. And now those who remained behind in Totonicapan are sending their children." (Suro, *Strangers among Us,* 31–32)

Migratory chains such as the one described here had, by 2000, attracted almost 48,000 El Salvadorans and 10,000 Guatemalans to Houston. Southern California was an even more popular destination, with approximately 127,000 Guatemalans and 250,000 El Salvadorans counted in Los Angeles as early as 1990. Given the dramatic increases in their numbers by the start of the twenty-first century, the new ethnic players had established beachheads in western barrios and were in the process of creating a fledgling leadership troupe; a cadre that was, by the early years of the twenty-first century, demanding a fair share of the American dream for their communities.

STATISTICAL TRENDS AMONG MEXICAN AMERICANS

Before moving on to a discussion of the individual topics noted above, it is necessary to quickly scrutinize some of the demographic changes that have taken place in the U.S. West in the years since the end of World War II, and how such trends have impacted the lives of Spanish speakers. Here again we turn to the work of Richard White who argues that, as the West of the postwar years became increasingly urban (and later on, suburban), so too has the Mexican American population (White, *"It's Your Misfortune,"* p. 592). According to the 1990 Census, 88 percent of all people of Mexican descent lived in urban areas, and more than 83 percent of them lived in just five states: California, Texas, Arizona, New Mexico, and Colorado. Thus, according to such figures, despite "the sometimes stereotyped rural origins of their past, Mexican Americans in 1990 were overwhelmingly an urban people," who faced the problems typical to urban cores in cities throughout the West (McKee, *Ethnicity in Contemporary America,* pp. 119 and 123). It is in such settings that the important promises of the Chicano era, increased education, better housing, economic improvement, and fuller inclusion in the American mainstream, encounter great difficulty in becoming reality.

The above is a significant and disturbing trend; however, further examination of census and other materials also reveals much economic progress by the Spanish-speaking people of the West in the past three decades. We will deal with specific figures and greater detail later, but now it is sufficient to note that part of this financial betterment is reflected by a growing number of Mexican descent familias who are becoming a part of the West's suburban landscape. As geographer Daniel D. Arreola states regarding this population in the Los Angeles area for example, there have been "ten suburbs in the county where Mexican Americans increased significantly between 1960 and 1990." Arreola also argues that this pattern is clearly visible in states such as Texas and Arizona as well since the 1960s. Thus, while large numbers of Hispanics live with and face the challenges of urban blight, a growing and not insignificant percentage are moving to the suburbs, improving their financial standing and effectively claiming a share of the American dream (McKee, *Ethnicity in Contemporary America,* p. 128).

Lastly, it is important to recognize that urban settings, while home to the majority of Hispanics, do not account for the totality of the Spanish speakers' regional existence. Another trend evident since the 1970s has been the increasing number of people of Spanish-surnamed descent migrating to the West's rural communities, primarily to work in commercial agriculture, food processing, and tourism. A study of this subject issued by the federal government notes that this development has "helped stem the pattern of long-term population decline in many rural communities . . . whose populations have been diminishing from natural decrease and economically motivated outmigration since the 1950s" (Kandel and Cromartie, "New Patterns of Hispanic Settlement in Rural America," p. 11).

HISPANICS AND EDUCATION IN THE WEST SINCE 1980

The voluminous research generated on Hispanic students and educational issues in the West over the past two and one-half decades can be seen as breaking down into competing schools of thought and analysis: one focusing on still common negative circumstances, the other (and certainly the minority interpretation) providing a more positive assessment of the educational state of this populace.

Recent studies by Jorge Chapa and Richard R. Valencia may serve as examples of the more pessimistic argument. In a 1993 essay published in the *Hispanic Journal of Behavioral Sciences,* the two scholars produced a descriptive overview of the 1990 Federal Census that highlights the chief concerns of academicians in this camp. For example, governmental statistics revealed that, of persons aged twenty-five and above, 15.5 percent of

Mexicanos had fewer than five years of schooling (as opposed to 1.7 percent for the non-Hispanic population), 55.9 percent had less than a high school diploma, and only 5.4 percent had earned a college degree (the corresponding figures for the nation's non-Hispanics were 20.4 and 22.2 percent) (Chapa and Valencia, "Latino Population Growth," p. 173). Not surprisingly, such low educational attainment was reflected in the socioeconomic status of this group, with median earnings for Mexican males (sixteen years old and above) standing at $12,527, versus $22,081 for non-Hispanics. A similar disparity is evident for Mexicanas, whose median earnings stood at $8,874, versus $11,885 for non-Hispanic women. Further, Chapa and Valencia argue, as this population becomes a larger percentage of the overall student body, especially in Western states, such predicaments are likely to increase, as more and more barrio children are funneled into increasingly segregated inner city schools. In sum, they believe that "the deleterious outcomes . . . especially low achievement, high dropout rates, and inferior college preparation—are likely to intensify."

Crowded portable classroom at Frey School, Edgewood, Texas. (Bob Daemmrich/The Image Works)

A recent investigation focused on this problem in Texas, a state with a long history of discrimination against and maltreatment of Mexican American schoolchildren. In a 2000 article, Richard Valencia revealed some of the glaring problems, such as segregation, high dropout rates, and low standardized test scores, which continue to plague these pupils in the Lone Star State. He notes, for example, that during the 1999–2000 academic year in the Austin school district, 77.6 percent of Mexicano children attend segregated schools, and not surprisingly, a disproportionate number of them underperformed in the TAAS (Texas Assessment of Academic Skills) test (recently renamed Texas Assessment of Knowledge and Skills, or TAKS). Additionally, other problems, such as a substantial percentage of uncertified teachers plying their trade in schools with high percentages of minority pupils, continue within Texas educational institutions (Valencia, "Inequalities and the Schooling of Minority Students in Texas," pp. 445–459).

A 2003 study by the Tomas Rivera Policy Institute revealed that Spanish-surnamed children in the Los Angeles area confronted similar issues. Researchers noted that, at the end of the 2001–2002 school year, only 26 percent of Hispanic graduates in Los Angeles County met the requirements for gaining admission into the California State University or the University of California systems (Tornatzky, Torres, and Caswell, "Education," p. 19). In fact, the percentage of Asian students who met such criteria exceeded the Hispanic number by an astounding 43 points (26 versus 69 percent). Other aspects of this academic undertaking divulged disheartening figures such as the following: 41 percent of all Hispanics drop out between enrollment in the ninth grade and expected graduation date; the percentage of Hispanic preschoolers enrolled in county nursery and preschool programs is far below the level for non-Hispanic populations (for example, 74 percent of white are enrolled, versus 42 percent of Hispanics); and finally, Spanish-surnamed children score well below all other groups in standardized math, language, and reading tests (Tornatzky, Torres, and Caswell, "Education," pp. 20–23).

Problems of low educational achievement are not limited to states with large Hispanic populations. In his research on Spanish-speaking people in Utah, for example, Jorge Iber noted that in 1990, even after an extensive and fairly successful Chicano/a era campaign for academic reform and improvement, the percentage of the Spanish-surnamed population with a high school diploma in the Beehive State still lagged behind the general population's figure by 25 points (61 versus 86 percent).

The litany of educational ills listed in previous paragraphs has elicited much consternation and anger among community leaders and the general population of western Hispanics. Clearly, at this moment it is appropriate to ask whether, given the seemingly dismal outcomes, the Chicano/a movement actually generated positive trends for these students at all. While the majority of authors in this field focus (and rightly so) on what remains to be done and where the system continues to fail, any answer to that question has to take into account some of the many improvements that have occurred since the 1960s. For such information, we turn to the research of economist Arturo González, and specifically to his recent book, *Mexican Americans and the U.S. Economy: The Quest for Buenos Días,* which offers a more positive appraisal of the educational outcomes of the Hispanic population of the West (and nationwide).

González's research traces educational outcome of Mexican Americans across generations, rather than assessing the entire group at a particular moment, and the process allows him to pinpoint differences between generations and unearths many positives. For example, from tabulations drawn from the 1999 Current Population Survey, González calculates that the average Mexican American has achieved an educational level of 10.1 years (compared to 13.3 years for the non-Hispanic white population). The ratio of these two numbers reveals a disparity of 3.2 years (or, roughly 24 percent less education for the average person of Mexican descent than for the average non-Hispanic white individual). In many ways, this affirms the conclusions of Chapa and Valencia. However, González then breaks down the total population into generations (the first generation consisting of the individuals who migrated to the United States, the second being the first contingent born in the United States, and so on) and age groups. This method generates the following two significant numbers: (1) persons 25–34 who are third-generation Mexican Americans averaged 12.4 years of schooling, roughly 90 percent of the majority's figure; and (2) persons 35–50 who are third-generation Mexican Americans averaged 12.2 years of schooling, approximately 89 percent of the non-Hispanic white amount (González, *Mexican Americans and the U.S. Economy,* pp. 62–68).

Lest we become complacent about the positive trend these statistics indicate, González's study offers a caveat regarding Mexican Americans and college education. Although more people of this background are attending, they still fail to earn degrees in high numbers. For example, 55.7 percent of the 25–34 third generation group who go on to post–high school studies did not graduate (18.7 percent earn associate degrees, and 25.5 receive four year or graduate diplomas). This figure is quite low when compared to that of non-Hispanic whites, whose corresponding totals are 31.8 percent who do not finish, 15.6 percent who earn associate degrees, and 52.6 percent who earn a BA or above (González, *Mexican Americans and the U.S. Economy,* pp. 68–72).

An example of this trend is visible in a recent publication by the Pew Hispanic Center that focuses on labor market and educational attainments in Texas in the year 2000. The research notes that almost one half (47.2 percent) of all Latinos in the state (age 16–66) have not completed high school (as opposed to 12.3 percent for non-Hispanic whites), and approximately one-quarter (26.1 percent) of Spanish-surnamed individuals have "some college" (as opposed to 60.8 percent of non-Hispanic whites). Not surprisingly, the educational gap generates a profound disparity in median weekly earnings. The 16–66 Latino group earns a median figure of $350 per week, while the non-Hispanic white population grosses $576.

Nevertheless, though parity has not been achieved, there has been improvement in the educational levels of second- and third-generation Hispanics in the West since the 1960s, and, as Professor González states, ultimately, "what matters is whether the educational situation of Mexican Americans is improving. . . . The evidence presented indicates that this is indeed taking place, but that future growth depends on college completion beyond the community college level" (González, *Mexican Americans and the U.S. Economy,* p. 78).

ECONOMICS: RESULTS AND TRENDS SINCE 1980

In a 1994 essay entitled "Latinos and the New Immigration: Mainstreaming and Polarization," historian Richard Griswold del Castillo argues that the 1980s, the so-called decade of the Hispanic, instead generated a "series of polarities and contradictions" in the majority population's view of Hispanics. The dichotomy is made evident through an examination of the economic statistics regarding Spanish speakers in the U.S. West in the years since 1980. For those on the lower end of the financial range, circumstances remained difficult. At the same time, however, the number of middle-class, affluent, and entrepreneurial Hispanics increased dramatically; and, as Griswold del Castillo sums it up, this period saw "the emergence of a new Latino middle class and upper class, one of the fastest growing economic groups in the United States" (Griswold del Castillo, "Latinos and the New Immigration," pp. 2 and 8).

The remainder of this section, then, fleshes out this summary. As with our earlier discussion on education, the academic research conducted on economics and Hispanic life in the West since the 1970s is voluminous and falls (primarily) into two schools of thought; academicians who believe that little has changed and who are highly critical of the nation's economic system versus scholars who recognize the reality of gains since the end of the Chicano/a era.

In a 1980s interview, Salt Lake City Chicano/a era leader Dr. Orlando Rivera argued that part of the reason for the decline in the movimiento in his state was because it had been so successful in opening opportunity to Spanish-surnamed people. Therefore, he argued, "A lot of our people are moving into better socioeconomic conditions, . . . they're assimilating to the culture, . . . they're moving into the professions. And probably 80, 85 percent [of them] are enjoying a good life" (Iber, *Hispanics in the Mormon Zion*, p. 112). Though Rivera's assessment is too optimistic, undeniably the movimiento increased opportunities and led to improved financial circumstances for many of the western states' Spanish-surnamed population. Equality, however, has not been achieved, and substantial numbers in barrios still face severe deprivation.

One of the most important academicians researching the economic standing of Hispanics since the 1970s is Princeton University sociologist Marta Tienda. She has published extensively on this topic, and she offers a concise overview of the field in a 1995 article entitled "Latinos and the American Pie: Can Latinos Achieve Economic Parity?" In this essay, Tienda summarizes important trends in Hispanic economic performance since 1980: "Latinos have made impressive gains in educational achievement, occupational mobility, and to a lesser extent income growth, but there are also disturbing signs of increased inequality among national origin groups and between natives and immigrants" (Tienda, "Latinos and the American Pie," p. 404). In sum, Tienda's studies reveal much Hispanic economic progress over the past three decades; however, though circumstances have improved for many, especially the native born, an increasing number of recent (documented and undocumented) immigrants means lower overall social and economic statistics of this population. Since many who come to the United States (particularly to places such as Los Angeles and elsewhere in the West) have limited education and can offer little more than strong arms and backs for menial labor, it is no wonder that the statistics quoted by many of the more "progressive" academicians and Hispanic organizations generate bleak pictures of economic health. As Tienda argues, it is the "combination of minority status, low levels of schooling, and limited English fluency [that] has extremely deleterious labor market consequences for Latinos" (Tienda, "Latinos and the American Pie," p. 416). In the last decade of the twentieth century, however, not all western Hispanics were automatically relegated to this end of the occupational spectrum.

The geographer Daniel D. Arreola, in encapsulating the economic patterns of Mexican Americans in a 2000 article, proffered the following figures: (1) the median income for families of Mexican descent was $23,609, versus $40,884 for all whites; (2) three times as many familias lived in poverty (12 percent) versus the number of white families (4 percent); (3) white families were more than twice as likely to earn above $50,000 than were Mexican American households; and (4) adults (both male and female) of Mexicano origin were far less likely to be employed in managerial and professional positions than whites (8.9 percent for men and 14.1 percent for mujeres versus 26.3 percent for white men and 27.2 for white women) (McKee, *Ethnicity in Contemporary America,* pp. 130–133). Although the numbers are disappointing, they are an improvement over past counts and, as Arreola argues, some of the negative "underclass characteristics" present are counterbalanced by much economic variability within this populace. Having presented some disheartening statistics, we now return, once again, to the work of Arturo

González for a more positive interpretation of Hispanic economic progress since 1980.

González's research focuses on a eclectic range of important financial indicators (revealed by the March 1999 current population survey), including wage assimilation, income distribution, poverty status, and occupational patterns. In general, through the use of the generation model described earlier, it is evident that Mexican Americans have made, and continue to make, economic progress.

Wage assimilation, defined by González as "wage parity with comparable U.S.-born workers," is a clear gauge of improving circumstances for Mexican Americans. His book cites a series of studies that indicate "that after ten to fifteen years . . . [an immigrant's] earnings matched those of natives, and soon thereafter actually passed natives' wages" (p. 47). To be evenhanded, González also identifies essays that challenge this assertion and suggest that Mexican immigrants who arrived after the 1980s have not achieved a level close to parity. While this may be true, overall, the trend since the 1970s is encouraging and reveals that economic progress is being made, especially by persons who have been in the United States a longer period of time:

> Even if the bleakest conclusions are true, immigrants still make significant gains over the course of their U.S. employment experience. . . . The implication from these studies is that the labor experiences of immigrants are dynamic rather than stable, and they improve with length of residence. . . . Even if immigrants do not achieve full wage parity, they eliminate most or all of the wage gap between themselves and native workers. The evidence for wage assimilation among Mexican immigrants is more positive than bleak. (González, *Mexican Americans and the U.S. Economy*, p.48)

Figures for the other indicators, likewise, do not reveal perfect economic equality, but demonstrate that the years since the Chicano/a era have generated enhancement in economic standing. For example, González notes, third-generation familias have mean incomes of $43,346 and median incomes of $34,000 (compared to $60,828 and $48,800 for non–Mexican American families). The per capita income mean for third-generation families of Mexican descent is $13,379 and the median figure is $10,267 (compared to $21,929 and $16,551 for non–Mexican

American families). In summary, in regard to wage assimilation and income distribution: "Although Mexican American families are poorer than other families, their average and median incomes do increase from one generation to the next" (González, *Mexican Americans and the U.S. Economy*, pp. 81–84).

Poverty status, living below a federally established threshold of household income, is "an absolute measure based on a combination of family size, family characteristics and income." A quick glance at various aspects of the indicator reveals much disheartening news: in 1998, for example, 16 percent of all families living in poverty in the United States were of Mexican descent (and such families accounted for only 6 percent of all families nationwide). Further, almost one-half of immigrant families who lived in poverty were of Mexicano origin. Finally, as González reveals, recent immigrants "account for only 52 percent of all Mexican American families but 60 percent of all Mexican American families in poverty" (González, *Mexican Americans and the U.S. Economy*, p. 85).

If we stopped at this point, it certainly appears that people of Mexican ancestry have made little progress in moving out of poverty. Again, however, the generational model proffers some positive results to include in our discussion. As we observed with income, the level of poverty for both Mexican American families and individuals tends to decline with the passage of time, as is evidenced by González's research, which indicates that 28 percent of first-generation families are in poverty, while 19 and 21 percent (respectively) of second- and third-generation familias exist below this threshold (compared to 13.3 percent, 4.3 percent, and 8.7 percent of each successive generation for non–Mexican American families). Additionally, his figures for personal poverty show a similar pattern. The first-generation individual poverty rate is 28.5 percent; for the second generation the number increases slightly to 29.1 percent, but the third-generation number drops to 23.9 percent (corresponding numbers for non–Mexican American individuals of each generation are 14.1, 11.1, and 11.1 percent). One final positive piece of information from this research is the finding that the percentage of Mexican American families on governmental assistance also declines with the passage of time. In summary, many of González's findings tend to support the contention of authors such as Linda Chávez, who states in her controversial 1991 study

Out of the Barrio: Toward a New Politics of Hispanic Assimilation: "The majority of Hispanics are in the process of acculturating and, therefore, should not be expected to have the same socioeconomic status as long-established ethnic groups" (quoted in González, *Mexican Americans and the U.S. Economy,* p. 29). Chávez points out, for example, that in the early twentieth century other immigrant groups started out at the bottom of the socioeconomic ladder, but they have now attained equal status with long-established ethnic groups.

The final aspect of the economic existence of Mexican Americans of the West (and elsewhere in the United States) that we discuss is occupational patterns, in particular, the distribution of occupation by type. A key question examined here is whether people of Mexican descent are moving out of lower-paying, less skilled (blue collar) positions and moving into higher-earning technical, managerial, and professional (white collar) occupations. As was the case with wage assimilation, income distribution, and poverty status, the results are mixed and yield reasons for both concern and optimism.

Before we move on to distribution of occupation by type, there are a few other patterns that we wish to note. As revealed by the figures in the paragraphs above, Mexican Americans tend to have less education and earn less than non-Hispanic whites. It should not be surprising, therefore, that this group should have greater difficulties finding full-time jobs. González's research presents the following important insights into extant circumstances: (1) Mexican Americans have the highest level of labor force participation (that is, people who are working or actively looking for work) rates in the nation; (2) first-generation Mexicanas have low rates of labor force participation rates, but this figure tends to increase dramatically (from around 60 percent for first-generation women to above 70 percent for mujeres (women) of the second and third generations); (3) in 1998, it took Mexican American men and women longer, on average, to find a job (8.5 weeks and 6.9 weeks, respectively) than non-Hispanic whites (7.3 weeks for men and 4.2 weeks for women); (4) Mexican Americans (both men and women) tend to have higher levels of unemployment than all other population groups in the United States, except African Americans; and finally, (5) the percentage of Mexican Americans men and women who work full-time and year-round was still lower than for non-Hispanic whites (71.9 and 53.6 percent, respectively, for Mexican Americans and 76.2 and 56.7 percent, respectively, for non-Hispanic whites) (González, *Mexican Americans and the U.S. Economy*, pp. 107–108). Clearly, two decades removed from the Chicano/a era, significant gaps in employment continue to exist between people of Mexican descent and the majority population.

Conversely, there are figures in the area of distribution of occupation type that indicate that conditions have improved since the 1970s. For example, the percentage of Mexican American men employed in professional, managerial, and specialized occupations (the highest-paying positions) expands from 4.1 percent of first-generation individuals to 14.3 percent of third-generation persons (the corresponding figures for third-generation non-Hispanic white men is 31 percent). The gains for women of Mexican descent are even more impressive, with the numbers of mujeres occupying such posts growing from 6.2 percent of first-generation members to 22.5 percent of third-generation women (the corresponding numbers for third generation non-Hispanic women is 35.6 percent) (González, *Mexican Americans and the U.S. Economy*, p. 112).

Additionally, the number of Mexican Americans (both men and women) who occupy the next two occupational category tiers (technical, sales, administrative support, and service) has also improved, especially among mujeres. For example, only 6.4 percent of first-generation men worked in the technical, sales, and administrative support area, while the same figure for third-generation members totaled 17.3 percent (corresponding figures for non-Hispanic white men were 16.8 and 19.7 percent). For Mexican American women, the same figures were 19.5 and 42.0 percent (corresponding figures for non-Hispanic white women were 31.9 and 40.9 percent) (González, *Mexican Americans and the U.S. Economy*, p. 112).

Having presented (and forced the reader to plow through) so many facts, figures, and trends, we now bring the focus down to the community level. Two recent studies, one examining the Spanish-speaking people of Los Angeles, the other focused on the same group in the state of Utah, provide a more localized sense of both positive and negative economic trends since the end of the Chicano/a era.

In 2003 Pepperdine University researchers Joel Kotkin and Erika Ozuna generated an overview of Latinos and economic development for the *Latino Scorecard: Grading the American Dream 2003* report published by the United Way of Greater Los Angeles. Not surprisingly, given the mixed data we have presented thus far, this report reveals that this population in southern California's metropolis has witnessed mixed results in their quest for the American dream. The researchers noted that, based on Census 2000 data, the median income for Latino familias in Los Angeles county stood at $33,820 (approximately 80.5 percent of the county as a whole). While this is an encouraging development, the comunidad lagged far behind in the category of per capita income. In 1999, this indicator stood at $11,100 for Hispanics, $35,785 for non-Hispanic whites, $20,595 for Asians, and $17,341 for African Americans. The unemployment rate for Hispanics stood at 7.3 percent in June of 2003, compared to 6.6 percent for all non-Hispanics. These figures, coupled with the educational problems mentioned in an earlier section of this chapter, likely means that the gap between Spanish speakers and other Los Angelinos will continue well into the twenty-first century (Kotkin and Ozuna, "Economic Development," pp. 41, 44, and 45).

One important positive trend noted by Kotkin and Ozuna was the increased amount of entrepreneurial activity among Latinos in the county. In 2000, there existed approximately 3,000 Hispanic-owned firms in the environs of Los Angeles. The most common kind of business, not surprisingly, were firms in the service industry, followed by construction companies and professional services establishments (such as engineering and accounting firms). In total, this cluster of companies employed more than 14,000 workers. In order for even more such firms to take flight in coming decades, the authors of this study called upon area banks to increase their outreach to such potential entrepreneurs as well for them to modify some of the requirements necessary for getting start-up loans for small businesses.

Research by historian Jorge Iber on the Spanish-speaking people of the state of Utah (mostly concentrated, not surprisingly, in the state's largest municipality, Salt Lake City) reveals similar gains and limitations. In 1990, for example, the median income for Hispanics in the state totaled $24,941, while the corresponding figure for non-Hispanic whites totaled $33,846. As noted in this chapter's discussion on education, a great deal of this difference is caused by the continued disparity in this field between the Hispanics and the broader population. Additionally, Iber asserts, the low median pay of single Hispanas (who often serve as primary caregivers to young children) was also responsible for reducing the median income figure of Hispanics in the Beehive State.

ELIUD PETE SUAZO: POLITICIAN AND CIVIC ACTIVIST IN SALT LAKE CITY, UTAH

One characteristic of previous studies about people of Mexican descent in the United States (from the 1960s through the 1980s) was an emphasis on portraying these historical actors as "faceless laborers, classes, and genders as reflected in the statistics of wages, occupations, and demographics" (Kreneck, *Mexican American Odyssey*, p. 14). Though such research was of value, by the middle of the 1990s a few scholars, such as Louise Ann Finch, Felix D. Almaraz Jr., and Mario T. Garcia, had begun writing biographies of important local and national personages of Mexican American descent and describing their roles in the struggle for greater opportunity and equality in the West. The movement from studies of groups to biographical studies evident within Mexican American historical studies is appropriately summarized by Thomas Kreneck (who recently published a biography of a Houston entrepreneur of Mexican descent) when he states that though he does not belittle the earlier studies, he does "suggest that biographies should always be part of the literatures, so that human dimension to Chicano history be reinforced and the individual be given proper credit" (Kreneck, *Mexican American Odyssey*, p. 14).

The story that follows is but one example of the many diligent persons of Mexican descent who worked to open doors in a variety of areas. In this case, we focus upon Eliud Pete Suazo, the first Mexican American to serve in the Utah State Senate. His story is an excellent case study of the value of biography within Mexican American historical research.

Eliud Pete Suazo was born in Salt Lake City, Utah, on June 4, 1951, the son of Patricio and Cecelia Suazo. The young Pete grew up on the tough west side of Utah's capital city during a time when people of Mexican descent had few job options (beyond working in agriculture, mining, or the railroad), and when few Spanish-surnamed youths graduated from the county's public schools. One of the only options open to kids such as Suazo was to work downtown selling papers or shining shoes in order to make a few extra dollars for themselves and their families. These difficult conditions did not, however, prevent Pete from succeeding in the classroom, and he graduated from Salt Lake City West High in 1969.

As was common during that time, the school counselor suggested that the young man seek opportunities to learn a trade or else join the military. Fortunately for Pete, the University of Utah had recently received a Ford Foundation grant designed to help the institution recruit talented minority students. Using these funds for scholarships, the University of Utah attracted a few dozen Chicanos/as and Native American pupils to their overwhelmingly lily-white campus. As a result, Pete, together with a few of his classmates from the west side, took the first step of a very difficult task by becoming a Mexican American earning a college degree from a Utah institution of higher learning.

Suazo graduated in 1973 with a degree in criminology and then started attending law school, but he did not finish a legal degree. He later pursued and earned a master's degree in Human Resource Management and Economics in 1978 from the University of Utah. These educational tools, as well is his involvement with the Chicano/a Movement, motivated Pete to pursue a career in public service. Among his various jobs in this field, he worked for the Boys and Girls Club and the Salt Lake City Housing Authority, and he served as an aide to Salt Lake mayor Palmer DePaulis. Further, he benefited his community by working with the oldest Mexican American organization in the state, the Centro Civico Mexicano, ultimately filling the role of the group's executive director. He also mentored barrio youths through his work with the neighborhood's boxing club. Finally, he used his business know-how and community connections to serve as a business consultant for aspiring minority entrepreneurs.

Suazo's efforts culminated in his decision, in 1992, to run for the Utah House of Representatives. Although Pete's district was represented by a Democrat, he believed that the individual in place was too conservative and out of touch with the growing Hispanic population in the area. Therefore, he mobilized the barrio and gay and lesbian communities and defeated his opponent (running on a platform calling for passage of a state hate crimes bill); he became one of the first Hispanic members of the state legislature.

Upon his arrival at the Capitol, Suazo confronted a difficult reality: he was a member of a minority (Hispanic) within another minority (the Democratic legislative contingent in conservative Utah is quite small). Would he be able to get any of his agenda items through the Republican-dominated body? Though he did not achieve most of his legislative goals (for example, he spoke out against the passage of legislation declaring English the official language of Utah), he earned the respect of many of his colleagues, and he worked feverishly to get his cohorts to think about the impact of their legislation upon the state's poor and minority populations. In this task he succeeded, eventually getting the Senate to pass a hate-crimes bill (although it died in the House) in the 2001 legislative session. In addition, Pete worked with his GOP colleagues in trying to change a previous redistricting decision that kept much of the west side of Salt Lake City (specifically, his neighborhood of Rose Park) out of the only urban congressional district in the state of Utah (the Second Congressional District).

Pete moved on to the State Senate in 1996, and it appeared that he would be able to continue to expand his influence and work for the betterment of the lives of all of Utah's citizens for many years to come. Tragically, this was not to be, for on August 21, 2001, Senator Pete Suazo was killed in a single-vehicle accident during a hunting trip in the Manti-La Sal National Forest, in the Uinta Mountains of central Utah. His colleagues, family, and supporters were stunned by his passing.

Even though much of the legislation that he supported still has not passed the Utah legislature, Suazo did accomplish much during his nine years of service. He broke down barriers to political participation and the quest for political office by Hispanics in an overwhelmingly white state and also championed the causes of some of Utah's forgotten peoples. In a sense, and here he succeeded overwhelmingly, Pete Suazo made it possible for some in the white majority to look at Utah through the eyes for a minority for the first time.

On the positive side of the equation, however, by the late 1990s it was also clear that this population was an important part of the state's economic and entrepreneurial life. Hispanics were important cogs in both the labor and management of industries such as tourism (especially in the skiing center of Park City), the service sector, and light manufacturing. In addition, by 1992 this population accounted for more than $2 billion in business transactions within the state. Finally, Hispanics were also establishing businesses that served the broader population as well as their comunidad. As Iber notes, by the end of the 1990s, "residents had the option of shopping in a growing number of *bodegas* (markets), *carnicerias* (butcher shops), *panaderias* (bakeries), *tiendas de ropa* (clothing stores), and *botánicas* (pharmaceutical and religious products) located in Salt Lake City, Murray, Midvale, Ogden, Provo, and even as far north as Logan (Cache Valley)" (Iber, *Hispanics in the Mormon Zion,* pp. 123–24).

An example of the dichotomy of opinion about this group's economic development in the West (and nationwide) can be found in recent publications by two organizations that focus much of their research on the circumstances confronting the Hispanic population of the United States: the Pew Hispanic Center and the Hispanic American Center for Economic Research (HACER).

In the 2004 Pew publication entitled "The Wealth of Hispanic Households: 1996 to 2002," researcher Rakesh Kochhar noted that conditions remain bleak, stating that, even with the gains of the 1980s and 1990s, most "Hispanics . . . fall into the lowest category of wealth and the size of their middle-class is relatively small. . . . The wealth gap between White households and Hispanic . . . households is much larger than the income gap." In other words, the "average" Hispanic household has far less in financial assets that does the "average" White household in the United States. Conversely, recent research by the Rand Corporation (a nonprofit think tank) and quoted in various HACER publications provides a totally different perspective on the economic life of Hispanics. HACER's leadership has ballyhooed financial gains by Spanish speakers under headline banners such as "Tracking Latino Progress," "U.S. Hispanics Reap the Benefits of a Strong Domestic Economy," and "Hispanic Wealth Growing above U.S. Average." These reports touted figures such as the growing number of Hispanic-owned businesses (up to 1.2 million by 2002), the increased number of *familias* earning above $100,000 (which grew by 126 percent in the years between 1991 and 2000), and the growing purchasing power of this community (currently estimated at $452 billion) (Garcia, "Tracking Latino Progress," p. 1, http://www.hacer .org/current/US002.php).

In summary, there have been many positive economic developments for the Mexican American population of the West since 1980. The middle class continues to grow, more and more Hispanic business firms are opening their doors, and greater numbers of Spanish-surnamed persons are moving into higher occupational levels. Conversely, newer immigrants are not doing as well financially as in previous generations, and a large disparity continues in per capita and family median and mean incomes (as compared with whites). These indicators reveal that equality has not been achieved, but many people of Mexican descent are inching closer to fulfillment of the American dream. As González argues:

> In the past, Mexican Americans were systematically denied economic opportunities and had to fight for even small improvements. Since the Civil Rights Movement of the 1960s, however, Mexican Americans have found that the road is becoming more and more a two-way street. The quest for *buenos días* may still succeed. (González, *Mexican Americans and the U.S. Economy*, p. 129)

ACCESS TO MEDICAL CARE

During the years of the Chicano/a movement, it was not uncommon for movimiento-inspired organizations to help establish health care facilities to service the needs of barrio dwellers throughout the West (see chapter 7). Such entities subsidized the costs of appointments (and other procedures) and offered Spanish-speaking people an opportunity to meet with medical personnel on a regular basis. In addition, many of the doctors and nurses at the clinics spoke Spanish and worked diligently to provide health care in a culturally sensitive way.

Although by the start of the twenty-first century, the majority (an estimated 60 percent in the year 2000) of Hispanics had coverage through employer-provided (and employee co-paid) private health insurance, a substantial percentage of this population remained burdened by the lack of affordable health care coverage. In addition, the percentage of Hispanics covered through this for-profit mechanism still lagged far behind the corresponding figure for the nation's non-Hispanics (estimated at 85 percent in 2000). Thus, as we continue our examination of the progress (or lack thereof) of the Spanish-surnamed peoples of the West, it is valuable to discuss the important medical issues and the current level of health care access for this group.

In earlier sections of this chapter we noted the large volume of scholarly research dealing with Hispanics (primarily of Mexican descent) in the areas of education and economics. Likewise, the number of studies undertaken dealing with this populace and health care over the past two decades is substantial. Thus, as we have done formerly, we limit ourselves to a few sources about the topic. Here, we turn to recent studies conduced by the Pew Hispanic Center and the Intercultural Cancer Council that deal with some of the principal medical problems confronting the Spanish-surnamed population of the West (and nation).

Three recent studies (conducted in 2000, 2002, and 2004) proffered readers a sense of both the negative and positive aspects of the relationship between this population and the health care system of the United States. Among the negative trends in recent years, the Pew Hispanic Center noted the following: (1) as of 2004, a substantial number of people of Mexican descent remained uninsured; with the Mexicano number (39 percent) much higher than the percentage of uninsured boriquas (18 percent) and Cubanos (20 percent), although lower than the percentage of Central Americans such as Salvadorans (41 percent); (2) a larger percentage of Spanish speakers in Texas were more likely to not have health insurance (43 percent) than the same population in California (36 percent) and the rest of the nation (32 percent); (3) approximately one-fifth of individuals in this survey pool stated that they encountered difficulties in paying bills or did not seek treatment for a medical condition due to economic considerations in the past year; and finally, (4) the report also noted that, even when they could afford to visit a doctor, 49 percent of Spanish-dominant individuals (most likely, the most recent immigrants, legal or undocumented) experienced a "problem" in communicating with attending medical personnel (Pew Hispanic Center, "Hispanic Health: Divergent and Changing," p. 2, and "Health Care Experiences," p. 3).

Mike Wright (right), *a volunteer at the Volunteer Healthcare Clinic, Austin, Texas, takes down vital statistics from Victor C. Rodriguez on the health of his son during their visit to the clinic for a routine checkup. (Larry Kolvoord/The Image Works)*

A 2002 survey by the same organization noted other negative trends: (1) obesity is more prevalent, and in particular among mujeres, in Hispanic communities (approximately one-third of Mexicanas are obese, versus one-fifth of white women) than in the broader population; (2) this group is twice as likely to develop diabetes (5.7 per 1,000) than non-Hispanic whites (3 per 1,000); (3) Latinos continue to be more likely to be uninsured (approximately one-third overall) than non-Hispanic whites (around one-tenth). We must offer one caveat here, however, and note a large difference in the percentage of uninsured individuals among Hispanics who are foreign-born and not citizens (about 55 percent), versus Hispanic foreign-born naturalized citizens (about 25 percent) and Hispanic native born (around 22 percent). Finally, (4) Hispanics have a higher rate of tuberculosis (13.6 per 1,000) than whites (2.3 per 1,000) and the general population (6.8 per 1,000) (Pew Hispanic Center, "Hispanic Health: Divergent and Changing," pp. 1-2 and "Health Care Experiences," pp. 1–3).

This same study, however, also revealed a number of positive trends: (1) Latinos have a lower mortality rate, overall, than the white-non Hispanic population (in part, due to the fact that this population is much younger than the broader group); (2) the infant mortality rate of Hispanic infants has dropped substantially over the past two decades, and the figures for Mexican Americans (less than 6 deaths per 1,000 live births), Cuban Americans (less than 4 deaths per 1,000 live births), and Central Americans (approximately 5.5 deaths per 1,000 live births) is now actually below that for white non-Hispanics (exactly 6 deaths per 1,000 live births); and, (3) nationwide, the Spanish-surnamed population tends to smoke less than the majority populace.

In 2003, UCLA researchers David E. Hayes-Bautista, Mariam I. Kahramanian, and Cristina Gamboa studied some of the patterns noted above in the large Hispanic population of Los Angeles. Their findings, based on figures for the years 1999–2001, were mostly in tune with results of research conducted elsewhere in the West. The trio noted that almost 38 percent of the Latino adults in the city did not have health insurance coverage; a bit higher than some of the figures cited previously, and most likely due to the large numbers of recent arrivals to the city. More unexpectedly, given the national figures, the percentage of Los Angeles' Hispanic adults who smoked (17.6 percent) was higher than any other group besides African Americans (20.6 percent). Perhaps most seriously, the community faced a serious shortages of physicians, and the trend appeared likely to continue, as few Hispanics (for example, only 38 percent, or 306 members, of the incoming class at the UCLA Medical School in 2002 were Latinos) were attending local academies for medical training. Surprisingly, given the limitations and concerns noted, the health outcomes for Los Angeles' Spanish-surnamed population were quite positive. For example, the infant death rate (5.2 per 1000) for Latinos was less than for non-Latinos (5.7 per 1000). Similarly, the rate for heart disease, cancer, and stroke deaths were all lower for Hispanics than for the rest of the city's inhabitants. Finally, the life expectancy of Spanish-surnamed people averaged more than 82 years, while that of non-Latinos was only 77 years (Hayes-Bautista, Kahramanian, and Gamboa, "Health," pp. 7, 8, 9, 13, and 14).

In summary, the picture for issues relating to health care and Mexican Americans (and other Spanish-surnamed groups) in the West is as muddled as that for education and economics. Though many positive strides have occurred, and indeed the health of the community is surprisingly good, major concerns regarding access (to both care and medical education) and cultural sensitivity remain and will continue to challenge the Hispanic comunidad of the West well into the twenty-first century.

POLITICS IN THE WEST SINCE 1980

In an October 2002 article entitled "Twin Peaks" in *Texas Monthly* magazine, author Cecilia Balli recounts the story of Rosie Castro and her twin sons Julian and Joaquín, and their journey through the state's political history since the early 1970s. The boys, serendipitously, were born during a La Raza Unida Party cook-off on September 16, 1974, in San Antonio, and have been (literally) enmeshed in Mexican American political life since then. Both parents, but especially Rosie, had worked long and hard to improve circumstances in San Antonio's West side, and the family "business" has now attracted both young men. The significance of the story, however, lies in an examination of the differences between how the Castro siblings achieved their political power (through the ballot box and traditional political campaigns), versus their parents' association with street protests, radical politics, and the LRUP (see chapter 7). In addition, the new generation did not have to struggle simply to gain recognition and fairer treatment from the Anglo political establishment (Julian became the youngest city councilman in San Antonio history, winning election in 2001). Unlike their parents' generation, Ju-

A Latino voter leaves a polling station in Hollywood, California, during the U.S. midterm elections, November 5, 2002. (Hector Mata/AFP/Getty Images)

lian and Joaquín's opportunity came courtesy of a Stanford undergraduate education and a Harvard law degree. In sum, this story tells us, much indeed has changed in regard to the political landscape and Mexican Americans in Texas, California, and elsewhere. The question, however, is whether increased political participation and power has generated a substantial economic and social change in barrio life. It is to that question we now turn.

During the years of the Chicano/a Movement, one of the principal goals of the leaders, whatever their philosophical stripes, was to increase the political power of the Mexican American population of the U.S. West. In many ways, they succeeded, and the number of Spanish-surnamed politicos elected throughout the region increased dramatically. In 2004 NALEO (National Association of Latino Elected and Appointed Officials) published its (now 230 pages long) *Directory of Latino Elected Officials* for a twentieth consecutive year. This document contains contact information and party affiliation for thousands of elected and appointed men and women who serve in federal, state, and local posts nationwide.

Still, has the increased representation benefited the community as a whole? The answer to this question is not clear. In his 1999 essay entitled "On the Future of Anglo-Mexican Relations in the United States," historian David Montejano summarizes the dichotomous political experiences of Mexican Americans since 1980:

> On the one hand, from a historical perspective, one must recognize a form of political inclusion, in the sense that most structural obstacles, such as the poll tax, at-large elections, and gerrymandered districts, have been removed. One must recognize that Mexican Americans have been granted effective citizenship and that this marks a departure from historical experience. . . . [But] political inclusion has not been a panacea, a general solution to the economic problems of most Mexican Americans. . . . The evidence suggests that the Mexican American community has been split into a socially incorporated middle class and a socially segregated lower class. (Montejano, *Chicano Politics and Society,* pp. 234–235)

As detailed in previous sections of this chapter, there are often sharp divisions within the academic community regarding the status of Hispanics. It is no different in regard to this population and politics. There are individuals who acknowledge that progress has been made and circumstances have improved. On the other hand, and this is the majority opinion, many hold that since the more radical versions of social and economic readjustment advocated during the years of the Chicano/a era have not come to pass, it follows that the Spanish-speaking people of the West remain mired in a state of political and economic oppression. A few examples will serve to illustrate the concerns raised about Hispanics and their political participation in the West over the past twenty-five years.

A major concern has been the tendency of politicos to use the ethnic card to gain power, but then to link themselves with business interests once they are in office, rather than embracing a progressive agenda. In the essay "Personality and Style in San Antonio Politics," from the collection of essays *Chicano Politics and Society in the Late Twentieth Century* (edited by David Montejano), Rodolfo Rosales argues that the election of Henry Cisneros as mayor of the Alamo City was a "turning point for Chicano politics in Texas and the Southwest" (Montejano, *Chicano Politics and Society,* p. 23). However, this momentous triumph became a Pyrrhic victory; Cisneros, it turned out, was "accountable only to . . . his own agenda—and, of course, to his . . . ties to particular sectors of interest—and only indirectly to the community" (Montejano, *Chicano Politics and Society,* p. 23). Instead of focusing on the needs of the poor, Rosales contends, Cisneros's administration concentrated on development and profit; for example, they put in place agreements to construct a Sea World theme park and the new home for the NBA's San Antonio Spurs, the Alamodome. Rosales argues, therefore, that having a Mexican American official who must maintain the "proper" business climate in a city really does not help bring about the "progressive" changes of which so many in academia are enamored.

This same collection offers yet another insightful piece regarding the political changes that have taken place among individual Mexican Americans since the end of the Chicano/a era. In his essay, "'Where Have All the Nationalists Gone?': Change and Persistence in Radical Political Attitudes Among Chicanos, 1976–1986," sociologist Martin Sánchez Jankowski, through the use of interviews conducted in 1976 and 1986, discusses how and why some persons involved with the *movimiento* changed their political perspectives. Sánchez Jankowski's research reveals that most of these men and women had, by the late 1980s, toned down their radicalism, and embraced the traditional two-party political system of the United States. Among the reasons cited for the changes were (1) the general climate of acceptance of a conservative agenda during the Reagan years, (2) where the subjects stood in the life cycle (it is much more difficult to devote oneself to radical politics when one has a mortgage to pay and a need to buy braces for children), and (3) the local political environment (some places simply did not lend themselves as well as others to continuing radical/nationalistic activism). This combination of factors, as one of Sánchez Jankowski's respondents asserts, ultimately influenced political beliefs; as the respondent put it, "What made me change from supporting nationalism was nothing dramatic, I just grew up" (Montejano, *Chicano Politics and Society*, p. 215).

As this study demonstrates, by the late 1980s many in the comunidad had left the more radical politics of the 1960s and 1970s far behind. Some had even embraced the more conservative notions of Reaganism; one respondent explained his reasons to Sánchez Jankowski:

> As I got older and realized that nationalism was not going to help anybody, I left both Chicano nationalism and the Raza Unida behind. . . . Now I am a Republican [because] after dropping any attachment I had for the Raza Unida, I didn't want to support the Democrats because I didn't think they really wanted to help Chicanos, they just get them to be happy with welfare. But the Republicans had policies that help people help themselves. I have helped myself, and other Chicanos should do the same. I think the Republicans help you to do that and I support them. (Montejano, *Chicano Politics and Society*, p. 224)

These men and women are, for better or worse, no longer looking to establish a separate nation and are willing to accept an opportunity to enter into the broader society's politics and work within the Democratic and Republican parties in order to achieve both personal and community goals. This form of political activity, however, is not enough for many scholars researching this history. One example is Ernesto Chávez, who, in his 2002 work *Mi Raza Primero: Nationalism, Identity, and Insurgency in the Chicano Movement in Los Angeles, 1966–1978,* complains that, having veered away from the radicalism of the Chicano/a era, the Spanish-surnamed community's politics have been "transformed into purely electoral efforts, the grassroots elements and their ability to truly redefine the American political landscape—to bring about days of revolution—has disappeared" (Chávez, *"My People First,"* p. 119).

As in the areas of education, economic development, and medical care, the political results for the Spanish-speaking people since 1980 have been mixed. Though the more traditional, and blatant, obstacles to participation (such as poll taxes and at-large districts) have largely been eliminated through legal and community action, there remain other impediments such as low rates of voter participation and citizenship (especially among more recent Mexican immigrants), which still limit the power of this ethnic group in the political arena. Such trends are particularly troublesome because of the continuing debate over the impact of Latino immigration to the U.S. West over the past three decades, a topic to which we now turn.

IMMIGRATION TO THE WEST SINCE *1980: A LOOK AT SOME NUMBERS*

There is little debate that immigration (both documented and undocumented) is the dominant issue regarding the Hispanic (but particularly, for those of Mexican descent) experience in the West since 1980. This subject is crucial to this history, and, in order to provide proper coverage, we have decided to split our treatment of the topic into two parts: in this chapter, we offer a cursory overview of the statistics regarding this immigration and note the dramatic increase in the number of Latinos in the West (both in urban and rural areas) over the past three and a half decades. Additionally, we proffer a brief account of the reaction by whites to the increased presence (and diversity) of Spanish speakers. This analysis sets the stage for an in-depth discussion of the myriad political, educational, social, and economic issues that have arisen from this substantial demographic change. In chapter 9, we will delve fully into matters such as Propositions 187, 209, and 227, in California, Proposition 200 in Arizona, bilingual education, affirmative action, and so on.

There are three vital points to remember about the wave of immigration that has swept the West from Latin America (especially from Mexico): first, it is in reaction to dramatic economic and other changes that have taken place in the United States and elsewhere; second, this wave is still ongoing; and finally, although it is overwhelmingly concentrated in the West (and in California and Texas particularly), the migratory surge has created comunidades of Latinos in many locales that had not previously contained substantial pockets of Hispanics, including rural areas of the West.

The Hart-Celler (Immigration) Act of 1965 is a crucial starting point for understanding the dramatic increase in this immigration over the past few decades. In an important 1998 work, *Unwelcome Strangers: American Identity and the Turn against Immigration,* historian David M. Reimers argues that this legislation, together with the end of the bracero program (see chapter 6), made it much more difficult for Mexicanos to enter the

United States. Because many thousands of these *trabajadores* wanted to continue working in the colossus of the north, they found a way "around" such hindrances. "Hence, they came without proper documentation. Later, Central Americans discovered how hard it was to immigrate to the United States, they too decided to enter illegally. Thus, in closing . . . [the] 'front door,' American policy fostered 'back door' illegal immigration" (Reimers, *Unwelcome Strangers,* p. 69). Simultaneously, the deindustrialization of the Northeast and parts of the Midwest, together with the movement of millions of Americans to the Southwest (and other parts of the Sun Belt), promoted the growth and expansion of the West's population and economy during the 1970s and 1980s. This development functioned as an additional magnet attracting immigrants to the region.

This trend was welcomed by many business interests of the West, as newly arrived illegal immigrants tended to work for low wages and to complain little about working conditions. It was the downturn in the California economy in the early 1990s, along with the arrival of more workers and their families (which increased the cost of education, medical care, and welfare programs) that helped raise concerns that the mostly Spanish-surnamed immigrants were becoming a drain on both state and national economies. The ultimate example of this backlash came in the form of Proposition 187 in California (and other propositions that followed in the Golden State and elsewhere) in the early 1990s, an act designed to limit the ability of undocumented immigrants to access publicly funded services such as schools and medical facilities.

A second important aspect of this wave is the fact that it reinforces Mexican (and other Latino) cultures in Western locales. The main question being debated regarding this issue is whether the acculturation of the newer Hispanic arrivals is being stunted by the fresh contact with individuals from the "old country" and by the belief of multiculturalists in the United States that it is beneficial for immigrants to maintain traditional cultures and nationalistic ties. This issue has generated intense debate over the past decade and has spawned a series of anti-immigrant books, among them, Samuel P. Huntington's *Who Are We?: The Challenges to America's National Identity,* and Victor Davis Hanson's *Mexifornia: A State of Becoming.* Although we will deal with such tomes in greater detail in chapter 9, it is important to note some general themes at this point. In brief, Huntington and Davis Hanson argue that the dramatic increase in the number of Hispanics in the West (and nationwide) is having a deleterious impact on U.S. society. These authors argue that the increased presence of Spanish speakers actively undermines the "American creed" and is damaging (or destroying) the ideas and beliefs that made our nation. In chapter 9 we deal with this issue more fully and suggest some of the kind of research that needs to be done in order to explore such claims in a rational manner.

One last impact of this migratory wave throughout the West is the movement of Hispanics, especially since the 1980s, into rural areas of the region (as well as into parts of the Midwest). An example of the research on this topic is the 2000 essay entitled "The Changing Geography of Mexican Immigration to the United States, 1910–1996," by Jorge Durand, Douglas S. Massey, and Fernando Charvet. In this study, the authors scrutinize where Mexicano immigrants settled during three separate eras: the "classic" and bracero period (1920–1960, where immigration to Texas and California was predominant, but which also produced pockets in other Western states, such as Arizona, as well as in the midwestern industrial states of Michigan and Illinois), the "undocumented" era (roughly 1965–1986, where the "traditional" states continued to be important, but with "newer" comunidades taking root and expanding in states such as Colorado, Nevada, Oregon, Utah, and Washington), and the post-IRCA (Immigration Reform and Control Act of 1986, which offered amnesty to undocumented workers meeting certain residency conditions), with a significant movement of Mexican trabajadores away from California to even more nontraditional destinations (in states like Florida and Georgia).

In brief, the authors argue that, especially since IRCA, immigrants from Mexico have "transformed a narrowly focused process affecting just three states into a nationwide movement with diffuse effects spread throughout the country" (Durand, Massey, and Charvet, "The Changing Geography of Mexican Immigration," p. 14). While many single men and families were attracted to urban areas, some moved to more rural parts of the West and Midwest; indeed, the Spanish-speaking newcomers have become the economic salvation of small communities that had been hemorrhaging population for most of the twentieth century. Following are three illustrations of the positive aspects and increased racial tensions caused by this trend.

Historian Jorge Iber, in his 2001 work *Hispanics in the Mormon Zion, 1912–1999,* provides an overview of the creation of three relatively new rural pockets of Mexicanos in the state of Utah. For example, he notes the way the establishment of processing plants (slaughtering cattle and turkeys) during the late 1980s and early 1990s pulled Mexicanos and Mexican Americans from more urban settings to smaller communities such as Hyrum (in northern Utah) and Moroni (in the southeastern part of the state). One of the immigrants living in Hyrum summarized his reason for moving to this locale: "'In this country you have a chance to succeed. In Mexico, we would live on beans, tortillas and coffee. Here we can feed our children. We wanted a better life for them. Now we have grandchildren and they only know America'" (Iber, *Hispanics in the Mormon Zion,* p. 119).

This positive experience, however, does not tell the whole story, as another instance of Mexicanos in rural Utah attests. During the 1980s people of Mexican descent began moving to more tourist-centered areas of the state; including the casino town of Wendover (located on the Utah-Nevada border, approximately 120 miles west of Salt Lake City). Beginning in 1980, one of the local gambling houses commenced an expansion, and many Mexicanos (primarily from the town of Juchipila in the state of Zacatecas) arrived to take up positions as change-makers, maids, and janitors. While the pay for such occupations was not great, they provided steady employment, as well as an opportunity to send children to area schools. Unfortunately, such hopes were dealt a severe blow in March of 1986, as Elko County (Nevada), Tooele County (Utah), and INS officers raided the town in search of "wetbacks." As a result of this event, many of the Mexicanos of Wendover were arrested, processed, and deported; the town's casinos protested vehemently regarding the loss of valued employees. Once the authorities' immigration "show" ended, not surprisingly, the town returned to normal. By the middle 1990s, using primarily Mexican labor, Wendover continued to grow (the town eventually split into a Utah side, Wendover, and a Nevada community named West Wendover), as more casinos moved into the area.

One final example of both the opportunities and tensions created by the movement of Spanish speakers into smaller western communities comes from the essay "Mexicans and 'Business as Usual': Small Town Politics in Oregon," by Robert C. Dash and Robert E. Hawkinson. Here, the authors examine the reaction of whites in what they describe as the previously "'idyllic' isolated agricultural community" (Dash and Hawkinson, "Mexicans and 'Business as Usual,'" p. 110) of Woodburn to the arrival and needs (educational and housing) of an increasingly diverse town population. Beginning in the 1950s and 1960s, many Hispanics began settling there, working in agriculture, local nurseries, food processing plants, and other industries. The comunidad grew until, by the early 1980s, downtown Woodburn had witnessed a cultural transformation, with *tiendas* (shops) now serving the needs of the Spanish-speaking population.

This transformation is but one area of concern for many local whites regarding their new neighbors. In addition, many of the Mexicanos have become involved with union activity and called for progressive changes in local schools (such as hiring teachers of diverse backgrounds and naming an elementary school in honor of César Chávez) and the development of adequate housing for farm workers. Dash and Hawkinson's concluding remarks pertain to one small town in Oregon, but could also apply to any of the many towns located all over the West that have experienced dramatic growth in their Hispanic populations: "Despite the dramatic demographic, economic and cultural changes that have remade the city since the 1960s, much of the leadership continues to practice the politics of exclusion. Future transformations of Woodburn's politics will inevitably be driven by the changes documented. . . . The important question remaining to be answered is what degree of civility and accommodation will mark those transformations" (Dash and Hawkinson, "Mexicans and 'Business as Usual,'" p. 110).

Now that we have provided a sense of the forces that have attracted such large numbers of immigrants, where they live, and how the majority population of the West has reacted to the migratory wave, we offer some statistics in order to quantify this trend. Obviously, the figures presented are based on statistical analysis and are subject to the limitations of that craft; nevertheless, a January 2004 publication by Jeffrey S. Passell, Randy Capps, and Michael Fix of the Urban Institute offers, we believe, an accurate account of current facts and figures relating to undocumented immigration in the United States.

The study revealed the following: (1) as of early 2002, there were approximately 9.3 million illegals in the United States; (2) Mexican nationals comprised 57 percent of this group (approximately 5.3 million people); (3) roughly 66 percent of the undocumented lived in just six states, with California and Texas accounting for 40 percent of this figure; (4) approximately 6 million such individuals are currently employed, accounting for roughly 5 percent of all workers; (5) labor force participation for undocumented men is around 96 percent; (6) approximately 2 of every 3 undocumented laborers earn less than twice the minimum wage; and (7) about 1.6 million children (less than 18 years of age) are undocumented immigrants (Passel, Capps, and Fix, "Undocumented Immigrants: Facts and Figures," pp. 1–3).

One final aspect of the study worth mentioning here is the estimated number of undocumented immigrants by state, and the large numbers of such persons concentrated in the West. For example, in early 2002, it is estimated that California contained approximately 2.4 million indocumentados and Texas had 1.1 million. Other states with significant undocumented populations included Arizona, with between 250,000 and 350,000 such persons; Colorado and Washington, with between 175,000 and 200,000 each; Nevada and Oregon, with between 120,000 and 150,000 each; Utah, with between 75,000 and 100,000; Kansas, New Mexico, and Oklahoma, with 50,000 to 75,000 each; and Idaho, with between 25,000 and 50,000 undocumented aliens (Passel, Capps, and Fix, "Undocumented Immigrants: Facts and Figures," p. 4).

In summary, the question of immigration (both documented and undocumented) is the major factor in considering the history of Hispanics in the West since 1980. As noted above, there have been many positive and negative outcomes of this tidal wave of humanity moving to the U.S. West. The political, academic, social, educational, and economic debate over this movement has spawned a myriad of causes, propositions, and arguments over the past twenty-five years. We will examine the events resulting from these changes in chapter 9.

CUBANS IN THE WEST SINCE 1980: GOLDEN EXILES AND MARIELITOS

An examination of federal census materials reveals that there were sixteen metropolitan areas in the West with Cuban American populations larger than 1,000 people in the year 2000. The western states with the largest number of Cuban American at this time were California, Texas, Arizona, and Nevada. Not surprisingly, the two specific locations we have discussed previously, Los Angeles and Las Vegas, top the list, with an estimated 39,000 and 11,200 Cubanos, respectively. Other substantial pockets of concentration include Houston (with about 8,900 Cuban Americans); San Francisco, California (with about 8,000); and Dallas (5,200) (McKee, *Ethnicity in Contemporary America,* p. 153). Although these are substantial numbers, the amount of research done on this population in the various metropolises has been quite limited. Still, a few researchers have endeavored to capture the sinews of Cubano life in the West, and we now turn to brief overviews of recent studies by William

Cuban Americans protest the downing of two unarmed, civilian-operated Brothers to the Rescue planes in the Florida straits in the Echo Park section of Los Angeles in March 1996. (AP Photo/John Hayes)

Clayson (Las Vegas), Richard Ferro (Seattle), and a broader study on the geographic and social mobility of Mariel refugees (including the largest pocket of western concentration in Los Angeles) by Emily Hayes Skop.

In a 1995 article entitled "Cubans in Las Vegas: Ethnic Identity, Success, and Urban Life in the Late Twentieth Century," William Clayson spends much of the first half of the essay discussing the arrival of the so-called "golden exile" generation of Cubans to Sin City during the early 1960s. His work documents much of the success the group experienced in getting settled in the Las Vegas metropolitan area, their participation in the establishment of the local Hispanic Chamber of Commerce, and their entry into the managerial level of casinos and other local industries. However, once Clayson begins discussing the post-1980 period and the arrival of Marielitos in the city, the tone of the study becomes more pessimistic.

While the exact number of refugees who arrived in the United States as a result of the 1980 Mariel boatlift and then came to Las Vegas is not known, it is known that these mostly young men arrived with significant baggage that hindered their economic and social progress. First, many had no relatives in the city, and thus, no one to introduce them to potential employers and social service agencies. Second, many Marielitos were mulattoes or black and were shunned by the overwhelmingly white members of the golden exile generation. Third, many of the newcomers practiced Santeria, the hybrid voodoo/Catholic religion of many Cubans of African descent, another cause of tension with the older Cubanos. Fourth, as persons who had reached maturity under a socialistic system, many Marielitos were ill prepared for the highly competitive nature of U.S., and particularly, Las Vegas society and economy. Finally, the Las Vegas Marielitos arrived at a time when the hysteria over the Al Pacino film *Scarface* was at its height. Needless to say, many of the recién llegados were stereotyped as criminals. Clayson's study cites numerous stories from local papers during the early 1980s that depict all Marielitos as thugs, killers, and drug dealers; the very incarnation of the Tony Montana character portrayed by Pacino.

This trend caused a dramatic shift in the economic success of the entire Cuban American population in this city. Whereas prior to the arrival of Marielitos, Cubanos had an average income that exceeded that of other local Hispanics by almost $7,000: by 1990, the "income of Mexicans, traditionally the lowest, exceeded that of Cubans by more than $4,000" (Clayson, "Cubans in Las Vegas," p. 13). Although there have been problems with the acceptance of the Mariel refugees, Clayson closes his piece on an optimistic note, arguing that in due time the Marielitos will experience success similar to that of their predecessors.

> Though the Cubans who came to Las Vegas during and after the Mariel boat-lift did not inherit the same advantages as those who came before, they are grateful to the United States and to Las Vegas for the opportunities and assistance they have received. One Mariel refugee who was living in Las Vegas in 1985 showed his gratitude by sending a money order for $1,000, which represented two-thirds of all he had, to the United States Treasury as a voluntary donation. (Clayson, "Cubans in Las Vegas," p. 15)

Richard Ferro's 1996 University of Washington dissertation, entitled "Perceptions of Discrimination: Cubans in the Pacific Northwest," offers readers an intimate examination of both the positive and negative aspects of Cuban American belief systems and life experiences in the Seattle area. As with the individuals described previously, the Cuban Americans living in this region are divided into two main groups, those who came in the 1960s and 1970s, and those who arrived in the 1980s.

As in Las Vegas (and Los Angeles, discussed in previous chapters) many of the older residents continue to see the United States as a land of limitless opportunity, where one can succeed through determination and effort. Although this is certainly a commendable attitude, it is also a bit unrealistic. Further, such a mind-set often leads Cuban Americans to take a condescending attitude, especially toward other Latinos (and in particular, toward Mexicanos and Mexican Americans). The greatest value of Ferro's research is that he documents various Cuban Americans expressing such negative views. Unfortunately, this kind of attitude can only perpetuate the bitterness and division between Cubanos and other Hispanics of the West that we discussed briefly in chapter 7.

The final recent study documenting the Cuban American experience in the West is a master's thesis by Emily Hayes Skop (produced at Arizona

State University in 1997) entitled "Segmented Paths: The Geographic and Social Mobility of Mariel Exiles." In this research, Hayes Skop focuses upon the success, or lack thereof, of Mariel refugees in comparison with that of previous generations of Cuban exiles. She focuses upon these individuals in Miami, Tampa, and various locales in the Northeast, as well as in the Los Angeles area. Although her research does not break down economic and occupational results down by individual locale, her conclusion does support Clayson's analysis for Las Vegas Marielitos. In summary, Hayes Skop notes that the white Cuban refugees in her study "are replicating the time-honored 'Cuban success story' of economic advancement, although perhaps at a slower rate than . . . earlier compatriots. Many nonwhite Mariels . . . while making some headway economically, are destined for a different path where advancement come less easily and where struggles are more frequent" (Skop, "Segmented Paths," pp. 74–75).

PUERTO RICANS IN THE WEST SINCE 1980

An examination of 2000 federal census materials reveals that, not surprisingly, California contained the largest Puerto Rican population of all states in the U.S. West; with a total of 140,570 boriquas (Census Bureau, Census 2000 Summary File 1, Hispanic or Latino by Type table for California). Other states with substantial numbers include Texas (with 69,504), Hawaii (30,005), Washington (16,140), and Colorado (12,993). Surprisingly, given such substantial numbers, we were unable to locate any research on this group in western states other than Hawaii and California. Therefore, and unfortunately, this section will be brief, dealing mainly with the existence of Puerto Rican organizations in various states of the West, as well as some anecdotal evidence, primarily from boriqua life in California and Hawaii.

The most thorough coverage regarding western Puerto Rican history since 1980 is offered through a series of articles that appeared in a special issue of *El Centro: Journal of Puerto Rican Studies,* published in the spring of 2001. Of these, the essay "Borinki Identity in Hawai'i: Present and Future," by Iris López and David Forbes, is most complete in examining circumstances for this comunidad over the past twenty-five years.

The Lopez and Forbes piece provides a brief overview of some of the activities of the various Puerto Rican organizations (such as the United Puerto Rican Association of Hawaii and the Puerto Rican Cultural Heritage Society). These and other island-based entities continue to stress aspects of boriqua ethnicity through educational programs, cultural affairs (such as Three Kings Day parades in Honolulu), and sport leagues. The most significant undertaking in recent years was the centennial celebration in 2000, designed to commemorate the arrival of the first Puerto Rican immigrants in Hawai'i in 1900–1901. Lopez and Forbes summarize the overall efforts of the various groups as aimed at "perpetuating cultural pride [rather] than . . . organizing Puerto Ricans politically and lobbying for their interests" (López and Forbes, "Borinki Identity in Hawai'i," p. 115).

The situation in California is similar. An on-line listing of Puerto Rican clubs and associations based in the Golden State revealed five groups, primarily based in the San Jose area. The oldest include the Club Cívico Social Puertorriqueño (started in 1966) and the Western Regional Puerto Rican Council (which began operation in 1972). Both are involved in charitable work, the promotion of educational achievement (through the issuing of scholarships) for boriqua youths, and cultural festivities such as the Día de San Juan festival and Three Kings Day parades. In addition to ethnic undertakings, however, the comunidad in California has also managed to flex a bit of political muscle, helping to move two Puerto Rican women, Lillian Barn and Yvette del Prado, into superintendent positions at two northern California school system during the 1980s.

The final bit of information on Puerto Ricans in the West comes from Texas, which is home to almost 70,000 boriquas (Census Bureau, Census 2000 Summary File 1, Hispanic or Latino by Type table for Texas). The activities of these Lone Star State associations are similar to that of their Hawai'i and California brethren; they aim to promote island culture, music, dance (here, in particular, it is important to note the existence of companies such as the Ballet Folklorico Borinken, the Nuestras Raices company based in San Antonio, and a similar group, Puerto Rican Folkloric Dance, headquartered in Austin), heritage, and education for community youth. In addition, there exist Puerto Rican civic and social groups in both Dallas and El Paso as well.

SALVADORANS AND GUATEMALANS: HISPANIC NEWCOMERS TO THE AMERICAN WEST

Two recent studies, joint efforts of the Tomas Rivera Policy Institute and the NALEO Educational Fund, provide an effective overview of the newest Latino populations, Salvadorans and Guatemalans, to arrive in the U.S. West, specifically, in the city of Los Angeles.

In the first study on people from El Salvador and Guatemala in Los Angeles, entitled "Constructing the Los Angeles Area Latino Mosaic: A Demographic Portrait of Guatemalans and Salvadorans in Los Angeles," the researchers explain that their goal is "to present baseline data on the sociodemographic indicators, economic status, labor force participation, and immigration . . . for these two populations" (Tomas Rivera Policy Institute, "Constructing the Los Angeles Area Latino Mosaic," p. 2). Among the key statistics presented are the following: (1) in 1990, the estimated population of Guatemalans in the metropolis was 127,000, and Salvadorans totaled 250,000; (2) very few of these individuals were born in the United States (only about 1 in 6); (3) the average age of both groups was twenty-six, much younger than the local African American population (by six years) and the white population (by thirteen years); (4) Guatemalans and Salvadorans in Los Angeles are very likely to have fewer than eight years of education; (5) almost all of the Guatemalans and Salvadorans in the city speak Spanish at home (more than 96 percent); (6) both groups have very high labor force participation rates; (7) the median individual salaries of members of both groups tend to be lower than that of whites, other Hispanics, and African Americans; (8) the percentage of home ownership is quite low by comparison with other ethnic groups; (9) as of the early 1990s, very few Guatemalans and Salvadorans in Los Angeles had become citizens of the United States (Tomas Rivera Policy Institute, "Constructing the Los Angeles Area Latino Mosaic," pp. 4–20). Though an examination of these figures tells us much about daily life in these comunidades, they really should not come as a surprise. The multitudes of Guatemalans and Salvadorans in

Los Angeles are beginning the same process that other ethnic groups have lived through (some would say endured) in this country in previous centuries.

The second study, entitled "Diversifying the Los Angeles Latino Mosaic: Salvadoran and Guatemalan Leaders' Assessment of Community Public Policy Needs," provides a synopsis of the developing leadership and organizational structure of both communities, as well as detailing the services that the cadres believe are necessary to improve circumstances for constituents. Not surprisingly, given the figures presented above, the public policy needs of both comunidades include the following: (1) increasing vocational training and other educational initiatives; (2) improving circumstances in the work place; (3) dealing with the violence among the various Latino youth groups, both in schools and neighborhoods; (4) finding ways to foster acculturation to American society, and (5) improving relations with local political and police officials.

Additionally, and much to their credit, both Salvadorans and Guatemalans had established by the mid-1990s a wide range of self-help organizations (researchers counted a total of eighty-nine different groups) designed to maintain their cultures, provide social services, and promote localized economic development. Among the most significant of these entities for Salvadorans are CARECEN (the Central American Resource Center), an immigrant rights advocacy organization, and COMUNIDADES (an umbrella group that brings together a collection of more than twenty "hometown associations" representing communities from all over El Salvador). Guatemalans have established similar entities, although their hometown groups tend to be divided into *ladino* (mestizo) and indigenous associations.

CONCLUSION

The dramatic growth of Latino populations, both documented and undocumented, in the U.S. West during the last twenty-five years has had both positive and negative impacts on the region's social and economic development. Since 1980, millions of hard working men, women, and children have come to the West in search of their slice of the American dream. These people have contributed much toil and sweat to further develop the region's resources. Though many arrived through legal means, a substantial percentage of them have broken U.S. law in order to arrive at the colossus of the north. This reality, in conjunction with associated increases in social costs, has stimulated much bitterness and debate among the inhabitants of western states, particularly in those areas that directly border Mexico. Further, the demands of academicians and ethnic activists since 1980 that the majority accept this uncontrolled and diverse wave has stimulated a negative, and often bone-headed and even violent, backlash against Latinos. In the final chapter of this work, we turn to an examination of the historical events that have resulted from the increased tensions, debates, and misunderstandings among the Spanish-speaking and other peoples living in the modern U.S. West.

BIBLIOGRAPHIC ESSAY

The *Washington Times* article we cite at the very start of this chapter was accessed at the following Web site: www.frontpagemag.com/Articles/Printable.asp? ID=14753. In this chapter we once again used Richard White's *"It's Your Misfortune and None of My Own": A New History of the American West* (Norman: University of Oklahoma Press, 1991) for broad coverage of the economic and social trends occurring in the West during the last decades of the twentieth century. One of the key points that White mentions is the increasing level of urbanization within the entire region, and, as other scholars have noted, the high percentage of Hispanics who lived in the metropolitan areas of the West.

In recent years, academicians and public policy researchers have noted not only the urbanization (and suburbanization) of Spanish speakers, but also the increased national and ethnic diversity (especially the increasing numbers of Guatemalans and Salvadorans) among the men, women, and children who now inhabit the barrios of cities such as Los Angeles and Houston. For more information on this topic, please see the following: Harry Pachon, "Diversifying the Los Angeles Area Latino Mosaic: Salvadoran and Guatemalan Leaders' Assessment of Community Public Policy Needs" (Claremont, CA: Tomas Rivera Policy Institute, 1997); "Constructing the Los Angeles Area Latino Mosaic: A Demographic Portrait of Guatemalans and Salvadorans in Los Angeles" (Claremont: Tomas Rivera Policy Institute, 1997); Daniel E. Arreola, "Mexican Americans," in *Ethnicity in Contemporary America: A Geographic Appraisal,* edited by Jesse O. McKee (Lanham, MD: Rowman and Littlefield, 2000); and Roberto Suro, *Strangers among Us: Latino Lives in a Changing America* (New York: Vintage Books, 1999).

For more information on the tendency of Mexican Americans and recent immigrants (primarily from Mexico, but from other Central American nations as well) in the past two or three decades to move to more rural locations, please see the following (by no means an exhaustive list): William Kandel and John Cromartie, "New Patterns of Hispanic Settlement in Rural America," Rural Development Research Report number 99 (Washington DC: United States Department of Agriculture, Economic Research Service, May 2004); Jorge Iber, "Mexican Workers in Utah: Life and Labor in Two Tourist Towns," *Journal of the West* 40, no. 2 (Spring 2001); Hal Rothman, *Devil's Bargain: Tourism in the Twentieth-Century American West* (Lawrence: University Press of Kansas, 1998).

After our brief examination of where Hispanics lived in the West during the last decades of the twentieth century, we turned to the signs of social and economic progress, as well as some of the continuing concerns and problems, which affected the lives of this population. The first topic examined was the area of educational attainment. Some of the works consulted included the following: Jorge Chapa and Richard R. Valencia, "Latino Population Growth, Demographic Characteristics, and Educational Segregation: An Examination of Recent Trends," *Hispanic Journal of Behavioral Sciences* 15, no. 2 (May 1993); Richard R. Valencia, "Inequalities and the Schooling of Minority Students in Texas: Historical and Contemporary Conditions," *Hispanic Journal of Behavioral Sciences* 22, no. 4 (November 2000); Louis G. Tornatzky, Celina Torres, and Traci L. Caswell, "Education," in United Way of Greater Los Angeles, *Latino Scorecard 2003: Grading the American Dream* (Los Angeles, CA: United Way of Greater Los Angeles, 2004); Jorge Iber, *Hispanics in the Mormon Zion, 1912–1999* (College Station: Texas A&M University Press, 2001); Gary Orfield, Daniel Losen, Johanna Wald, and Christopher B. Swanson, "Losing Our Future: How Minority Youth Are Being Left Behind by the Graduation Rate Crisis" (Cambridge, MA: Civil Rights Project at Harvard University, 2004); National Council of La Raza, "State of Hispanic America" (Washington, DC: National Council of La Raza, 2004); Arturo González, *Mexican Americans and the U.S. Economy: The Quest for Buenos Dias* (Tucson: University of Arizona Press, 2002); Pew Hispanic Center, "Texas Labor and Educational Outcomes, 1995–2000" (Washington, DC: Pew Hispanic Center, 2001); and "Special Report: Academe's Hispanic Future," *Chronicle of Higher Education,* November 28, 2003.

The next topic examined was the economic development of the Spanish-surnamed population in the years since 1980. Among the works consulted in this section were the following: Richard Griswold del Castillo, "Latinos and the New Immigration: Mainstreaming and Polarization," Renato Rosaldo Lecture Series Monograph (Tucson: University of Arizona, 1992–1993); Jorge Iber, *Hispanics in the Mormon Zion, 1912–1999* (College Station: Texas A&M University Press, 2001); Marta Tienda, "Latinos and the American Pie: Can Latinos Achieve Economic Parity?" *Hispanic Journal of Behavioral Sciences* 17, no. 4 (November 1995); Daniel D. Arreola, "Mexican Americans," in *Ethnicity in Contemporary America: A Geographical Appraisal,* edited by Jesse O. McKee (Lanham, MD:

Rowman and Littlefield, 2000); Arturo González, *Mexican Americans and the U.S. Economy: The Quest for Buenos Días* (Tucson: University of Arizona Press, 2002); Joel Kotkin and Erika Ozuna, "Economic Development," in the United Way of Greater Los Angeles, "Latino Scorecard 2003: Grading the American Dream," (Los Angeles, CA: United Way of Greater Los Angeles, 2004); Rakesh Kochhar, "The Wealth of Hispanic Households: 1996–2002" (Washington DC: Pew Hispanic Center, 2004); the materials from the Hispanic American Center for Economic Research (HACER) can be found at the following Web sites: http://www .hacer.org/US2002.php; http://www.hacer.org/US85.php; and http://www .hacer.org/US004.php.

The next discussion focused on Hispanics and access to health care in the U.S. West. Among the works consulted here were the following: Intercultural Cancer Council (ICC), "Hispanic/Latinos and Cancer," which can be accessed at http://www.iccnetwork.org/cancerfacts/cfs4.htm; Pew Hispanic Center, "Health Care Experiences: Survey Brief," March 2004, which can be accessed at http://www.pewhispanic.org; Pew Hispanic Center, "Hispanic Health: Divergent and Changing," January 2002, this report can be accessed at http://www .pewhispanic.org; David E. Hayes-Bautista, Mariam I. Kahramanian, and Cristina Gamboa, "Health," in the United Way of Greater Los Angeles, "Latino Scorecard 2003: Grading the American Dream" (Los Angeles, CA: United Way of Greater Los Angeles, 2004); and Adela de la Torre and Antonio Estrada, *Mexican Americans and Health: Sana! Sana!* (Tucson: University of Arizona Press, 2001).

There are many excellent studies about the role of Hispanics in the politics of the U.S. West since the end of the Chicano/a era. Among the materials consulted for this section were the following: *Chicano Politics and Society in the Late Twentieth Century,* edited by David Montejano (Austin: University of Texas Press, 1999). From this book, we used materials from the following essays: David Montejano, "Conclusion: On the Future of Anglo-Mexican Relations in the United States"; Rodolfo Rosales, "Personality and Style in San Antonio Politics: Henry Cisneros and Bernardo Eureste, 1975–1985"; and Martin Sánchez Jankowski, "'Where Have all the Nationalists Gone?': Change and Persistence in Radical Political Attitudes Among Chicanos, 1976–1986." Lastly, we also utilized Ernesto Chávez, '*My People First!' 'Mi Raza Primero': Nationalism, Identity, and Insurgency in the Chicano Movement in Los Angeles, 1966–1978* (Berkeley: University of California Press, 2002).

In this chapter, we provided a brief overview of the estimated numbers of immigrants, both legal and illegal, many of whom have settled in the West since 1980. Some of the works consulted for this section of the chapter included the following: David M. Reimers, *Unwelcome Strangers: American Identity and the Turn against Immigration* (New York: Columbia University Press, 1998); Jorge Durand, Douglas S. Massey, and Fernando Charvet, "The Changing Geography of Mexican Immigration to the United States, 1910–1996," *Social Science Quarterly* 81, no. 1 (March 2000); Robert C. Dash and Robert E. Hawkinson, "Mexicans and 'Business as Usual': Small Town Politics in Oregon," *Aztlán* 26, no. 2 (Fall 2001); and Jeffery S. Passel, Randy Capps, and Michael Fix, "Undocumented Immigrants: Facts and Figures" (Urban Institute Immigration Studies Program, January 12, 2004).

For the section on Cuban Americans in the late twentieth-century West, we utilized the following: William Clayson, "Cubans in Las Vegas: Ethnic Identity, Success, and Urban Life in the Late Twentieth Century," *Nevada Historical Society Quarterly* 38, no. 1 (Spring 1995); Richard Ferro, "Perceptions of Discrimination: Cubans in the Pacific Northwest," Ph.D. dissertation, University of Washington, 1996; Emily Hayes Skop, "Segmented Paths: The Geographic and Social Mobility of Mariel Exiles," Master's thesis, Arizona State University, 1997.

The information for the section on Puerto Ricans in the post-1980 West was gleaned from the following: Iris López and David Forbes, "Borinki Identity in Hawai'i: Present and Future," *El Centro: Journal for Puerto Rican Studies* 13, no. 1 (Spring 2001); Jorge Piñero, "Extended Roots: San Jose, California," in *Extended Roots: From Hawaii to New York, Migraciones Puertorriqueñas á los Estados Unidos,* edited by Blanca Vasquez (New York: Hunter College, 1985). Information on the various contemporary organizations for Puerto Ricans in the West came from the directory at http://www.elboriqua.com/Directory.html.

The materials for the biographical sketch of Eliud Pete Suazo were drawn from the following: Jorge Iber, *Hispanics in the Mormon Zion, 1912–1999* (College Station: Texas A&M University Press, 2001); Greg Burton and Jacob Santini, "ATV Accident Claims Suazo," *Salt Lake Tribune,* August 21, 2001, A1; Greg Burton and Jesus López, "Remembering a Favorite Son," *Salt Lake Tribune,* August 22, 2001, A1; Greg Burton, "Suazo Remembered for Reaching Out," *Salt Lake Tribune,* August 25, 2001, A1; Leslie Mitchell, "Suazo Business Center Opens," *Salt Lake Tribune,* August 22, 2003, C7; Paul Rolly, "Suazo's Disarming Demeanor Brought GOP to His Side," *Salt Lake Tribune,* August 26, 2001, AA3; obituary for Eliud Pete Suazo, *Salt Lake Tribune,* August 22, 2001, A9.

HISPANIC
HISTORIOGRAPHY AND
CURRENT ISSUES

As has been made plain by the bibliographic essays that follow each chapter, the body of historical literature on Hispanics is extensive. To be sure, Mexican Americans constitute the major focus of research on Hispanics, and for obvious reasons. Compared to that of other Latino subgroups, the history of Mexican Americans is a lengthy one, extending from the colonial era to the present, and it has been the subject of study for a longer period of time. By now, historians have probed into just about every aspect of the Mexican American experience, and the several monographs, articles and dissertations on the topic have not only situated the history of Hispanic Mexicans in the context of the history of the U.S. West but have explored its importance in relation to other developments in the West, such as violence, urbanization, regionalism, and labor movements. Chicano/a history, as the study of Mexican Americans is sometimes called, is today commonly incorporated into school curricula, conference programs, and academic anthologies written on the West. Awards and other forms of recognition won by Chicano scholars continue to increase the perceived legitimacy of this relatively fresh and exciting field of study.

Many are the issues that keep Hispanics before the public spotlight. On the one hand, Hispanics make themselves noticeable by bringing before the public forum political and social concerns apropos to the group. On the other hand, defenders of tradition react in fear that Hispanics imperil American institutions and established social conventions. Among other things, these guardians of an old America attempt to regulate immigration from Latin America, question the use of the Spanish language in formal settings, and launch unrelenting attacks on affirmative action policies. Certainly, Americans in this camp do not take lightly to what is termed the "Browning of America."

Yet, there are others in the West (and in the rest of the nation for that matter) that see possible benefits from this so-called "browning." Advertisers target the growing Hispanic market, the food industry too eagerly co-opts varieties of Hispanic foods, and musicians keep adding a Latin sound to their repertoire. With growing visibility in the marketplace, as well as in the political arena, the corporate world, and in the educational system, aspects of Hispanic life demand better answers from academicians to new and old questions. Those issues in continued need of study are discussed later in this chapter.

HISTORIOGRAPHY

Historians have focused almost exclusively on Mexican Americans until relatively recently, and so in what follows, Hispanic will essentially mean Mexican American unless otherwise indicated. There is general agreement that the initial serious study of Mexican Americans started during the Chicano/a movement of the 1960s and 1970s. Before then, professional historians gave little consideration to those of Mexican descent in the West. Scholars did focus on the Spanish presence in the borderlands, though the attention tended to be on exploration, administration, and the founding of frontier institutions. For many of these pre-1960s writers, the history of Spain and Mexico in the Far North seemed to have ceased with the successful Texas war for independence in 1836 and with the Treaty of Guadalupe Hidalgo of 1848.

Several factors explain the neglect of the post-1836 and post-1848 Spanish-Mexican experience. To begin with, many Americans looked upon Hispanics as stepchildren of society, as constituting a proletarian class, as a people unworthy of political and social equality, and by extension, as a people with no significant history. Sociologists, anthropologists, psychologists, and educators in that epoch saw Mexican Americans not much differently. Recent studies show the social science literature of that period as considering Mexican Americans to be culturally and intellectually disadvantaged, responding to obstacles before them with acquiescence and surrender. Historians believed Mexicans to have been nonplayers in western history, as were other peoples of color like African Americans and Asians. Historical perspectives that recognized the agency of ordinary individuals, furthermore, did not come into their own until sometime after the mid–twentieth century. Any history written on Mexican Americans in the West before the 1960s came from the pen of lay historians such as Benjamín Read (of New Mexico) or J. T. Canales (of Texas), from a handful of scholars (among them historian Carlos E. Castañeda and folklorist Aurelio M. Espinosa) in the academy, or from journalists like Carey McWilliams, credited with writing the first significant history book on Mexican Americans, *North from Mexico: The Spanish-speaking People of the United States* (Philadelphia: J. B. Lipppincott, 1949).

During the decade of the 1960s, however, various currents merged that gave significant impetus to the study of Hispanics as a group. Primary among these was the Chicano movement, a liberal (and at times radical) political eruption within Hispanic communities that among other things, called for school curricula to incorporate Chicanos into the pages of U.S. history. The general liberalism of the age acted as a second catalyst promoting research on Mexican Americans, as it fostered a more sensitive understanding of oppressed people in history. Innovative historical approaches during that time further expedited the process of historical inquiry among Mexican Americans, as now ordinary people (such as Hispanics) were thought to merit as much attention as the high and the mighty.

So what thoughts did the first scholars writing on Hispanics have of them as a group? Some of the earliest writers in the 1970s saw Mexican Americans as part of an immense working class, held captive in a colonial dependence. According to this view, Mexican Americans became colonial subjects of the United States following the conquest of the West. Since 1848, the colonial model posited, Mexican Americans had been an oppressed group, victimized by Anglo discrimination, political disfranchisement, and labor exploitation. Despite their grim circumstances, Mexican Americans counteracted victimization, fending off domination by individual acts of resistance, community uprisings, and labor activism. The

most prominent book to advance this thesis was Rodolfo Acuña's *Occu-*
pied America: The Chicanos' Struggle toward Liberation (San Francisco:
Canfield Press, 1972).

During this initial phase of Chicano history, not all historians viewed
Mexican Americans as a monolithic population and one almost helpless
to resist the racial order. In their quest to recover Chicano history and to
portray Mexicans as historical actors, some historians offered countless
examples showing Hispanics participating in the West's development,
practicing free enterprise by embarking on successful business ventures,
or freely advancing political platforms intended to improve circumstances
for local neighborhoods or villages, all of which would not have been possible under a colonial structure. Other writers saw differentiation within
Mexican American communities, noting variation in the experiences of
people living in specific geographic regions of the West, identifying disparate levels of acculturation and degrees of education, seeing Hispanics
in sundry occupations including professional ones, and observing divergent family structures. Since such findings conflicted with the portrayal
of an inert, apathetic, and homogeneous community, writers suggested,
the understanding of the Chicano experience as well as the applicability
of the colonial model seemed in need of rethinking.

Diversity indeed came to be a key historical description of the Hispanic community during the 1980s and 1990s, as scholars explored
newer themes and topics. For one thing, a middle class seemed always to
have existed, though it had assumed contradictory historical roles, at
times speaking in behalf of the Hispanic community, at times accommodating itself to white society for the sake of material progress. Clashes between working class folks and those of middling status seemed common,
especially during the period of the Chicano movement, when youthful
militants referred to their elders, who cautioned patience and modera-
tion, as vendidos (sellouts). Historians found further diversity among
generations, as the younger set, at least up to the 1950s, had almost always quarreled with the nationalist postures of their parents and grandparents, particularly when the older group was foreign born. Within the
ranks of community members, furthermore, there prevailed perceptible
variation in language usage and fluency (in both Spanish and English), in
entrepreneurial spirit, in party politics, and in rural versus urban orienta-

tion. Mexicans who had migrated to the urban areas of the Midwest, or to communities in the Northwest, had pursued multifaceted strategies in adapting to their surroundings. This steady stream of studies showed the initial impression of a monolithic Hispanic community to have been patently distorted.

The publication of these stimulating and sophisticated studies also led historians to revisit the old supposition that the history of Hispanics started at the ending of the Mexican War. Earlier, historians had pointed to the Treaty of Guadalupe Hidalgo of 1848 as the pivotal event that had transformed the history of Mexico in the borderlands to that of the history of the U.S. West, with the old pobladores (settlers) becoming U.S. citizens that year. But some scholars noted that to divide Chicano history then made little sense, for no disconnection occurred between one era and the other. Social and cultural tenets prevalent among the pobladores prior to 1848 crossed sovereignties unaltered, for instance, though the Mexicans in the conquered territories made appropriate adjustments thereafter.

In New Mexico specifically, Ramón A. Gutiérrez's award-winning *When Jesus Came, the Corn Mothers Went Away: Marriage, Sexuality, and Power in New Mexico, 1500–1846* (Stanford, CA: Stanford University Press, 1991) noted that the colonial caste system that separated the Spanish well-to-do from the lower class and the sense of honor and family values that defined gender roles hardly ceased functioning in 1848. Then, as has recently been shown by literary scholars, among them Louis Gerard Mendoza in *Historia: The Literary Making of Chicana and Chicano History* (College Station: Texas A&M University Press, 2001), the writings of novelists and poets do not recognize the same watershed dates as do those who make up the historical community. Instead, fiction writers treat emotions, character types, and story lines, with no particular historical demarcation in mind. Another school of thought, advanced by Gilbert G. Gonzalez and Raul A. Fernandez in *A Century of Chicano History: Empire, Nations, and Migration* (New York: Routledge, 2003), points to the year 1900 as a more accurate date for the key turning point in Chicano history, for it was in the early years of the twentieth century that immigration, technology, and urbanization produced a society in the West clearly distinguishable from the pastoral society of the preceding century.

The rise of Chicana history during this era also helped amend the old periodization. Historians who focused on Hispanic women's history noted that the oppression (or "colonization") of Hispanas did not begin in 1848, nor was it solely a tenet of Anglo American ideology. If women had always been victimized by male oppression, then the history of Chicanas ought to be pushed back, at least going back to the period of the Spanish conquest of Mexico (1519–1521), taking in all of European history, when Spanish males began the subordination of mestizas, that is, the female progeny of their sexual contacts with Indian women.

The study of women during the 1980s and 1990s went far beyond questions of turning points in the Chicano narrative. By the latter decades of the twentieth century, indeed, historians had attributed to women a legitimate place in the historical record. The stream of new studies on women, such as Vicki L. Ruiz's *From out of the Shadows: Mexican Women in Twentieth Century America* (New York: Oxford University Press, 1998), found them active participants in neighborhood politics, volunteer projects, church parishes, farm and ranch management, labor unionism, and on other fronts. Historians discovered women pursuing various avenues, at times cautiously, at others boldly, in efforts to end domination by men. Defiance of male (and parental) authority was manifest in the adoption of new fashions (perhaps bobbed hair in the 1920s, the miniskirt in the 1960s, or the body piercing of today), in discourse contained in literary works by women, in frank talk about sexual orientation, in the debate over women's issues at conferences, and in other arenas. After the 1980s, historians had shattered the old stereotype of passive Mexican women content with their role as housewives, and a more nuanced image of women had emerged.

Increasingly, researchers in the 1980s and 1990s came to accept the history of Mexican Americans as resembling that of other groups also contending for a livelihood in the West. It was true that the Mexican experience had been shaped by unique forces, among them racism, lynching, and disfranchisement. But like their counterparts around them (including Native Americans, Anglo American citizens, African Americans, foreign-born Europeans, and Asians), Mexican-origin residents had survived frontier uncertainty by relying on time-tested strategies. Like other inhabitants of the West, furthermore, Hispanics had introduced and pre-served long-lasting social and cultural institutions, such as the Catholic Church. Following the Civil War, literate members of Hispanic society had founded an increased number of newspapers, as another example, which they used as a medium for disseminating their thoughts on issues of the day, if not their responses to Anglo American governance. Further, Mexican Americans had sustained an ethnic lifestyle that, while not al-ways the best option for success in an Anglo milieu, served them well in the competition for human existence. On the other hand, historians began to point out the problems within Hispanic society, just as they did with other groups in the West, specifically noting the way rancheros had rejected the need to modernize their estates, community members had engaged in political infighting and even internecine violence, and His-panics had not always engaged in good faith efforts to improve their con-dition in a bountiful land. Overall, historians now viewed their Hispanic subjects in a more realistic light than had their predecessors.

What accounted for the revisionism that occurred during the wan-ing decades of the twentieth century? Several things did. For one, the general conservatism that followed the 1960s and 1970s led to a re-assessment of some of the approaches that had driven earlier interpreta-tions, among them the colonial model, the focus on racism to explain Chicano subordination, and the preoccupation with the labor exploita-tion that was held to account for perpetual poverty within colonias. Fresh perspectives and techniques in the 1980s and 1990s now comple-mented the New Social History of the 1970s, permitting historians to probe into neglected dimensions of Chicano communities. Armed with revisionist premises, the benefit of accumulated knowledge, and of course computer skills, researchers launched investigations into episodes of collective dissent, intellectual currents, demographic shifts, and an array of other occurrences to find precedent for just about every happening in their own day. Folklorists, anthropologists, ethnologists, cultural geographers, and literary scholars, among others, chimed in with their own methodologies, theories, and frameworks to recapture and reconstruct the many-sided Chicano past. By the 1990s, the nu-merous advances made in Chicano history had rendered archaic old views that had prevailed unchallenged for generations among educators, sociologists, and anthropologists.

Interdisciplinary approaches, postmodern analyses, feminist perspectives, and gay and lesbian viewpoints, among other avenues of study, have continued to shape an image of Hispanics as a multidimensional group not to be captured by facile caricature. This portrayal comes from the works of senior scholars who pioneered the field, as well as from a younger cohort whose formative years were the conservative or moderate post-1970s. Raised in an era when institutional obstacles to upward mobility were crumbling, the newer generations of scholars tend to pass over older issues, such as racism, and instead consider questions of more recent vintage, among them transnationalism, identity formation across borders and time, and the place of entertainment (as for example, the theater, athletics, music, and dancing).

As has our book, historians in recent years have also acknowledged the presence of various Latino group in the West, and have incorporated them into the general configuration of Hispanic history. Latino scholars are increasingly turning their attention to the immigrants' respective country of origin (be it Puerto Rico, Cuba, or Mexico) to better understand and explain each group's history in the West. They have observed the similarity in the way peoples from different Latin American countries have been incorporated into the United States, that is, by imperial conquest (Puerto Rico, or the U.S. Southwest) or through economic colonialism (as in the case of Mexico or the Central American countries). Another common ingredient among the history of Latinos in the West is immigration from abroad (rather than from east of the Mississippi River), especially since the last decades of the twentieth century. Further attracting contemporary scholars are such issues as intermarriage among the several Latino groups, interaction among Hispanics in social settings such as the baseball diamond, and the distinctions made (or not made) among them, considering the wide variations in racial constitution prevalent in Latin American countries.

Historical thought on Hispanics has indeed made much headway over the last few decades, recognizing the role Hispanics have played in transforming society as bona fide historical players and acknowledging their membership in an increasingly multicultural setting. It might seem that it is time to end the study of Hispanics as a separate group, but in fact the part Hispanics have played in the so-called culture wars of recent years suggests that all too many Americans are still not ready to accept Hispanics completely as bona fide Americans. Before we turn to the future of the study of Hispanics in the West, we must consider the conflicts that show so clearly the need for that study.

HISPANICS AND THE CULTURE WARS

The numerous changes that occurred within Hispanic communities in the West following the 1960s and 1970s engendered dismay among many Americans. Those of a conservative political bent in particular worried about the threat posed to the old WASP America by the growing political power of Hispanics, a fear made even more real by the Latino population boom discussed in chapter 8. Since the 1960s and 1970s, Hispanics had made strides in numerous areas, persuading mainstream society to implement innovative educational curricula for Hispanic children, establish race-based admissions policies, launch multicultural studies programs, translate official documents into Spanish, and so on. Was this the old America, many (including Hispanics) wondered? Should Latinos, as with immigrants before them, not be expected to conform and accept a conventional American lifestyle based on old-fashioned U.S. values and standards? The anxiety many felt about the course of events involving Mexican Americans and other Latinos eventually manifested itself in a racial backlash focused on immigration, assimilation, the use of English in public discourse, bilingual education, affirmative action, and other Hispanic-specific social issues. The culture wars of the late twentieth and early twenty-first century expanded to include Hispanics.

California became the center of contention regarding immigration, with the debate spilling over to neighboring Arizona. Opponents of immigration blamed the Latino foreign-born for taking scarce jobs away from U.S. citizens, burdening the welfare system, increasing the cost of education, contributing to crime, and in general leading the country toward moral waywardness. In 1994, therefore, California voters approved the Save Our State initiative (known more widely as Proposition 187). Of those who voted, 60 percent (including about 23 percent of Latino voters) endorsed the contents of the measure, which mandated that social services and schooling be denied to undocumented residents of California. The proposition also called on teachers and others working in social service agencies to disclose the presence of those in the country illegally.

Critics of Proposition 187 marshaled a strong case (both during the campaign and after) against the plan, affirming its unfairness. By no means did the immigrants threaten the American fiber, they noted, as most newcomers generally expressed sincere appreciation for the country they had just entered and were committed to upholding mainstream values. Instead of being economic hazards, immigrants actually contributed to the country's economic stability by assuming job positions shunned by others. Immigrants served as maids, hotel and restaurant workers, construction hands, roofers, plumbers' helpers, field laborers, and the like. Moreover, the immigrants paid their fair share of taxes that sustained the public good. The courts listened and agreed, declaring that the provisions of Proposition 187 counteracted guarantees extended by federal statutes and that services that were prohibited by the recently approved plan could not be denied the immigrants. But by no means was this the last fight over the issue of immigration, for in 2004 the people of Arizona backed their own proposition containing restrictions similar to those approved a decade earlier in the Golden State.

The question of Latino assimilation (or lack of it) also preoccupied Americans who advocated cultural homogenization for the country. For their own good, the argument went, Hispanics should accept U.S. cultural conventions and values, lest they be perceived as stepchildren of society and lest they themselves feel that they were less than full citizens. If people made the decision to live in the United States, then logic dictated that they embrace the core culture of their adopted country and reject allegiance to those institutions and traditions left behind. Once immigrants opted for assimilation they would become—having acquired essential skills and familiarity with U.S. institutions—worthy rivals in a highly competitive U.S. society. Failure to accept mainstream culture doomed one to a lower standard of living, political disfranchisement, and the reputation of an ingrate. Society should not have a responsibility to help those unwilling to accept the tenets of the host culture. Government certainly ought not to be a party to insuring the perpetuation of a nonnative way of life, as it did if it accepted the obligation to translate political literature into Spanish. Should people wish to maintain the old culture, let them do so in the privacy of their homes, their churches, and Hispanic enclaves (if that was where they opted to live).

Critics of such an ethnocentric stance advanced persuasive arguments in behalf of retaining Hispanic culture. For one thing, Spanish-Mexican civilization, they insisted, was almost indigenous to the West, having existed in areas such as New Mexico for almost two centuries before Americans superimposed their own way of life on that of Mexicans. There existed a continuous link between Hispanic settlements of the earliest entradas (expeditions) to present-day communities, so that if Hispanics wanted to be Hispanics, what right did outsiders have to demand assimilation? Mainstream culture inclined to be abrasive, callous, and judgmental, whereas the culture of the home surroundings tended to be gentle, nurturing, and compassionate. A Hispanic environment served as a refuge and retreat from an otherwise unkind world. Why abandon it?

A Hispanic preference for maintaining their home language, at the expense of mastering English, further infuriated Anglophiles. During the late 1970s, interest groups predicting dire consequences for the "balkanization" of the United States raised alarms. English served as the language of government, education, and formal communication, they declared. It functioned as a venue unifying millions of people under one flag. Why strive to maintain another language that did not equip citizens with the proper tools essential for life struggles in the United States? Furthermore, it was the language of red-blooded Americans. To renounce the importance of English, or to subordinate it to a foreign tongue, was to reject the country that extended its beneficence to all, including immigrants.

By the end of the 1980s, some twenty states had enacted English-only statutes. California seemed to have attracted the most attention in its anti-foreign language stance. Voters there in November 1986 by a large percentage approved of Proposition 63, which made English the official state language.

But Hispanics determined on loyalty to the language of their upbringing had answered English-only proponents with reasoned conviction. First, the Spanish language buffered cultural chauvinism, shielding Hispanics from cultural imperialists determined to eradicate ways of life that did not fit into the American milieu. Second, Spanish speakers should be commended for their bilingualism and not criticized for it; after all, did not most European countries encourage mastery of more than one language? To belittle Spanish was to suggest the superiority of English. Not only should American society commend the knowledge of Spanish, but government had the duty to assure its usage. After all, there existed inherent guarantees in the Constitution protecting one's right to expression. Realistically, most Latinos would settle for a compromise, accepting bilingualism as a fair concession to their opponents if critics would only stop their unreasonable onslaught.

The English-only movement quite naturally extended to education programs such as bilingual instruction. Opponents argued that it was not in the American tradition to financially assist a non-English speaking group to keep using a foreign language. Some of them complained that much of the teaching in bilingual programs emphasized Spanish instead of English, thereby exacerbating an already serious communications problem. They warned that bilingual education remained an untested and unproven pedagogical framework for bringing those who still speak the language that is their heritage into the mainstream. Bilingual education's adversaries remained adamant in their position that loyalty to a language other than English only fostered fragmentation. Further, they argued, fidelity to the language of the old country could only beget ethnic or nationalist sentiment, even separatist movements. As had been the case earlier with immigration and English-only, California became one of several states taking steps to discontinue bilingual education. Detractors there in 1998 sponsored Proposition 227, known officially as the English-Language Initiative for Immigrant Children. Some 60 percent of the voters approved of it, and the measure abolished bilingual education in the state. Teaching those speaking a foreign tongue would now be done through an immersion approach in an early grade; thereafter, they would be integrated into the rest of the student body. Arizona followed suit in 2000, and at the national level, the Bilingual Education Act of 1968 expired on January 8, 2002, replaced by new approaches passed by Congress to teach the foreign-born. The English Language Acquisition Act of 2002 dictated teaching solely in English.

A California State University student demonstrates during a speech given by former Ku Klux Klan leader David Duke. Duke is speaking in support of Proposition 209, which, if passed, would abolish affirmative action in the state of California. September 1996. (Kim Kulish/Corbis)

Proponents of bilingual education had offered compelling points for maintaining the program. For one thing, the approach had the beneficial effect of desegregating the schools. It offered a rational and pragmatic method of instruction for teaching those who could not understand the lessons of the classroom. Further, advocates noted, it served as a means of helping youngsters make the transition into speaking fluent English. Teaching in a person's native language would boost a student's self-esteem. To teach only in English would be demoralizing to the learner and could only foster feelings of helplessness and despair.

A further issue of debate in the 1990s and the early twenty-first century with Hispanics at its center was affirmative action. Since the 1960s, minority groups and women had pushed for ways by which government, private companies, and educational institutions might take stronger measures to ensure their inclusion in these sectors. Government bureaucracies, businesses, and university campuses had in turn implemented policies to bring about fair representation of women and minorities.

But to many, affirmative action programs just did not square with the American ethic of hard work and the philosophy of self-help. Honest and law-abiding Americans made something of themselves, not by receiving preferential treatment from those in power, but by following a regimen of industry, discipline, enterprise, and commitment to goals that often took self-sacrifice and dogged resolve to achieve. Affirmative action plans permitted the less qualified to obtain an edge over superior talent, so that students who won admission into the professional schools, or minority businessmen who received government contracts, did so due to their status in society as an "oppressed minority" and not on the basis of individual worthiness. Critics further noted that affirmative action stigmatized those who profited from it, casting them as inferior recipients lacking real merit. Furthermore, noted affirmative action program opponents, to favor one group over another because of past discriminatory practices was simply discrimination in reverse, as better-qualified whites, usually males, were at a disadvantage in recruitment or employment. Lastly, these critics warned, affirmative action was so odious to many that it could not help dividing the nation politically.

Many were the defenders of affirmative action practices. First of all, such strategies served to bring about remediation for generations of overt discrimination against people of color and of women. How else could amends be made, if not by taking extra recruitment initiatives and making aggressive attempts to assure that historically oppressed people got an even break in their wish to attain the American dream? To erase affirmative action mechanisms would mean returning to the discrimination of the old days, when minorities and women were overlooked in hiring and admission to college life. Affirmative action policies had proven effective over the decades, proponents argued. Since the 1960s, an unprecedented number of Hispanics had successfully completed their education in professional schools, and most now were contributing to the general welfare as chain store managers, attorneys, physicians, professors, teachers and administrators, and a wide range of other high-profile occupations. Many of these minority success stories involved bilingual individuals able to offer an important service to society, especially in the economic sector, where Hispanic buying power was increasing. Then, advocates of affirmative action pointed out, there existed a need everywhere to have a proper representation of the general makeup of the American population. What sense did it make to have white males in positions of influence and people of color and women relegated to secondary roles?

ALBERTO R. GONZALES, ATTORNEY GENERAL

Among westerners who reached the ultimate in political success during the early years of the twenty-first century was the Tejano Alberto R. Gonzales. Certainly, he was not the first Hispanic Texan to engage in government service at the national level. As early as the 1920s and 1930s, Alfonso S. Perales of San Antonio was a participant in diplomatic missions to Latin American countries. During the period from 1961 to 1967, Raymond L. Telles of El Paso served as ambassador to Costa Rica. In the 1960s, Henry B. González (no relation to Alberto) of San Antonio began his long career (1961–1999) as a Democratic legislator in the U.S. House of Representatives, and during the 1990s Lauro Cavazos and Henry Cisneros occupied Cabinet positions. But Alberto R. Gonzales was the first to gain an appointment as attorney general. Moreover, he did so as a Republican, while the other Hispanics in high government posts have been Democrats.

U.S. President George W. Bush looks on as Alberto Gonzales (center) *is sworn in as attorney general by Associate Supreme Court Justice Sandra Day O'Connor during a ceremony on February 14, 2005, at the Department of Justice in Washington, D.C. (Tim Sloan/AFP/Getty Images)*

Traditionally, Hispanics in Texas voted Democratic, and continued doing so even after the state went heavily Republican during the 1980s. Mexican Americans continued supporting the party of Franklin D. Roosevelt and Lyndon B. Johnson, the party responsible for Social Security, Medicare, and Head Start, pro-labor laws and civil rights legislation, for student loans and other programs designed to assist the disadvantaged and downtrodden, such as Mexican Americans.

But as did the majority of Anglo Texans, many Hispanics during the late twentieth century found appeal in the platform of the Republicans. Traditional Catholics approved of the anti-abortionist stance of the party, as did those who liked the Republicans' emphasis on family values or believed gay unions to be blasphemous. Hispanic entrepreneurs resentful of government intervention and private citizens who found talk of gun control an infringement on their constitutional rights turned Republican. Successful professionals (perhaps forgetful of the social programs responsible for their achievements and of the civil rights movements that had removed barriers to their advancement) rejected the notion of government assistance and instead accepted the dictum that anyone, despite race or ethnicity, can make it in America. Among those who accepted Republican principles was Alberto R. Gonzales.

Little in Gonzales's childhood would have predicted his rise to power. Born in 1955, he spent his early years in Houston in poverty, just as did many other Hispanic Houstonians of that generation. But following graduation, he entered the U.S. military, then attended Rice University, where in 1979 he received a degree in political science. Off to Harvard Law School he went next, receiving his J.D. degree three years later. He returned to Houston in 1982 and joined one of the most prestigious law firms in the city. He worked doggedly to earn a partnership in the firm, and at the same time he got involved in community projects, won election as president of the Houston Hispanic Bar Association (1990–1991), and (in 1992) was selected as the Outstanding Young Lawyer in Texas. Numerous other awards and recognitions came his way during this time period.

In the mid-1990s, he began the ride that would take him to Washington and the position of Attorney General. In 1995, he became general counsel to Texas governor George W. Bush, with an appointment to an interim vacancy in the Texas Supreme Court and, subsequently, an election to the Texas high court. When Governor Bush won the presidency in 2001, he took Gonzales with him as White House counsel. In February 2005, the Congress confirmed Gonzales as Attorney General.

Many thought Gonzales a model candidate for the post. The moderate stance he took while serving on the Texas Supreme Court (1999–2001) earned him backing from pro-abortion groups, for he ruled in favor of a young woman's right to have an abortion without parental knowledge. Latino leaders savored his appointment as the first top lawman. So did many of the most powerful and influential Hispanic civil rights organizations, seeing him as a sign of the success of their historic efforts to force equality upon the nation. Groups endorsing him as attorney general included the Mexican American Legal Defense and Education Fund (MALDEF), the League of United Latin American Citizens (LULAC), and the National Council of La Raza (NCLR).

Still, Gonzales faced detractors. Concerned for what his conservatism portended were those mindful of the former White House counsel's willingness to sidestep constitutional guarantees of civil rights in order to counter terrorist threats. Leftists and liberals saw him as in league with rich Republicans bent on dismantling social programs crucial to ensuring a passable way of life for the working poor. Some alarmists even saw him as part of ominous new developments in American society. The attorney general, the ranks of the Texas Rangers and Border Patrol, and the preponderance of prison staffs had once upon a time been mainly Anglos who collectively guarded white supremacy. Now by the early twenty-first century, law enforcement agencies were becoming ethnic and were being staffed by assimilated Hispanics who were being used to keep other Hispanics under control.

Gonzales the attorney general seemed a metaphor for the inner conflicts and incongruities that typified Latino communities after generations of life in the West. For decades, civil rights activists had demanded that conservative America open up doors to Hispanics in government, yet Gonzales—like other Latinos—was himself conservative. Many had argued that it made sense to elect (or appoint) persons to high places in light of demographic changes, yet Gonzales represented a Latino constituency that opposed policies that made special provisions for Hispanics to make such gains. He recognized that his ethnicity in part explained his success, yet he argued against preferential treatment, saying one's ethnic background should not be considered in advancements. The State Bar of Texas had recognized Gonzales for his legal work among the indigent, yet he had received substantial contributions from big business and from rich donors indifferent to the plight of the poor. But Gonzales's remarkable achievement could not be denied. He had seen the West as a region of boundless possibility, set his goals high, and reached them.

By the 1990s, the argument against affirmative action had persuaded many, and the most prominent revolts occurred in Texas and California. In what came to be termed the Hopwood case (March 1996), the U.S. Circuit Court of Appeals ruled that the University of Texas could no longer permit race-based preferences in an effort to achieve multicultural representation in its law school. On November 5, 1996, voters in the Golden State approved by 54 percent Proposition 209 (formally known as the California Civil Rights Initiative). Thenceforth, state-supported institutions, organizations, and establishments were to reject preferences based on race, nationality, and sex. In Texas, minority advocates scored a coup in 1997 when they got the legislature to adopt the top 10 percent plan as a replacement for the defunct affirmative action policies. Now, students graduating in the top 10 percent of their class would automatically be admitted into the state university of their choosing, including the University of Texas and Texas A&M University. Previously, the student body at these elite universities consisted of (mainly white) students who came from well-to-do backgrounds and had attended wealthy schools and were thus prepared to score well on entrance exams. The top 10 percent plan attempted to equalize the situation and diversify college campuses. But many white students still raised the specter of discrimination, and it was not long before the 10 percent plan also came under attack.

FUTURE DIRECTIONS FOR STUDYING HISPANICS

Whether seen as a people whose heritage and way of life place them outside the mainstream (as illustrated by the culture wars) or regarded as ones contributing constructively to U.S. culture, Hispanics are certain to shape the future course of American history in years to come. Because of that, they will (and should) remain a subject for investigation by academicians. Scholars, after all, devote themselves to the serious investigation of society's concerns, and Americans have indeed made Hispanics very much an issue.

In studying the group, then, older but pertinent topics should remain at the center of inquiry, among them immigration. By keeping an eye on population trends, demographers can offer insights, and even answers, to old and new questions. Why for instance, does nativism persist? Is that nativism correlated to economic downturns, or is it more associated with the West's history of racism? What are the causes for immigration? Is it poverty in the respective homeland of the immigrants, or is it the fact that countries such as Mexico have become economic colonies of the United States and simply provide a cheap labor source for Americans who need construction workers, hotel maids, farm hands, restaurant helpers, gardeners, and the like? How do the immigrants disperse? In the early twenty-first century, Hispanic newcomers to the United States headed into the South (in states such as North Carolina and Alabama), a region that they had previously avoided. Is the immigrants' preference for rural or urban areas? If Americans have ambivalent feelings about immigration, then what might be done to produce a more enlightened and compassionate immigration policy?

Since Hispanics living in the West derive from diverse nationalities, it seems wise to examine the subject of ethnicity more scrupulously. What common traits do those born in Latin America share, and how do their respective cultures differ? What does each group contribute to the American economy, or what problems does each create? Have recent arrivals in the West from places such as Puerto Rico, the Dominican Republic, and Honduras, or Cubans from Florida, settled in historically Mexican American colonias such as Los Angeles, Tucson, or San Antonio, or have they preferred other regions? Has the coming of Central Americans, Puerto Ricans, or Cuban Americans to the trans-Mississippi region caused friction with Mexican Americans, or is pan-ethnicity the rule? Scholars see pan-ethnicity as involving coexistence and cooperation among Hispanic groups of differing backgrounds. Since these groups (though each maintains its own nationality) share similar problems and concerns, they form coalitions in efforts to focus society's attention on their common needs. Have such alliance proved constructive or unsuccessful?

Women's role in history, a long-standing subject of investigation, should also remain in the forefront of analysis. Determining how women have contributed to the history of Hispanics in the West is important for a number of reasons, not the least of which is overturning the generally held view that they are submissive figures in the family and that they consequently shape a family structure that somehow departs from the Anglo American model. Though studies already exist portraying Hispanic women as successful heads of households, entrepreneurs, ranch and farm owners, community leaders, and political advocates, the topic is far from having been fully explored, and future studies will no doubt depict women as self-confident figures who contribute to family stability as do parents universally. Making women the focus of attention should not mean studying only their traditional duties as mothers and wives, but should underscore their part as determined individuals or as group activists committed to one cause or another. How have women improved community life over the generations, for instance, as promoters of quality education, as agitators for fair political representation, or as campaigners for municipal improvement? How have they kept up the religious faith of communities by their involvement in parish organizations, such as Las Guadalupanas? In short, how have women attempted their own empowerment?

If mainstream thought holds that Hispanics threaten national homogeneity by retaining homeland cultural patterns, then the current work of academicians such as sociologists, psychologists, linguists, and folklorists should persist. Over the years, social scientists have refuted a lengthy list of fallacies associated with Mexican American culture. Nevertheless, there are still those in the academic community, as well as in society at large, who insist that Hispanics are underachievers, and that they are so because of deficiencies in their value system. Are the following common assertions correct: that Hispanics constitute an inordinate number on the welfare roles, that cases of teenage pregnancies are higher among Hispanics, and that Hispanic youths are inclined to gang association? Further, is the Hispanic mind so laden with a Latin American psychological ethos that those of Hispanic descent are hampered from competing adeptly in the United States? Is speaking two languages not a hindrance to progress, especially when so many youngster mix languages in a type of Hispanic ebonics? What of the Hispanic propensity for wanting to perpetuate old beliefs systems, among them curanderismo and Santería? These many questions continue to divide Americans, and they demand serious scholarly assessment.

The education of Hispanics, and particularly of Mexican Americans, has certainly been a matter of legitimate concern and discussion for both parents and school officials since at least the early twentieth century. The essential questions in that long-standing debate appear as pertinent today as they were earlier. What explains high dropout rates and low scores on achievement tests? Is it race, culture, environment, or class? Should the blame be placed on schools, which are often underfunded or at times staffed by teachers hostile toward Hispanic students? Should the method of instruction be different for those coming from a Hispanic home environment? For many years Hispanic activists contended that bilingual education was an appropriate and rational method for instruction when Hispanics constituted the bulk of the student body. Yet voters (including

First and second grade students at Manzanita Elementary School, Oakland, California. Many of the students are native Spanish speakers. They are taught in both English and Spanish. (David Butow/Corbis Saba)

Hispanics) have discarded such a notion. Is the No Child Left Behind Act of January 2002 (which mandated sweeping reform for the nation's educational system) proving to be the universal solution to the problems that hinder quality instruction in America, as its advocates argue, or is this approach simply producing greater gaps between rich school systems prepared to implement its directives and those less capable of doing so? There are many Mexican Americans, on the other hand, who find little fault with the nation's public school system as it currently exists, for they go on to become exemplary success stories upon graduation. Who and what is right on this point? Such lingering questions call for a diligent hunt for the truth.

Also to be studied assiduously is institutional racism, something that has stalked Hispanics in the West since the mid–nineteenth century. Certainly, racism today is not manifest in the uninhibited name-calling, segregation, and lynching of yesteryear. Does racism still exist, then, though in more subtle and less virulent forms? Many Latino spokespersons today view immigrant bashing, the English-only movement, redistricting efforts, and actions to curtail social programs as racism in a new guise. They note that the persistence of unequal school funding, the elimination of bilingual education, and the weakening of affirmative action policies manifest a modern strain of bigotry. But those unwilling to tolerate special privilege (among them some Hispanics) argue simply that years of commitment to helping the disadvantaged and downtrodden through special programs is enough and that Hispanics should make concessions to American society by accepting U.S. beneficence and integrating themselves gratefully into the general citizenry. What better indicators of Jim Crow's decline than the increased rate of exogamous marriages with Anglos, the support the Hispanic community gave to Propositions 187, 63, and 227 in California, and the presence of Hispanics in high places (including Cabinet posts). Many believe that, in the twenty-first century, it is time for Hispanics to stop invoking the race card. Since this quarrel over racism will remain contentious for years to come, it should continue to be an important theme of academic debate.

Not to be neglected for further study is politics. As has been noted throughout this book, Hispanics have historically struggled against political obstacles like gerrymandering, disfranchisement, poll taxes, and other mechanisms designed to control the Hispanic electorate. Such impediments to political participation fell by the wayside during the latter decades of the twentieth century, yet Latinos still feel the need to rally Hispanic communities, to battle their determined opponents in the culture wars, for instance. Many organizations presently exist throughout the United States committed to defending the rights of immigrants, to insuring the security of Hispanic laborers and farm workers, to seeing that Hispanics gain greater access to higher education, and to winning visible political representation. The Southwest Voter Registration Education Project (SVREP), founded in 1974 by Willie Velásquez in Texas, is one example of an old organization still certain that many political fights over Hispanic issues lie ahead. Why do matters such as these linger, scholars should ask. Is it because the majority consciously seeks to maintain Hispanics in a status of dependency? Or is it, as many critics maintain, that Hispanics are politically apathetic? Is the acculturated Hispanic middle class more likely to be politicized than the lower class? What explains the gradual but discernible drift of Hispanics from the Democratic to the Republican Party? What is the future of Hispanic politics?

Quality time also should be spent on clarifying the notion of identity as it applies to the Hispanic community. The many subgroups generally categorized as Hispanics have assorted identities. Because identity is shaped by one's experience in the home and the immediate environment, by socializing agents such as the schools or the mass media, and by the culture of the homeland, as well as by various other forces, not all Hispanic groups share the same identity. Anglos, Mexicans, and African Americans growing up in the same town, for instance, might very well develop a different racial (or ethnic) consciousness, for each group might have had discrete experiences involving prejudice, poverty, or adversity. Their home life—which included eating particular foods, abiding by the long-standing customs and traditions of their parents, speaking a different language, or placing faith on one religion or another—also influenced the manner in which they define themselves. Even after generations of living in the United States, therefore, Hispanic subgroups relate to nationality, so that Mexicans consider themselves distinct from Cubans, Cubans from Puerto Ricans, Puerto Ricans from Colombians, and so on. Recognizing that diverse identities exist within the Hispanic community, as well as realizing that people who opt for maintaining an old heritage do not threaten American institutions (indeed defend them) would at least reassure those fearing the "Browning of America." Scholarly work can help assuage such fears.

Aside from older salient questions, there exist several other more contemporary issues in need of research scrutiny. Labeling, closely associated with identity, lingers as an article of debate, for as of this date no one label pleases all ethnic groups. The U.S. government uses the term "Hispanic" for official purposes, and many Anglo Americans apply it generically to those with Latin American origins, as noted above. Often, speakers will use the term because it is less offensive than others, such as "Mexican," which can have a racially charged connotation. Not knowing any better, they use the term "Hispanic," believing it to be the name people of Latin American heritage prefer. What to call themselves can be a conundrum for Hispanics as well. Over the course of the twentieth century, people of Mexican origin have referred to themselves as Latin American, Mexican American, Chicano, Hispanic, or Latino, without much consensus as to which is most correct. "Hispanic" seems currently the most popular term for a number of reasons: it has apparently been officially sanctified, it simplifies and facilitates dialogue among different parties, and it permits groups such as Mexican Americans the luxury of being considered Caucasian while simultaneously retaining ethnic loyalties. Still, many Mexican Americans reject the term, as do scores within the Cuban American, Puerto Rican, and various other Latino communities. It does not adequately capture their particular experience, and so the label appears inappropriate. As the Hispanic community continues to diversify, some way of solving the complex problem of appropriate labels seems requisite.

Diversity also begs for more thorough interrogation. By no means do Hispanics constitute a monolithic entity. They differ in place of birth. While most are U.S.-born, recent arrivals come from Mexico, Puerto Rico, or the Central America nations, so that enclaves almost always consist of both native-born residents and immigrants. Further, racial differences pervade the Hispanic community. Mexican Americans for the most part derive from a Spanish-Indian mixture (and thus census officials list them as Caucasian), while Caribbean-descent people span a racial spectrum from light to dark colorations. Class differences within each subcommunity further prevents typecasting. Although it is true that a disproportionate number of Hispanics struggle daily to make ends meet, a respectable mass belong to the Hispanic middle class, and another more fortunate cohort live in affluent comfort. Even cultural differences distinguish one Hispanic group from another. Though the Spanish language binds most Hispanics together, for instance, historical setting, vocabulary, and intonation make for variation. Even if there existed a physical resemblance, it would be simple enough to determine whether a speaker's background was Mexican, Honduran, or Cuban. Explaining the existence of diversity within Hispanic communities would help eliminate vile stereotypes, allay suspicions of "foreigners," and hopefully promote racial harmony.

Rates of assimilation and acculturation among Hispanics have recently achieved new importance, given the resurgence of migration from Mexico and the arrival of groups that had not been part of the West's history until late in the twentieth century. Does immigration from Mexico reverse or delay acculturation trends among those who have lived in the United States for generations? Or is the American capitalist and democratic system so seductive as to co-opt any foreign arrival within years? Do immigrants from some points of origin adapt more quickly? Are some groups more willing to jettison components of their old culture, and why? Do the children of immigrants have a greater desire to succeed at education than do students who are native born? What specifically are the indicators of acculturation for immigrants? Is acculturation for immigrants, as well as for those who have lived in the United States for decades, desirable? Do Hispanics gauge acculturation in the same way as do Anglo Americans? Mexican- and Cuban-descent citizens measure their Americanization by their ability to function adequately in the mainstream while simultaneously being able to speak Spanish, to work in professional positions while retaining ties to ethnic enclaves, or to act as power brokers within the major political parties while pressing for ethnic needs.

A miscellany of other issues has only recently emerged, and researchers might well focus upon them. What accounts for the success of evangelical Protestants in recruiting Hispanics, who have historically been faithful Catholic parishioners? Does this movement into the Protestant camp reflect other developments unfolding in the country, such as demographic change in the West? What are the implications of such defections, especially as they involve movement into the more conservative fundamentalist and evangelical denominations? Should one expect Hispanics to vote for those who emphasize the issues of life, family, and morality instead of politicians who stress the need to ensure the social welfare of citizens? Will conversion to Protestantism affect identity within the Latino community? Would Anglo Protestants be more willing to marry Hispanic Protestants than Hispanic Catholics?

But many issues aside from religion have forced themselves upon us lately. What is it about the Republican Party that appeals to the Hispanic community? Why do Hispanics take political stands that conflict with their own self-interest, as in the case of English-only or anti-affirmative action propositions, to name the most obvious? Is the nativist reaction of recent decades an incorrect demonstrator of racial prejudice, since the rate of intermarriage between Hispanics and Anglos is increasing? Will marriages between African Americans and Hispanics become more common as time goes on? What is the future for U.S. West in terms of culture? Will the region forever host people of differing nationalities, each faithful to the culture of their respective motherland while at the same time loyal defenders of the American flag? Or will people therein one day forego their once uncompromising belief that it is best to live in a milieu that embraces the best of both worlds? Other issues, among them the Hispanic interest in American music crazes (such as hip-hop) and the more serious subject of Hispanic reaction to gay marriages, stand out as ones warranting fundamental study.

FINDING ANSWERS

Presently, a cadre of researchers is actively pursuing answers to some of the lingering questions mentioned above, as well as to newer ones that have surfaced as the Hispanic experience in the West unfolds. Scholars have already offered clues for dealing with many of these questions, as adduced by the existence of numerous bibliographies and historiographical essays that have appeared during the last few decades as scholars have begun seriously studying the Hispanic presence in the United States. But other kinds of information and sources aside from these research tools exist to address these engaging matters. The Internet is a most convenient storehouse of information, for it contains an inexhaustible amount of data on any subject regarding Hispanics. Readers must be discriminating in their use of the 'Net, however, lest they find themselves misled by opinions, editorials, and other kinds of nonacademic discourses. Anthologies, which appear with greater frequency these days, suggest article-length solutions to many questions that have been identified here. In such collections of essays, educators, sociologists, political scientists, and other academicians provide their most recent research conclusions, giving answers, suggesting solutions, or revising old beliefs on whatever issue most concerns them.

Periodicals specializing in one academic field or another similarly facilitate the distribution of research findings. Journals, whether they be national or regional in scope, openly invite the submission of essays on Hispanics for consideration. Sociologists, political scientists, and educators, for example, have been able to make recommendations for solving problems in the pages of academic publications such as the *Social Science Quarterly* or the *Hispanic Journal of Behavioral Sciences*. Historians have similarly found friendly outlets in recent years in the *Western Historical Quarterly, Southwestern Historical Quarterly,* and *Pacific Historical Review,* to name only a few of these professional journals.

The historians' own contribution to old and new issues comes via interpretations, such as those discussed at the beginning of this chapter. Historical writing is ever prone to change, offering newer perspectives (and therefore answers) as the decades pass. Historians dutifully altered the old views of Hispanics being a problem population and an ahistoric group, for example. They did so by conducting vast research in archival depositories, keeping up with revisionist historical trends, and—swayed by their own experience growing up—giving agency to their historical subjects. Still, more answers to pressing issues can come from a willingness to embrace evolving research strategies such as interdisciplinary approaches. Political science models, among others, have much to offer, and accepting them can provide more persuasive explanations for Hispanic political diversity, for instance. The techniques introduced by folklorists and literary critics are of immeasurable value to historians wanting to give a more holistic portrayal of the Hispanic past. As indicated in the previous chapters, numerous lost or heretofore unknown literary texts have recently been recovered, creating a more complete picture of the Hispanics of previous centuries, who used to be thought of as almost universally illiterate.

Answers may also derive from the work produced by alliances forged among social providers, doctors, politicians, and the many other professionals who attend to the Hispanic community. The general tendency has been for people in different lines of work to act independently of each other, even as they have the same aim: to improve the lives of the disadvantaged. Building ties between professionals of disparate backgrounds makes it more likely that they will identify old and new problems, suggest remedies, and disseminate proposed solutions. Scholarly findings, for instance, could in this manner be effectively implemented by those who have direct regular contact with Hispanics in need, whether they are the indigent, the elderly, students, or immigrants.

HISPANICS IN THE WEST

This book has shown that the Hispanic presence in the trans-Mississippi west has been long-standing and resilient. The contribution that Hispanics have made to the development of western America has been generally positive and constructive. Hispanics of Spanish-Mexican ancestry have left an indelible mark on the region—its culture, its economy, and its geography—and more recently Hispanics from various countries in Latin America have continued adding to that legacy. There is every indication that Hispanics will continue to play a role in forging the West's economic and political destiny.

Historically, however, Anglo Americans have not been openly hospitable to fellow citizens who are Hispanics. Though Americans moving into the frontier after 1848 found an already entrenched Hispanic civilization, they considered those settlers and migrants that subsequently arrived from Mexico as outsiders. Moreover, they looked on Mexicans as racial inferiors and persons unworthy of entering into economic competition with white citizens, and they placed onerous barriers before Mexican Americans in order to obstruct their upward climb. Even today, many in the United States regard Latinos as a problem, think of them as too ready to depend on the welfare state, and view them as a people with special needs.

To better understand the history of the West, we must recognize that people from across the globe have long viewed the wide expanse from the Mississippi River to the Pacific Ocean as a place where high ambitions might indeed materialize. Like U.S. citizens, Europeans, African Americans, and Asians, Latinos entered the West wanting only the chance to join the contest for individual and community well-being. Most have not seen their ethnicity as a disqualification in the pursuit of the American dream, and like others in the land, whether they be of Asian, African, or another ancestry, they have not seen it as a deterrent to loyalty and allegiance. The common thread in the history of the West has been all peoples' desire to further their own and the region's progress.

BIBLIOGRAPHIC ESSAY

Periodically, historians pause to see what exactly their works on a particular area of study have said. In that manner, they are able to determine patterns of thought in their field of interest and ascertain how exactly interpretations have changed as time passes. Among the earliest essays published on the historiography of the Mexican American was one by Juan Gómez-Quiñones and Luis Leobardo Arroyo, "On the State of Chicano History: Observations on Its Development, Interpretations, and Theory, 1970–1974," *Western Historical Quarterly* 7 (April 1976). It recapped and assessed the arguments advanced in the earliest publications written about Hispanics. Profiting from hindsight, historians by the 1980s questioned some of the first analyses of the subject, for example, Alex M. Saragoza in "The Significance of Recent Chicano-Related Historical Writings: An Appraisal," *Ethnic Affairs* 1 (Fall 1987). Other historiographical pieces in the 1980s to review publications and identify the interpretations that had driven Mexican American history during the previous twenty-year span of time were Richard Griswold del Castillo's "Chicano Historical Discourse: An Overview and Evaluation of the 1980s," *Perspectives in Mexican American Studies* 4 (1993), and Arnoldo De León's "Texas Mexicans: Twentieth Century Interpretations," in *Texas through Time: Evolving Interpretations,* edited by Walter L. Buenger and Robert A. Calvert (College Station: Texas A&M University, 1991).

During the 1990s and the early twenty-first century, Chicano historiography had become important enough that some targeted it for constructive criticism and others made it the focus of extensive scholarly discourse either in essays or at colloquia; at the same time, a vocal constituency cited a need to broaden its scope. Two well-informed reviews on the state of Chicano history as of the 1990s were that of David G. Gutiérrez, in "Significant to Whom?: Mexican Americans and the History of the American West," *Western Historical Quarterly* 24 (November 1993), and that of Manuel G. Gonzales and Cynthia M. Gonzales in the introduction to *En Aquel Entonces: Readings in Mexican American History* (Bloomington: Indiana University Press, 2000). Those calling for reconsiderations of old thinking included Gilbert G. González and Raúl A. Fernández, who, in "Chicano History: Transcending Cultural Models," *Pacific Historical Review* 43 (November 1994), questioned the continued preference for using a cultural model to interpret Chicano history when it made better sense to employ an economic framework, especially for the twentieth century. Then, several of the papers read before a conference titled "Toward a New Chicana/o History," held at Michigan State University in 1996, which collectively appeared in *Voices of a New Chicana/o History,* edited by Refugio I. Rochín and Dennis N. Valdes (East Lansing: Michigan State University Press, 2000), raised further questions about old premises and conclusions. Some of the essays, especially those written by younger scholars, suggested possible new avenues for research and others ways of ensuring Chicano history's continued vibrancy and success. Such revisionist views of

Chicano history indicated the common patterns of changing thought familiar to historiography, and such reconsiderations will continue. A common trend today, for instance, is appealing for the incorporation of the West's many Latino sub-communities into the corpus of Chicano history. Such a call is to be found in George J. Sánchez's, *"Y Tú Qué? (Y2K): Latino History in the New Millennium,"* in *Latinos: Remaking America,* edited by Marcelo M. Suárez-Orozco and Mariela M. Paez (Berkeley: University of California Press, 2002). An earlier generation probably would not have issued such a summons.

As for the contemporary issues discussed in the next section, a mountain of literature exists on them, including from scholarly works, editorials from every camp in the political spectrum, and materials issued by the U.S. government, state legislatures, and local social service agencies. Some of the academic works we consulted for writing this chapter may serve as useful guides to further readings. A good introduction to the more contentious issues that divide Americans in our day is *Culture Wars: Opposing Viewpoints,* edited by Mary E. Williams (San Diego, CA: Greenhaven Press, 1999). Also helpful are the informative essays in *Pursuing Power: Latinos and the Political System,* edited by F. Chris García (Notre Dame: University of Notre Dame Press, 1997). John A. García's *Latino Politics in America: Community, Culture, and Interests* (Lanham, MA: Rowman and Littlefield, 2003) offers a fairly comprehensive portrait of Hispanics as a social and political force and speculates on the political future of the several subgroups. Further elaborating on the impact that Hispanics are making on the United States and the West is the anthology *Latinos: Remaking America,* edited by Marcelo M. Suárez-Orozco and Mariela M. Paez (Berkeley: University of California Press, 2002). From these works (and others like them), one can acquire an informed idea of how Hispanics remain an integral element of life in the U.S. West.

To research present-day personalities, such as Alberto S. Gonzales, scholars have a variety of sources at their disposal. Magazines for the general reading public often carry stories on these individuals: for example, on Gonzales, Michael Duffy's, "Bush's Man from Humble," *Time,* November 22, 2004, p. 56. Then there are reference volumes on living figures of national importance. We were able to find an entry on Attorney General Gonzales in *Current Biography Yearbook 2002,* edited by Clifford Thompson (New York: H. W. Wilson, 2002). One of many Internet sources available on Gonzales would be www.histpanicvista .com/HVC/Columnist/rlovato/011705rlovato.htm.

CHRONOLOGY

711–1492   Muslims occupy Spain, and Spaniards attempt the recapture of their country in what is called *La Reconquista.*

900   Spaniards believe they have found the tomb of St. James (Santiago) in what is today Galicia and are stirred to carry on their religious crusade to oust the Muslims.

1521   Hernando Cortes conquers Tenochtitlán, the capital city of the Aztecs.

1528   Alvar Nuñez Cabeza de Vaca is marooned on Galveston Island. He is the first European to set foot in Texas.

1541   Francisco Vásquez de Coronado leads an entrada (expedition) into the Far North looking for fabled cities of gold.

1598   Juan de Oñate establishes the first Hispanic settlement in New Mexico.

1609   Pedro de Peralta founds Santa Fe.

1680   The Pueblo Revolt, a bloody uprising against the Spanish presence in New Mexico, occurs.

1706   Albuquerque established as part of Spain's resettlement of New Mexico following the Pueblo Revolt.

1718   San Antonio, Texas, is founded.

1775   A presidio to guard the hinterland is established at San Agustín de Tucson. It becomes modern-day Tucson, Arizona.

1776   Monterey, California, settled by colonists under Juan Bautista de Anza.

1781   Los Angeles, California, founded.

1810   Mexico declares its independence from Spain when Father Miguel Hidalgo issues the Grito de Dolores.

1821   Mexico wins its independence from the mother country. The Far North now falls under Mexico's sovereignty.

1834   Spanish-language journalism arrives in New Mexico with publication of *El Crepúsculo de la Libertad.*

1836   Texans declared independence from Mexico. Among signers of the Declaration of Independence are José Francisco Ruiz, José Antonio Navarro, and Lorenzo de Zavala.

1848   Treaty of Guadalupe Hidalgo ends the War with Mexico. The Far North falls under the sovereignty of the United States.

1853   Death of Joaquin Murrieta, the Californio who had terrorized Anglo Americans in retaliation for atrocities inflicted upon his loved ones.

1855   *El Clamor Público* editorializes against the Yankee presence in California.

1859   Juan Cortina leads a rebellion in South Texas against Anglo Americans whom he accuses of corruption and villainy against Tejanos.

1862   Ignacio Zaragosa repulses the French at Pueblo on the Cinco de Mayo (Fifth of May).

1863   Chipita Rodríguez convicted and hanged in Texas for murder.

1865–1866 At the New Almadén mine in California, Mexican miners strike against job dangers, low pay, and poor housing.

1872	María Amparo Ruiz de Burton of California publishes *Who Would Have Thought It?* (Philadelphia: J. B. Lippincott, 1872).
1877	In the Salt War, Hispanic settlers in the El Paso Valley resist Anglo American attempts to control the local salt lakes.
	Rio Grande Railway arrives in the San Luis Valley of Colorado.
1880	Due to dispossession of their lands, about 80 percent of Hispanics in Santa Barbara, California, are now classified as unskilled laborers.
1881	U.S. Indian Service orders Mexican ranchers and farmers off lands near Tucson, which these families had occupied for decades.
1882	Passage of Chinese Exclusion Act.
1886	Hawaii enacts a Chinese Exclusion Act.
1880s	Paniolos of Mexican descent are working on ranches in Oahu, Hawaii, Maui, and Kauai.
1890	The *Partido del Pueblo Unido,* in conjunction with the efforts of the *Gorras Blancas,* sweeps to victory in San Miguel County, New Mexico.
1890s	The largest network of mutual aid societies, the *Alianza Hispano Americana,* is established in Tucson, Arizona. The group continues to function until the 1940s.
1900	On December 14, a group of 55 Puerto Ricans, on their way to Hawaii, escape from their employers in San Francisco; this group serves as the genesis of the Puerto Rican community in California. On December 23, the first group of Puerto Ricans arrives in Honolulu.

1902   Passage of Newlands Reclamation Act helps bring millions of acres in the West under cultivation, eventually turning many formally arid areas into rich farmlands and increasing the demand for cheap labor to work upon these lands.

1903   Workers of Mexican descent participate in the Oxnard, California betabelero strike.

1905   Arrival of St. Louis, Brownsville, and Mexico Railway into South Texas ushers in new economic opportunities for whites and dramatically changes social relations between whites and people of Mexican descent in the region.

1910   California Immigration Commission reports that Mexican railroad workers generally earn 25 percent less than do non-Mexican descent employees.

1911   *El Primer Congreso Mexicanista,* a group that sought to challenge the maltreatment of persons of Mexican descent, meets in Laredo, Texas.

1912   New Mexico and Arizona admitted as states into the Union.

1913   Passage of Alien Land Law in California, designed to stop "foreigners" (mostly Japanese immigrants) from purchasing farmland.

1915   The Plan de San Diego, which called (in part) for the taking back of the lands lost as a result of the Treaty of Guadalupe-Hidalgo, leads to increased tensions, and outright hostilities, between Anglos and Mexican Americans in South Texas.

1917   Passage of Jones Act, which makes Puerto Ricans U.S. citizens.

1921   Establishment of Sons of America, a Mexican American veterans group in San Antonio, Texas. This is one of several such organizations that will unite to form LULAC in 1929.

1923	Great Western Sugar Company (of Montana) begins recruiting Mexicans to work as betabeleros.
	Establishment of Rama Mexicana (Mexican Branch) of the LDS Church in Salt Lake City, Utah.
1930	Federal Census reports the presence of more than 7,000 individuals of Mexican descent in Wyoming.
1931	*Alvarez v. Lemon Grove School District* and *Independent School District v. Salvatierra* decisions.
1938	Emma Tenayuca and Luisa Moreno help lead a strike by pecan shellers in San Antonio.
1930s	Some 250,000 persons of Mexican descent leave the state of Texas due to deportation or repatriation.
1941–1945	An estimated 250,000 to 500,000 Spanish-surnamed individuals serve in uniform during World War II.
1942	José Díaz is murdered at Sleepy Lagoon on August 1–2.
1943	Zoot-suit riots take place in June in California and elsewhere in the West.
1947	*Méndez v. Westminster School District* decision in California.
	The encyclical *Mediator Dei,* which challenged Catholic clergy to fight against social injustice, is issued by Pope Pius XIII.
1948	*Delgado v. Bastrop Independent School District* decision in Texas.
	American GI Forum established by Dr. Héctor P. García in Corpus Christi, Texas.
1949	Funeral director in Three Rivers, Texas, refuses to allow the family of Felix Longoria to hold his wake at his facility.

1958   LULAC President Felix Tijerina helps create the "Little School of the 400," a program intended to teach children of Mexican descent 400 "basic" English words necessary to complete first grade.

The cursillo movement, designed to engage Catholic men in the fight for social justice and to increase their ties to the Catholic Church, begins in Texas.

1959   Fidel Castro establishes his control over Cuba, leading to the exodus of 215,000 Cubans, many to Los Angeles and Las Vegas, by 1962.

1960   "Viva Kennedy" clubs established to turn out the Mexican American vote for Senator John F. Kennedy.

1962   César Chávez resigns from the CSO and, with Dolores Huerta, begins operation of the National Farm Workers Association.

1963   Los cinco candidatos win elections in Crystal City, Texas.

1965   Hart-Celler Immigration Act passed.

1966   NFWA (later to become the UFW) signs first labor agreement with grape grower.

Members of the Alianza movement take over the Echo Amphitheater within the Kit Carson National Forest.

1967   Tierra Amarilla County courthouse incident.

Brown Berets founded in Los Angeles, California.

Mexican American Youth Organization founded in San Antonio, Texas.

1968   Corky Gonzales and members of the Crusade for Justice participate in the Poor People's March alongside Dr. Martin Luther King Jr. Puerto Ricans from California also participate in this event.

Mexican American Legal Defense and Educational Fund begins operation.

1969   Corky Gonzales issues *El Plan Espiritual de Aztlán.*

Members of MEChA issue the *Plan de Santa Barbara.*

1970   National Chicano Moratorium Committee march in Los Angeles on August 29.

1972   La Raza Unida Party holds its only national convention in El Paso, Texas.

Publication of Rodolfo Acuña's *Occupied America: The Chicanos' Struggle toward Liberation.*

1973   *White et al. v. Regester et al.* decision helps establish single member districts throughout Texas.

1980   Mariel Boatlift brings approximately 125,000 Cubans to the United States. Many of these men and women eventually migrate to the West.

1981   Henry Cisneros elected mayor of San Antonio.

1982   *Plyler v. Doe* decision makes it possible for children of undocumented workers to receive a public education.

1986   Immigration Reform and Control Act passed.

1996   Eluid "Pete" Suazo becomes the first Hispanic ever elected to the Utah State Senate.

1990s   Propositions 187, 209, and 227 passed in California.

2000   Census Bureau estimates that there are 127,000 Salvadorans and 250,000 Guatemalans in Los Angeles as early as 1990.

2004   Ken Salazar elected to the U.S. Senate for Colorado.

2005   Alberto Gonzales sworn in as Attorney General of the United States.

SELECT BIBLIOGRAPHY

BOOKS

Acuña, Rodolfo. *Occupied America: A History of Chicanos.* 5th ed. New York: Pearson Longman, 2004.

Alonzo, Armando. *Tejano Legacy: Ranchers and Settlers in South Texas, 1734–1900.* Albuquerque: University of New Mexico Press, 1998.

Balderrama, Francisco È., and Raymond Rodríguez. *A Decade of Betrayal: Mexican Repatriation in the 1930s.* Albuquerque: University of New Mexico Press, 1995.

Bannon, John Francis. *The Spanish Borderlands Frontier, 1513–1821.* New York: Holt, Rinehart, and Winston, 1970.

Barrera, Mario. *Race and Class in the Southwest: A Theory of Racial Inequality.* Notre Dame, IN: University of Notre Dame Press, 1979.

Blackwelder, Kirk. *Women of the Depression: Caste and Culture in San Antonio, 1929–1939.* College Station: Texas A&M University Press, 1998.

Boyle, Susan Calafate. *Los Capitalistas: Hispano Merchants and the Santa Fe Trade.* Albuquerque: University of New Mexico Press, 1997.

Camarillo, Albert. *Chicanos in a Changing Society: From Mexican Pueblos to American Barrios in Santa Barbara and Southern California, 1848–1930.* Cambridge: Harvard University Press, 1979.

Campa, Arthur L. *Hispanic Culture in the Southwest.* Norman: University of Oklahoma Press, 1979.

Cardona, Luis Antonio. *A History of Puerto Ricans in the United States of America.* Bethesda, MD: Carreta Press, 1995.

Cardoso, Lawrence A. *Mexican Emigration to the United States, 1897–1931: Socio-Economic Patterns.* Tucson: University of Arizona Press, 1980.

Carroll, Patrick J. *Felix Longoria's Wake: Bereavement, Racism, and the Rise of Mexican American Activism.* Austin: University of Texas Press, 2003.

Castro, Américo. *The Spaniards: An Introduction to Their History.* Los Angeles: University of California Press, 1971.

Castro, Max J. *The New Cuban Immigration in Context.* Coral Gables, FL: Dante B. Fascell North-South Center, University of Miami, 2002.

Chávez, Ernesto. *"My People First!" "Mi Raza Primero": Nationalism, Identity, and Insurgency in the Chicano Movement in Los Angeles, 1966–1978.* Berkeley: University of California Press, 2002.

Chipman, Donald E. *Spanish Texas, 1519–1821.* Austin: University of Texas at Austin, 1992.

Corwin, Arthur F. *Immigrants and Immigrants: Perspectives on Mexican Labor Migration to the United States.* Westport, CT: Greenwood Press, 1978.

Cruz, Gilbert R. *Let There Be Towns: Spanish Municipal Origins in the American Southwest, 1610–1810.* College Station: Texas A&M University Press, 1988.

Cuello, José. *Latinos and Hispanics: A Primer on Terminology.* Detroit, MI: Wayne State University Press, 1996.

de la Teja, Jesús F. *San Antonio de Béxar: A Community on New Spain's Northern Frontier.* Albuquerque: University of New Mexico Press, 1995.

De León, Arnoldo. *Ethnicity in the Sunbelt.* 2nd ed.; College Station: Texas A&M University Press, 2001.

———. *Racial Frontiers: Africans, Chinese, and Mexicans in Western America, 1848–1890.* Albuquerque: University of New Mexico Press, 2002.

Deutsch, Sarah. *No Separate Refuge: Culture, Class and Gender on an Anglo Hispanic Frontier, 1880–1940.* New York: Oxford University Press, 1987.

Díaz-Stevens, Ana Maria, and Anthony M. Stevens-Arroyo. *Recognizing the Latino Resurgence in U.S. Religion: The Emmaus Paradigm.* Boulder, CO: Westview Press, 1998.

Dolan, Jay P. *Hispanic Catholic Culture in the U.S.: Issues and Concerns. Notre Dame History of Hispanic Catholics in the U.S.* Vol. 3. Notre Dame, IN: University of Notre Dame Press, 1997.

Dolan, Jay P., and Gilberto Hinojosa, eds. *Mexican Americans and the Catholic Church.* Notre Dame, IN: University of Notre Dame Press, 1994.

Escobar, Edward J. *Race, Police, and the Making of a Political Identity: Mexican Americans and the Los Angeles Police Department.* Berkeley: University of California Press, 1999.

Foley, Neil. *The White Scourge: Mexicans, Blacks, and Poor Whites in Texas Cotton Culture.* Berkeley: University of California Press, 1997.

Frazier, Donald S., ed. *The United States and Mexico at War: Nineteenth-Century Expansionism and Conflict.* New York: Macmillan Reference Books, 1998.

Fuentes, Carlos. *The Buried Mirror: Reflections on Spain and the New World.* New York: Houghton Mifflin, 1992.

Gamboa, Erasmo. *Mexican Labor and World War II: Braceros in the Pacific Northwest, 1942–1947.* Austin: University of Texas Press, 1990.

Gamboa, Erasmo, and Carolyn M. Baun, eds. *Nosotros: The Hispanic People of Oregon: Essays and Recollections.* Portland: Oregon Council for the Humanities, 1995.

García, F. Chris, ed. *Pursuing Power: Latino and the Political System.* Notre Dame, IN: University of Notre Dame Press, 1997.

García, Ignacio M. *Chicanismo: The Forging of a Militant Ethos among Mexican Americans.* Tucson: University of Arizona Press, 1997.

————. *Hector P. García: In Relentless Pursuit of Justice.* Houston, TX: Arte Público Press, 2002.

————. *United We Win: The Rise and Fall of La Raza Unida Party.* Tucson: University of Arizona Press, 1989.

————. *Viva Kennedy: Mexican Americans in Search of Camelot.* College Station: Texas A&M University Press, 2000.

García, John A. *Latino Politics in America: Community, Culture, and Interests.* Lanham, MD: Rowman and Littlefield Publishers, Inc., 2003.

García, Juan R. *Mexicans in the Midwest, 1900–1932.* Tucson: University of Arizona Press, 1996.

García, Manuel. *An Accidental Soldier: Memoirs of a Mestizo in Vietnam.* Albuquerque: University of New Mexico Press, 2003.

García, Mario T. *Memories of Chicano History: The Life and Narrative of Bert Corona.* Berkeley: University of California Press, 1995.

Gómez-Quiñones, Juan. *Chicano Politics: Reality and Promise, 1940–1990.* Albuquerque: University of New Mexico Press, 1990.

————. *Roots of Chicano Politics, 1600–1940.* Albuquerque: University of New Mexico Press, 1994.

Gonzales, Manuel G. *Mexicanos: A History of Mexicans in the United States.* Bloomington: Indiana University Press, 1999.

González, Arturo. *Mexican Americans and the U.S. Economy: The Quest for Buenos Dias.* Tucson: University of Arizona Press, 2002.

González, Deena J. *Refusing the Favor: The Spanish-Mexican Women of Santa Fe, 1820–1880.* New York: Oxford University Press, 1999.

Gonzalez, Gilbert G. *Labor and Community: Mexican Citrus Worker Villages in a Southern California County, 1900–1950.* Urbana and Chicago: University of Illinois Press, 1994.

Gonzalez, Gilbert G., and Raul A. Fernandez. *A Century of Chicano History: Empire, Nations, and Migration.* New York: Routledge, 2003.

González, Juan. *Harvest of Empire: A History of Latinos in America.* New York: Penguin Books, 2000.

Griswold del Castillo, Richard. *La Familia: Chicano Families in the Urban Southwest, 1848 to the Present.* Notre Dame, IN: University of Notre Dame Press, 1984.

————. *The Los Angeles Barrio, 1850–1890: A Social History.* Berkeley: University of California Press, 1979.

————. *The Treaty of Guadalupe Hidalgo: A Legacy of Conflict.* Norman: University of Oklahoma Press, 1990.

Griswold del Castillo, Richard, and Richard García. *César Chávez: A Triumph of Spirit.* Norman: University of Oklahoma Press, 1995.

Guerin-Gonzales, Camille. *Mexican Workers and American Dream: Immigration, Repatriation, and California Farm Labor, 1900–1939.* New Brunswick, NJ: Rutgers University Press, 1994.

Gutiérrez, David G. *Walls and Mirrors: Mexican Americans, Mexicans and the Politics of Ethnicity.* Berkeley: University of California Press, 1995.

Gutiérrez, José Angel. *The Making of a Chicano Militant: Lessons from Cristal.* Madison: University of Wisconsin Press, 1998.

Gutiérrez, Ramón A. *When Jesus Came, the Corn Mothers Went Away: Marriage, Sexuality, and Power in New Mexico, 1500–1846.* Stanford, CA: Stanford University Press, 1991.

Guzmán, Betsy. *The Hispanic Population: Census 2000 Brief.* Washington, DC: U.S. Bureau of the Census, 2001.

Haas, Lisbeth. *Conquest and Historical Identities in California, 1769–1936.* Berkeley: University of California Press, 1995.

Hernández, Jose A. *Mutual Aid for Survival: The Case of the Mexican American.* Malabar, FL: Krieger, 1983.

Hernández, Ramona. *The Mobility of Workers under Advanced Capitalism: Dominican Migration to the United States.* New York: Columbia University Press, 2002.

Hoffman, Abraham. *Unwanted Mexican Americans in the Great Depression: Repatriation Pressures, 1929–1939.* Tucson: University of Arizona Press, 1974.

Iber, Jorge. *Hispanics in the Mormon Zion, 1912–1999.* College Station: Texas A&M University Press, 2001.

Jackson, Jack. *Los Mesteños: Spanish Ranching in Texas, 1721–1821.* College Station: Texas A&M University Press, 1986.

Johnson, Benjamin Heber. *Revolution in Texas: How a Forgotten Rebellion and Its Bloody Repression Turned Mexicans into Americans.* New Haven, CT: Yale University Press, 2003.

Jones, Oakah L. *Los Paisanos: Spanish Settlers in the North Frontier of New Spain.* Norman: University of Oklahoma Press, 1979.

Kandel, William, and John Cromartie. "New Patterns of Hispanic Settlement in Rural America." Rural Development Research Report, no. 99. Washington DC: United States Department of Agriculture, Economic Research Service, May 2004.

Kanellos, Nicolas, ed. *Hispanic Theater in the United States.* Houston, TX: Arte Público Press, 1984.

Kessell, John L. *Spain in the Southwest: A Narrative History of Colonial New Mexico, Arizona, Texas and California.* Norman: University of Oklahoma Press, 2002.

Kreneck, Thomas H. *Mexican American Odyssey: Felix Tijerina, Entrepreneur and Civic Leader, 1900–1965.* College Station: Texas A&M University Press, 2001.

Lamar, Howard Roberts. *The Far Southwest, 1846–1912: A Territorial History.* New Haven, CT: Yale University Press, 1966.

Luckingham, Bradford. *Minorities in Phoenix: A Profile of Mexican American, Chinese American, and African American Communities, 1880–1992.* Tucson: University of Arizona Press, 1994.

MacLachlan, Colin M., and Jaime E. Rodríguez O. *The Forging of the Cosmic Race: A Reinterpretation of Colonial Mexico.* Berkeley: University of California Press, 1980.

Mares, E. A., ed. *Padre Martínez: New Perspectives from Taos.* Taos, NM: Millicent Rogers Museum, 1988.

Mariscal, George, ed. *Aztlán and Vietnam: Chicano and Chicana Experiences of the War.* Berkeley: University of California Press, 1999.

Márquez, Benjamin. *LULAC: The Evolution of a Mexican American Political Organization.* Austin: University of Texas Press, 1993.

Martínez, Oscar J. *Mexican Origin People in the United States.* Tucson: University of Arizona Press, 2001.

Mazón, Mauricio. *The Zoot Suit Riots: The Psychology of Symbolic Annihilation.* Austin: University of Texas Press, 1984.

McDonald, David R., and Timothy M. Matovina, eds. *Defending Mexican Valor in Texas: José Antonio Navarro's Historical Writings, 1853–1857.* Austin, TX: State House Press, 1995.

Meléndez, A. Gabriel. *So All Is Not Lost: The Poetics of Print in Nuevomexicano Communities, 1834–1958.* Albuquerque: University of New Mexico Press, 1997.

Meyer, Doris. *Speaking for Themselves: NeoMexicano Cultural Identity and the Spanish-Language Press, 1880–1920.* Albuquerque: University of New Mexico Press, 1996.

Meyer, Michael C., William L. Sherman, and Susan M. Deeds. *The Course of Mexican History.* 7th ed.; New York: Oxford University Press, 2003.

Miranda, M. L. *A History of Hispanics in Southern Nevada.* Reno: University of Nevada Press, 1997.

Monroy, Douglas. *Rebirth: Mexican Los Angeles from the Great Migration to the Great Depression.* Berkeley: University of California Press, 1999.

———. *Thrown among Strangers: The Making of Mexican Cultures in Frontier California.* Berkeley: University of California Press, 1990.

Montejano, David. *Anglos and Mexicans in the Making of Texas, 1836–1986.* Austin: University of Texas Press, 1987.

———. *Chicano Politics and Society in the Late Twentieth Century.* Austin: University of Texas Press, 1999.

Montoya, María E. *Translating Property: The Maxwell Land Grant and the Conflict over Land in the American West, 1840–1900.* Berkeley: University of California Press, 2002.

Moraga, Cherie, and Gloria Anzaldua. *This Bridge Called My Back: Writings by Radical Women of Color.* New York: Kitchen Table Women of Color Press, 1983.

Morín, Raúl. *Among the Valiant: Mexican Americans in WWII and Korea.* Alhambra, CA: Borden Publishing, 1966.

Muñoz, Carlos. *Youth, Identity and Power: The Chicano Movement.* New York: Verso, 1989.

Nash, Gerald D. *The American West in the Twentieth Century: A Short History of an Urban Oasis.* Englewood Cliffs, NJ: Prentice-Hall, Inc., 1973.

Navarro, Armando. *The Cristal Experiment: A Chicano Struggle for Community Control.* Madison: University of Wisconsin Press, 1998.

———. *Mexican American Youth Organization: Avant Garde of the Chicano Movement in Texas.* Austin: University of Texas Press, 1995.

Nostrand, Richard L. *The Hispano Homeland.* Norman: University of Oklahoma Press, 1992.

O'Callaghan, Joseph F. *A History of Medieval Spain.* Ithaca, NY: Cornell University Press, 1975.

Olson, James S., and Judith E. Olson. *Cuban Americans: From Trauma to Triumph.* New York: Twayne Publishers, 1995.

Pagán, Eduardo Obregón. *Murder at the Sleepy Lagoon: Zoot Suits, Race, and Riot in Wartime Los Angeles.* Chapel Hill: University of North Carolina Press, 2003.

Paredes, Américo. *A Texas-Mexican Cancionero: Folksongs of the Lower Border.* Austin: University of Texas Press, 1976.

Pew Hispanic Center. "Health Care Experiences: Survey Brief," March 2004. Accessed at http://www.pewhispanic.org.

————. "Hispanic Health: Divergent and Changing," January 2002. Accessed at http://www.pewhispanic.org.

Pitt, Leonard. *The Decline of the Californios: A Social History of the Spanish-Speaking Californians, 1846–1900.* Berkeley: University of California Press, 1966.

Pitti, Stephen J. *The Devil in Silicon Valley: Northern California, Race, and Mexican Americans.* Princeton, NJ: Princeton University Press, 2003.

Quezada, Gilberto J. *Border Boss: Manuel B. Bravo and Zapata County.* College Station: Texas A&M University Press, 1999.

Ramírez, Juan. *A Patriot After All: The Story of a Chicano Vietnam Vet.* Albuquerque: University of New Mexico Press, 1999.

Reimers, David M. *Unwelcome Strangers: American Identity and the Turn against Immigration.* New York: Columbia University Press, 1998.

Reyes, David, and Tom Waldman. *Land of a Thousand Dances: Chicano Rock 'n' Roll from Southern California.* Albuquerque: University of New Mexico Press, 1998.

Rochín, Refugio I., and Dennis N. Valdes, eds. *Voices of a New Chicana/o History.* East Lansing: Michigan State University Press, 2000.

Romo, Ricardo. *History of a Barrio: East Los Angeles.* Austin: University of Texas Press, 1983.

Rosales, F. Arturo. *Chicano: The History of the Mexican American Civil Struggle.* Houston, TX: Arte Público Press, 1997.

Rosenbaum, Robert J. *Mexicano Resistance in the Southwest: "The Sacred Right of Self-Preservation."* Austin: University of Texas Press, 1981.

Ruiz, Ramón Eduardo. *Triumphs and Tragedies: A History of the Mexican People.* New York: W.W. Norton and Company, 1992.

Ruiz, Vicki L. *Cannery Women, Cannery Lives: Mexican Women, Unionization, and the California Food Processing Industry, 1930–1950.* Albuquerque: University of New Mexico Press, 1987.

————. *From out of the Shadows: Mexican Women in Twentieth Century America.* New York: Oxford University Press, 1998.

Ruiz, Vicki L., and Virginia Sánchez-Korrol. *Latina Legacies: Identity, Biography, and Community.* New York: Oxford University Press, 2005.

Sánchez, George J. *Becoming Mexican American: Ethnicity, Culture, and Identity in Chicano Los Angeles, 1900–1945.* New York: Oxford University Press, 1993.

Sánchez-Korrol, Virginia. *Teaching U.S. Puerto Rican History.* Washington, DC: Publication Sales, American Historical Society, 1999.

San Miguel, Guadalupe, Jr. *"Let All of Them Take Heed": Mexican Americans and the Campaign for Educational Equality in Texas, 1910–1981.* Austin: University of Texas Press, 1987.

Sheridan, Thomas E. *Arizona: A History.* Tucson: University of Arizona Press, 1995.

———. *Los Tucsonenses: The Mexican Community in Tucson, 1854–1941.* Tucson: University of Arizona Press, 1986.

Simmons, Marc. *The Last Conquistador: Juan de Oñate and the Settling of the Far Southwest.* Albuquerque: University of New Mexico Press, 1991.

Smith, Michael M. *The Mexicans of Oklahoma.* Norman: University of Oklahoma Press, 1980.

Stewart, Kenneth L., and Arnoldo De León. *Not Room Enough: Mexicans, Anglos, and Socio-Economic Change in Texas, 1850–1900.* Albuquerque: University of New Mexico Press, 1983.

Suárez-Orozco, Marcelo M., and Mariela M. Paez, eds. *Latinos: Remaking America.* Berkeley: University of California Press, 2002.

Suro, Roberto. *Strangers among Us: Latino Lives in a Changing America.* New York: Vintage Books, 1999.

Takaki, Ronald. *A Different Mirror: A History of Multicultural America.* Boston: Little, Brown, and Company, 1993.

Tatum, Charles M. *Chicano Popular Culture: "Que Hable el Pueblo."* Tucson: University of Arizona Press, 2001.

———. *Chicano Literature.* Boston: Twayne Publishers, 1982.

Thompson, Jerry D. *Juan Cortina and the Texas-Mexico Frontier, 1859–1877.* El Paso: Texas Western Press, 1994.

Tijerina, Reies López, and José Angel Gutiérrez, trans. *They Call Me "King Tiger": My Struggle for the Land and Our Rights.* Houston, TX: Arte Público Press, 2000.

United Way of Greater Los Angeles. *Latino Scorecard 2003: Grading the American Dream.* Los Angeles, CA: United Way of Greater Los Angeles, 2004.

U.S. Bureau of the Census. *1980 Census of Population, General Social and Economic Characteristics, Texas, Section 1.* Washington, DC: Department of Commerce.

Valdés, Dionicio Nodín. *Barrios Norteños: St. Paul and Midwestern Mexican Communities in the Twentieth Century.* Austin: University of Texas Press, 2000.

Vargas, Zaragoza. *Proletarians of the North: A History of Mexican Industrial Workers in Detroit and the Midwest, 1917–1933.* Berkeley: University of California Press, 1993.

Vigil, Ernesto. *Crusade for Justice: Chicano Militancy and the Government's War on Dissent.* Madison: University of Wisconsin Press, 1999.

Weber, David J. *The Mexican Frontier, 1821–1846: The American Southwest under Mexico.* Albuquerque: University of New Mexico Press, 1982.

———. *The Spanish Frontier in North America.* New Haven, CT: Yale University Press, 1992.

White, Richard. *"It's Your Misfortune and None of My Own": A History of the American West.* Norman: University of Oklahoma Press, 1991.

Williams, Mary E., ed. *Culture Wars: Opposing Viewpoints.* San Diego, CA: Greenhaven Press Inc, 1999.

Wyckoff, William. *Creating Colorado: The Making of a Western American Landscape, 1860–1940.* New Haven, CT: Yale University Press, 1999.

Ybarra, Lea, ed. *Vietnam Veteranos: Chicanos Recall the War.* Austin: University of Texas Press, 2004.

Zamora, Emilio. *The World of the Mexican Worker in Texas.* College Station: Texas A&M University Press, 1993.

Zavella, Patricia. *Women's Work and Chicano Families: Cannery Workers of the Santa Clara Valley.* New York: Cornell University Press, 1987.

ARTICLES

Alamillo, José M. "More Than a Fiesta: Ethnic Identity, Cultural Politics, and the Cinco de Mayo Festivals in Corona, California, 1930–1950." *Aztlán: A Journal of Chicano Studies* 28 (Fall 2003).

———. "*Peloteros* in Paradise: Mexican American Baseball and Oppositional Politics in Southern California, 1930–1950," *Western Historical Quarterly* 34 (Summer 2003).

Almaguer, Tomas. "Racial Domination and Class Conflict in Capitalist Agriculture: The Oxnard Sugar Beet Workers' Strike of 1903." *Labor History* 25, no. 3 (Summer 1984).

Barajas, Frank P. "Resistance, Radicalism, and Repression on the Oxnard Plain: The Social Context of the *Betabelero* Strike of 1933." *Western Historical Quarterly* 35, no. 1 (Spring 2004).

Benavides, Ferol E. "The Saint among the Saints: A Study of Curanderismo in Utah." *Utah Historical Quarterly* 41 (Autumn 1973).

Boessenecker, John. "California Bandidos: Social Bandits or Sociopaths?" *Southern California Quarterly* 80 (1998).

Camacho Souza, Blasé. "'Trabajo y Tristesa,' 'Work and Sorrow': The Puerto Ricans of Hawaii, 1900–1902." *Hawaiian Journal of History* 18 (1984).

Candelaria, Cordelia. "La Malinche, Feminist Prototype." *Frontiers* 5 (1980).

———. "La Malinche, Feminist Prototype." *Journal of Women Studies* 5, no. 2 (1980).

Chapa, Jorge, and Richard R. Valencia. "Latino Population Growth, Demographic Characteristics, and Educational Segregation: An Examination of Recent Trends." *Hispanic Journal of Behavioral Sciences* 15, no. 2 (May 1993).

Chávez, Carmen R. "Coming of Age During the War: Reminiscences of an Albuquerque Hispana." *New Mexico Historical Review* 70, no. 4 (October 1995).

Christian, Carole E. "Joining the American Mainstream: Texas' Mexican Americans During World War I." *Southwestern Historical Quarterly* 93 (April 1989).

Clayson, William. "Cubans in Las Vegas: Ethnic Identity, Success, and Urban Life in the Late Twentieth Century." *Nevada Historical Society Quarterly* 38 (Spring 1995).

Dash, R. C., and R. E. Hawkinson. "Mexicans and 'Business as Usual': Small Town Politics in Oregon." *Aztlán* 26, no. 2 (2001).

Dias, Austin. "Carlo Mario Fraticelli: A Puerto Rican Poet on the Sugar Plantations of Hawai`i." *Centro: Journal for Puerto Rican Studies* 1 (Spring 2001).

Durand, Jorge, Douglas S. Massey, and Fernando Charvet. "The Changing Geography of Mexican Immigration to the United States, 1910–1996." *Social Science Quarterly* 81 (March 2000).

Espinoza, Dionne. "'Revolutionary Sisters': Women's Solidarity and Collective Identification Among Chicana Brown Berets in East Los Angeles." *Aztlán* 26, no. 1 (Spring 2001).

Fogel, Walter. "Mexican American Study Project: Education and Income of Mexican Americans in the Southwest." Los Angeles: Division of Research, Graduate School of Business Administration, UCLA, 1966.

García, Richard A. "Dolores Huerta: Woman, Organizer, and Symbol." *California History* 72 (Spring 1993).

Griswold del Castillo, Richard. "Chicano Historical Discourse: An Overview and Evaluation of the 1980s." *Perspectives in Mexican American Studies* 4 (1993).

———. "Latinos and the New Immigration: Mainstreaming and Polarization." Renato Rosaldo Lecture Series Monograph. Tucson: University of Arizona, 1992–1993.

Gutiérrez, David G. "'Sin Fronteras': Mexican Americans and the Emergence of the Contemporary Mexican Immigration Debate." *Journal of American Ethnic History* 10, no. 4 (Summer 1991).

Hayes-Bautista, David E., Mariam I. Kahramanian, and Cristina Gamboa. "Health." In United Way of Greater Los Angeles, *Latino Scorecard 2003: Grading the American Dream*. Los Angeles: United Way of Greater Los Angeles, 2004.

Iber, Jorge. "Bidal Agüero and *El Editor* Newspaper: The Varied Roles of a Spanish-Surnamed Entrepreneur in a Lubbock, Texas, Barrio, 1977–1999." *West Texas Historical Association Yearbook* 75 (1999).

————. "Mexican Americans of South Texas Football: The Athletic and Coaching Careers of E. C. Lerma and Bobby Cavazos, 1932–1965." *Southwestern Historical Quarterly* 55 (April 2002).

————. "On-Field Foes and Racial Misconceptions: The 1961 Donna Redskins and Their Drive to the Texas State Football Championship." *International Journal of the History of Sport* 21 (March 2004).

Kotkin, Joel, and Erika Ozuna. "Economic Development." In United Way of Greater Los Angeles, *Latino Scorecard 2003: Grading the American Dream*. Los Angeles: United Way of Greater Los Angeles, 2004.

Lecompte, Janet. "The Independent Women of Hispanic New Mexico, 1821–1846." *New Mexico Historical Review* 12 (January 1981).

López, Iris. "Introduction: Puerto Ricans in Hawai'i." *Centro: Journal of the Center for Puerto Rican Studies* 13 (Spring 2001).

López, Iris, and David Forbes. "Borinki Identity in Hawai'i: Present and Future." *Centro: Journal of the Center for Puerto Rican Studies* 13 (Spring 2001).

Marín, Christine. "Mexican Americans on the Home Front: Community Organizations in Arizona During World War II." *Perspectives in Mexican American Studies* 4 (1994).

Marotta, Sylvia A., and Jorge G. García. "Latinos in the United States in 2000." *Hispanic Journal of Behavioral Sciences* 25, no. 1 (February 2003).

Martinez, Oscar J. "On the Size of the Chicano Population: New Estimates, 1850–1900." *Aztlán* 6 (Spring 1975).

Massmann, Ann M. "Adelina 'Nina' Otero-Warren: A Spanish American Cultural Broker." *Journal of the Southwest* 42 (Winter 2000).

McKay, R. Reynolds. "The Federal Deportation Campaign in Texas: Mexican Deportation from the Lower Rio Grande Valley during the Great Depression." *Borderlands Journal* 5, no. 1 (Fall 1981).

Medina, Nitza C. "Rebellion in the Bay: California's First Puerto Ricans," *Centro: Journal of the Center for Puerto Rican Studies* 13, no. 1 (Spring 2001).

Mittlebach, Frank G., and Grace Marshall. "Mexican American Study Project: The Burden of Poverty." Los Angeles: Division of Research, Graduate School of Business Administration, UCLA, 1965.

Montgomery, Charles. "Becoming 'Spanish-American': Race and Rhetoric in New Mexico Politics, 1880–1928." *Journal of American Ethnic History* 20, no. 4 (Summer 2001).

Moustafa, A. Taher, and Gertrud Weiss. "Mexican American Study Project: Health Status and Practices of Mexican Americans." Los Angeles: Division of Research, Graduate School of Business Administration, UCLA, 1968.

Paredes, Raymund. "The Origins of Anti-Mexican Sentiment in the United States." In *New Directions in Chicano Scholarship.* Ricardo Romo and Raymund Paredes, eds. La Jolla: University of California at San Diego, 1978.

Pinero, Jorge. "Extended Roots: San Jose, California." In *Extended Roots: From Hawaii to New York, Migraciones Puertorriqueñas a los Estados Unidos.* New York: Centro de Estudios Puertorriqueños, Hunter College, 1984.

Regalado, Samuel O. "Baseball in the Barrios: The Scene in East Los Angeles Since World War II." *Baseball History* 1 (Summer 1996).

Richardson, Valerie. "Denver, Mexico?" *Washington Times,* August 24, 2004.

Ríos-Bustamante, Antonio José. "New Mexico in the Eighteenth Century: Life, Labor and Trade in la Villa de San Felipe de Albuquerque, 1706–1790." *Aztlán: International Journal of Chicano Studies Research* 7 (Fall 1976).

———. "Wyoming's Mexican Hispanic History." *Annals of Wyoming: The Wyoming History Journal* 73 (Spring 2001).

Sánchez, George J. "'Y Tú Qué?' (Y2K): Latino History in the New Millennium." Marcelo M. Suárez-Orozco and Mariela M. Paez, eds. *Latinos: Remaking America.* Berkeley: University of California Press, 2002.

Saragoza, Alex M. "Recent Chicano Historiography: An Interpretive Essay." *Aztlán* 19 (Spring 1988–1990).

———. "The Significance of Recent Chicano-Related Historical Writings: An Appraisal." *Ethnic Affairs* No. 1 (Fall 1987).

Scholes, France V. "Civil Government and Society in New Mexico in the Seventeenth Century." *New Mexico Historical Review* 10 (April 1935).

Slatta, Richard W. "Chicanos in the Pacific Northwest: A Historical Overview of Oregon's Chicanos." *Aztlán* 6 (Fall 1975).

Tienda, Marta. "Latinos and the American Pie: Can Latinos Achieve Economic Parity?" *Hispanic Journal of Behavioral Sciences* 17, no. 4 (November 1995).

Tornatzky, Louis G., Celina Torres, and Traci L. Caswell. "Education." In United Way of Greater Los Angeles, *Latino Scorecard 2003: Grading the American Dream*. Los Angeles: United Way of Greater Los Angeles, 2004.

Torres, David L. "Dynamics Behind the Formation of a Business Class: Tucson's Hispanic Business Elite." *Renato Rosaldo Lecture Series Monograph* (1989).

Treviño, Roberto R. "Facing Jim Crow: Catholic Sisters and the 'Mexican Problem' in Texas." *Western Historical Quarterly* 34 (Summer 2003).

Ulibarri, Richard O. "Utah's Unassimilated Minorities." In *Utah's History*. Richard D. Poll, ed. Logan: Utah State University Press, 1989.

Valencia, Richard R. "Inequalities and the Schooling of Minority Students in Texas: Historical and Contemporary Conditions." *Hispanic Journal of Behavioral Sciences* 22, no. 4 (November 2000).

Zamora, Emilio. "The Failed Promise of Wartime Opportunity for Mexicans in the Texas Oil Industry." *Southwestern Historical Quarterly* 95 (January 1992).

DISSERTATIONS

Carr, Norma. "The Puerto Ricans in Hawaii: 1900–1958." Ph.D. dissertation, University of Hawaii, 1989.

Ferro, Richard. "Perceptions of Discrimination: Cubans in the Pacific Northwest." Ph.D. dissertation, University of Washington, 1996.

Gil, Vincent Edward. "The Personal Adjustment and Acculturation of Cuban Immigrants in Los Angeles." Ph.D. dissertation, University of California at Los Angeles, 1976.

Hunt, Rebecca Ann. "Urban Pioneers: Continuity and Change in Ethnic Communities in Two Denver, Colorado, Neighborhoods, 1875–1998." Ph.D. dissertation, University of Colorado, 1999.

Laird, Judith F. "Argentine, Kansas: The Evolution of a Mexican American Community, 1875–1940." Ph.D. dissertation, University of Kansas, 1975.

Martínez, Ana Luisa. "Voice of the People: Pablo Cruz, *El Regidor,* and Mexican American Identity." Ph.D. dissertation, Texas Tech University, 2003.

Shinseki, Kyle Ko Francisco. "El Pueblo Mexicano de Hawai'i: Comunidades en Formación." Master's thesis, University of California, Los Angeles, 1997.

Zamora, Emilio. "Mexican Labor Activity in South Texas, 1900–1920," Ph.D. dissertation, University of Texas, Austin, 1983.

PAMPHLETS

Oropeza, Lorena. "Making History: The Chicano Movement." Julian Samora Research Institute Occasional Paper, No. 17. *Latino Studies Series* (December 1997).

Orozco, Cynthia E. "Beyond Machismo, La Familia, and Ladies Auxiliaries: A Historiography of Mexican-Origin Women's Participation in Voluntary Association and Politics in the United States." *Renato Rosaldo Lecture Monograph Series.* Tucson: University of Arizona, 1994.

Pachón, Harry. "Diversifying the Los Angeles Area Latino Mosaic: Salvadoran and Guatemalan Leaders' Assessment of Community Public Policy Needs." Claremont, CA: Tomas Rivera Policy Institute, 1997.

Passel, Jeffery S., Randy Capps, and Michael Fix. "Undocumented Immigrants: Facts and Figures." Urban Institute Immigration Studies Program, January 12, 2004.

Tomas Rivera Policy Institute. "Constructing the Los Angeles Area Latino Mosaic: A Demographic Portrait of Guatemalans and Salvadorans in Los Angeles." Claremont, CA: Tomas Rivera Policy Institute, 1997.

INDEX

ABOUT THE AUTHORS

Jorge Iber, born in Cuba and reared in Miami, is a graduate of the University of Utah and currently serves as chair of the Department of History at Texas Tech University, Lubbock. He is the author of numerous scholarly articles on Hispanics in the West, with a particular emphasis upon the impact of high school football on the lives of Mexican Americans in southern Texas. He is the author of *Hispanics in the Mormon Zion* (2001) and is the coeditor of an upcoming collection of essays entitled *Mexican Americans and Deportes*.

Recognized as a leading authority on the history of Texas-Mexicans, Arnoldo De León is C. J. "Red" Davidson Professor of History at Angelo State University, San Angelo, Texas. On the faculty at ASU since 1973, his many publications include *The Tejano Community, 1836–1900* (1982); *North to Aztlán: A History of Mexican Americans in the United States* (coauthored with Richard Griswold del Castillo, 1996); *Mexican Americans in Texas: A Brief History* (1999); *Ethnicity in the Sunbelt: Mexican Americans in Houston* (1989); and *Racial Frontiers: Africans, Chinese, and Mexicans in Western America, 1848–1890* (2002).